To Mary, for her patience and support

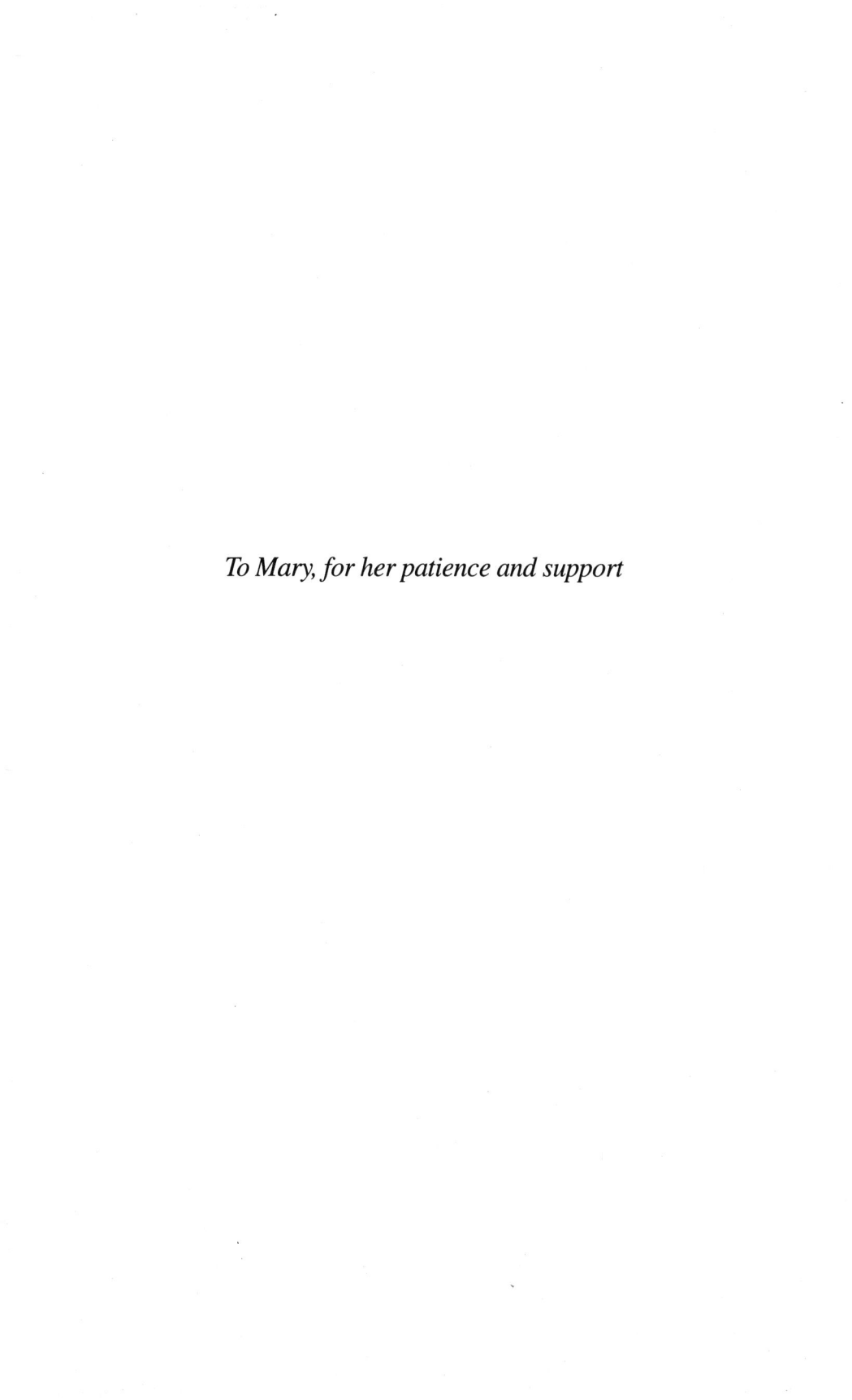

Tomorrow's Global Community

Tomorrow's Global Community

How the Information Deluge is Transforming Business & Government

By

Jim Mann

with an Introduction by
Harlan Cleveland

BainBridgeBooks

Philadelphia

Published November 1998
by
BainBridgeBooks
an imprint of
Trans-Atlantic Publications Inc.
Philadelphia PA
Website: www.transatlanticpub.com

PRINTED IN THE UNITED STATES OF AMERICA

ISBN: 1-891696-06-8

Notice about the lack of copyright protection
The author abdicates his intellectual property rights, since he believes that, in the forthcoming "knowledge-based economy," ideas should be shared freely in amiable partnerships without the scourge of litigation.
Please see Chapter 21 for more details.

Library of Congress Cataloging-in-Publication Data

Mann, Jim, 1919 -

Tomorrow's global community : how the information deluge is transforming business & government / by Jim Mann.

    p.   cm.
Includes biographical references and index.
ISBN 1-891696-06-8 (hc.)
1. Communications—Social aspects. 2. Information society.
3. Business networks. 4. Knowledge management. I. Title
    HM259.M36   1998
    302.2—dc21   98-29812
                                                      CIP

NOTICE TO READERS:
The author welcomes comments and constructive criticisms of this book. You may e-mail him at:
jim-mann@transatlanticpub.com
or write to the publisher at:
311 Bainbridge Street, Philadelphia PA 19147

Book design by Graphic Decisions Inc.
Cover design by Drawing Board Studios

CONTENTS

Introduction By Harlan Cleveland: *The Information Volcano* 9
Foreword 13

Part One
The Information Deluge and its Consequences

1. We're Drowning in Information 19
2. Information Overdose: The Side Effects 26
3. Information, Knowledge and Wisdom 57
4. Communication Creates Society 72
5. Information, Authority and Democracy 84
6. Adam Smith's Arthritic Invisible Hand 108
7. The Media: Formed, Fed and Foiled by Information 128

Part Two
The Rise of Partnership Networks

8. Managing Information in the Workplace 153
9. Networks of Partnerships 169
10. Organic Networks: Complex Adaptive Systems 192
11. Superpartnering: Operations and Knowledge Networks 210
12. Three Economies 226

Part Three
The Application of Partnership Networks to Social Structures

13. Rediscovering Government 249
14. Restoring the Supremacy of the Individual 270
15. The Death Struggle of Government 286
16. Solving the Problem of Social Insurance 303
17. Transforming Education 316

Part Four
Toward New Paradigms

18. The Need for Paradigm Change 341
19. The Bottom Line—A Deception 347
20. The Corporation—Legalized Irresponsibility 355
21. Intellectual Property—Unfair and Unenforceable 368
22. Preparing for the New Global Community 378
23. Tomorrow's Global Community: A Family of Families 394

Addendum: The World in 2301 A.D.—A Story 405
Bibliography 435
Notes and References 449
Index 472
About the Author 480

Introduction

The Information Volcano

I learned in Hawaii, where I once lived in the shadow of a volcano, that long before it blows seismologists can hear it rumble: the volcano is clearing its throat. In trying to detect the seismic rumbling of our human futures, social observers such as Jim Mann or myself also learn to look for relevant clues. Our clues are the tools we humans fashion ahead of the eruptions that follow, because human tools always seem to be invented before we know how they will come to be used.

In the great social event of recent times, we married computers to electronic telecommunications. That touched off an eruption of change which will deeply influence everything—and I mean everything—that you and I will be trying to do in the years and decades just ahead of us. This book is about the colossal changes the information eruption now clearly portends.

Jim Mann has spent his life in the midst of the information volcano. He sees in the overdose of information new, elusive opportunities. To catch them requires a new kind of wisdom—not just political savvy, economic theory, cultural sensitivity or spiritual insight, but a way of thinking about the situation as a whole. In this meticulously researched book, Mann boldly predicts that the ever-increasing volume and accessibility to information will eventually bring down some of the Western world's most entrenched paradigms in society, culture and politics.

This information explosion, coupled with the new-found pastime of conjuring tomorrow, has opened a Pandora's box in our society that couldn't have even been comprehended only a few decades ago. As Mann says, distrust of our institutions in both business and government is spreading like a cancer. It's too late to put the genie back in the lamp; all we can do now is listen to the rumble and plan for the eruption.

* * * *

Mann's view of the near future is optimistic. It is centered about the individual in a series of amiable partnerships where knowledge and information flow freely, permitting greater choice and freedom than are currently found in today's top-heavy, centralized bureaucracies. He predicts changes in government, business, the economy, education, and welfare that will greatly benefit humankind.

The systematic study of the future is a very recent breakthrough in the long history of thinking. "The intellectual construction of a likely future is a work of art," one of the early futurist pioneers, Bertrand de Jouvenel, wrote in 1967. He called it not planning or forecasting, but "the art of conjecture."

All around us, metaphors about the Year 2000 and more safely distant goal lines have become a popular framework for planning by schools, scholars, public authorities, corporate executives, one-issue lobbies and citizens' groups. Simulation techniques are routinely taught in graduate schools of planning and public affairs. Trouble in the global environment, even if foreseen only in the calculations of nuclear physicists and atmospheric chemists, have come to be cover-story fare.

Millions of people now use popularized models of the future as guidance on whether or when to have babies, practice safe sex, buy aerosol hair spray, eat more fiber, or even plan an outdoor picnic for next weekend. Meanwhile, as this book points out, it becomes increasingly easier to lose track of one's sense of purpose in this torrent of data. It is imperative we take the time to analyze what's going on around us in these most tempestuous of times.

The study of the future, at best, has developed a fresh angle of vision on the whole range of human knowledge, and a fresh reason to thread together the compartmentalized disciplines into which we have divided the life of the mind. Indeed, Mann argues that the digital age will blur the line between private and public life in many respects.

Futurism is not an effort to predict a unique and inevitable future, but to construct alternative futures, then work back from preferred outcomes to guide decisions about what we ought to be doing, starting right now. That's precisely what Jim Mann has done by practicing de Jouvenel's art of conjecture in creating his futures and formulating his vision of partnerships and networks.

Introduction

The prime temptation, to emulate Cassandra, is always lurking in the wings. Among the conceivable futures for a person, group, nation or civilization, it is still the catastrophic threat—the nuclear holocaust, the poisoned Earth or the atmospheric heat trap—that wins the ratings contest. If Cassandra were living today, she couldn't be checkmated by Apollo; she could instead make a very good living hosting a talk show about catastrophe.

However, gloomy preoccupation with what might go wrong can too easily frustrate the actions that need to be taken soon to make sure that whatever is wrong goes right. It's also true, of course, that paralysis can be induced by rosy sentimentality, that of Pollyanna: We'll surely manage to get out of the rut we're in, so why should I help push?

What's left is the role of the practical visionary, dedicated to steering us through the deep but narrow channel that divides Pollyanna from Cassandra. It's the world's highest calling. By writing this important book from a practical standpoint, Jim Mann has answered that calling.

* * * *

During the years immediately ahead, we citizens of the high-technology world are going to have to aim our science and technology at higher human deeds and purposes, with a good deal less guidance from "leaders." As Mann points out, the eventual death of bureaucracy makes the individual the all-important member of society, with all the corresponding responsibility. If nobody is fully in charge (and nobody is anymore), each of us is partly in charge.

We have come to a moment in world history when, as Albert Einstein may have been the first to say, "imagination and creativity are more important than knowledge." That means our next and crucial learnings will be integrative thought, reflective practice, and the art of "getting it all together."

A practical visionary, Jim Mann is rare in his willingness to tackle the whole schmear at once, to think through the fundamental changes that together constitute "the information revolution." It is equally rare to discover a thinker who can write about such complex fundamentals in readable prose—as if the choices and chances are really meant to be understood by us all.

In the final analysis, Mann has re-discovered for us that the very foundation of tomorrow's global community rests upon the virtues of the family—the most fundamental, universal and time-honored social unit of all.

The Norwegian explorer Thor Heyerdahl once told me he had edited his personal philosophy down to seven words: Translate ideas into events to serve people. Those words well express why this book needed to be written.

Harlan Cleveland
Sterling, Virginia
August 1998

Foreword

This is a book about the universal problems of our time. But it is also the completion of a very personal adventure.

During 15 years of working as a teacher and 40 years of working with and for the media, I became increasingly disturbed by what I saw happening to myself, my friends, my country and my world. Individuals and society seemed to be facing problems never faced before.

I read books like Alvin Toffler's *Future Shock*, Senator Daniel Patrick Moynihan's *Pandaemonium*, and William Greider's *Who Will Tell the People?* Toffler argued that the runaway acceleration of change was overturning our institutions and shifting our values; Moynihan, that the world can expect 50 or even 150 new countries as ever smaller groups fight for self-determination; Greider, that American democracy had been betrayed.

I agreed with what they said. They described the turmoil accurately. But I wanted to know *why*. Worldwide changes, worldwide confusion, and worldwide strain must have a worldwide cause. Only by understanding the cause, can we answer what H. G. Wells, almost six decades ago, called the universal problem: "How are we to adapt ourselves to these mighty disruptive forces that are shattering human society as it is at present constituted?"[1]

This book is the result of my search to find out *why*. The search began in dismay but ended in hope. In analyzing the cause of these problems I discovered that many people were working on solutions. What follows discusses the underlying problem, the solutions that address it, and how I believe both the underlying problem—and most of the derivative problems—will ultimately be resolved to humankind's benefit.

FELLOW TRAVELERS

Every book is a product of its time, and this one certainly is. My first discovery was a remarkable convergence in the thinking of authors concerned with current problems. Each in his or her own way focused on the growing ability and desire of individuals to do their own thing, to make their own decisions. Daniel Yankelovich[2] discovered this trend in opinion polls. Vaclav Havel[3] celebrated it as "respect for the unique human being and his or her liberties and inalienable rights" and "the principle that all power derives from the people." John Naisbitt[4] and William Greider[5] pleaded for it in politics. Rosabeth Kanter,[6] Peter Drucker[7] and Tom Peters[8] showed business adapting to it. Psychologists Nathaniel Branden,[9] Howard Gardner[10] and Robert Kegan defended the right of individuals to use knowledge and express their wills on the basis of personal ability rather than community standards, particularly in today's changing world.

I found Kegan's *In Over Our Heads* especially revealing. Kegan theorizes that as human beings grow in age and experience they can develop different levels of consciousness each more reflective and less dependent on social environment than the one before. He believes, the spread of knowledge and cultural turmoil requires—and to some extent is creating—more and more people with higher levels of consciousness.

In other words, all the major signs seem to point to a recognition that the flood of information can lift the human race into a higher state of being, where equality and diversity are not only reconcilable but complementary. If we become victims of the information deluge, it is because we are unable—or unwilling—to build and board the ark. This book is about how that ark is being built and boarded.

The book can be read in three ways. The patient reader, who wishes to take the same journey I took, will start at the beginning and persevere. Less patient readers can skip Part One and move immediately to the emerging solutions in Part Two. Readers reluctant to undertake a journey unless someone shows them pictures of where it will end can read the *Addendum* first.

A MINI-MAP OF THE JOURNEY

The book is arranged pretty much as my search took place.

Part One explains the problem and how we humans got where we are. It starts by describing the extent of the information deluge (Chapter 1) and specific problems it causes (Chapter 2). It then analyzes the way communication, knowledge and wisdom work (Chapter 3) and how advances in communication determine the nature of society (Chapter 4). Part One ends with three historical chapters tracing the effects of the constantly rising flood of information on government (Chapter 5), the economy (Chapter 6) and the media (Chapter 7).

Part Two describes the search for solutions and tries to explain and evaluate them. We see why innovators are managing information through partnering and networking (Chapter 8), how they are beginning to organize the economy in partnership networks (Chapter 9) and what has led to rejection of bureaucracy (Chapter 10). These trends lead to the substitution of a superior form of business management (Chapter 11), which will be widely accepted despite resistance (Chapter 12).

Part Three argues that the information deluge is having a similar effect on government, making civil bureaucracy obsolete (Chapter 13) and requiring a higher form of democracy (Chapter 14). Like business, society resists yet moves inevitably toward these new forms of governance (Chapter 15) with new approaches to public welfare (Chapter 16) and new methods in education (Chapter 17).

Part Four summarizes conclusions I arrived at in the course of the journey. I now believe we have to abandon some important outdated paradigms (Chapter 18), i.e., the bottom line as the measure of success (Chapter 19), the legal corporation as a limit on responsibility (Chapter 20) and the idea that individuals can buy and sell intellectual property (Chapter 21). With sufficient self-confidence and self-reliance we can solve the crucial problems of society while developing a strategy for personal success in our changing world (Chapter 22).

The book closes with a sketch of what we can expect our world to become: a virtual single community—the extended human family (Chapter 23).

THOSE WHO GAVE DIRECTIONS ALONG THE WAY

There is much on the following pages about partnering—collaboration between different minds to arrive at greater wisdom. This book is the result of much partnering. Some of it was direct, face to face, by phone, and by mail. Russ Anderson, Leo Bogart, Gil Chapman, Al Eisenpreis, Oz Elliott, Norman Glenn, Allen Hammond, Beverly Hori-Akron, Jim Horton, Dave Keil, Red Quinlan, Martin Tarcher, Scott Tilden, Sam Vitt, Wally Wood and Hrisey Zegger were active partners who deserve special thanks.

As the notes and bibliography attest, there were also some 200 authors with whom I was a passive partner. Although I take complete responsibility for the way the ideas in this book are presented, very few of them are totally mine. Hundreds of minds have been wrestling with the underlying problem and its consequences. An impressive number of them saw what was happening many years earlier and predicted much of what has happened. If I have made any original contribution, it is to highlight these unifying patterns by gathering their ideas in one place.

Jim Mann
Gales Ferry, Connecticut
July 1998

Part One

The Information Deluge And Its Consequences

Like water, information is refreshing, invigorating and an essential good. As the body cannot live without water, the mind cannot function without information.

But just as out-of-control water can destroy homes and drown people, so out-of-control information can disorganize society and disorient individuals. It is this book's contention that the information deluge has reached a crisis point, the most fundamental crisis humankind has ever faced. As the deluge is both widespread and deep, so are the problems. Part One explores why increasing information causes problems, how information, communication, understanding and wisdom work, the ways they affect us individually and as a society, and how the rising information flood has created or aggravated the disruptive forces that are shattering today's society.

1

WE'RE DROWNING IN INFORMATION

> *"All our knowledge brings us nearer to our ignorance....*
> *Where is the knowledge we have lost in information? Where is*
> *the wisdom we have lost in knowledge?"*
> — T. S. Eliot, 1934[1]

Today's world provides all of us with more information than we can manage, simply because each generation has added what it learned to the knowledge of previous generations. Even though our learning capacity has grown greatly over the centuries, the pileup of information has reached a point where modern men and women have difficulty managing this surfeit of facts and ideas.

A PARABLE FOR OUR TIME

About four decades ago, Ken Purdy wrote a short story called "The Noise."[2] A man goes to a psychiatrist because he has the "gift" of hearing what other people are thinking. As this ability becomes more acute and he hears the thoughts of more and more people, the information that used to be very helpful in small doses is now driving him crazy. I have no idea whether Purdy realized it, but he was writing a parable for our time. We are all receiving more information than we can absorb. The result is disorientation, confusion, inability to make decisions, intellectual paralysis and, in extreme cases, violence and insanity. As Marshall McLuhan put it in *Understanding*

Media, "Mental breakdown of varying degrees is the very common result of uprooting and inundation with new information and endless new patterns of information."[3]

How could the flow of information, once considered an infallible escalator to human progress, become a stumbling block?

Primitive humans learned to survive by sharpening their senses, remaining ever alert, searching constantly for signs that might provide information about the presence of food or water, the animal they were hunting, or the danger they had to avoid. Today, modern humans learn to survive by dulling the mind, closing down the senses. We give little or no attention to much of what we see and hear. We watch television without seeing the commercials. We carry on conversations while the radio chatters. We even read differently than we used to, with more scanning and less concentration.

NOBODY'S FAULT

The first fact underlying this problem is there is so much more to know. Forty years ago, when I was a high-school teacher, I taught a course called "World History." We joked then about covering the history of the world in one year. The course had nothing about China, Japan or anything outside western civilization. Today, history covers not only more years but a much broader field. We know a lot more about the past than we used to know.

Compared to the growth of historical studies, scientific knowledge has grown even more. According to education critic Lewis J. Perelman, "in fast-paced fields, available information doubles every few years—or even months," and "rapid advances in science and technology have reduced the 'half-life' of valid knowledge in many areas to as little as eighteen months."[4] Today a student can spend a lifetime studying just one scientific field—whether astronomy, biology, engineering, geology, mathematics, medicine, physics or psychology—and find that the field chosen embraces a number of specialties, each demanding another lifetime of learning.

Today's news coverage asks us to pay attention to events all over the world, and in much greater detail, than it did 50 years ago. In December 1941, CBS Radio sponsored a dinner in the ballroom of New York's Waldorf-Astoria to honor its top reporter, Edward R. Murrow, who had just returned from London, where he had held Americans entranced with his broadcast accounts of the London Blitz. One of the speakers, Congressional Librarian Archibald MacLeish, told Murrow he had "accomplished one of the great miracles of the world" by destroying "the superstition that what is done beyond 3,000 miles of water is not really done at all."[5]

Fifty years ago instant reporting from Europe was a miracle. Today we get pictures in color of a comet's debris crashing into the planet Jupiter, some 390 million miles away.

Consider the information that is being added to food packaging: besides ingredients, serving size and number of calories, there is percentage of fat, cholesterol, sodium, carbohydrates, sugar, protein and fiber content along with the vitamins by percentage of recommended daily requirement. The government orders automakers to provide window-sticker information on the percentage of parts of the car made in the United States and Canada plus names of other countries which added 15 percent or more to the vehicle's value. In a good-hearted attempt to prevent discrimination by insurance companies, the U.S. House of Representatives passed a bill requiring insurers to report the number of policies they issue, where issued, both claims and losses and even the number of agents by area according to ZIP code in the 25 largest metropolitan areas.

THE DIFFICULTY OF KEEPING UP

On a single day, November 16, 1994, the Associated Press reported two startling facts: The Social Security System had just discovered that for over 16 years it had underpaid hundreds of thousands of retired Americans nearly a half-billion dollars because of a mistake in its computer system, and General Motors asked employees to return money it had mistakenly overpaid as a performance bonus.

The U.S. General Accounting Office claims that the 1990 census contains a minimum of 14.1 million gross errors.[6] The U.S. Department of Commerce reports that our country's 1991 balance of trade was minus $28 billion, plus $28 billion, plus $24.3 billion or plus $164.1 billion "depending on how it is measured."[7]

Each year Congress faces about a hundred bills related to managing information. This is a bit of a joke, since our elected federal legislators cannot possibly keep up with the information needed to evaluate the new bills they pass. And "sunset legislation" requires that Congress review old legislation and decide whether to extend it or allow it to expire. A new Congress can open its first session with more than a thousand reviews on its agenda.

THE ACCELERATION OF COMMUNICATIONS

We humans have greatly increased our ability to transmit and absorb information since Johann Gutenberg invented movable type a little over 500 years ago. Today the printed word has become so essential to business, government and social relations that we consider it a national disgrace that there are adult Americans who cannot read. In addition non-literary media introduced since Reginald Fessenden's 1901 first wireless transmission of the human voice bring more information to those who cannot read than was available a century ago to those who could.

Pictures were added to sound when RCA opened the first television station, W2XBS, in 1930. Today the average American household has a television set operating for nearly 50 hours a week, and three out of every five American homes subscribe to cable television. Television content was once dominated by three broadcast networks. We now have direct access to satellite transmission with a choice of 200 video channels. And everybody is talking about 500 channels in the years to come.

By the year 2000, the Internet, a worldwide web of interconnected computer networks, will enable a user to communicate with more than 250 million people and reach each of them instantaneously no matter where they are. As Intel Corp. chief executive Andrew S. Grove told stockholders, "It's called the processor-communications spiral. Faster communications call for faster processors, and faster processors call for faster communications."[8] He said nothing about the need for faster minds.

FORCE-FEEDING

Not only has it become more difficult to decide what information deserves our attention, but much of it is forced upon us. Advances in technology have made communication so easy, so prevalent and so difficult to ignore that our minds are being stuffed with data and ideas even when we are not looking for them. This, of course, is nothing new. Communicators have been forcing us to pay attention since Stentor used a horn to rally the Greeks during the battle for Troy. It is just that today there are so many more horns. According to the American Association of Advertising Agencies, an average of 1600 advertising messages are directed at the individual consumer every day.[9] Both G.K. Chesterton and George Bernard Shaw have been quoted as observing that New York's Times Square at night would be so beautiful "if you couldn't read."

Meanwhile the media, the professional deliverers and evaluators of public information, are moving more and more from functional to frantic. Journalists are caught in the jaws of an inescapable vise. On one side, as Northeastern University School of Journalism Director Nicholas Danilof has written: "Reporters are inundated with faxes, press releases and official reports. Writers are wooed by politicians, lobbyists, spin doctors, press conferences and media pseudo-events."[10] On the other side, the working press faces growing audience apathy. With the multiplication of media it has become harder and harder to hold the public's attention. This is why so many of today's reporters resort to sensationalism, and why the press goes into excess-mode the minute some subject captures public interest.

Audience apathy and sensationalism are only a small part of the damage done to the media by the rising information deluge. There will be much more about this in Chapter 7.

INFORMATION VS. UNDERSTANDING

At a "town hall" broadcast in Tampa, Florida, television commentator Ted Koppel complained to President Clinton: "This is a curious criticism to make, but sometimes I think you're so specific in your answers or so detailed in your answers, that it's a little hard to know what the answer to the questions was."[11] An excess of detail interferes with clear thinking, just as many people speaking at once can make it difficult to understand anyone.

As the abundance of food has led to an increase in cases of anorexia and bulimia, so the flood of information can occasion a sort of intellectual anorexia, where the patient loses all appetite for learning, or mental bulimia, where the victim swallows information voraciously with no interest in digesting it, as we shall see when we discuss "tuneout" in Chapter 2.

We make decisions by evaluating data relevant enough to form a judgment as to what should be done. Decisions become difficult not only when we cannot get enough data, but also when we get too much. In the mid-80s, direct marketing expert John Miglautsch discovered that no matter how much information data processing departments provided, "additional information opened new vistas and generated more questions." His conclusion: "mountains of data can immobilize corporations."[12]

Miglautsch confirms what I learned in the 70s. I was hired to conduct a study for Broadcast Advertising Reports, a company that provided detailed information on where and when television commercials were broadcast. My job was to interview decision makers at companies that paid millions of dollars for these advertisements to find out if my client could develop other reports that the advertisers might buy. Almost to a man, the executives I interviewed told me that they did not want more data. They already had too much. The excess of information was keeping middle managers from making decisions.

OUR UNQUENCHABLE THIRST FOR KNOWLEDGE

A core conundrum of human nature is our unquenchable thirst for knowledge, our need to know. We spend our entire lives learning, yet are condemned to go to our graves never knowing all that there is to know—or even learning how much of what we think is, really is not.

Even the most dogmatic believers agree that only God can know everything. And, since we are constantly learning, there is always the chance that something we learn tomorrow might throw new light on what we learned today. As Benjamin Franklin put it in a speech before the Continental Congress:

> Having lived long, I have experienced many instances of being obliged, by better information or fuller consideration, to change my opinions even on important subjects, which I once thought right, but found to be otherwise. It is therefore that, the older I grow, the more apt I am to doubt my own judgment of others.[13]

It is easy to say that strong minds handle this problem by growing in humility, while weak minds surrender to despair. But that does not answer the question I have wrestled with all these years: How do we survive this cacophony? What is the best way to use the multitude of modern media and the flood of information they provide without losing our sanity? What is this barrage of information doing to each of us as individuals and to the society in which we live? And who, if anyone, controls—or can control—this phenomenon?

This is scary. So scary that many people run away from it. Some follow the first strong voice they hear and surrender to intellectual demagoguery.

1. We're Drowning in Information

Others scoff at the intellectual life as an exercise in futility and let their minds lie fallow. Still others substitute information for understanding and bury the life of reason under a mountain of facts. Yet we have to keep swimming in the ocean of information even though what was a calm, tranquil lake for our forefathers has become for us a storm-tossed sea.

Most of us have been trained to think that knowledge is good and the more information we have the better. But that traditional attitude was simplistic. Like water, information can cleanse, refresh and nourish. It makes life possible. The growth of information, like the abundance of clean, drinkable water, has been a great blessing to individuals and society. But, like water, information can also swamp, suffocate and kill. The next chapter examines some of the more important ways in which the flood of information can do and has done its damage.

2

INFORMATION OVERDOSE: THE SIDE EFFECTS

"The result of more knowledge may be greater ignorance—or, at least, the feeling of ignorance—about where we are and where we are heading, and particularly where we should head, than was true when in fact we knew less but thought we knew more."
— *Zbigniew Brzezinski, 1970*[1]

An overdose of information causes serious psychological side effects. It increases uncertainty and multiplies our fears. It undermines confidence in authority. It causes some people to become unbalanced in their approach to reality as they substitute partial information for the whole, while it causes others to withdraw from reality either by not trying to understand and apply information or by allowing others to do their thinking for them. Finally, it intensifies the alienation of groups isolated from mainstream society.

MORE SEEPING FLOOD THAN TIDAL WAVE

It is important to remember two things when analyzing the harmful effects of the information deluge. First, the deluge is more of a seeping flood than tidal wave. It did not happen all at once. Many of the problems it causes have been creeping up on us for more than a hundred years. Second, these consequences seldom act in isolation. Most problems, including problems related to overdoses of information, have multiple contributing causes. Not everything that is wrong in our lives or society is caused by the information deluge. But almost always the information deluge magnifies the problem's importance or makes solving it more difficult.

There are seven serious side effects of information overdose: uncertainty, fear, distrust, knowledge warp, tuneout, groupthink and alienation.

1. UNCERTAINTY

The growing flood of information has greatly increased the amount of uncertainty in our world, and the spread of uncertainty is causing multiple changes and difficulties in how we run our lives and our society.

A CHILD OF IGNORANCE

This is not a plea for more certainty. Certainty is useful, but too often it is the child of ignorance. Not too many centuries ago most of humankind was certain that the world was flat. A little child is certain that his mother is the greatest and smartest woman in the world. This type of certainty, of course, is frequently replaced by other certainties. Most people now know that the world is round. The adult son realizes that his mother, no matter how important to him, is not the world's smartest woman.

As knowledge grows, certainty is increasingly replaced by doubt. Ignorant people tend to be more intolerant than broadly educated people, not because they are mean or evil, but because they do not know enough. We rightly admire tolerance or the humility in admitting one might be wrong. Under certain conditions doubt is good. The wise realize how much they do not know.

DISRUPTIVE

In practical life uncertainty can also be disruptive. For one thing, it gets in the way of making decisions. Consider the proliferation of consultants and study groups. It has become customary for executives to bring in consultants or hire research firms before making major decisions. At the secondary management level it is even worse. Executives are afraid to make decisions before they consider all the information, while all the information is now too much to consider.

The acme of dependence on consultants was reached in the 1988 leveraged buyout of RJR Nabisco. Advisors to the parties in the transaction "earned" $461 million. Drexel Burnham was paid $227 million, Merrill Lynch $109 million, Kohlberg, Kravis & Roberts $75 million, Morgan Stanley $25 million, and $25 million was given to Wasserstein-Perella chiefly to prevent them from giving advice to other parties.[2]

A standing joke about our government is that, when Congress is faced with a problem, it doesn't make a decision, it sets up a committee. There is validity in the complaint. Legislators do appoint committees and study groups to postpone or avoid decisions. But there is also a good deal of justification in this. Decisions are more difficult today precisely because there is so much more information to study—and so much more information available to critics.

ENDANGERING OUR JURY SYSTEM

The spread of uncertainty has also invaded our courts and could, eventually, undermine our jury system. First, it takes longer and longer to select an "unbiased" jury, since jurors know so much more about what has happened and lawyers know so much more about how jurors perform. Second, the jurors, once selected, have a harder time making up their minds. With everything jurors know (and realize they don't know) about sociology, psychology and psychiatry, they are far more likely to give the criminal the benefit of the doubt.

Psychological states, once considered irrelevant, are now seen as mitigating circumstances. In Los Angeles, Moose Hanoukai, who bludgeoned his wife to death, was found guilty of voluntary manslaughter instead of second-degree murder because his lawyer claimed he was a victim of husband battering and years of abuse. For similar reasons juries acquitted Lorena Bobbit, who cut off her husband's penis, and decided Aurelia Macias's castration of her husband was a case of simple battery.

The use of expert testimony in trials has not helped. As *The Economist* observed, after a jury decided that baby sitter Louise Woodward was guilty of second-degree murder and the judged changed the verdict to manslaughter:

> There are just too many experts and facts and arguments around these days: nobody is sure which of them to trust. More and more trials hinge on intricate scientific evidence.... And so, by a paradox,

the introduction of ever more sophisticated information into trials undermines faith in their outcomes.[3]

NORMLESSNESS

Uncertainty is at the root of what French sociologist Emile Durkheim called "anomie" (normlessness), a breakdown of traditional social restraints. Over 27 years ago Zbigniew Brzezinski, whose quote heads this chapter, warned that:

> The threat of intellectual fragmentation, posed by the gap between the pace in the expansion of knowledge and the rate of its assimilation, raises a perplexing question concerning the prospects for mankind's intellectual unity. It has generally been assumed that the modern world, shaped increasingly by the industrial and urban revolutions, will become more homogeneous in its outlook. This may be so, but it could be the homogeneity of insecurity, of uncertainty, and of intellectual anarchy.[4]

This uncertainty erodes social cohesion, undermines civil discipline and considerably weakens established religions. It is very difficult to hold fast to a creed rejected by people all around you. A 1967 opinion poll found that 85 percent of Americans considered premarital sex morally wrong.[5] Yet less than three decades later public opinion had changed so radically that there were 3.7 million unmarried male-female couples openly living together in the United States.[6]

Because there is such a diversity of opinion in our society, the average American is reluctant to appear certain about moral principles even when he or she believes in them. In his book, *Spirit of Community*, Amitai Etzioni, the founder of the Communitarian movement, uses an incident at Harvard to illustrate the fear many liberals have of taking moral stands. As a participant in a faculty seminar on the ethical condition of America, he suggested that the group discuss the moral implications of the decline of the American family. Although no one objected, his suggestion was ignored. Later two of those present told him why: "If a high-profiled group of ethicists at Harvard would form a consensus on the matter, it might put a lot of pressure on people, and it might even be used to change the laws."[7]

This attitude has grown in recent years precisely because there is so much information not only concerning the relationships under discussion, but on how other people think about these relationships. The result is that most people either have doubts themselves or do not want to appear as if they do not.

ANXIETY, GUILT, STRESS

One of the effects of uncertainty is anxiety, fear of making a mistake. The more we know about the ideal way to do something (whether the ideal proposed is correct or not), the more we fear falling short. And that uncertainty generates guilt, stress, discouragement and fear.

Consider the plight of the well-meaning mother faced with the duty of raising a child. What used to be predominantly a matter of instinct, supplemented by advice from one's mother and other more experienced females, has now become the occasion for anxious research. Back in 1950, David Riesman's *The Lonely Crowd* pointed out that parents lack the self-assurance they used to have, and that "the loss of old certainties in the spheres of work and social relations is accompanied by doubt as to how to bring up children." Hence mothers and fathers turned to others, like the late Doctor Spock, for advice, "but even these authorities speak vaguely."[8]

In the words of psychologist Shari L. Thurer, "There are just too many books. Not only does the wide range of advice confuse parents, but the vast quantity of data suggests that mothering is far more complicated and awesome than ever suspected."[9] As in other fields, there are constantly new theories and research to plague mothers and others with uncertainty.

2. FEAR

Closely related to uncertainty is the second side effect of information overdose: fear. Ignorance does not frighten us until we are aware that we do not know. So long as a hunter walking in the woods hears nothing he fears nothing. If he hears a sound and does not know what it is, he panics.

Although fear is a protective instinct useful in itself, an excess of fear interferes with rational decision-making.

HALF A MILLION MURDERS

In Rwanda thousands of peasant Hutus who lived peaceful, if primitive, lives became ferocious murderers of half a million Tutsis. The only explanation given is that they were motivated by fear due to government radio broadcasts. As one native put it, "I did not believe the Tutsis were coming to kill us, but when the government radio continued to broadcast that they were coming to take our land, were coming to kill the Hutus—when this was repeated over and over—I began to feel some kind of fear."[10] The immediacy and reach of radio makes it a powerful promoter of panic, particularly among the uneducated.

Of course, balanced information can restore sanity. Emmanuel Kamuhanda, who admitted killing 15 fellow villagers, said later: "The government told us that the RPF (Rwandan Patriotic Front) is Tutsi and if it wins the war all the Hutus will be killed. As of now, I don't believe this is true. At the time, I believed that the government was telling the truth."[11] The problem with fear is that, though it is usually based either on misinformation or on too little information, it cannot wait for correction or complete information.

AMERICA TOO

But we need not go to Rwanda for examples of the damage caused by fear. Consider the unfair, even cruel, treatment of fellow Americans infected with the HIV virus, children as well as adults. When the public is subject to an avalanche of news about a fearful subject, the facts about the danger will always be absorbed and applied more quickly than reassurances qualifying the nature of the danger.

As Richard Saul Wurman points out in *Information Anxiety,*

> Most Americans feel more at risk in an airplane than in a car, based on the extensive and often gruesome coverage of plane crashes. Yet the number of passenger deaths per mile traveled is much greater in an automobile—about 2,154 deaths per billion miles compared to only 214 in an airplane.[12]

In 1994, *Newsweek* featured a lengthy article on "Kids Growing Up Scared."[13] In a poll conducted by *Newsweek* and the Children's Defense Fund, more than half the children and 73 percent of adults said they were afraid of violent crime against them or a family member. Yet there is only one chance in 70,000 that a child will be murdered. Years ago most parents and children would not have heard about that one victim. Today almost everybody hears.

As the magazine points out, "The fear of crime is almost a separate phenomenon from the real danger it poses." The flood of information has made crime in America more fearful than it really is. Violent crimes get major attention in the news media. International coverage makes people aware of crimes in other parts of the country and the world. Much of the rise in recorded crimes may be due to greater diligence in recording. The police have better equipment and systems for record keeping. Telephones make reporting of crimes easier. Insurance policies give property owners incentive to report each theft, even thefts that never happened.

FOSTERING FEAR FOR PROFIT

What makes fear difficult to manage is not only that it is contagious but that there is almost always someone who can benefit by fostering fear in others. The information deluge has been a bonanza for insurance companies, for it has made people more aware of the possibility of catastrophe, whether by accident or illness. Few holders of accident or health insurance policies know precisely what their policy covers, to say nothing about the odds of their having an accident or becoming ill. Most sign up out of fear—better to be safe than sorry.

Profit opportunities generated by fear are usually found on both sides of the street. Take, for example, the controversy over whether electromagnetic fields cause cancer. In 1974, Nancy Wertheimer, an experimental psychologist, noted an unusual incidence of childhood cancer in certain areas of Denver and conducted a study that found a relationship with proximity to high-current electrical power lines. After her findings were publicized by science writer Paul Brodeur, first in a 1989 *New Yorker* series, then in a book titled *Currents of Death,* an avalanche of research grants followed, including $5 million from the National Cancer Institute and a total of $55 million from the U.S. Department of Energy and the National Institute of Environmental Health Sciences. In July, 1992, an article in *Science* calculated that the cost of public anxiety about the harmful effects of electromagnetic fields had risen to more than $1 billion a year, and the Electric Power Research Industry has spent from $6 million to $14 million each year since then.[14]

The point here is that the tremendous research outlay created by this controversy came from both sides—nourished equally by fear of possible harm to children and fear of possible harm to business. To date, nothing has been proven either way,[15] but the fear remains. After California parents asked that children in a school near power lines be bused to other schools, epidemiologist Charles Poole observed: "The buses don't have seat belts and kids die every year in bus crashes. We don't know there's any risk at all in electromagnetic fields from power lines. But people have a fear of the unknown."[16] Inability to manage the information leads parents to expose their children to a proven danger to avoid an unproven one.

PARALYZING GOVERNMENT

Chapter 5 will deal with the impact of the information deluge on our government, including the crippling pressures caused by fear. Washington is crowded with pressure groups, and almost all of them are kept alive—often very prosperously—by their clients' fears. Businesses are afraid government regulations may hurt them. Individuals are afraid of higher taxes or loss of government benefits, and they all have lobbyists fighting to get the attention of overburdened legislators.

If you need proof of the leverage in fear, just study the latest fund-raising letter from Washington, whether from an organization to save Social Security or an alliance to defend civil rights. Democracy is being smothered by its own "success," as fear turns the people's right to be heard into a deafening din.

3. DISTRUST

Coupled with the growing fear that government may do something to hurt them is a significant decline in the faith citizens used to have in authorities—whether individuals or institutions.

NO MORE LEADERS

We hear often that our nation no longer produces the kind of leaders we had years ago. There are no more George Washingtons, Abraham Lincolns, or Theodore Roosevelts. But the problem lies not in the caliber of our leaders, but in how we see them. There is no real evidence that today's politicians are less honest or more stupid than leaders of yesteryear, though some may be.

The real problem is that we know too much about them. Charismatic leadership requires a certain amount of public ignorance. The reason no man is a hero to his wife (or as they used to say, valet) is that his wife (or valet) knows him too well. Even John F. Kennedy, the last hero to live in the White House, would have lost his charisma if Americans had known in 1961 everything we know about him today. As Amitai Etzioni put it, "Since the 1950s we have cut our authority figures down to size."[17]

Opinion polls confirm his observation. In 1958, 55 percent of Americans felt they could "trust the government in Washington to do what's right." By 1978 fewer than 30 percent felt that way. In 1966, only five out of every 20 respondents believed that "people running the country don't care what happens to people like me." By 1977 that number had risen to 12 in 20.[18] In 1991, a Time-CNN poll found that 91 percent had little or no faith in the ability of Washington to solve problems and get things done.[19] In 1996, a Harris Poll sponsored by *Business Week* reported that almost seven out of every 10 Americans felt it was harder to attain the American dream of equal opportunity, personal freedom and social mobility, with even more blaming the government.[20]

> In *No Sense of Place*, Joshua Meyerowitz theorizes:
> One of the reasons for our general loss of faith in powerful central leadership may be that the new communication environment coupled with our expectations of the office make impossible demands on a President. By revealing more, the new media demand more manipulation and control. And yet the new media reveal so much that they also make the President's need for control and advice more visible. As a result, people have become more cynical about the presidency as they begin to become more aware both of the manipulation of symbols and images and of the management of personal impressions. The new media create a dilemma for politicians: They demand the smooth performance of a professional actor, yet they also make such performance appear to be a sham.[21]

DECLINE OF AUTHORITY

The more we know about authority figures, the less power they have. This is true of individuals and institutions. As reverence for politicians, teachers and clergymen declined, so did respect for government, schools and religion. The number of teachers and clergymen accused of child molestation has grown way out of proportion to the reality not only because children know more about such crimes but because the public is more ready to believe.

Something similar has happened in law enforcement. It is not so much that there are more corrupt police as it is that the public know more about corrupt police. In fact, even a simple and forgivable problem like overwork (in California the average detective's case load has doubled, in some cases tripled, in the last 15 years) has a pernicious effect in that the public has less confidence in the police because it knows they are overloaded (which may explain why the number of private detectives working in California rose from some 2,500 to about 7,500 in the same period).

Disrespect is a single step from distrust, which in turn feeds the uncertainty and fear already mentioned. The press, our principal source of day-by-day information, is itself caught in this dilemma. As *Newsweek* columnist Meg Greenfield wrote not long ago, the press' relentlessly cynical depictions of what goes on in government has not only "lessened respect for politics and government, but has generated 'plenty of richly deserved cynicism' about the press itself."[22]

This distrust has even turned against scientists. In 1978, the entire Spring issue of *Daedalus* was devoted to "The Limits of Scientific Inquiry." In the introduction, Robert Morison wrote of how the decline in public esteem for authority figures has affected scientists, who are...

> suspect, not only as authorities in their own right, but also because the scientific establishment has become identified with the general power structure, which to some of our citizens at least appears to become ever more overbearing and untrustworthy.[23]

The more information we absorb about the media or about the government, the more conscious we become of their shortcomings and the more reason we have to distrust. But it is not only information about the venality of authorities that breeds distrust. Even useful information can lead to distrust if the recipients do not fully understand it. This is why the more information the government releases on the state of the economy, the more reasons ordinary citizens find to distrust the government.

The official statistics announce healthy consumer-purchasing patterns, but that news does not jibe with the consumer's experience. The Federal Reserve increases interest rates because government figures show the U.S. economy in high gear. But the ordinary Joe sees his brother without a job and his wallet a lot thinner than it used to be. As business analyst John Cunniff said in an Associated Press feature: "The Fed has its reasons, legitimate ones for hiking interest rates. But those reasons are very difficult for millions of people to understand."[24] That brings us to a fourth harmful side effect of information overdose.

4. KNOWLEDGE WARP

Because there is so much information and it flows so freely, many individuals have access to advanced knowledge before they are ready for it. They become knowledgeable in one area but remain ignorant about related areas. They obtain wherewithal without wisdom.

BOMBS AWAY

The son of a couple I know was arrested for manufacturing bombs and setting them off where they damaged property and endangered lives. He had learned how to make a bomb, but he had not learned his social obligations or even what the law would do to him as a result of his actions.

That may seem an extreme case. Yet all around us we find incidents of children buying and using guns. One reason for the spread of drugs among youngsters is that it so easy for children to learn how to obtain and use drugs before they understand the long-range consequences of drug use. A similar explanation is given for the spread of sexual diseases and the 1.1 million pregnancies among young unmarried women in the United States.[25]

Knowledge warp intensifies the shock and chaos of introducing "civilization" into primitive societies. Primitives still act like primitives, but now the young men of Sierra Leone wreck Mercedes, Volvos and BMWs instead of ox-carts. There is an incongruous wedding of primitive values and sophisticated knowledge. Solomon Anthony Joseph Musa justifies the murder of his benefactors by saying he did it "to erase the humiliation and mitigate the power his middle-class sponsors held over him," and guerrilla leader Prince Johnson makes a video as he tortures and kills Liberian president Samuel Doe.[26]

Using the fire of modern technology to illuminate the uneducated mind almost always results in an explosion.

EVEN THE EDUCATED

But knowledge warp is a problem as much for the adult and educated as it is for the young or uneducated. The absent-minded professor and the ivory tower are symbols of how specialized knowledge can crowd out vital information in other areas. The more information we have to juggle, the harder it becomes to maintain intellectual balance and give proper attention to information outside our field, like the specialist in a Florida hospital who paid so much attention to the intricacies of cleanly amputating a patient's foot that he did not realize he was cutting off the wrong foot.[27]

With the rapid growth of technology ability to act is galloping ahead of understanding the social consequences of acting. Gene alteration, test-tube conception, surrogate motherhood, organ transplants, the Internet and the ease of pirating intellectual property are a few examples.

A sociology professor, Raymond Murphy of the University of Ottawa, has written a book accusing his fellow sociologists of knowledge warp. His *Rationality and Nature* argues that "sociology has been constructed as if nature didn't matter" and tries to develop an alternative sociology blending what is distinctly human with what humans share with other forms of life.[28]

The late Professor Julian L. Simon of the University of Maryland[29] and Gregg Easterbrook of *Newsweek*[30] have accused environmentalists of knowledge warp leading to unwarranted alarmism. Business people complain that environmentalists ignore the economic and business effects of their proposals. Environmentalists, in turn, accuse their critics of knowledge warp because of the concentration on technology and business interests.

IN COURTS OF LAW

I mentioned earlier how uncertainty threatens the American jury system. Knowledge warp is another threat. Since our jury system relies on the common sense and unbiased judgment of average citizens, the courts disqualify jurors who have knowledge of the case that may lead to prejudgment. But the information flood has filled the average mind with half truths and misleading information that can affect judgment.

Defense lawyers now look for jurors who watch daytime talk shows. To play on the pseudo psychology viewers absorb from such shows lawyers have actually pleaded "pornographic intoxication" ("drunk" from looking at dirty pictures) as a mitigating circumstance for rape and murder, "cultural psychosis," (traumatic childhood) to excuse one girl's killing another for her leather coat, and "urban survival syndrome" (living in a tough neighborhood) to explain how fear compelled a man to end an argument with two unarmed men by murdering them.

IN LEGISLATURES

On another level, knowledge warp among legislators is the reason for the promulgation of laws that do not work and laws that do more harm than good. Lawmakers know a lot about the needs of our society but, too frequently, not enough. One reason for our ever-increasing national debt is that the public—and most legislators—have a better knowledge of government-bestowed benefits than they have of government-imposed costs.

A primary explanation given by former defense secretary Robert S. McNamara for the mistake of the Vietnam War perfectly describes knowledge warp:

> When it came to Vietnam, we found ourselves setting policy for a region that was terra incognita. Worse, our government lacked experts for us to consult to compensate for our ignorance about Southeast Asia.... The foundations of our decision-making were gravely flawed.[31]

Like my neighbors' kid, our leaders knew all about applying explosive force but far too little about its consequences.

ACCEPTING UNREALITY

A pernicious consequence of knowledge warp is that its distortion of reality is frequently accepted even after people are aware of it. Our government, for instance, measures inflation and the cost of living largely by the Consumer Price Index (CPI), calculated by the average price of a predetermined cross-section of goods and services that is supposed to represent the purchases of average Americans. The list is updated about once every 10 years. The CPI has been criticized by Senator Patrick Moynihan and others not only because it is not updated frequently enough, but even more because it does not reflect the way consumers adapt their purchasing patterns to price changes and other external factors. As *The Economist* observed, "the problem is that the economy is changing too quickly for the statisticians to keep up."[32]

2. Information Overdose: The Side Effects

Even though everyone admits the measurement is warped, there are a whole range of government decisions being made on the basis of the CPI, from cost-of-living increases in Social Security payments to contingent clauses in labor contracts. Hence the government is forced to use what it knows is fiction as if it were a significant fact. A commission of scholars estimated that the CPI's overestimating inflation by only one percent a year will add almost $140 billion to the U.S. annual deficit and $634 billion to the national debt by the year 2005. The commission called that warped information "the fourth largest Federal program, after Social Security, health care and defense."[33]

This is not an isolated example. Businesses frequently use unreliable data to make crucial decisions. Million-dollar advertising decisions are made regularly on the basis of A.C. Nielsen ratings of television audiences and Simmons Market Research Bureau measurement of magazine readership, though both have been widely criticized as inaccurate and misleading.

SPECIALISTS AND SUPER-SIMPLIFIERS

In the 1970 best seller that made Alvin Toffler famous, he describes four victims of future shock: *the denier*, who blocks out unwelcome reality; *the specialist*, who accepts change but only in a narrow sector of life; *the reversionist*, who clings to the past; and finally *the super-simplifier*, who seeks a single explanation for all the changes going on.[34] The specialist and the super-simplifier are victims of knowledge warp.

Specialization was the first major response to the information deluge. It was a new and usually effective way to manage information. The only problem, as Toffler indicates, is that it is easy for the specialist to make use of all the latest information in his profession while closing his eyes to what is new in other fields. The result is knowledge warp.

Thus even so sagacious a specialist as Peter Drucker can get too close to his material. In *The New Realities*,[35] Drucker distinguishes between microeconomies, macroeconomies, transnational economies and the world economy, but does not seem to realize that these definitions exist as separate systems only in the minds of economists and their students. The real economy is organic and worldwide, with every economic activity, whether micro or macro, influencing every other.

Toffler's super-simplifier plugs into one explanation and refuses to consider all others in an attempt to escape a multifaceted dilemma. Unfortunately the approach can do a lot of damage when trying to solve problems—whether it be the man who blames every car problem on the quality of the gasoline or Alvin Toffler himself who ends his book prescribing the impossible—that we somehow halt the acceleration of change:

> Our first and most pressing need, therefore, before we can begin to gently guide our evolutionary destiny, before we can build a humane future, is to halt the runaway acceleration that is subjecting multitudes to the threat of future shock while, at the very same moment, intensifying all the problems they must deal with.[36]

Despite my insistence that the information deluge is not the only cause of society's and the individual's many problems, including the fast pace of change, I am sure there will be readers who feel this book makes me a super-simplifier. At least, I do not think we can dam the deluge. I am convinced we must accept the flood and find ways to manage it.

5. TUNEOUT

Tuneout is a form of denial. It tries to survive the flood of information by floating on it. Its symbol is the couch potato who sits before the television set seeing and hearing but not really absorbing or understanding.

APATHY AND EMOTIONAL WITHDRAWAL

In *Future Shock,* Toffler devotes an entire chapter to the psychological effects of the shock of extreme change, how overstimulation may lead to bizarre behavior:

> First, we find the same evidences of confusion, disorientation, or distortion of reality. Second, there are the same signs of fatigue, anxiety, tenseness, or extreme irritability. Third, in all cases there appears to be a point of no return—a point at which apathy and emotional withdrawal set in.[37]

Information overstimulation can cause such involuntary symptoms but more commonly the effect is voluntary: what I call "tuneout." Toffler's denier, for example, solves the problem of too much change by making believe it is not happening.

Yet one does not have to be a couch potato to take refuge in tuneout. Because the information flood makes it so difficult to retain control, many people surrender to extreme passivity—at least in wide areas of their lives. This is why so many people attend the nearest church or no church at all. It is also why so few American citizens vote. In his 1950 classic, *The Lonely Crowd,* psychologist David Riesman tried to explain the growing indifference to politics. He acknowledged that one can ignore politics because no action seems needed for a good outcome, and that prosperity and security can breed political indifference. But he argued that complete withdrawal can also mean that "the scene looks so confused that no action seems adequate, or so hopeless that no action looks promising."[38] He went on to argue that such withdrawal can spread to other spheres and affect character formation.

VANNATIZING AMERICA

Another effect of tuneout is failure to distinguish between the trivial and the important, what Ted Koppel called "the Vannatizing of America," after television game show star Vanna White, who became an "important personality" by walking back and forth turning blocks from their blank side to their lettered side on "Wheel of Fortune."[39] More and more Americans deal with the flood of information by trivializing it.

This "Trivial Pursuit" attitude provides the feeling of managing information without taxing the mind with understanding or sorting it for significance. I once asked an acquaintance how he thought a new five-story building would affect the neighborhood. He told me he had no idea, but he had calculated the number of bricks used in its construction.

Dilettantism has taken on a new and pernicious form. People flit from information source to information source with no intention of using what they learn. Education has been reduced to a form of entertainment. In *Amusing Ourselves to Death,* Neil Postman explains this form of tuneout as using amusement to provide meaning to information with no genuine personal relevance:

> Where people once sought information to manage the real contexts of their lives, now they had to invent contexts in which otherwise useless information might be put to some apparent use.

He blames the electronic media, principally television, for creating ...

a world without much coherence or sense; a world that does not ask us, indeed, does not permit us to do anything; a world that is, like the child's game of peek-a-boo, entirely self-contained. But, like peek-a-boo, it is also endlessly entertaining.[40]

But humans used tuneout long before television. As long as there have been classrooms, students have tuned out teachers in the spring, and as long as there has been marriage, husbands have tuned out chattering wives (and vice versa). In fact, selective tuneout is a useful tool in managing unwanted information. My wife has the ability to watch television without seeing or hearing the commercials.

Turning off attention can be a deliberate technique in managing the information one neither wants nor needs. It becomes dangerous only when the individual pays attention only to information that allows him to feel comfortable, and tunes out whatever makes him feel uncomfortable—a temptation that always existed but that becomes more seductive as the volume of information grows.

RELYING ON THE UNRELIABLE

Information availability coupled with the natural human tendency to avoid both worrisome work and difficult decisions can seduce executives to tune out vital information. Thus, as employee counselor David W. Foerster warned, "Hiring decisions have become data-driven and not values-driven." Some 3,000 companies have used the CompuScore System from National CompuScreen Inc. in Portland, Oregon. By administering an online 80-question survey, the hiring executive gets an immediate prediction on the candidate's propensity for substance abuse, theft or violence. National CompuScreen boasts a minimum 96 percent success rate, a claim difficult to prove, since it would require following the lives of applicants who took the test over a period of several years.[41]

As information services tempt executives to tune out knowledge they really need in business decisions, so modern technology has caused tuneout in military decisions of life and death. As *The Economist* wrote recently, "The new warfare will be 'multi-dimensional,' meaning not only that air, sea and land operations will be increasingly integrated, but also that information and outer space will be part of modern war."[42] The magazine is talking about "information warfare" made possible by superior technology, electronic systems like the U.S. Navy's Cooperative Engagement Capability or the Force Threat Evaluation & Weapon Assignment. Yet I cannot help wondering whether over-reliance on technology was the reason a U.S. commander blasted an Iranian passenger jet out of the mid-morning sky in 1988,[43] and why an American pilot shot down a U.S. helicopter three years later during the Persian Gulf War, killing 24 of his countrymen.

DODGING RESPONSIBILITY

In his book, *The Knowledge Executive*, Harlan Cleveland points out that tuning out information is an easy way to avoid responsibility.

> In ancient China no one wanted to notice a dead body, let alone pick it up from the street; by social custom, the person who betrayed knowledge of the death became responsible for the funeral. We don't need to go all the way back to biblical times to find examples of people who avoided knowledge of nearby poverty or distress, "passed on the other side," leaving the problem for some Good Samaritan willing to take the responsibility that goes with knowledge.... During the Watergate hearings, I lost count of the number of government officials who had evidently said to themselves (and perhaps to their spouses), "I don't really want to know what that money is being spent for."[44]

Sidestepping responsibility by tuneout is closely related to our sixth serious side effect.

6. GROUPTHINK

There is a natural tendency in every human to follow the crowd or "authorities" on the assumption that others probably have more or better information. Allowing a group, large or small, to do our thinking for us is what I call groupthink.

THE BAY OF PIGS

In 1983, Irving Janis published an interesting book called *Groupthink, Psychological Studies of Policy Decisions and Fiascoes*. Janis was interested in how decisions made by small groups are affected by a group psychology in which members of the group defer to group thinking even when they would have arrived at a different opinion if they had been operating independently.

One of the author's studies centers on the Bay of Pigs fiasco. After the invasion of Cuba failed, Arthur Schlesinger wrote that he had hesitated to bring up his objections for fear that others would regard it as presumptuous for him, a college professor, to take issue with august heads of major government institutions. Even President Kennedy himself said that he was wrong to assume "that the military and intelligence people have some secret skill not available to ordinary mortals."[45]

Although Janis seemed to think of groupthinking as a very distinct process from independent thinking, groupthink, in my much wider definition, always influences everyone's thinking to some degree. It would be the height of folly as much as egotism to try to live in denial that there are others with knowledge superior to ours. Moreover, as some scholars have pointed out, groupthink can be an economical manner of making a decision when the decision does not warrant the effort an independent decision requires.

But here I am talking about groupthink when, as a dangerous side effect of information overdose, it surrenders mental independence in important decisions out of fear or sloth.

Why is it that so many people sell stocks when everybody else is selling, and buy stocks when everyone else is buying—even though experts continually point our that the real money lies in bucking trends? Why is it that so many advertisements emphasize the popularity or success of a product when all that should count is its value and price? Why do women presuppose that they will look better in dresses that are in style?

As the flood of information makes decisions more difficult the temptation becomes stronger and stronger to let others make decisions for us. We are more likely to follow the crowd, to accept ideas because everyone else seems to accept them. This is not the place to debate the value and virtue of religious faith. But we must admit that, in many cases, people have joined cults and let some guru do their thinking in order to avoid the hard job of thinking for themselves. One of the rules of the Heaven's Gate cult, revealed after the 1997 mass suicide, was that members were not to trust their own judgment or use their own minds.[46]

Toffler described "life style" as a form of groupthink: "the choice of a life style model to emulate is a crucial strategy in our private war against the crowding pressures of overchoice."[47] The irony is that, as the young learn enough to lose respect for their parents and revolt against their family's life style, they do not become independent thinkers, which is very difficult. Instead they leap from one groupthink to another, adopting customs, styles and tastes of their teenage peers.

I believe that more than 90 percent of all racial, ethnic and religious prejudice in the world is the result of groupthink. Unreasonable dislike or fear of others may have its roots in some historical fact but it is perpetuated—sometimes for centuries—by groupthink.

PECULIARLY AMERICAN?

In *Democracy in America*, that very perceptive Frenchman, Alexis de Tocqueville, concluded that groupthink is a peculiarly American disease. He did not call it groupthink, but he argued that, because every American thinks himself the equal of every other man, it will be difficult for most Americans to resist accepting the opinion of the majority. In *The Closing of the American Mind*, Allan Bloom paraphrases de Tocqueville's argument:

> If all opinions are equal, then the majority of opinions, on the psychological analogy of politics, should hold sway. It is very well to say that each should follow his own opinion, but since consensus is required for social and political life, accommodation is necessary. So, unless there is some strong ground for opposition to majority opinion, it inevitably prevails. This is the really dangerous form of the tyranny of the majority, not the kind that actively persecutes minorities but the kind that breaks the inner will to resist because there is no qualified source of nonconforming principles and no sense of superior right. The majority is all there is.[48]

But neither de Toqueville nor, I fear, Professor Bloom foresaw the effects of the information deluge on the need for an authoritative community to provide social values. Americans—and people throughout the world—had no problem so long as their countries had homogeneous sets of values.

But the flood of knowledge has undermined national consensus, splintered social value structures, and forced individuals to look elsewhere for a lodestar. And the natural place to turn was to more homogeneous islands of community. Some were ethnic, some religious, some tribal and some created by sharing the terror and misery of life in the ghetto. Groupthink explains why the global village is fragmenting into so many ethnic groups, unruly gangs and hostile communities.

That brings us to the last and most troublesome side effect of information overdose: alienation.

7. ALIENATION

The spread of information has deepened the divisions that fragment our society. More and more minorities with characteristics that put them at a disadvantage in the larger society withdraw from or revolt against the majority.

ENVY IS A PART OF IT

Though desire may be considered the reverse of fear, it can be just as destructive. One complaint about advertising—perhaps the principal complaint—is that it creates desires and thereby dissatisfaction. But advertising is not alone in breeding dissatisfaction. Television, movies, newspapers and magazines constantly remind each of us that others have desirable things that we do not. Because they know what they are missing, 1998's poor—whether in urban ghettos or third-world countries—have "needs" that were not even in the dreams of 1898's poor.

Astandard dictionary defines envy as a "painful or resentful awareness of an advantage enjoyed by another joined with a desire to possess the same advantage." Though not the sole cause, envy certainly played a major role in the 1993 Los Angeles riots. But we need not rely on social explosion to show how the spread of information lies at the roots of over-urbanization and the growth of ghettos.

Population shifts always result from people learning (truly or falsely) that life is better someplace else. Such population flows, of course, go way back in history. But today they have become an incredible torrent. Nowhere can this be seen more clearly than in Africa, where the coastal cities have become huge nests of slums populated by peasants from the continent's interior.

TRIBALISM

Many social commentators, including Senator Patrick Moynihan,[49] *Newsweek's* Joe Klein,[50] The Manhattan Institute's Myron Magnet,[51] and management guru Peter Drucker,[52] have commented on the growth of "tribalism" in modern society. We no longer speak of the United States as a melting pot. Instead we have Jesse Jackson's "rainbow coalition" (with rainbow a fact and coalition a dream).

What happened? The information deluge has forced minorities to see themselves as others see them. That is why there was such terrified response to a book like Charles Murray's *The Bell Curve*,[53] which reiterated the "finding" that blacks do less well than whites in Intelligence Quotient testing. It was useless for Murray and others to point out that many blacks have higher IQs than many whites, and that each individual exists as a unique individual, not as an average. Blacks know how the white majority looks at them and, willy nilly, that changes the way they look at themselves. As the Jesuit scholar Walter J. Ong observed in *The Presence of the Word* (written before Apartheid was outlawed):

> The white racist or Black Muslim is more preoccupied (even if negatively) with members of the other race than are most of those who favor integration. In the present situation, such a society as the whites of the Republic of South Africa is not only a retarded culture but a self-deceived one. The white South African psyche is structured around and enslaved to the Negro.[54]

SEEING OURSELVES AS OTHERS SEE US

Back in the 1930s, an American philosopher/psychologist by the name of George Herbert Mead explained why we see ourselves largely in the way others see us. Hugh G. Duncan's *Communication and Social Order* describes Mead's reasoning:

> The individual experiences himself as a self, not directly, but indirectly, from the standpoints of other members of the same group or from the standpoint of the social group as a whole to which he belongs. He becomes an object to himself by taking the attitudes of other individuals toward himself within a social world in which both he and they are involved. He can take these attitudes because what he says to others can mean the same to himself as it does to them. For when he speaks he hears his own words, and thus learns what words mean because he can observe how they affect others, as well as how they affect him.[55]

In *No Sense of Place*, Joshua Meyrowitz, describes the paradox that resulted when modern communications disrupted the isolated information systems of minority affiliations:

> Many people take renewed pride in their special identity, yet the heightened consciousness of the special group is the result of being able to view one's group from the outside; that is, it is the result of no longer being fully in the group.... People sense they are in a minority group because they feel excluded from the larger reference group.[56]

Meyrowitz says in another place:

> Television has helped change the deferential Negro into the proud Black, merged the Miss and Mrs. into a Ms, transformed the child into a 'human being' with natural rights. Television has fostered the rise of hundreds of 'minorities'—people who, in perceiving a wider world, begin to see themselves as unfairly isolated in some pocket of it.[57]

Though other media as well as television were behind these changes, I agree that this analysis offers at least a partial explanation for the recent rise of minorities as potent social and political forces. The more they are alienated the stronger will be their desire—and ability—to fight.

FIVE CONSEQUENCES

Learning how others look down on you has a five-pronged effect.

1. It widens the social world in which you are involved. Centuries ago people were conscious only of how their neighbors saw them. Today most people are concerned about the opinions of people throughout the world. This can affect small groups and whole countries. It has added to the moral breakdown in Russia and is evident in much of the modern Islamic world.

2. It encourages isolation to protect yourself, whether psychological or physical. Let the world think you are inferior. You salvage your self respect by turning your back on the world and withdrawing into yourself or into a community of people who consider you an equal. Iran is a prime example of the latter, but this sort of retreat happens in groups large and small, from the whole of Islam to the Pennsylvania Amish. As to psychological retreat, Riesman provided an example in *The Lonely Crowd*:

> Among Sioux reservation children, as described by Erik H. Erikson, there seem to be two reactions to white culture: one is resentful resistance, the other is what might be termed compliant resistance. The behavior of the former seems, to the white educator, incorrigible; of the latter, almost too ingratiating, too angelic. In

both cases, because he has at least the tacit approval of his parents and other Sioux adults, the child preserves something of the Sioux character and tradition whether or not he yields overtly to the whites. The conflict, however, drains the child of emotional energy; often he appears to be lazy. Both the resistant and the seemingly compliant are apathetic toward the white culture and white politics.[58]

3. **It curdles hope and ambition into despair and resentment.** Conscious that many think you cannot achieve what they have achieved you rescue your self respect by blaming your misfortune on them. This attitude can be found among many of the black underclass in American cities—and almost as many of the white underclass dependent on welfare. It is at the heart of the phenomenon described in *A Nation of Victims: The Decay of the American Character*,[59] a 1992 book by Charles J. Sykes, who argues that more and more American groups and individuals define themselves as victims to avoid responsibility and project guilt onto others.

4. **It inspires you to fight for your rights.** The battle takes many different forms, from assassination and terrorism to boycotts, picketing and infiltration. Anwar Sadat in Egypt, Indira Ghandi in India and David Gunn, the abortion physician in the United States, were murdered by extremist members of alienated groups. The infiltration strategies of the Pakistani fundamentalist Maulana Abul Ala Maududi (died 1979), the Roman Catholic Opus Dei (founded in Spain in 1928), the Israeli Gush Emunim followers of Rabbi Zvi Yehuda Kook (died 1982), and the Protestant fundamentalist Operation Rescue of the United States are remarkably similar.[60]

5. **It creates attitudes that breech the boundaries of the alienated culture to influence other cultures,** thereby reaffirming their validity in the alienated group. Religious fundamentalists, for instance, are helping to maintain, and even restore, religion's place in the Islamic East and the Christian West. Professed outlaws in the alienated underclass, like Snoop Doggy Dogg, sing rampage and revolution and become popular stars in the majority culture. As *Newsweek* commentator Joe Klein observes,

> We are living in the Golden Age of Attitude. Rantings reverberate, politics and entertainment conflate. Louis Farrakhan was a calypso performer; his protege Khalid Abdul Muhammad struts his stuff like a gangsta-rapper. Both exist somewhere on the media spectrum between Ice-T and the Ayatollah Khomeini.... Poses struck in

Hollywood and on CNN become real life on the frontiers of civility: "Mad Max" videos become how-to manuals for road warriors in the anarchy of Somalia.[61]

Examples of alienation, deepened—if not created—by the flood of information, are almost too many to mention. They range from feminists to African tribes, from homosexuals to Bosnians, Muslims and Serbs, from the disabled to American Indians, from Quebec separatists in Canada to Catholics and Protestants in Northern Island to the militia groups in our western states. Consider here just three of these, very different, alienated groups:

1. GHETTO GANGS

In 1970, a University of Pennsylvania black sociologist, Elijah Anderson, spent three years living in the Chicago ghetto to observe the street culture. His study resulted in two books[62] and an article in *The Atlantic Monthly*.[63] Anderson speaks of "an oppositional culture" governed by the "code of the streets." It exists side by side with "decent" poor families, bolstered by the churches, who cling to traditional middle-class values. The important point here is that what looks, to the outsider, like total anarchy is not that at all. It is a well-formed culture that has grown spontaneously out of the need of society's refugees to nourish their self respect.

The violence itself is integral to the cultural code. You prove yourself and earn respect in the eyes of fellow gang members by punishing, even killing, those who treat you with disrespect. "If someone disses you, you got to straighten them out." And to survive in the environment even "decent" people have to conform to the code. So valued is being esteemed by oneself and others that many "street men" are willing to die in defense of "their honor." What outsiders consider a desperado is in his own eyes a kind of martyr.

In summary Anderson writes:

> The extent to which some children—particularly those who through upbringing have become most alienated and those lacking in strong and conventional social support—experience, feel, and internalize racist rejection and contempt from more conventional society may strongly encourage them to express contempt for the more conventional society in turn. In dealing with this contempt and rejection, some youngsters will consciously invest themselves and their considerable mental resources in what amounts to an oppositional culture to preserve themselves and their self-respect.

Once they do, any respect they might be able to garner in the wider system pales in comparison with the respect available in the local system; thus they often lose interest in even attempting to negotiate the mainstream system.[64]

Interviewing a youngster in a Chicago West Side housing project, *Newsweek* quotes her explanation for admiring rapper Snoop Doggy Dogg: "He grew up like us and he says we're all in the same gang. To me he's saying you gotta take what's yours."[65]

As will become evident in Part Two, the solution to the problem of the alienated lies in enabling the hostile underclass to achieve self esteem in the broader culture.

2. RELIGIOUS FUNDAMENTALISTS

I define "fundamentalism" somewhat as Martin E. Marty does in the book he wrote with R. Scott Appleby, *The Glory and the Power*. Although the term fundamentalism originated in American Protestantism in the early 20th Century, Marty uses it to describe any religious minority that is united by charismatic leadership, clings to a most radical interpretation of its religious beliefs and is willing to fight for those beliefs.

The book discusses examples from American Christianity, Israeli Judaism and Egyptian Islamism and defines fundamentalism as a habit of mind and pattern of behavior, "a religious way of being that manifests itself as a strategy by which beleaguered believers attempt to preserve their distinctive identity as a people or group."[66]

Fundamentalists in this sense have been called extremists, ultra-orthodox, radical-reformists, neo-traditionalists and the religious right. As Marty and Appleby point out, fundamentalists use modern techniques to defend ancient beliefs. They are fervent proselytizers; and, whether Sikhs in India, IRA supporters in Belfast, or abortion foes in the United States, they are willing to use guns to prove their point.

What they have in common with other alienated groups is the realization that the majority looks down on them, the decision to hold themselves apart, the conviction that major problems would disappear if everybody thought as they do, and the willingness to fight for what they believe. The emphasis may vary from group to group, but the basic outlines are always there. Naturally, the methodology of each group will be colored by their social environment. While alienated religious groups in Egypt and India assassinate national leaders, their counterparts in the U.S. take over school boards, run radio programs and march in picket lines.

Fundamentalism is a good example of how groupthink becomes a refuge from the uncertainty and confusion created by the information deluge. At the heart of every fundamentalist group is the need for absolute authority. In theory the authority is always God. In practice it is some interpreter, usually a charismatic leader. Like the gangs described above, "the inner core and sympathizers alike follow a rigorous socio-moral code that sets them apart from nonbelievers and from compromisers."[67]

3. JAPAN INC.

The rise of Japan as a major economic power is seldom seen as a consequence of tribalism—or the the information deluge. But it is.

In his insightful *Looking at the Sun*, James Fallows argued that "Asia's modern success is the latest stage of a process that started when the European colonialists spread out through Africa, Asia, and Latin America five centuries ago." Because the Westerner had superior resources, machinery and firepower, they could and did push the Asians around. "To most Westerners," Fallows explained, "this episode is part of the distant past. In Asia its aftereffects live on today. Having seen the consequences of being weak, many of these countries resolved at all costs to become strong."[68]

Nowhere is this more true than in Japan. The Japanese have always felt, with good reason, that Westerners considered them inferiors and much of the history of the last century can be explained by that fact. For two and a half centuries before the arrival of Commodore Matthew C. Perry in 1853, Japan was closed to the world. Japanese citizens were executed for trying to leave Japan. A shogun's edict proclaimed:

> All Southern Barbarians and Westerners, not only the English, worship Christianity, that wicked cult prohibited in our land. Henceforth, whenever a foreign ship is sighted approaching any point on our coast, all persons on hand should fire on it and drive it off.[69]

Perry's arrival and increased information about the west resulted in a new attitude. The Japanese had to catch up to prove their superiority. Military fail-

2. Information Overdose: The Side Effects 53

ure in the Second World War forced their leaders to recognize that the real strength of the Aryan world lay in economic supremacy. Although Americans may consider the U.S. occupation of Japan under General Douglas MacArthur and later George Kennan to be one of history's great successes, to the Japanese it was a confirmation of the perception that America and the rest of the Western world considered them inferior. This perception was the principal motive propelling Japan's impressive drive to economic power.

Today Japan is the dominant economic power in Asia and, despite recent setbacks, many of its leaders are talking about an Asian regional trading bloc in which the yen will replace the dollar as the currency for international transactions.[70] Japan plans to become the dominant economic power in the world. To this end, as Fallows insisted repeatedly, the Japanese have milked the information stream to learn the knowledge of the West to use it against the West. As he also stressed, the success of Japan's economic strategy lay in holding down the living standards of its citizens to increase its power as a nation.

Some 20 years ago, as a consultant to Matsushita Corporation of America (the manufacturer and marketer of Panasonic products), I witnessed Japanese pride and hunger for information firsthand. Nine out of 10 employees at Panasonic's New Jersey headquarters were Americans, but they worked side by side on every level with Japanese, all brought from Japan by the company and all destined to return after they had served their stint abroad. The top managers of the American subsidiary were all Japanese.

I had been hired by the communications director, who was an American. So my request to interview the Japanese president of the U.S. subsidiary was unexpected. But an interview was arranged and I came away with two lasting impressions. He was extremely proud of the company and its founder, who built a one-man shop making electrical sockets into a diversified international corporation. But he was even more intrigued about how I operated and wanted to know every detail of what I was doing and why.

For almost a hundred years, Japan has held to a policy of producing "purely" Japanese products and reducing dependence on the rest of the world. Since it will always be dependent on other countries for food and oil, its strategy has been to compensate by becoming independent in high technology. Most of this technological knowhow came from the United States until, in the late 1980s, Japan achieved a positive trade balance in high-tech products, and its Ministry of International Trade and Industry was able to report that "Japan's technology will soon be overtaking U.S. technology."[71]

This "purity" in manufacturing has extended to Japan's immigration policies. According to a 1991 Japanese government survey, there are only about 1 million foreigners (almost all Koreans) living in Japan, not even one percent of the country's population of 122 million.[72]

What neither the Japanese nor *Looking at the Sun* foresaw was how the information deluge would overwhelm Japan's economic strategy. As recent surveys indicate,[73] the famed docility and diligence of the Japanese citizenry is being undermined by information from the West. There are an estimated 1 million Japanese on the Internet. In Tokyo alone Internet connection services have gone from one to 45 in two years.[74] Resistance to immigration is under pressure as Japanese companies complain of labor shortages. In 1988, only 80,000 immigrants were allowed to enter the islands. Three years later the influx was up to 210,000 a year. The International Labor Organization estimates that it is now close to half a million.[75] Even more significant, the total value of foreign mergers with and acquisitions of Japanese companies went from $585 million in 1995 to more than $2.5 billion in 1996.[76]

Meanwhile many Japanese companies are moving overseas to avoid their country's high production and labor costs and the impact of the high yen. Toyota has manufacturing plants in other parts of Asia as well as the United States and Europe, and plans to build a new $1.6 billion plant somewhere in the European Community. As these firms involve more and more non-Japanese (Toyota president Hiroshi Okuda wants foreign plants to hire more local designers.[77]), it will be increasingly difficult to maintain 100% Japanese control. As Harvard University professor and former Secretary of Labor Robert B. Reich explained it,

> The logic of the global web is so powerful that the Japanese will either be forced to comply over time or else face a stiff penalty from the marketplace, the talent pool, and competitors and governments.... Japanese-owned companies that have been notoriously slow to open their top executive ranks to non-Japanese will operate at a competitive disadvantage.[78]

The Japanese have argued that America is weak because it is made up of so many diverse races and nationalities. If that is a weakness, it is a weakness no modern nation, including Japan, can avoid forever.

2. Information Overdose: The Side Effects 55

THE PROBLEM IS TEMPORARY

The accelerating, worldwide fusion of diverse cultures and concerns tells us what is likely to happen to minority groups, whether gangs, the urban underclass, religious fundamentalists, the disadvantaged, American Indians, Africans, or Bosnians, Muslims and Serbs.

Though it might take another century or more, the spread of information and freedom of movement will eventually undermine the economic, cultural and psychological causes of group alienation. Consider how frequently intermarriage has broken through these boundaries. America's Indians quarrel over what percentage of Indian blood makes one a member of the tribe. The Massapequa Pequots currently accept anyone who can prove he or she is one-sixteenth Pequot, and Bruce Kirchner, a tribal elder, foresees the need to reduce the requirement to one-thirty-second.[79]

The spread of knowledge—via social understanding, rights legislation, medical science and prosthetic technology—has already mainstreamed many of the disabled. And, as we shall see in later chapters, new ways of managing information may reconcile, if not eliminate, many other conflicting claims of minorities. But this will take time—lots of time. In *Culture of Complaint*, Robert Hughes protests the coarse generalization of terms like Latin-American Culture:

> There is no "Latin-American literature" as such, any more than there is a place called "Asia" with a common literature that somehow connects the Ramayana, the works of Confucius and the Pillow-Book of Sei Shonagon. There are only the cultures of various and distinct Latin-American countries, diverse in themselves.... All are the products of long, intense, unpredictable hybridization between three continents, Africa, Europe and America—the process which, more and more, is seen at the center of "Eurocentric" culture as well.[80]

It is hard to tell whether Hughes is complaining about blindness to cultural differences or efforts to make cultural hybridization conform to political divisions instead of waiting for its "long, intense, unpredictable" development. What is significant here is his realization that cultural dissipation and commingling always took place, though it used to happen much more slowly. Today, with the accelerating information flood, it happens so fast that we have difficulty tracking it—so much difficulty that the French are making themselves the butt of international laughter by trying to legislate foreign words out of their language.

The information deluge has magnified the problems caused by uncertainty, fear, distrust, knowledge warp, tuneout, groupthink and alienation. Is there a solution to this growing problem, a new antidote, immunization shot or a social system that can defuse these bombs or lessen their effects?

I think there is. And I think society is already feeling its way to the solution. But before we can grasp how and why such a solution might work, we have to go back to basics, as we do in the next chapter, in order to understand, as much as possible, the nature of information, knowledge and communication.

3

INFORMATION, KNOWLEDGE AND WISDOM

"We spend our lives at learning things, yet always find exceptions and mistakes. Certainty seems always out of reach. This means that we have to take some risks to keep from being paralyzed by cowardice."
—Marvin Minsky, 1985[1]

To manage information we must understand how we receive it and pass it to others. In every communication both the communicator and the communicatee manipulate the information. I ask readers (1) to accept specific definitions of the terms information, idea, knowledge, judgment, design, argument, wisdom, interest and community, (2) to guard against two common fallacies in reasoning and (3) to be aware of the differences in logical, rhetorical and esthetic communication. This should help us to evaluate specific communication, to discount distortion common to all communication and to use a five-step regimen in managing information.

BLAMING THE MESSENGER

We have seen how the growth of human knowledge has brought the flow of information to a flood stage spreading uncertainty, fear, distrust, knowledge warp, tuneout, groupthink and alienation. Now we pause for a chapter of self-analysis, to examine what information is and how it is communicated, to consider how learning or the exchange of information affects each of us. Its affects on society we leave for Chapter 4.

A number of years ago, as an adjunct professor of marketing, I had the unpleasant experience of facing a class revolt for the first time. My students were all employees of a major corporation, which not only encouraged them to improve themselves by taking business courses but also paid their tuition—provided they passed the course.

Despite several years of teaching at both the high school and university levels, I had relatively little experience with employer-financed education and made the mistake of expecting the students to do substantial work in connection with the course. When, after a couple of preliminary tests, it became evident that failure was a possibility if they did not study, three of the students—all adults over 30—walked out of class and complained to the university administration that I was a poor teacher, my marking system was unfair and they found it impossible to understand what I wanted.

I invited a representative of the university to sit in on my class and he had no complaints (or even suggestions for improvement). The remaining students passed the course and turned in some remarkable papers on marketing projects. But my teaching ability or lack of it is not the point here. The students who left were an example of a common phenomenon: the tendency we all have to blame the source when we have a problem with information.

One of the reasons I wrote this book is that, as both a member and observer of the press, I was troubled by the ever-increasing volume of complaints about the pernicious influence of the media. These complaints even came from the most-respected members of our society: leaders in government, religion and education.

Having made my living for 40 years by advising, criticizing and writing about editors, advertisers, journalists and media managers, I have no illusions that journalists are all saints, or even all smart. What bothered me was that much, if not most, of what the press is blamed for is not caused by the press at all. In fact, in many cases people in the media are as distressed by it as their critics.

Why does this happen? Sometimes the critics are surrendering to the urge we all have to break the mirror when we are unhappy with what we see. But most of the time the undeserved criticism is due to human pride, which prefers blaming the communicator to accepting the responsibility for understanding. The public media are especially open to this type of criticism,

3. Information, Knowledge and Wisdom

first, because their job is both to reflect and anticipate the problems of society and, second, because it is so easy to find instances in which the media deceived or misled us.

YET ALL COMMUNICATION IS MANIPULATIVE

One of the earliest lessons a child learns is not to take the observations of its senses at face value. Two balls may appear the same to the eye, but touch teaches that one is hard, the other soft. As infants, we learn to correlate the observations of one sense with those of our other senses. Eventually, we also learn that human communication too cannot be accepted at face value. Every individual communication must be tested against and correlated with all the other things we have learned.

Communication requires even more diligence than observation, for it involves a new element: the human communicator. Someone else is deciding the content and structure of the message.

Hence the most important step in learning how to deal with communication—and, therefore, the media—is to realize that all communication is manipulative, for every communication package is selective. The teacher is limited in what she can communicate, by time as well as by knowledge and skill. The student too is limited in what he can absorb, by attention as well as by interest and capacity. A skillful communicator adapts the medium to the audience—not only the message, but even more the method.

In a way, it takes even more skill to be a successful audience. It requires understanding and discipline to sharpen attention, sustain interest and develop capacity, all of which I expect my readers to do independently of this book. What we should try to do here is understand the method so that we can more clearly comprehend the message.

As Marshall McLuhan pointed out over 40 years ago, the medium is often an integral part of the message.[2] There was no MTV at the time, but MTV certainly illustrates his point. McLuhan, however, became so enamored with his "discovery" of the impact of medium abstracted from content, that he almost completely ignored the impact of content and, to a large extent, the interplay of medium and content.

But we have always had, and now need more than ever, the ability to distinguish—never totally, but sufficiently to make the effort worthwhile—

between message and method, between the information or ideas conveyed and the way in which they are transmitted, between substance and style.

DEFINING SOME TERMS

There are a number of critical terms that appear in almost every discussion of thought and communication, yet are extremely vague because they have, even in the dictionary, many different meanings. The following definitions are mine, for purposes of this book. I have tried to make each very precise to prevent confusion.

INFORMATION: *Anything a mind has perceived whether from observation or communication.*

Note that I do not call something information until some mind has perceived it, whether my mind or another's. I realize that Harlan Cleveland, in *The Knowledge Executive,* requires externality and organization, for he defines information as "organized data—organized by others, not by me."[3] I also know that the information theory used by scientists, since Norbert Wiener created cybernetics, interprets many instances of cause and effect as signal and response so that any series of signals is called information whether perceived by a human being or not, a definition so broad it implies that information is and always has been infinite and, therefore, cannot increase. In fact, since the DNA research of James Watson and Francis Crick in 1952, the analogy of causation as communication has been carried over into biology which now speaks of genetic codes and chemical messages. I do not say these definitions and word uses are correct or incorrect, just that my definitions are different and purposefully so.

IDEA: *A mental pattern which imperfectly but usefully represents existing things by generalizing perceptions common to a number of those things.*

This is almost the opposite of the primary definition in the *Merriam-Webster Dictionary*: "a transcendent entity that is a real pattern of which existing things are imperfect representations." The dictionary concept is identical with that of Plato in his analogy of the cave where we poor humans live and have to settle for the flickering shadows of a divine reality. If ideas are real patterns and existing things are imperfect representations, then the mind becomes the measure of all reality. I am an objectivist in that I believe reality is something outside of our mind and that our minds are imperfect instruments that have to

3. Information, Knowledge and Wisdom

reformulate reality in order to grasp it. Even "thing" is an idea, a static form that we abstract from the constant flow of reality so that our minds can handle it.

KNOWLEDGE: *The mind's translation and retention of information as an idea.*

The dictionary gives knowledge at least ten meanings including mere cognizance, sexual intercourse and the entire body of truth, information and principles acquired by humankind. My definition is more limited. Cleveland describes knowledge as information that has been put to use in one's mind, but adds that most knowledge is expertise.[4] Theodore Roszak says an idea becomes knowledge "when it gathers to itself a certain broad consensus in the society."[5] But then his concept of idea is closer to what I call a judgment.

JUDGMENT: *The forming of a proposition that establishes a mental relationship between two or more ideas.*

Relationships themselves are ideas abstracted from experience, whether identity (this thing is not that thing), similarity (that thing is like this thing) or value (this is bad; that is good). Such judgments are the first step in processing ideas for use.

DESIGN: *A mental construct made up of interrelated judgments.*

A design can be as simple as a syllogism or as complex as the federal budget.

ARGUMENT: *A design constructed for the purpose of arriving at a judgment, whether to convince oneself or others.*

WISDOM: *A mind's accumulation of judgments and designs that have been tested by practical use.*

Usually we do not speak of wisdom unless the accumulation is manifold and significant. (Cleveland calls wisdom "integrated knowledge, information made superuseful by theory."[6]) But in my sense even a small accumulation can be considered a bit of wisdom.

INTEREST: *The motivating force that drives human beings to pursue knowledge.*

The motivation may be inspired by many things, including need, curiosity, desire to please another or the sheer joy of using one's perceptive faculties. This definition is not identical to any of the several found in most dictionaries. I am defining here precisely for epistomological relevance.

COMMUNITY: *The interrelation of a number of individuals brought about by sharing one or more interests.*

Note that I do not include locality in this definition. As we shall see later, the essential element in community is common interest, which is why increased information has so much impact on the structure and operation of society.

FALLACIES THAT FLOW FROM THE WAY THE MIND WORKS

The phrase, "tested by practical use," in the definition of wisdom is very important because it is ultimately the only measure of value in information. Due to the way it operates, the mind has a strong tendency to make two fundamental errors in its efforts to understand, i.e., to grasp reality.

1. Because human beings use knowledge to make things happen—I pull up a chair because I want to sit down—the mind tends to look for a similar process in the world outside. This leads to what I call the *animistic fallacy*: Nothing happens unless some mind wills it to happen. Animism was one of the earliest forms of religion because primitive minds sought an explanation for things they saw happen. Trees grow, therefore there must be a spirit inside each tree that makes it grow. Out of this type of thinking grew the *teleological fallacy*: Because there is a purpose behind everything we do, everything must have a purpose.

Darwin's great contribution to biology was to point out that all the various species we see around us could have come about by what we call accident, and what he called natural selection. He showed that their existence could be explained without presuming a preexisting mental design, a teleological cause. But the animistic and teleological fallacies are so strong that even a dyed-in-the-wool Darwinist, biologist Richard Dawkins, wrote an entire book, *The Selfish Gene*, explaining evolution as if genes had some sort of mental capacity and could do things on purpose.[7]

2. Because the mind has no other way to test the validity of what it knows but to put it to use, the mind's second weakness is its inclination to slip into the *experimentalistic fallacy*: if it works, it has to be true. When a scientist comes out of a laboratory with a new scientific discovery, fellow scientists will not accept the theory until they can reproduce the experiment in their laboratories. They want proof. The fallacy lies not in confirming the evidence, a necessary though fallible test, but in the frequent assumption that the test proves that the judgment conforms absolutely with reality.

On May 9, 1994, *Newsweek* reported:

> Last week physicists announced the first experimental evidence ever for the existence of a long-sought elementary particle called the top quark. In doing so, they completed a 2,000-year-old search for the fundamental, indivisible bits of which all matter, from stars to slugs, is made.[8]

When I copied this item, I noted next to it: "I could be wrong, but I bet someday other scientists will discover the bits out of which top quarks are made." Sure enough, 21 months later *Newsweek* announced:

> According to a paper made public last week, certain results suggested that quarks may actually be composed by even smaller and more fundamental particles. If true,...this raises the disturbing possibility that the universe will never surrender its ultimate material, that beneath every level of particles lurks another, still more esoteric and inaccessible.[9]

As thousands of years of experience have shown, no matter how sure we think we are, we could be wrong. The earth is not flat; it is not the center of the universe; and the recipe for chocolate cake that always works at sea level does not work on top of Mount Everest. "Like evolution itself," as Mihaly Csikszentmihalyi has written,"the quest for truth never ends. Certainties are always revised, and entirely new vistas open up when we least expect it."[10]

THE MIND AS A LIMITED INSTRUMENT

The human mind is a limited instrument. Just as the eye changes light waves into color and the ear, vibrations into sound, so the mind refashions what it perceives. Information, ideas, and judgments are mental constructs, useful for practical dealings with reality but always distortions of reality. The great German philosopher Immanuel Kant was talking about religion and moral sense when he used the term "practical reason," but all reason has to be practical in that it must say: "This is knowledge I can work with," never: "This is absolutely true."

This limitation of the mind is what quantum physicists are arguing about when they speak of the paradox of Schroedinger's cat, a speculated animal in a speculated box who could be dead or alive depending not upon what we do, but upon what we observe.[11] This scientific puzzle echoes the medieval argument on how many angels can dance on the point of a pin or Bishop George Berkeley's question in the 18th Century whether a tree falling in the forest really makes a noise, if no one hears it.[12]

The mind's stubborn refusal to accept its own limitations is what leads very learned men like physicists Eugene Wigner and John Wheeler to theorize that information is the basic ingredient of the universe and that the universe may owe its existence to the fact that it is observed by intelligent beings.[13] We find a more recent example of this projection of the mind's shortcomings onto reality among superficial admirers of chaos theory, who speak of disorder as if it were a state of reality rather than an admission that we do not understand a real state.[14] Thus Irene Sanders wrote that chaos "is the way the world creates the rich diversity that we see all around us."[15]

THREE WAYS OF COMMUNICATING

Back in the Fifth Century before the Christian era, Aristotle wrote treatises on three different ways of communicating, distinguished by the purpose of the communicator. He referred to them as Logic, Rhetoric and Poetics. In today's language I would call these three communications techniques: the logical approach, the rhetorical approach and the aesthetic approach.

The logical approach is the tool of the teacher. It aims at helping the audience to understand. It appeals to reason and is satisfied if it is accepted by the minds of the audience.

The rhetorical approach is the weapon of the orator. It aims at getting the audience to do something. It appeals to emotions as well as the mind and it fails unless the audience responds by action.

The aesthetic approach is the instrument of the artist. It aims at pleasurable perception. It involves one or more of the audience's perceptive faculties (mind, emotions, imagination, senses) in such a way as to share the communicator's vision.

These approaches are, of course, abstractions. Very seldom, if ever, are they employed alone, logic unblemished by rhetoric or rhetoric unembellished by esthetic. In fact, in this age of fictionalized documentaries and re-enacted events, it is becoming more and more difficult to isolate the three approaches.

What is important to remember is that in each case the communicator manipulates both substance and style. The substance is selected, pruned and groomed not only to fit the communicator's purpose, but also to fit the limitations of his knowledge and the requirements of the medium. What remains is then styled through order, omission and embellishment.

Aristotle himself was very much aware of this. In his definition of rhetoric he observed that:

> rhetoric is a combination of the science of logic and of the ethical branch of politics; and it is partly like dialectic, partly like sophistical reasoning. But the more we try to make either dialectic or rhetoric sciences, instead of the practical faculties they really are, the more we shall inadvertently be destroying their true nature.[16]

If, as I have shown above, science rests on practical tests that are never infallible, we find even more reason to agree with Aristotle that communication is a "practical faculty." Even the teacher, appealing to reason, manipulates—with dialectic to arrive at the truth or sophistical reasoning to deceive. And the politician, a manipulator by profession, uses rhetoric—including these techniques and, as Aristotle said, all other "available means of persuasion" to promote or defend normative judgments as to what is good or bad for his constituents.

TO PROTECT OURSELVES

From a practical point of view, to protect ourselves against manipulation in any communications we should realize that every communicator distorts the information offered by the way it is selected, the order in which it is presented, and the manner in which it is embellished.

Selection is dictated by knowledge, motive and attitude.

Before accepting new information that is important to us, we should question the source. Did the information come from someone who really knows? And, if the information involves judgment, is the source someone whose judgment we have reason to trust? This is extremely important when dealing with the media. As we shall discuss in a later chapter, much of what is presented by professional communicators is distorted less by malice than by the need to deliver information before all the facts are available.

The more we understand the motive behind a communication, the easier it is to evaluate it. The majority of readers know that an advertisement is trying to sell something, and discount its message accordingly. More of a problem arises in nonadvertising matter, particularly straight news reporting. For years, American journalists naively promoted the idea that they could and would be completely objective in the news columns. In 1939, before the United States became directly involved in World War II, CBS radio distributed a four-page directive to its staff on how the war was to be covered in its news broadcasts. It said, in part:

> Columbia's announced policy of having no editorial views of its own and not seeking to maintain or advance the views of others will be rigidly continued.... Those, therefore, who are its voice in presenting or analyzing the news must not express their own feelings. This does not preclude informed appraisals of the meaning of facts.... What news analysts are entitled to do and should do is to elucidate and illuminate the news out of common knowledge or special knowledge.... Their function is to help the listener to understand, to weigh, and to judge, but not to do the judging for him.[17]

Today, news departments still strive for objectivity, as KXAS (Fort Worth, Texas) television news co-anchor Mike Snyder learned, in October 1994, when he was suspended for two weeks without pay for taking sides in the race for Texas governor.[18] But news managers today are far more circumspect in policy statements than they were in 1939. They realize how much judgment precedes the help they give listeners to understand, weigh and judge. They agree with ex-newspapermen and now journalism professors John C. Merrill and Ralph D. Barney that "news media naturally distort reality; it is the nature of abstracting from that reality and creating verbal and pictorial representations for second-hand consumption."[19]

As we shall see later, the simple motive of keeping one's audience interested is a major factor in undermining journalistic objectivity.

In 1983, Dr. Carl A. Galloway brought a $30 million libel suit against CBS-TV's Dan Rather and "60 Minutes." The plaintiff's lawyer argued not that the TV program was dishonest, but that editing—especially editing for excitement and drama—distorted the facts and was unfair to Galloway.[20] It was a curious point to be made by a lawyer. Can one imagine a good trial lawyer purging every element of drama from his courtroom presentation? If editing for drama is reprehensible in a TV program or a magazine article, how can we defend its use in a court of law? Galloway lost the case.

Rhetoric, as much as logic, is a valid and necessary tool in human communications. Both are open to misuse, but neither can be forbidden in the name of justice. In fact, it is the human condition that, while logic helps us to challenge and evaluate information, logic is helpless unless emotion and will—rhetoric's province—convince the mind to pay attention. Journalists who bring us information through the media are humans informing humans. The intelligent realize that, and they do not read publications or listen to broadcasts as if they were the Bible (which, by the way, never stints on rhetoric).

This brings us to distortion caused by the communicator's attitude. Attitude is less conscious than motive, and frequently harder to recognize. But it can influence both what the communicator knows (for it directs attention) and what he uses (for it colors the communicator's judgment). A major corruptor of objectivity, for instance, is the self-aggrandizement reporters find in familiarity with celebrities—politicians, movie stars and sports heroes.

An important facet of attitude is taste, what can be defined as one's perception as to what is aesthetically appropriate. Communicators are influenced not only by their own tastes, but almost as much by what they consider to be the taste of their audience. Men, for instance, frequently use different language when communicating with women than they use with other men.

CULTURE AS COMMUNICATION CORRUPTER

Underlying attitude, and usually its least conscious element, is culture. Human beings are molded by their social environment not only in what they think but as much in how they think and in how they communicate with each other. As Edward T. Hall puts it in *Beyond Culture*:

> Culturally based paradigms place obstacles in the path to understanding [others, particularly people from different cultures] because culture equips each of us with built-in blinders, hidden and unstated assumptions that control our thoughts and block the unraveling of cultural processes.[21]

A most important theory about the impact of culture on the way we think as well as on how we communicate was developed by Benjamin Lee Whorf and Edward Sapir in the 1930s. Sapir explained the cultural biases built into language, which is a cultural construct that "actually defines experience for us by reason of its formal completeness and because of our unconscious projection of its implicit expectations into the field of experience."[22]

This influence on how we think is almost impossible to control, since the community agreement on speech is largely unconscious.

Add to all this the warning of John Locke in 1690: "Words have naturally no signification, the idea which each stands for must be learned and retained by those who would exchange thoughts and hold intelligible discourse."[23] Furthermore, as Colin Cherry explains in *On Human Communication,*

> Language cannot give precise representation of things or ideas because there are simply not enough different words to express the subtlety of every shade of thought. If we had words for everything, their numbers would be astronomically large and beyond our powers of memory or our skill to use them.[24]

This arbitrary and changing meaning of words is only the beginning of what we have to worry about in communication.

It is important to realize that when I say that style always manipulates meaning, I am not talking about something sinister. In fact, in many instances the writer or speaker may be unconscious of what he or she is doing. Like most things humans do, the process of communicating is largely instinctive. So much so that it is extremely difficult (some would say impossible) to talk or write with complete objectivity. It is natural to let our feelings, prejudices, and desires color the meaning of what we say or write. Much of this manipulation takes place unconsciously. And, for that matter, much of what the audience hears or reads is similarly manipulated by the recipient's feelings, prejudices and desires, also operating unconsciously.

Added to the possibility of being misled by one-on-one communication, we also have to deal with the subconscious messages we absorb daily. Back in the 1970s the aforementioned Oxford zoologist, Richard Dawkins, advanced an interesting theory of how cultural transformations take place in human society. He called it "memetics" and explained it in his book, *The Selfish Gene.*

3. Information, Knowledge and Wisdom

Dawkins builds his theory on a biological analogy. He theorizes that there are ideas and attitudes that spread from one mind to another "just as genes propagate themselves in the gene pool by leaping from body to body via sperm or eggs."[25] He gives these intellectual "genes" a name: "memes." Examples of memes for our purposes would be tunes, fashions, catch phrases, theories, attitudes, standards that spread from mind to mind and become prevalent enough to influence the way a society thinks. "Communism is evil." "Makeup improves a woman's appearance." "Natural is good." These are all memes widely accepted in today's American culture.

Dawkins hit upon an important truth about human communication, though I believe he chose a misleading analogy. What he calls memes are more like viruses than genes, highly contagious viruses. They do not require sperm or eggs for transmission, only an unguarded mind. It is possible to build immunity against particular memes, but no one is immune to every meme, and some memes are more contagious than others. African-Americans, for example, are so influenced by the prevalent memes of physical beauty (white beauty) that they have to make a conscious effort to adopt "black is beautiful" standards. Groups that try to segregate themselves from the rest of America (the Amish, the Hasidic Jews) are less afraid of their countrymen's arguments and proselytizing than they are of their memes.

A THREEFOLD OBLIGATION

Since all communication is manipulative and no communication is without distortion, truth-seekers—that is, all of us—have a threefold obligation both to ourselves and to anyone who learns from us:

- We have to discount the biases in every communicator.
- We have to compensate for our shortcomings in learning.
- We have to become more efficient in using what we learn.

It is this last point that presents our biggest problem and which is the principal subject of this book. Because there is so much information, fed to us from so many sources, it has become extremely important that individuals— and organizations—learn to manage information. Just as our physical health depends on eating the right food in the right quantities, so our mental well-being depends on selecting the right information in the right quantities. We do not all have to eat the same things; some need some kinds of food more than others. We do not all have to know the same things; some need certain kinds of information more than others.

This life-long learning regimen has five elements:

1. Control of attention. Our attention span may seem infinite. It isn't. Human beings have remarkable abilities to do several things at once. Most of us can drive a car in traffic and keep up an unrelated conversation at the same time. Teenagers can do their homework while they listen to music. It is also possible, for some more than others, to absorb information subconsciously and consciously at the same time. But there are always limits. And, usually, the more attention is dissipated, the less effective the learning.

2. Information evaluation. Just as it is natural for a baby to put everything in her mouth, so it is natural for her to open her mind to everything. But, as she grows older, she learns that certain things belong in the mouth and others do not. So, too, we must learn that we cannot open our minds to everything.

3. Information storage. As any student studying for exams knows, the memory is a tricky faculty that sometimes works the way we want it to and sometimes does not. As any scholar knows, there are other ways to store information than by memorization. It is important to put what is important where you can get it when you need it.

4. Information relations. Understanding is more useful than just knowing, largely because it enables us to relate the bits of information our minds have gathered. Information relationships help us determine what we should pay attention to—what is important and where to store it.

5. Information application. It is not what you know but how you use it that makes a difference. Success in life, no matter how you define it, depends largely on ability to use information. Some people use what they learn. Others let it lay fallow. One of the most important shortcomings in our educational system is that most of the time is devoted to imparting information and very little time is spent teaching children how to use it. More on this in Chapter 17.

THE FLOOD MAKES EACH STEP MORE DIFFICULT

The heavier the stream of information coming our way, the more difficult it is to manage the information. The very volume distracts and confuses. It is

3. Information, Knowledge and Wisdom 71

easier to listen for the footfall of someone following you in a quiet wood than in Times Square at noon. It is easier to evaluate the value of information you receive when there are only a few facts to consider. It is much harder when there are hundreds of interrelated facts. Unless you learn how to evaluate and select what is important for you, you will be so swamped with information that you will soon find it impossible to store what you have learned and to understand relationships, to say nothing about using the information effectively.

Everything said here regarding management of information by individuals applies equally to management of information by institutions. As we shall see in the following chapters, management of information determines how societies operate and whether they grow or die. This is true of any cooperative venture of human beings, whether nation states, city governments, school systems, business corporations or individual families.

Information management is an extremely complicated, easily damaged way of dealing with reality. As the next chapter explains, humankind has continually reorganized its information-management tools to handle the amount of information available. So far, we have always succeeded, though not without failed experiments and individual disasters caused by resistance to change.

Today, in what everyone calls "the information age," information management is not only more important than it has ever been, but the changes information management requires are greater and more urgent than any society has ever undertaken.

4

COMMUNICATION CREATES SOCIETY

"The interactions of new technologies and new ideologies ... are the forces driving the economic system in new directions. Together they are producing a new economic game with new rules requiring new strategies ...."

— *Lester C. Thurow, 1996*[1]

Not only does the exchange of information enable and qualify community, but every major advance in civilization can be traced to a significant advance in communication methods, almost always directly related to the tools men invent. Rulers learned early on the importance of information in exercising power. As the flow of information increased, they tried again and again to dam or rechannel it—with diminishing success. These facts help us understand what is happening today.

COMMUNICATION CREATES COMMUNITY

Communication is as natural to human beings as sex. The need for both is undoubtedly among the primary reasons why men and women have always lived in communities. It was natural to mate. It was natural to bear children and care for them. Neither was possible without communication.

Community and communication have the same root, historically as well as etymologically. Whether family or village, a community cannot happen unless people share some values, agree on how they will cooperate and manage

4. Communication Creates Society

to compromise when total agreement becomes elusive. All this is achieved through communication.

Furthermore, to function effectively communities require organization, and, as cybernetics theorist Norbert Wiener put it, "Communication is the cement that makes organisations. Communication alone enables a group to think together, to see together, and to act together."[2] The first step in organization is leadership. It need not reside in a single individual. From the beginning the father tended to lead in providing food, the mother in caring for the children. Leadership may have arisen out of physical characteristics and circumstance, but ultimately it was exercised and recognized through communication.

Authority and government, no matter how primitive, required communication. As communities grew in size and complexity the position of leader was won more often through skill in communication than by physical strength. As an Egyptian scribe wrote 2,200 years before Christ: "Speech was mightier than any fighting."[3]

My purpose here is not to trace the development of primitive society, but to point out how much the very concept of society, of community living, depends on information or communication. I use the words "information" and "communication" almost interchangeably because information without communication has no social value and communication without information is meaningless.

COMMUNICATION ADVANCES LAUNCH NEW SOCIETIES

Michael Rothschild, president of The Bionomics Institute in San Francisco, marks the progress of civilization by four major information revolutions.

The first happened 32,000 years ago: The Cro-Magnon's discovery of the lunar calendar. Archaeologist Alexander Marshack calls these scratches on a piece of reindeer antler the first writing. He argues that the reason why Cro-Magnons survived and developed into modern humans while their competitors, the Neanderthals, died out, was that the Neanderthals never developed writing. Both groups lived by hunting (or scavenging, if we are to believe more recent archeologists). Knowing where game would be at certain times of year was critical to getting enough to eat. That calendar scratched on a piece of horn enabled the Cro-Magnons to track seasons and migrations, thus making them more efficient hunters. In the reasoning of archaeologists, the Cro-Magnon's ability to bring more meat to the family cave gave them the edge in the race for survival.

Rothschild's second information revolution took place some 5,000 years ago in the land of Sumer (now southern Iraq). A trader sending 10 sheep to his client would enclose 10 tiny clay "sheep" in a sealed clay container. Upon receipt the client broke the container and counted the token sheep to make sure none of the real sheep had been sold or eaten in transit. Then some trader found it more convenient to scratch "pictures" of the tokens in a clay tablet. Since reeds served as scratching tools, a shorthand developed by pressing the end of the reed into the soft clay to make different wedge-shaped (cuneiform) designs. Then the Sumerians started using some of the symbols to represent syllables as well as things, and combined syllables to represent other things. (E.g., if the Sumerians had spoken modern English, a Sumerian trader might have combined the symbol for "plow" and the symbol for "man" to write "plowman.")

Thus the Sumerians had invented writing, the ability to represent language in permanent visible form, a major advance over hieroglyphics, which used pictures to represent things. Now men could talk to each other not only farther than the sound of their voices, but in permanent records—simultaneously breaking both the sound and the time barriers to communication. This new medium, written communication, made possible the codifying of laws, the keeping of books, and all the other communication paraphernalia essential for developing wider governments and more extensive trade.

The third information revolution, according to Rothschild, took place much more recently—a little over 500 years ago. A German goldsmith, Johann Gutenberg, invented, or perfected, movable-type printing. Rothschild argues that movable type made possible the rise of modern science and the machine age. What it really did was create mass media, which, in turn, made possible modern science, the machine age, the Renaissance and the Protestant Reformation.

Rothschild's fourth information revolution is currently underway: the explosion of electronic communications set off by the invention of the microprocessor.

4. Communication Creates Society

Rothschild's summary:

> By exploiting our unique biological potential for literacy, the first Information Revolution turned scattered bands of hunter/gatherers into coordinate clans of hunters. The second made possible the villages and cities of the Agricultural Age. The third led to science, industry and the nation-states of the Machine Age. And this, the fourth Information Revolution, is creating the electronic global village of the Information Age.[4]

MEDIA, BUSINESS AND SOCIAL STRUCTURE

Rothschild's four watersheds of history are a bit of an oversimplification. He does not distinguish the invention of picture writing (Egyptian hieroglyphics) from the invention of syllable writing (Sumerian cuneiform) from the invention of today's phonetic writing. Undoubtedly there were many other critical advances in communication techniques in addition to Rothschild's four. But his observations are important in that they highlight three important facts:

First, the communication revolutions that had major social effects were all media revolutions that triggered an exponential increase in human knowledge. Both the Cro-Magnons and the Sumerians used symbols. But the former designed their system for record keeping, while the latter designed theirs for sending messages. Gutenberg was also using symbols, the letters of the alphabet. What he changed was the facility to multiply messages. In each case, it was the invention of a better way to communicate that released a new flood of information. It was the increase in information that changed how people thought, what people did, how people lived and eventually how they organized the societies in which they lived.

Second, all of these inventions were related to numbers and motivated by business. The Cro-Magnons were counting the days between phases of the moon to improve their hunting. The Sumerians were counting the number of livestock, sacks of wheat or barrels of wine to track sales. Gutenberg was counting the copies he could print, for that was his business (although, like many technical wizards, he was a lousy businessman and lost his invention to a money lender).

Media developments, as we shall see, are almost always propelled by, and unable to shake free from, business interests. In fact, Rothschild could have added the invention of money to his list of information revolutions. For money—whether coin, paper or wampum—is nothing more than a communication technique. A symbol of value-owed, developed to facilitate communication and record keeping in conducting business.

Third, every major increase in information had a tremendous impact on social structures—coordinated clans, villages and cities, nation states and the global village. The flow of information determines how people live, the way they interrelate and, ultimately, the kind of government they accept.

SOCIETIES, CIVILIZATIONS AND CULTURES

If information flow determines the nature of society, how does it affect the ebb and flow of civilizations? In his *Study of History*, Arnold Toynbee wrote:

> A growing civilization may be defined as one in which the components of its culture are in harmony with each other and form an integral whole; on the same principle, a disintegrating civilization can be defined as one in which these same elements have fallen into discord.[5]

But what precisely is a civilization? Of the four definitions given in Webster,[6] the nearest to this use is "the total culture of a people, nation, period." There is a bewildering amount of subjectivity both in this definition and Toynbee's use. Nations may fix boundaries, but peoples and periods constantly spill over, mixing and melding with each other. And precisely what does Webster mean by "total culture," or Toynbee by "harmony of culture's components"?

In his 1981 extended homily, *Voluntary Simplicity*,[7] under the heading of "Civilizations in Transition," Duane Elgin theorized that every civilization lives its life in four stages: (1) Springtime, an era of faith and high growth, (2) Summer, an era of reason and full blossoming, (3) Autumn, an era of cynicism and initial decline, and (4) Winter, an era of despair and breakdown. Unfortunately the only detailed example he gave was what he called "western industrial civilizations" (the plural is his), which he saw as currently in stage three, since "the powerful engine of economic and technological growth is running out of steam," and the "compelling sense of social purpose" is rapidly dissolving.

4. Communication Creates Society

I agree with Toynbee's observation that the cultures of particular groups can be more or less harmonious, and with Elgin in that our current culture contains a good deal of cynicism and that the bureaucratic industrial economy is running out of steam. However, I believe it is much easier to understand what is happening if we think of civilization as synonymous with human progress, i.e., Webster's first definition: "the process of civilizing or becoming civilized," with civilized meaning "advanced in social organization and the arts and sciences."

Social organization, arts and sciences are all manifestations of knowledge, the flow of information as refined, rearranged, developed and applied by humankind. Admittedly this flow is never even. There are ups and downs which Toynbee sees as periods of harmony or discord, and Elgin sees as growth, blossoming, decline and breakdown. There are also lateral shifts in cultural trends, as the process of refining, rearranging, developing and applying information is done in various ways by different groups of people. Although these different cultural currents frequently clash, they more often filter into each other through the cultural osmosis we call communication.

Because specific or individual cultures or civilizations are difficult to segregate and impossible to define, many historians distinguish the different steps in human progress by the type of tools men and women use.

INFORMATION AND TOOLS

Tools are so closely allied with knowledge and communication that traditional historians have named civilization's eras by the materials most commonly used for tools: the Stone Age, Bronze Age, Iron Age. Perhaps the new modern era should be called the Electronic or Digital Age rather than the Information Age because information, which set the stage for every age, is so much more than a tool.

That is not to say that tools are unimportant to the pursuit and application of knowledge. In *The Cult of Information*, Theodore Roszak wrote that the "mind has never been dependent on machinery to reach the peaks of achievement."[8] I disagree. If machinery includes tools, there is every evidence that most of the heights of achievement in art, philosophy, science and government could not have been reached without tools. Painting required pigments; sculpture, chisels. Even the most primitive vocal music seems to have been accompanied by drums. Advances in science were dependent on lenses and laboratories, scales and scalpels. Neither city-states nor empires could function without weapons and writing. Psychologists are still trying to analyze how the different tools for word processing—from quill to computer—influence thought processes.

In her book, *The Art of Memory*,[9] Frances A. Yates showed in extensive detail how important memory was to the ancients, how they organized knowledge to assist memory, and how memory became less important as humankind developed tools to store and transmit information.

The tool, a human's physical extension, almost as much as communication, a human's mental extension, has determined the course of civilization. That was the message of Lewis Mumford's 1934 masterwork, *Technics and Civilization*. The Industrial Revolution with its need for massive machinery was responsible for nation-state competition, global colonialism and bureaucracy in both business and government. It was also responsible for Jeremy Bentham's Utilitarianism, which made investigation and fact gathering a major function of government, and ultimately Karl Marx's Socialism, which proposed that government take over the means of production.

In this last half of the 20th Century the new electronic/digital tools are pulling us out of the Industrial Age and into the Digital Age. Even popular music, as Theodore Roszak pointed out, has become dependent on digitalizing machines. The immediate effect of the change has been to "democratize" key economic tools. In 1952, John Kenneth Galbraith was still insisting, in *American Capitalism*,[10] that the research and development necessary for product innovation and business success required large corporations with extensive capital resources. Today MIT professor Nicholas Negroponte argues that the era is gone when size was a prerequisite for success in global markets and that no country or company is too poor or too small to contribute to the scientific pool of human knowledge, because miniaturization and the low prices of computers and computer peripherals enables anyone, no matter how small, to go global.[11]

It was always true that anyone could have an idea, form a judgment or create a design. What has changed today is that it has become easier for anyone to communicate and apply ideas, judgments and designs. This means not only that there is more rapid and wider spread of information, but also that the

4. Communication Creates Society

consequent mixing and melding of information generates more new information than ever before.

It also means that geographical boundaries are becoming less significant. Electronic/digital tools do more than bridge the gaps of time, they eliminate the barriers of space and distance. Individuals on opposite sides of the globe communicate with each other in real time. Not only has mental work become a greater proportion of all work, but mental work no longer requires physical proximity whether to access sources of information or to interact with other minds.

As we shall see in Chapter 13, this gradual diminution of time and distance will affect power structures not only in industry and commerce but even more in government, where the edifice of authority and responsibility rests on now-obsolete concepts about the relevance of time (e.g., elected personnel serve for specified terms) and space (e.g., the range of government authority is determined by geography).

COMMUNICATION AND AUTHORITY

Because communication is the essential instrument for exercising authority—the leader must persuade his followers, and the followers must listen to the leader—rulers learned early the importance of using and controlling the flow of information. Under China's Ch'in Dynasty in 213 B.C. a minister proposed that all books not sponsored by the ruling party be burned, with the exception of books in the imperial library and manuals on agriculture, medicine, pharmacy, and divination.[12]

Controlling information flow by edict may work for a time, but it did not prevail in China nor has it since. Information is like running water. No matter how high the dam, the river will sooner or later spill over the top or find another channel.

But here it is more important to understand how information, or the lack of it, affects leadership and authority than to trace the history and folly of censorship and other attempts to suppress communication.

Ignorance has always been the ally of tyranny. In 1834, a French revolutionary by the name of Auguste Blanqui explained to his fellow revolutionaries that: "The poor do not know the source of their miseries. Ignorance, the daughter of bondage, makes them a docile instrument of the privileged."[13] In China, 124 years later, Chairman Mao echoed Blanqui:

> Apart from their other characteristics, the outstanding thing about China's 600 million people is that they are "poor and blank." This may seem a bad thing but in reality it is a good thing. Poverty gives rise to the desire for change, the desire for action and the desire for revolution. On a blank sheet of paper, free from any marks, the freshest and most beautiful characters can be written, the freshest and most beautiful pictures can be painted.[14]

Power over others is based on knowledge—or, more to the point here, on the existence of ignorance. It is easy for one person to dominate another, if the dominator knows more than the dominated. No matter how much violence and physical force is used, the dominator must ultimately depend on superior knowledge. This is why parents find it more difficult to manage teenagers than little children. This is why dictators work so hard to control the means of communication. And this is why the first victims of the information deluge were suppressive governments. It was the free flow of information that tore down the Iron Curtain in Eastern Europe and undermined apartheid in South Africa.

A vital factor in the failure of the 1994 attempt to restore Communism in Russia was the rapid flow of information through modern communication technology. In his autobiographical memoir Boris Yeltsin described his response when news of the coup attempt reached his vacation dacha:

> While all this was going on, the phones and the fax at Arkhangelskoye were working, if intermittently. There was actually nothing surprising in this. In the two or three years of burgeoning business in our country, an incredible number of new communication lines had been installed. An hour after my daughters typed our appeal, it was being read in Moscow and other cities. The Western wire services sent it out, professional and amateur computer networks transmitted it and independent radio stations, stock-market lines and the correspondents' network of many national publications also passed it on. And many Xerox machines, previously banned, mysteriously appeared. I think the middle-aged coup plotters simply could not imagine the extent and volume of the information age, which was so new to them.[15]

The Internet undermines all attempts to control information, which is underscored by the presence and global access to specialized bulletin boards like Digital Freedom Net, PeaceNet and Usenet's newsgroups on human rights.

IS ANARCHY THE ALTERNATIVE?

It is certainly a great blessing that the widespread access to information has undermined totalitarianism. But, as we shall see, it has also undermined other forms of centralized control—in business, in government and in most of our social structures.

Is anarchy the alternative? If we cannot build new structures to withstand the information deluge, it could be. The horrors of anarchy and defiance of law have already appeared in Eastern Europe, in Africa and in American cities—riots in Los Angeles, bombings in New York and Oklahoma City. In fact, today's foreign policy, for the United States as well as other countries, consists largely of trying, however futilely, to extinguish the brush fires of anarchy.

At this writing, a number of press pundits and, of course, the Republicans are blaming many of the administration's problems on the character of President Clinton. Yet I doubt there is a man or woman in our country today who could solve our domestic and international problems. There is just too much to know.

The same trend that undermined totalitarianism has sapped the power of our leaders by fostering distrust, as we saw in Chapter 2. The imperfections of politicians have always caused and will always cause problems, but today even superior politicians cannot operate effectively, because the basic problem they face is one of structure. Rothschild's "fourth revolution" is upon us and a new form of social order is required to deal with the flood of information let loose by today's technologies. To avoid chaos and anarchy we have to define this new social structure and get it in place quickly.

A multitude of fundamental questions rides the information deluge. In government, is federalism the appropriate social structure? If so, why does it seem so clumsy in meeting today's problems? Is it possible that we need a new form of democracy or that democracy has to change into something else? In business, is benevolent bureaucracy, even with profit sharing and flex-plan benefits, still a workable management structure? If the information superhighway is turning the world into a global village, why are ethnic enclaves clawing at each other's throats and howling for independence?

KNOWLEDGE AND COMMUNITY

The three major conclusions of this chapter provide an insight into what is wrong.

1. Information flow defines the nature of society.

2. Tools, particularly the tools that facilitate communication, determine the extent of information flow.

3. The information available to the managers and the managed decides how authority is exercised, whether in business or government.

Since information creates community, we can discover and define the cement that unifies society by the way its members share information. For centuries information spread slowly and was restricted by distance. Since communities and cultures took years to change and were limited by geography, authority was identified with families and dynasties and consolidated by roads and walls. Changes in the nature of communities and coherence of culture directly paralleled changes in the spread of information both as to speed (time) and distance (geography).

The relation of the tools of communication and the stability of society was discussed almost 50 years ago by political economist Harold Adams Innis, who argued in *The Bias of Communications* that hard-to-move stone hieroglyphics resulted in small, stable societies, whereas easily-transported papyrus documents enabled the Romans to build a faster changing and more extensive empire.[16]

Today our electronic communication tools have demolished the space and time barriers that once controlled the flow of information. Does this mean that we are now one global community? Unfortunately, no, for the volume of information is too large and individual minds are too small. Instead we have multiple communities and multiple allegiances no longer separated by space and time, with all the conflicts and confusion that such a situation generates.

4. Communication Creates Society

KNOWLEDGE AND INDEPENDENCE

Even communities have changed, for it is harder to reach consensus. The information flood has undermined social docility. The more people know, the more they want to make their own decisions, the more independent they become and the less likely they are to accept dictation whether from cruel tyrants or solicitous guardians. As a consequence, many of those in authority, from presidents and prime ministers to businessmen and bankers, find themselves bewildered and impotent, unable to understand the rapidly changing demands of their constituents and customers and helpless to muster the consensus they need to be effective.

Since the Age of Englightenment universal education has been seen as a desirable social goal. Much was written about the desirability of knowledge; and little about the problems that might arise from everyone being knowledgable. Education, the sharing of information, is the bedrock of democracy: the system of community organization that assumes individual citizens have sufficient information to decide for themselves.

How this worked out in the development of our government is the subject of Chapter 5; how it worked out in developing our economy, is the subject of Chapter 6.

5

INFORMATION, AUTHORITY AND DEMOCRACY

"In framing a government which is to be administered by men over men, the great difficulty lies in this: You must first enable the government to control the governed; and in the next place oblige it to control itself."

— *James Madison, 1787*[1]

We have seen how new civilizations evolved out of increases in the flow of information. Now we examine more closely how the advance of information over the last 300 years created American democracy: our concepts of freedom and cooperation, the growth of the federal government at the expense of the states, immigration and the settling of the West, the transformation of American culture from optimistic melting pot to pessimistic diversity, the deepening morass in Washington and the increasingly drastic changes in our value systems.

THE ROOTS OF DEMOCRACY

No system of government better exemplifies how information flow determines the nature of society than American democracy. The evolution of the modern concept of human nature, society and government can be traced back to Niccolo Machiavelli and Martin Luther in the 16th Century. It was further developed by John Locke and Thomas Hobbes in the 17th, and applied to society with considerable detail by a large number of 18th Century writers, notably Francois Marie Arouet Voltaire, Charles Louis Montesquieu, Jean Jacques Rousseau and Edmund Burke.

Their theories and insights resulted from many minds cooperating through the printed word, and spread across the Western world through pamphlets, treatises and other publications, such as the periodical on law and economics edited by Cesare Bonesma de Beccaria and a group of young Italian scholars and the even more influential *Encyclopedie, ou Dictionnaire raisonné des arts, des sciences et des métiers*, published by Denis Diderot.[2]

AMERICAN DEMOCRACY UNIQUE

Although the roots of democracy lie in Europe and the tremendous flood of information released by the printing press, American democracy, as expressed and applied by the revolutionaries who founded the United States, is unique. European governments, hobbled by centuries-long histories and entrenched sources of power, were never able to apply those Enlightenment ideas as purely or directly.

America provided virgin soil for planting the principles of freedom and equality, a political synthesis that tempered Rousseau's ideal of complete human equality with Locke's ideal of individual political freedom. These principles were considered particularly relevant at the time, for the population of the 13 American colonies was exceptionally heterogeneous for the age.

Massachusetts was founded by Puritan separatists from the Church of England, Virginia by Episcopalians, Pennsylvania by Quakers, New York by Dutch Reformed, Maryland by Catholics. Rhode Island was established by Roger Williams to give freedom of religion to Puritan dissenters. Jews came to Manhattan Island in 1654. A black, Crispus Attacks, died in the Boston Massacre, and an estimated 5,000 blacks fought alongside whites in the American Revolution.

More important, especially in the minds of the country's early leaders, the colonists were free from the bonds of hereditary nobility as expressed in the British monarchy and peerage. This did not mean, as we shall see, that they were not influenced by the political climate and class system of Great Britain. But there was unanimous fear and repugnance regarding the trappings of nobility and the transfer of authority through heredity.

The small group of men whom the colonies sent to Philadelphia to set up the United States government were the world's first information autocracy, empowered by the knowledge and ideas they shared rather than by wealth, land ownership or inherited power.. The Declaration of Independence on July 4, 1776, the Constitution presented on September 17, 1787, and the Bill of Rights put in force on December 15, 1791, were all composed by scholars, men who were great readers and thinkers though mostly self-educated.

The result was that the structure of American democracy rested on two principles distilled from the ferment of political philosophy that had risen in Europe over two centuries. Both were clearly stated in the Declaration of Independence and declared "self-evident." The first was "that all Men are created equal, that they are endowed by their Creator with certain unalienable Rights"; the second, "that to secure these Rights, Governments are instituted among Men, deriving their just Powers from the Consent of the Governed."

EQUALITY AND INALIENABLE RIGHTS

At the time a mere six percent of Americans had the right to vote. All of the Founding Fathers took for granted that, when it came to political power, women had no more rights than children. As to the equality of blacks and Native Americans, not only was slavery tolerated and slaves denied the vote but, in basing the number of Representatives on each state's population, the Constitution counted each slave as three-fifths of a person. Native Americans, unless they paid taxes, were not counted at all.

What then did our Founding Fathers believe when they wrote that "all men are created equal?" They meant that men are born with certain inalienable rights. They generally described these rights as "Life, Liberty and the Pursuit of Happiness," and presumed that liberty meant that...

> Congress shall make no law respecting an establishment of religion, or prohibiting the free exercise thereof; or abridging of the freedom of speech, or of the press; or the right of the people peaceably to assemble, and to petition the Government for a redress of grievances.

Freedom of religion was a natural concern, since so many of America's early settlers had arrived in search of religious freedom. As for freedom of speech, the press and assembly, the Founding Fathers realized the critical role played by freedom of expression in bringing about the American Revolution. Pamphleteering in the second half of the 18th Century was almost as pervasive and influential as network television in the second half of the 20th. The Declaration of Independence might never have been written if *Common*

5. Information, Authority and Democracy

Sense, a little pamphlet by Thomas Paine, had not convinced so many colonists that independence from the British crown was not only conceivable but necessary. *Common Sense* appeared in January of 1776. In a few months more than 150,000 copies had been sold.[3]

Thus the keystone of democratic rights was the free flow of information, whether by speech, press, peaceable assembly or public petition. In fact, even the First Amendment's position on religion was carefully crafted to protect freedom of ideas and beliefs rather than to encourage the practice of religion. The Fourth Amendment protects citizens against unwarranted search and seizure; it seems to go out of its way to mention their "papers" as well as their persons, houses and effects. It is impossible to understand what "created equal" means unless you understand how freedom of speech defines what is meant by human equality and inalienable rights. What makes us human is the ability to think and speak for ourselves, and anything that blocks that ability is a violation of human rights. Equality begins, and in many ways ends, with freedom of speech.

Since the United States Constitution was created "to secure these Rights," the Continental Congress envisioned the federal government as a political device geared more to protecting rights than to initiating projects for the commonweal. As its Preamble explains, the Constitution was established "to form a more perfect Union, establish justice, insure domestic tranquility, provide for the common defense, promote the general welfare, and secure the blessings of liberty to ourselves and our posterity."

The purpose of this chapter is to show how the interplay of these democratic principles with the multiplication of information and its effects on society gradually transformed the idea of "establishing justice and promoting the general welfare" from a reactive to a proactive polity.

GOVERNMENT BY COOPERATION THROUGH COMPROMISE

During the Continental Congress an extremely important meme, or master idea, became the lodestar for the development of American democracy: "Compromise is a virtue." That idea was something new in human society. When everybody agrees on a principle, virtue lies in accepting its consequences absolutely, and compromise is considered weakness. Patrick Henry could move his fellow men with "Give me liberty or give me death." A couple of centuries later, Barry Goldwater would proclaim that "extremism in the defense of liberty is no vice" and "moderation in the pursuit of justice is no virtue." But the Founding Fathers were establishing a government on the consent of the governed, and that consent would have to be arrived at without threatening the inalienable right of every citizen to think and speak as he pleased.

The catalyst for the system of cooperation we call American democracy was compromise. Only by compromise could the Founding Fathers manage the flood of ideas and information—often in conflict—with which they had to deal. The inspiration for the Revolutionary War may have been Patrick Henry's absolutism, but foundation for the revolutionary government lay in the attitude of that most sagacious of Americans, Benjamin Franklin, in his last speech at the Constitutional Convention already quoted in Chapter 1: "The opinions I have ... I sacrifice to the public good."

Sacrificing one's opinions to achieving consensus is as essential to American democracy as individual freedom. In fact, it is the other side of the same coin, for freedom without compromise inevitably leads to anarchy. This tension between the rights of the individual and the rights of the community exists in every government. What American democracy did was provide a process to resolve it amicably. Compromise characterizes both the strengths and weaknesses of the American system, for it places centrism at the heart of our politics. How else can a large number of different opinions be reconciled than by settling somewhere in the middle? This is why so many of our politicians seem to be cut from the same cloth, and why the safest road to election runs down the center.

The problem with centrism is that it is so easy to forget the difference between compromise and indifference, especially in a world flooded by information beyond our comprehension. The danger in governing by compromise is that it encourages voting for candidates offensive to no one. This is not a problem exclusive to democracy. One reason the U.S.S.R. collapsed so completely was that the compromises engineered by Communist Party's internal politics put dullards like Brezhnev in the Kremlin.

As we shall see in later chapters, there is a danger that democracy will grow flabby without the tensions created by outside value systems and, since past value systems are primary victims of the information explosion, a new, more relevant value system must be found. I believe this new system will embody both inalienable human rights and the virtue of cooperating through compromise.

THE MOVE AWAY FROM INDIVIDUAL STATE SOVEREIGNTY

Now, however, we are interested in how the flow of information affected and gradually changed the form of government that the American revolutionaries constructed. The amazing thing about the new country was how quickly the 13 sovereign colonies began to think of themselves as a single nation despite the 10th Amendment's reserving to the states (or the people) all "powers not delegated to the United States by the Constitution, nor prohibited by it to the States," and the 11th's warning that "the judicial power of the United States should not be construed to extend to any suit in law or equity" brought against an individual state by another state or foreign government.

There were still, at the time John Jay wrote the second Federalist Paper, many influential politicians who believed "that instead of looking for safety and happiness in union, we ought to see it in a division of the States into distinct confederacies or sovereignties."[4] A group of extremists, typified by John Taylor and John Randolph, considered themselves "Pure Republicans" and wanted to keep the federal government as weak as possible.

Though the unity required to win the war against England was a major factor in making the 13 "sovereign" colonies one nation, what kept governance from slipping back to the individual states and made average citizens more interested in national than state politics was the volume of information reaching Americans from overseas. From the fall of the Bastille in 1789 to the battle of Waterloo in 1815 Europe was in constant turmoil and the news from abroad, despite the distance, was frequent enough to generate intense political heat on this side of the Atlantic.

Americans were first enthused, then bewildered by the news about the French Revolution, which began with cries of freedom and equality but soon degenerated into a barbarism very different from the way America had conducted its revolution. But France was still considered the ally and England the enemy. Feeling against everything British was especially high in the coastal cities of Boston, New York, Philadelphia and Charleston because the British navy, trying to enforce a blockade of Napoleon's Europe, was interfering with American shipping, searching U.S. vessels and impressing seamen to serve in the British navy unless they had proof that they were not Englishmen. In addition, there were constant reports of attacks on American frontier settlements by Indian allies of the British.

The rising temperature of anti-British sentiment finally exploded into the War of 1812, three years of painfully erratic hostilities that resulted in little change between the two countries but did a lot to consolidate nationalistic feeling in the U.S. Albert Gallatin, then secretary of the treasury, observed that, because of the war, the people "are more American; they feel and act more like a nation; and I hope that the permanency of the Union is thereby better secured."[5]

In 1865 the end of the Civil War rang the death knell of states' rights. The argument between the North and the South was really about the individual state's right to self-determination. The Northern states denied that right and won. It was a painful and divisive way to settle the argument, but it established once and for all that the center of popular allegiance, interest and power was in Washington, not the state capitals.

THE MOVE TO AN ACTIVIST CENTRAL GOVERNMENT

Our country was settled, and later enlarged, almost entirely by refugees—first from religious persecution, then from economic persecution, finally from political persecution. These refugees brought most of their habits from the old country, not only habits in clothing, eating and organizing, but also habits in thinking.

Since most of the early Americans were from England, they were very much Englishmen and very much convinced that there had to be a governing class, if not the repudiated nobility, then "a people descended from the same ancestors ... very similar in their manners and customs," as suggested by John Jay.[6] Even Thomas Jefferson, the most populist of the early leaders, felt that "there is a natural aristocracy among men," though grounded "in virtue and talent" rather than birth.[7]

In early colonial times, being a landowner meant you made your living through agriculture, whether on the huge plantations in the south or the smaller farms of the north. But, even before the Revolution, more and more of the property owners in the coastal cities made their money not through agriculture but through trade. Before Washington retired, there was a clear political split in Congress with two parties, Alexander Hamilton's Federalists favoring mercantile interests and a strong central government and Thomas Jefferson's Democrats (then called Democratic Republicans) on the side of agriculture and less central government.

In 1804, Alexander Hamilton, the primary advocate of an active federal government, was killed in a duel with Aaron Burr. But 15 years later the dead Hamilton won his major victory when Chief Justice John Marshall opened the door to active government by declaring, in McCulloch v. Maryland, that the federal government had the right to use "all means which are appropriate...and not prohibited, but consistent with the letter and spirit of the constitution."[8]

Nevertheless, by 1828, when the Democratic Party's Andrew Jackson was elected president, the Federalist Party was dead, colonial elitism had disappeared, and the president had been elected on a platform of greater popular participation in government. Within a few years, most states gave the vote to all white adult males. The party of less federal government had triumphed, yet Jackson and Congress were involved in far more of the nation's business than any of the Founding Fathers had ever dreamed possible.

What had happened to the fight for less government in Washington?

It had been overwhelmed by a flood of information that shifted the average American's interests and allegiance from his state to the national government. This burst of information was the result of two uniquely American traits: the love of learning and the lure of monetary gain; and two historical events: the opening of the American West and the Industrial Revolution.

LITERACY, LEARNING AND ENTERTAINMENT

Americans have always loved learning. Our public schools and public libraries sprang up almost spontaneously due to popular enthusiasm and government support. The goal of universal literacy took root in the United States long before it was widely accepted in Europe, partly because reading the Bible was important to many of the early settlers, and partly because a large number of America's earliest entrepreneurs started print shops. By 1840 there were some 2,000 people employed in printing and publishing in New York City alone.[9] Widespread literacy dovetailed nicely with the Founding

Fathers' faith in individual independence and government empowered by the people.

But information favoring the national government over state sovereignty would not have reached such influential proportions had it not been facilitated by entertainment.

In recent years a number of scholars have deplored the popular trend to use the media more for entertainment than for education. Neil Postman's *Amusing Ourselves to Death* is an example. What Postman and his fellows seem to overlook is that people have always preferred entertainment to education, and that education of the populace (the learning that influences social trends and government structure) is more a fringe benefit of entertainment than the other way around. For proof that this was true in the early 19th Century, consider that popular repugnance to slavery was crystallized by a novel, Harriet Beecher Stowe's *Uncle Tom's Cabin*, and that the influential Lincoln-Douglas debates had many aspects of a traveling circus.

The first half of the 19th Century was the era of orators. Daniel Webster, Henry Clay, Stephen Arnold Douglas and Abraham Lincoln drew huge crowds from miles around and held their attention for days at a time because they provided a form of popular entertainment. Unfortunately, all that we have today of the Lincoln-Douglas debates are written words, without the speakers' vocal embellishments, gestures and grimaces or the audience's laughter, cheers and catcalls. These political gatherings were successful for the same reason (at the same time, 1800 to 1840) that religious "camp meetings," featuring effective preachers, were sweeping frontier communities, and lectures, headlining scholars like Ralph Waldo Emerson, were so popular in more sedate New England.

At the same time, another form of popular entertainment was growing in America: the newspaper. With the invention of print-shop, entrepreneurs were trying to make their presses profitable. Many of these printers, like Benjamin Franklin, started by handling type but soon moved into handling ideas, sometimes those of others, more often their own. In Chapter 7 we shall examine the way the media influenced America and America influenced the media while the information deluge transformed both.

MORE POWERFUL THAN POLITICS

Here it is important to note how the power of information and the ideas it creates transcended political power in range and influence. The Founding Fathers were unique in that many of them were both politicians and writers. But government by philosophers, in the rare instances it has happened, seldom lasts beyond a single generation.

Peter Drucker makes a strong point of what he calls "the futility of politics,"[10] contending that the principal social transformations of the 20th Century were not caused by politicians or political events. He is speaking about the work force shift from farm and home to factory and office, and then from a predominance of industrial labor to a predominance of technological workers. These changes were effected not by government but by the development and application of information and the ideas it generated.

Ideas, or the intellectual designs that become habits of thinking and determine a society's sense of values, are largely formulated by journalists and other professional communicators, not necessarily because they are smarter or more powerful than everybody else, but because their livelihood depends on how well they can hold public attention by gathering and focusing information.

By 1847 it was very clear that the range of the printed word could exceed the range of oratory. In 1833, Benjamin H. Day launched the *New York Sun*, the first newspaper sold for a penny. By 1836, a competitive penny paper, James Gordon Bennett's *New York Herald*, was selling 30,000 copies every day. The Hoe cylindrical press was invented in 1847. Two years later Bennett was using a 12,000-impressions-an-hour six-cylinder version.

With daily frequency and wide distribution, newspaper editors became highly influential and were courted more and more by politicians. Andrew Jackson doled out federal appointments to at least 57 journalists.[11] Jackson was the first president to depend on a "kitchen cabinet," and his coterie of unofficial advisors was dominated by newspapermen: Amos Kendall, former editor of the Frankfort, Illinois, *Argus of Western America,* who was given a job in the Treasury department; Francis Preston Blair, Kendall's successor at the *Argus* who had since become editor of the *Washington Globe*; and Isaac Hillers, who came to Washington from Concord, New Hampshire, where he edited a well-read weekly.[12]

INFORMATION AS LURE: A PARADISE OF PROMISE

If information from Europe had a great influence in centralizing American government in Washington prior to the Civil War, information from America to Europe had an even greater effect in the years that followed. Between 1830 and 1924 an estimated 35 million immigrants moved from Europe to the United States lured by the news of higher wages and greater opportunities. These new citizens, most of them in their 20s or 30s, transferred their allegiance from their European homelands not to individual states but to the United States.

Had the U.S. remained only 13 states, it might have preserved the original idea of a very limited central government. But the 1803 Louisiana Purchase made Americans more interested in the whole country than in their home states. Suddenly the size of the country was doubled, opening up thousands of acres of opportunity, and creating a whole series of new states: Kentucky in 1792, Tennessee in 1796, Ohio in 1803, Louisiana in 1812, Indiana in 1816, Mississippi in 1817, Illinois in 1818, Missouri in 1821.

This not only weakened the voting power of the 13 original states, but forced the government in Washington to take on more responsibilities than could have been foreseen when the authors of the Constitution wrote that Congress shall have the power "to regulate commerce with foreign nations, and among the several States, and with the Indian tribes."

Few things helped to accelerate this trend more than the steam locomotive. The Baltimore & Ohio railroad was founded in 1828. Railroads played a major part in the Civil War, and eventually had as much or more influence than the Conestoga covered wagon in opening up the west.

The railways were also a major factor in accelerating the flow of information. Not only did they move people and information across huge distances more rapidly than ever before, but they created the first major commercial justification for the telegraph, an invention perfected by an American, Samuel Morse, and demonstrated before Congress in 1844.

The energy that sustained America's growth years was created almost entirely by stories of individual successes and news of frontier opportunities. Horatio Alger (1834-1899) wrote and sold more than 100 novels with heroes who rose from rags to riches on honest hard work. News of the 1848 discovery of gold at Sutter's Mill brought more than 40,000 prospectors to

5. Information, Authority and Democracy

California in two years. And in Europe, Alexis de Tocqueville told his countrymen that in America artistocracy "if at the present day it is not actually destroyed, it is at any rate so completely disabled that we can scarcely assign to it any degree of influence."[13]

That lack of an aristocracy had nothing to do with economics. When de Tocqueville visited America in 1831, there was a greater financial gap between rich and poor than there is today. Two-thirds of the nation's wealth was owned by less than 10 percent of its families.[14]

During most of that half century, there were numerous Americans with little money, insufficient food and abysmal shelter, but there were very few without hope. That accounts for the enormous difference between the information climate of America in the 19th Century and that of America on the eve of the 21st. No matter how poor he might be, that century's average American lived in an aura of hope. He saw himself as equal because he was convinced he had equal opportunity.

This consummate American optimism was largely responsible for the "melting pot" phenomenon that turned so many diverse immigrants into productive U.S. citizens. In the May 1995 issue of the *Atlantic Monthly*,[15] Benjamin Schwarz approvingly quotes Randolph Bourne's 1916 condemnation of the American Anglo-Saxon elite as "guilty of just what every dominant race is guilty of in every European country: the imposition of its own culture upon the minority peoples." Bourne felt that the American elite were forcing immigrants to accept "English snobberies, English religion, English literary styles, English literary reverences and canons, English ethics, English superiorities."

Admittedly an English bias in American culture exists even to this day, but both Bourne in 1916 and Schwarz in 1995 seem to forget that culture is never imposed, it is always adopted, and that it is natural, in any society, for the minority to emulate the majority; the hopeful to imitate the successful; the weak to admire the powerful. No matter how faithfully first-generation immigrants cling to the culture of the old country, their progeny, whether for good or ill, inevitably adopt more and more of the culture surrounding them.

There can be a difference, however, in the rate at which this change takes place. An upbeat, promising culture will be adopted more readily, and therefore more quickly, than an insecure, discouraging culture, which is why the

U.S. melting pot seems to have operated so much more efficiently a century ago than it does today.

FROM OPTIMISM TO PESSIMISM

American culture has shifted from faith in the future to doubt about its outcome because of a revolution in public information. In the 1800s the predominant news was about opportunity and success. In the 1900s, particularly after World War II, it has been increasingly about problems and failures: the need for farm supports, the danger of another depression, fear of Communism, blacklists and McCarthyism, the Korean War, the Bay of Pigs, Vietnam, Watergate, the Club of Rome's 1972 *Limits to Growth* report, OPEC and the gasoline shortage, environmental abuse, drugs, crime, AIDS, the collapse of major corporations, Somalia and Bosnia.

How did we reach this new watershed, what Robert Hughes calls the *Culture of Complaint*? How did we cross this spiritual continental divide from good news to bad, from optimism to pessimism? Undoubtedly the Great Depression in the 1930s changed a lot of thinking about the ability of the United States, and particularly American business, to sustain an ever-growing economy. Some analysts trace the change to American intellectuals' fascination with Sigmund Freud and Max Weber after World War II. Others, like John Galbraith, have pointed to the post-war business schizophrenics who complained more and more about creeping socialism, while lobbying more and more for government protection and subsidies.

Finally, as Steven Stark and others have argued, government was increasingly attempting to fix economic and social problems, and the more government moved into those areas, the higher public expectations rose and the lower chances of success fell. Stark quotes UCLA professor James Q. Wilson:

> First, no one really knows how to solve these problems. Second, the public itself is deeply conflicted about most of these issues; you rarely have a consensus from which to act. Third, these issues tend to be so complex that they overwhelm the process. And finally, when these measures fail to do much to solve something like crime—which is what inevitably happens—they greatly reinforce the general disillusionment with government.[16]

5. Information, Authority and Democracy

Ultimately there were two underlying causes for the growth of pessimism. The first was geographical. Americans had exhausted the natural opportunities of a wide-open, unexploited frontier. The second, and even more fundamental cause, was that Americans and the world were learning more and more about the long-term effects of our actions—information which bore the uncertainty of all predictions and, therefore, tended to feed fear more often than hope.

Nurturing this trend to pessimism was the growing dependence on numbers to measure progress and economic health. The trouble with measurements is that they evaluate the future with the values of the past, and are therefore intrinsically biased against change. Because our standards for measuring the Gross National Product, inflation, employment, the balance of payments, and family income are obsolete, they make our economic condition look worse than it is, thereby feeding public pessimism.

The information flood has had profound negative impact on how America understands—and evaluates—itself.

RIGHTS, PRIVILEGES AND DEFENSIVE COMMUNICATION

One of the consequences of flooding water is that it carries silt, which not only soils everything but usually damages the inner workings of automobiles and other machines. The rising flood of information did something similar to the machinery of government.

Someone has said that the seeds of lobbying were planted by our founding fathers when they wrote the Constitution. James Madison worried lest the national government be taken over by a single faction, whether majority or minority. His solution, as he described it in the 51st Federalist Paper, was the separation of House, Senate, executive and judiciary so that each of the four branches would have a separate constituency, "giving to those who administer each department the necessary constitutional means and personal motives to resist encroachments of the others."[17]

Unfortunately none of the Founding Fathers foresaw that, while the division of powers protected the United States from any group that wanted to seize power, it would help groups to slow down or prevent government decisions they opposed. This condition grew worse as the flood of information increased the chances of average citizens learning about government activities, encouraging the tendency to defensive organization.

In 1982, economist Mancur Olson proposed a theory to explain why the national economies of the victors in World War II stagnated, while the economies of the losers prospered. In *The Rise and Decline of Nations,* Olson provided evidence to prove that under democratic governments with long periods of stability the citizenry has the opportunity to organize groups with the purpose of promoting and protecting special interests.

A 1990 survey sponsored by the American Society of Association Executives showed seven out of 10 Americans belonging to at least one association, and half the respondents said the main function of most associations was to influence the government.[18] These organizations are predominantly organized to defend existing partisan interests. In *The Lonely Crowd,* David Reisman calls them "Veto Groups."[19] Thus they are usually foes of change. This makes innovation and experimentation extremely difficult. Yet innovation and experimentation are necessary for economic growth and progress.

Countries that have to "start over" because they have gone through a period of major instability, such as Germany and Japan after the war, can do a lot of experimenting and innovating before there are many specific benefits to protect and before their citizens have time to organize lobbying groups to protect them. The fact that the economies of both Germany and Japan grew vigorously after the war but are now slowing down seems to confirm Olson's theory.

In 1994, Jonathan Rauch wrote *Demosclerosis: the Silent Killer of American Government,* a book that builds on Olson's theory by showing how we Americans have so crowded Washington with organizations defending different special interests that the U.S. government has ground to a standstill. In 1920, there were an estimated 400 lobbying groups in Washington. Today there are, at last estimate, more than 20,000. Issue groups are the largest employer in Washington after the government.

The government encouraged these organizations by moving more and more into programs with clear-cut constituencies, which naturally organized to protect the programs. So now, in the words of Charles Schultze, a former Council of Economic Advisors president, "the legislative process is structured to increase the difficulty of passing legislation in proportion to the size of the

5. Information, Authority and Democracy

harm it may do to a particular group,"[20] making it much easier to pass laws benefitting specific groups than it is to rescind them.

TAXATION AS ECONOMIC TAXIDERMY

There is a parallel explanation as to why the economies of stable societies tend to slow down. Taxes are almost always designed to protect current businesses, which are already organized, while there is little or no incentive to protect or encourage future businesses, which are not. As a government matures its need for tax revenue increases. The tax structure becomes more complex to accomodate the special-interest groups who rush to protect their interests as soon as a new tax or tax increase is proposed.

Therefore, the longer a nation remains stable the more its taxation system will artificially favor the established, frequently preserve the outdated, and unhealthily discourage experimenters and innovators.

America's tax system is only one example of how increases in information have brought decreases in Washington wisdom.

LOUD VOICES AREN'T NECESSARILY CLEAR VOICES

In a sense, up until the middle of this century one of the principal problems of democracy was how to make the citizenry's voice strong enough to reach the government. Then, as mass communication techniques improved, associations moved to Washington, professional communicators took over and broadcast talk-shows multiplied, the problem reversed itself. Now the problem is making the government's ears strong enough to decipher the din.

The outcry against lobbying and lobbyists usually concentrates on the amount of money lobbyists funnel to Congressmen through PACs, lecture fees, free trips, entertainment and other gifts. These abuses are far less important than people think. Not only are most politicians relatively honest, but no politician can afford to allow even the appearance that he or she can be bought. Moreover, as Herbert E. Alexander of the University of Southern California has pointed out, most of the money tends to follow the legislator's opinion rather than the legislator's opinion following the money.

The real power of lobbyists lies in their ability to manipulate information. They are particularly powerful today because we have given our elected representatives a job that requires more knowledge than any human being can possibly master. If the great majority of the senators and representatives find it an impossible task to read most of the bills they vote on, how can we expect them to learn all they need to know to evaluate those bills? That is what makes the job of today's lobbyists so easy. When a legislator is trying to make a decision in an area about which he or she knows relatively little, the lobbyist is an expert willing to help him or her understand—in a way, of course, that is favorable to the lobbyist's client.

The growing need for more information is one reason why there are so many more people employed by government today than there were a century ago. Members of Congress have justifiably added to their staffs. Between the late 1940s and the early 1990s the Washington population of congressional and committee staffers rose from 2,400 to 11,000. Most of these staffers gather and process information to help senators and representatives understand the needs of their constituents and learn enough about what is going on to protect those interests. Few manifestations of the pernicious possibilities in too much information are clearer than the situation where a biased expert has the opportunity to educate an ignorant legislator's aide in search of a few clear ideas.

GROWING GOVERNMENT COMPLEXITY

Parallel with the growth of legislators' staffs was the growth of government bureaus. As the functions of the federal government increased, the manpower necessary to oversee and administer increased, both because there was more to do, but even more because the information required to do it was becoming more and more complex. The *Federal Register* now publishes close to 7,000 pages a year on federal law proposals, rules and regulations compared with less than 2700 pages in 1930. The number of pages of law entered in the 1991-1992 session was 250 percent more than the number entered in the 1965-1966 session. This blizzard of regulation has given birth to an army of specialists, lawyers, accountants and other consultants to help ordinary citizens (and lawmakers) understand and follow the rules. Eventually these specialists, in defense of their livelihood, became the principal foes of deregulation and other proposals to simplify government.

Specialization occasions another information phenomenon that distorts the workings of government: the natural tendency of people who work with the same information to develop an attitude of alliance. From gourmet chefs

5. Information, Authority and Democracy 101

to computer hackers, from journalists to astrophysicists, bonding always results between specialists who understand each other in a world that does not understand them. It is natural, therefore, that the government's watchdog agencies soon become very friendly with the industries they are assigned to watch. Though the Civil Service system was set up early in this century to rescue government employment from political patronage, it also made these nonelected officials less responsive to the "ignorant" public and more likely to side with the industry people whose expertise they share.[21]

It is no surprise that, upon retirement from government service, many members of regulatory commissions find jobs in the industries they have regulated. So common did this practice become that in 1993 President Clinton required 1,100 officials in his new administration to pledge in writing that they would not lobby their former agencies for five years after leaving government service.

The government so carefully crafted by James Madison, Alexander Hamilton, Benjamin Franklin and their co-workers has become a babble of partisan voices, information manipulators, confused legislators, entrenched bureaucrats, specialist cliques and ineffective politicians. This sad situation is aptly summarized by Alvin Toffler: "The quality of our decision-making is deteriorating across the board. Not because the people in charge are stupid. But because they're all running too fast, making too many decisions, too fast, about too many things they know too little about."[22]

BLINDFOLDED LAWS

Congress has also encouraged the administrative bureaucracy by passing more and more laws that have to be arbitrated by the government's executive branch—laws that cannot function without a bureaucratic seeing-eye. While the flood of information has made Congressmen more aware of areas requiring legislation, it has also made them more aware of how impossible it is to foresee all the consequences of the laws they write. So they pass laws that have to be applied and interpreted by administrators.

In his 1992 book, *Who Will Tell The People: The Betrayal of American Democracy,* William Greider provides many examples of how the laws on energy, environmental protection and occupational safety have been eviscerated by adminstrative subjective interpretation and random application. He calls such legislation "hollow laws," and concludes that:

> The general political climate is now infected with a cynical understanding that things need not be real in order to satisfy the public's desires and demands. Instead, both political parties and the webs of client-representative relationships surrounding them have perfected the practice of concocting hollow laws—promises the government makes to the people which it does not necessarily intend to keep.[23]

Although there is considerable justification for this analysis, these "hollow laws" are less the invention of a conspiracy than the result of legislators trying to deal with more information than they can handle. The more difficult it is to make decisions, the stronger the temptation to pass the buck. If the legislature, the administration and everyone else in Washington seems to have lost their sense of America's values, maybe it is because they have.

THE RISE AND FALL OF VALUE SYSTEMS

There are at least two nonprofit organizations in the United States that call themselves American Values[24] and are dedicated to preserving the same. I am not sure whether either has defined clearly what is meant by American values and how they compare with English values, French values or Japanese values. What I am sure about is that the value system that is accepted by most Americans today is considerably different than the value system of most Americans two centuries ago.

I am convinced that there is an underlying ethic that arises from the nature of the human person and is, therefore, a permanent norm against which we can evaluate the great variety of moral systems developed by ethicists and the even greater variety of value systems by which human beings live. But the legitimacy of my belief is irrelevant here. What interests us is how information flow changes value systems and, in particular, how it has changed the value systems of Americans.

Moral tenets such as the Ten Commandments tend to persist so long as society considers them a benefit, and to fade away as soon as society loses interest in defending them. The great majority of human beings are conformists and well-intentioned. They do not like to break rules, particularly if breaking them will result in disapproval by the people with whom they associate.

But the majority of human beings are also weak. There is always temptation to break rules. When peer pressure fades or is confused, there is less fear of disapproval, and rules are broken more frequently. And rules that are broken frequently, especially when hardly anybody cares, are soon considered no rules at all. That is how particular moral principles lose their power and how value systems change.

Value systems also change because people tend to interpret principles differently depending on the type of information that dominates their daily lives. In the early history of the United States, Herbert Spencer's dictum, "Every man has freedom to do all that he wills, provided he infringes not on the equal freedom of any other man," was interpreted very differently by Americans on the frontier and Americans in the East Coast cities.

Value systems, of course, encompass much more than morality. They impregnate and qualify the entire culture. Taste in art, literature and music, respect for learning, attitudes toward age and position, etiquette, manner of dress, even eating habits and the way people spend their leisure time are each subsystems in a culture's total value system. Although value systems are integral to what we call culture, the cultural context usually includes knowledge, customs, lifestyles and economic practices and structures that are influenced by but extend beyond value systems.

HOW VALUES AND CULTURES CHANGE

Some, like Serge Latouche in his *In The Wake of the Affluent Society*, accuse the "techno-economic megamachine" of assassinating cultures. Although Latouche admits that the economic dimension is "an historical and cultural invention," he fears that, in the West at least, "it is tending to become a substitute for culture."[25]

We shall consider the economic ramifications of spreading information and their impact on culture in the next chapter. Here we are trying to understand how value systems change. This is important not only because what people know influences value systems, but also because value systems are critical in formulating the cultural forces that manage information. A society's values can change in three ways: erratically, imperceptibly or cumulatively.

1. Values tend to change erratically when they are under high social tension due to a clash of opinion between groups with disparate interests.

Popular attitudes toward Native Americans and African-Americans are an example. There has been a tremendous shift from the way the average white American looked at Indians and blacks when the Constitution was written and the way the average white American does today. But the change was neither gradual nor smooth.

The sad history of the U.S. government's relations with Native Americans began with good intentions, despite the widely accepted presumption that the Indians were basically savages and somehow inferior. Most of the early government's negotiations with Indian tribes were conducted honorably. One of the last acts of the American Confederation was the 1787 Northwest Ordinance, which proclaimed that "utmost good faith shall always be observed towards the Indians; their lands and property shall never be taken from them without their consent." There were occasions when the U.S. government treated Indian chiefs as dignitaries. And there were tribes that fought as our allies in the Revolutionary War.

But there were other tribes who allied with the British, as there were tribes on both sides earlier, when the British were fighting the French in the French and Indian Wars. Most important, the value system of white Americans was quite different from that of the Indians. (Whites, for example, considered blowing off an enemy's head much more civilized than cutting off his scalp.)

Whenever the red man's use of land interfered with the white man's land use, popular values shifted, as they frequently do, from upholding human rights to pursuing economic advantage. Since white men had the vote and Indians did not, there were few politicians willing to fight for Indian rights. When the Supreme Court decided in favor of the autonomy of the Cherokee Indians, President Jackson refused to support the decision.[26]

The slavery question in the United States was another example of erratic changes in human values. Attitudes on whether slavery was right or wrong differed widely, depending on how necessary slavery was to the local economy. Most of the framers of the Constitution saw some difficulty in reconciling slavery with their ideas of liberty and equality, but were willing to compromise with slavery's defenders. Nevertheless, in 1808, the government, following Britain's lead, banned the importation of slaves.

5. Information, Authority and Democracy

The outcries of the Abolitionists, who had nothing to lose if the slaves were freed, were little appreciated by the plantation owners, whose economic world depended on slavery. As usual, there were politicians on both sides and many in the middle. Even the Great Emancipator, Abraham Lincoln, considered white men superior to black, compromised for years on the issue of slavery, and issued his Emancipation Proclamation not as an unequivocal stroke for human equality, but as a war-time strategy and only against the states in rebellion. Today, the legal system says black citizens are free and equal but the white man's value system, changed though it is, still lags considerably behind the law.

2. Values change imperceptibly when their underlying necessity for the social structure is removed or weakened, even though there is no conscious attack on the values themselves. Consider how the American attitude regarding the family has changed.

When the Founding Fathers rejected royalty and the transmittal of authority by inheritance in favor of the equality and independence of all men, they may not have realized it, but they were also eliminating much of the foundation that traditionally made the family important. Not only royalty but the entire social structure of medieval society was built on the authoritarian concept of the family, with the father as despot ("lord of the house") and the first-born male his successor. Family relationships were everything. Treaties between countries were often sealed with marriages. The family was the basic legal and social unit of medieval society.

All that changed in America. The new democratic system made the individual its basic legal and social unit. This decision was made with no intention of changing family law or customs. Exclusion of women from the vote was a natural consequence of the old concept of the family, as were most of the laws regarding heredity. But now sons could vote independently of their fathers, and there was less emphasis on the importance of being first-born.

Simultaneously with this ideological/legal emphasis on the individual, economic changes in society made the family less important. The availability of land in the United States helped make grown sons independent of their fathers. Social and financial success depended less on the family in which you were born. The move to the frontier made families more mobile, initiating a trend away from multigenerational families and diminishing the number of communities consisting solely of interrelated families. The industrial revolution made family businesses less important, forcing most people to earn their living outside the family.

All these changes prepared the way for a gradual progression to woman's suffrage, children's rights, the feminist movement, and eventually what today is so often called the "collapse of family values."

3. Values change cumulatively when new rules are introduced to protect society against new or newly recognized dangers. The American value system regarding the rights of business and how it should be conducted has been changing cumulatively since the close of the Constitutional Convention.

In the beginning most of the new government's concern about business was to encourage and protect it. Alexander Hamilton was the leader in fighting for a federal bank and tariffs to protect young American industries. But by the time Andrew Jackson was elected president, Amos Kendall was warning him that business was threatening the freedom of man by increasing "the number of his masters."[27]

In 1890, the Sherman Antitrust Act declared illegal all business agreements aimed at restraining interstate or foreign trade. In 1911, the Supreme Court forced the dismemberment of the Standard Oil Company. In 1914, the Clayton Antitrust Act prohibited sales contracts, intercorporate stock holdings and price cutting to hurt competition. The Federal Trade Commission was set up as watchdog.

This gradual shift from looking at business and mercantile interests as social assets to seeing big business and barons of industry as public enemies continued through the 19th Century with laws against child labor and sweatshops and for a minimum wage in certain occupations. In 1916, to strengthen labor unions against corporate power, the federal government exempted them from the antitrust laws. By 1935, employers were obliged to accept collective bargaining. In turn, when the unions became too strong, public attitudes changed toward them until the 1947 Taft-Hartley Labor Act restricted their power by outlawing the closed shop, secondary boycotts and jurisdictional strikes.

Eventually, defending the public against business extended to action against deceptive advertising, labeling and packaging, consumer protection, the Food and Drug Administration, dismemberment of the American Telephone & Telegraph Company, environmental impact studies and penalties for polluting. Of course, laws themselves do not make a value system, but they do reflect prevailing values, especially in a society with elected lawmakers, even when the law seems to keep several steps ahead of the value system, as in the case of racial prejudice.

THE DELUGE AND VALUES

It is difficult to exaggerate the psychic importance of value systems in determining how society operates. The faster value systems change, the more likely society will become disoriented. That is why the information deluge is so threatening. The more turbulent the information flow, the more rapid and confusing the shifts in our value systems.

We already see signs of disorientation in Washington, in academia, and in the media. Arguments over values are becoming louder and louder. Communitarian leader Amitai Etzioni complains of "rampant moral confusion and social anarchy."[28] We can already diagnose the first symptom of panic: the cries for destruction are beginning to drown out proposals for construction.

I believe there is a solution, and I think it lies in solving the riddle of how our society can develop a value system to control the information flow before the information flow swamps what is left of our value system.

I promise an outline of that solution in Part Two, but first we will examine how information has undermined another pillar of our society, the economy.

6

ADAM SMITH'S ARTHRITIC INVISIBLE HAND

"The information revolution has stormed the ramparts of the nation-state, and most of our favorite economic theories, capitalist as well as Marxist, have been trampled in the rush."
— Harlan Cleveland, 1993[1]

The same information flow that created democracy was responsible for Adam Smith's free-market theory. But the free market was immediately undermined by growing information, which gave sellers advantages over buyers, created economic pressure groups, encouraged oligopoly, perverted money management, confused economists, crippled private and public insurance, fueled speculation, diverted business energies from productivity to manipulation and handicapped government in policing the economy. Analysts like Alvin Toffler and Peter Drucker see the problem but miss its real cause.

WANDERING FINANCIAL PATHS AND MURDERED MONEY

Nowhere are the effects of ever-increasing information more evident than in the world of economics and finance. Our country's balance of payments and national debt are beyond redemption. The value of the dollar fluctuates daily, while *The Economist* magazine tells us that its "future path could be up, down or sideways" and Joel Kurtzman's book announces *The Death of Money*.

To understand how this happened, we go back again to the time when liberty became the rallying cry of Western civilization: financial liberty as well as political liberty. In 1776, the same year America's founding fathers promulgated the Declaration of Independence, a British professor of moral philosophy by the name of Adam Smith published a very influential dissertation called *The Wealth of Nations*. Smith's ideas were not entirely new, but they were expressed clearly and in terms that blended wonderfully with the wave of democratic thinking washing across Europe and America.

Since Smith was a morals professor, it is not surprising that he was very precise about obligations, in this case the government's obligations. Thus he clearly stated that the government in the person of the sovereign had the duty:

(1) to defend society from violence and invasion,

(2) to protect individuals from injustice or oppression in their relations with other individuals,

(3) to erect and maintain public works and institutions that cannot be provided by the private sector.[2]

But, when it came to commerce or business, the moralist turned economist felt strongly that government should leave people alone. So long as they did not violate the laws of justice, he wanted citizens to be left free to pursue their own interests in their own ways, free to bring both "their industry and their capital" into competition with the work and wealth of others.

Smith gave two reasons for his conclusion. First, government should not attempt a function "for the proper performance of which no human wisdom or knowledge could ever be sufficient."[3]

The second, better-known rationale was Smith's theory that government interference was unnecessary because the "natural effort of every individual to better his own position" will carry society "to wealth and prosperity." Unfortunately, posterity heralded this position while ignoring the first.

WHY DEMOCRACY CLASPED THE INVISIBLE HAND

Smith was convinced that this innate tendency of buyers and sellers to watch out for their own interests would create an economic balance to the benefit of all. In describing this unconscious management of the economy Smith described it as being "led by an invisible hand,"[4] a simile that caught the public imagination and is part of the language of economists.

Smith's concepts, as presented in both his earlier *Theory of Moral Sentiments* as well as *The Wealth of Nations*, were more qualified and complex than the idea that ignited the popular imagination and fueled Western business and government policies for two centuries. In fact, Smith developed his theories to explain economic phenomena he observed, not to prescribe ways of managing economies. But that has never kept his disciples from transmuting the explanations of phenomena into formulae for action.

To put it another way: Adam Smith was a seminal thinker, but like almost every seminal thinker, from Plato and Aristotle through Darwin, Kant and Freud, the seed that took root was not the one the thinker intended to sow nor a seed he would have approved. An inevitable consequence of the way information flows is that conceptual currents create an undertow more powerful than the splash of specific theory or the wave of qualified argument. Conceptual currents, alas, are not only more influential but also more liable to misinterpretation.

If Smith's "simple system of natural liberty" had enormous appeal in England, it was even more attractive to Americans whose battle for independence had been ignited and fueled by resentment against attempts by King George III and the British Parliament to restrict commerce in the colonies. Thus the dogma that market freedom is always good and interference with market freedom is always bad became a benchmark for American business and politics throughout the 19th and 20th Centuries.

FREE MARKET WAS A CHIMERA

There are those who argue, and they have plenty of historical evidence to back them up, that there has never been a free market that achieved healthy growth unless it was planted in a commercial environment created by government interference. The principal economist to develop that argument was a German: Friedrich List in his 1841 treatise, *The National System of Political Economy*. England's late-19th Century free market prospered because the British crown had first built a powerful merchant marine, then restricted textile imports and finally promulgated strict laws (not repealed until 1843) against the exportation of English machines and manufacturing processes.

In America, government interference by protective tariffs, championed by our first Secretary of the Treasury Alexander Hamilton, and 1844 presidential candidate Henry Clay, began long before the free market took hold. The most

6. Adam Smith's Arthritic Invisible Hand 111

noteworthy bill passed by the U.S. Congress in 1828 was protectionist legislation known as the "Tariff of Abominations." Almost a century later, the booming American free-market decade (1919-1929, when industrial output doubled) was launched by President Warren G. Harding with the erection of extensive tariff barriers. For more examples see William Lazonick's 1991 book, *Business Organization and the Myth of the Market Economy*.

The reason we can find no example of Adam Smith's theory working without conditioning is that it cannot. In Neil Postman's words,

> Capitalism, like science and liberal democracy, was an outgrowth of the Enlightenment. Its principal theorists, even its most prosperous practitioners, believed capitalism to be based on the idea that both buyers and seller are sufficiently mature, well informed and reasonable to engage in transactions of mutual self-interest.[5]

But that was an illusion. Distribution of information is always uneven. It is unlikely, if not impossible, for any two persons to have identical knowledge. And the instant one party in a marketing transaction has better information than the other, that negotiator has an advantage, and cheating becomes not only possible but likely.

In *American Capitalism*, John Kenneth Galbraith denies this, arguing that Adam Smith and other economists of the 19th Century were realists, for in their day the larger part of the national product was contributed by agriculture, the cotton, coal-mining, metal and metal-working industries, all of which had too many producers for any single producer to influence prices.[6] Yet Galbraith admits that "this did not remain the case," and develops his theory of countervailing power to explain economic developments that cannot be explained by Smith's invisible hand.

Early in his analysis Galbraith observes that "man cannot live without an economic theology—without some rationalization of the abstract and seemingly inchoate arrangements which provide him with his livelihood."[7] He more or less agrees that the righteousness of the free market is a central dogma of that theology. But he is more interested in its effect on economic modeling—what economists teach and preach. My interest is more on how such dogmas affect the general public's store of information.

TRANSFORMING THE MORAL CODE

Economic "theology," people's presumptions about the "rules" that govern their livelihood, can make a tremendous difference in all human relations, so much so that it can transform the moral code by which men live. We find an extreme example in America's first critical cultural conflict, the way the U.S. government, backed by popular opinion, treated the American Indian.

The underlying cause for that infamous injustice was the clash of two diametrically opposed economic dogmas. The colonists came to America with an economic structure based entirely on ownership of land. The Indians, in contrast, believed that human beings could no more own land than they could own air or sunshine. Negotiation between the white man and the Indian was impossible, for neither could accept, nor even understand, the attitude of the other.

The growth of information had a similar influence on the marketplace, for it taught business people how to manage multiple motives so as to manipulate buying behavior. By its very definition marketing requires purposeful influence on how and why buyers buy. Marketing presumes intentional interference with Adam Smith's economic balance.

Economists are aware of this, which is why, when they talk about free markets, they mean markets free from government interference, not from business interference. But, as we shall see later, expecting the marketplace to stay free of government also makes little sense, for government is so much a part of the commercial world that it cannot avoid influencing the market even when it follows an avowed *laissez-faire* policy.

With the spread of knowledge, selling techniques grew from the primitive hucksterism of the snake-oil salesman to the sophisticated marketing of Madison Avenue. The playing field between the marketer, a professional, and the consumer, an amateur, became more and more uneven, making Adam Smith's "invisible hand" more and more arthritic.

THE RISE OF MARKETING

By the dawn of the 20th Century there was a major shift in the way manufacturers peddled goods. The industrial revolution had taught business how to mass manufacture. Henry Ford figured out how to make cars that could be sold at prices most Americans could afford. It was the first step into modern

6. Adam Smith's Arthritic Invisible Hand

marketing; instead of first making products and then looking for buyers, marketing sets out to learn what buyers want and designs the products to fit that need.

But in studying people's needs and wants, sellers quickly figured out how to influence what people wanted. Soon marketers were not only designing products to fit wants but designing wants to create demand for products. These advances sent business careening along the very thin line that separates persuasion from manipulation. One such maneuver was planned obsolescence. Another was advertising perfected to mold public taste, frequently with methods that lost sight of the difference between information and misinformation.

Soon millions of women were convinced that lipstick was a necessity. Then millions more could not appear in public without dying their hair. And men whose forefathers had lived entire lives unoffended by the smell of their fellows suddenly were compelled to fight B.O. As Galbraith so felicitiously commented, the result was that competition, which was supposed to reward us with lower prices and greater efficiency, now became "an exercise in uniquely ostentatious waste," assailing our ears "with rhymed commercials and soap opera and rendering the countryside hideous with commercial art."[8]

ADVERTISING DISCOVERS PSYCHOLOGY

By mid-century, advertising professionals were importing information from science and academia to analyze the behavior of consumers. There was a sudden influx of Ph.D.s into the advertising business. George Gallup taught marketers how to measure public opinion. Ernest Dichter made lots of money selling motivational research (e.g., prunes are hard to sell because they arouse feelings of old age and insecurity).

Advertising agencies discussed "models of buyer behavior," debating how marketing plans could incorporate Alfred Marshall's appeal to buyer utility, Ivan Pavlov's manipulation of learning behavior, Sigmund Freud's use of symbols to arouse the subconscious, Thorstein Veblen's insights into the impact of cultural concerns and Thomas Hobbes' description of how buyers reconcile social and personal goals.

All this new information generated some useful insights and much useless confusion. Many companies prospered. But many more spent millions of dollars on information they did not need or know how to use. The number of products (supermarkets for example now have to decide whether to carry some 20,000 new products every year) and the amount of information about consumers has made marketing much more difficult.

Today two more techniques for abusing buyers have added to all this sleight of hand (or should I say, sleight of mind?). The first is a new alliance between the entertainment and advertising industries. Comics, movies, TV shows and games are used to create multiple-product franchises that invade adult pocketbooks through the hearts of children. Cabbage Patch Kids, Teenage Mutant Ninja Turtles and Power Rangers are less toys than tweezers applied to children to squeeze money out of parents.

The second is less obvious but just as pernicious. While politicians and media worry about what the new communications technology is doing to secrecy and privacy, the more serious danger lies in the way truth is being distorted or buried under avalanches of specialized information. Patients can no longer understand all that their doctors are doing. Investors get lost in the intricacies of finance. Policy holders despair of learning what insurance benefits are their due. Owners of computerized cars are at the mercy of their mechanics.

INFORMATION EMPOWERS PRESSURE GROUPS

But persuasion is not the only technique overshadowing price competition. There is also pressure. The more business people and customers learned about how commerce works, the more both sides realized that competitive power could be amplified through cooperation. The medieval guilds were early pressure groups used by tradesmen to keep competition down and prices up. As the industrial revolution took hold, the workers formed unions to counter the power of their bosses—a reaction to a more powerful, if less organized, pressure group, the owners and managers of the mills, mines and machines: Karl Marx's capitalists.

It is impossible to exaggerate the importance of information in creating, strengthening and perpetuating pressure groups. The function of the union organizer was largely educational, to teach the workers the power in united action and the hope in exercising that power. On the other side, the bourgeoisie were a social class and as such owed their rise as much to communication as to commerce. Knowledge spread the industrial revolution, not just the sci-

6. Adam Smith's Arthritic Invisible Hand 115

ence and engineering that created machines, but the opportunities for profit in machines and cheap labor.

In his *Spirit of Community,* Amitai Etzioni points out that "the advantages of using information over and over again gives a great advantage to the established and the large."[9] But the reuse of information also proved to be a trap. As knowledge grew, so did ability to analyze and imitate new products and techniques.

In the late 19th Century Britain was able to control textile trade because its mills required less than half the manpower of its nearest competitor (Germany). Today information flows so rapidly that competitors can quickly adapt, if not copy, the cleverest new machines, processes and products. So much so that competing companies often spend much more on advertising than on product innovation, for they have learned that share of market depends less on product differences than on how consumers think about the product and the company. (I shall return to this in Chapter 21.)

In practice, however, competition between firms frequently gave way to connivance. As Galbraith explains, although there are exceptions,

> ...the number of firms participating in a business is likely to be at its maximum within a few years or even a few months after the business is born. Thereafter there is, typically, a steady decline until a point of stability is reached with a handful of massive survivors and, usually, a fringe of smaller hangers-on.[10]

Thus, in the United States, the automobile, steel, rubber, tobacco, liquor and chemical industries all became oligopolies. When the field is dominated by a few large manufacturers pricing is usually determined, not by competition, but by a covert conspiracy. One of the companies—usually the largest—raises or lowers a price, and the others see that it is to their advantage to follow. This is not always as evident as it is with airline passenger fares and bank interest rates, but is widespread in both consumer and industrial markets.

The more I study economic history, the more convinced I become that information flow is a more basic determinant of economic stability than competition. Although information flows unevenly, it does flow irrevocably and eventually becomes the great leveler. Galbraith's principal theme in his 1939 classic, *American Capitalism,* is his theory of what he calls "countervailing power"—that the marketing power of a few strong firms working in tacit agreement is usually countered by the development of buyers with enough economic leverage to balance the power of the sellers.

This means, in Galbraith's words, that "competition which, at least since the time of Adam Smith, has been viewed as the autonomous regulator of economic activity and as the only available regulatory mechanism apart from the state, has, in fact, been superseded."[11] He quickly adds that competition still plays a role, but that, in addition to competitors, strong or organized buyers also provide a regulatory mechanism. A modern example: the supermarket chains, whose ability to grant or refuse shelf space gives them enormous leverage with packaged-goods manufacturers.

MONEY MANAGEMENT BECOMES AN ECONOMIC CANCER

To really understand how communication and information flow affect our way of life both socially and economically, we must go back once more to the way of thinking that glorified Smith's invisible hand. Smith's entire free market idea rested on a further dogma that human beings always act out of self-interest. This was not a denial of the possibility of good Samaritans or saintly self-sacrifice, but economists agreed with Max Weber's pessimistic observation that such acts of benevolence did not affect general economic conclusions, because "it is even more certain that the mass of men do not act in this way . . . and never will."[12]

Thus the social ineffectiveness of altruism was basic to Western economic theory. The majority of economists restricted their consideration of human motivation even further by interpreting self-interest as the pursuit of wealth or money. As economist James Q. Wilson explains in *Political Organizations*,

> Economics rests on the assumption that persons and firms will rationally seek to maximize their utility. In principle, utility refers to anything a person values—not only money, but honor, power, fame, or compassion. In fact, economics almost never deals with any of these other values; it treats instead of one value, money. There are two reasons for this. The first is that money is a common measuring rod by which a large number of other values, but not all other values, can be compared. . . . The second reason for money measure is that it permits one to make a highly simplified, but not unrealistic, motivational assumption—namely, men prefer more money to less, other things, such as effort, being equal.[13]

The problem is that once you accept money as the dominant motivator in society, you have to wrestle with the economic conundrum that macro-management of the free-market economy rests on micro-mismanagement, because the great majority of human beings are incompetent in the management of money. Mancur Olson even criticized the great John Maynard Keynes for developing macroeconomic theory without adequate basis in microeconomic theory.[14]

To illustrate the incredibly complex nature of natural systems or causal relations, physicists point out that the flutter of a butterfly's wings in the Amazon jungle affects the weather in Chicago. So, too, the national (and world) economy is affected by the way my spendthrift uncle and your penny-pinching aunt manage their finances. Recent studies prove that money illusion is widespread. People prefer monetary value over real value.[15] No wonder economics is called "the dismal science."

THE MYSTERY OF MONEY

Money, as I said earlier, is a form of communication. It is a way of expressing worth. Like all forms of communication, it is an abstraction. Humans cannot transmit information to anyone without first processing it—turning it into an idea, a mental creation related to, but never the same as, reality. But money is an abstraction more removed from reality than most of our ideas, because it says, "This stands for value, not the color, the taste, the shape or the feel of the object, but its value." And unlike color, taste, shape and feel, value is not an objective trait. It is not determined by the object. It is determined by the desires and needs of someone outside the object. Value is by definition relative. Nothing in life has the same value to everybody— except, by an outrageous legal fiction, money.

Of course, in reality, not even money has the same value to everyone. Misers and philanthropists look at it differently. Where its real value lies is in the tricks we can perform with it. Humans learned early that they could do things with money that they could never do with reality. While the alchemists searched for the mythical philosopher's stone to turn base metals into gold, businessmen found its equivalent in money. The imaginative science of finance was developed years before the physical sciences. By the mid-1500s, before Galileo, Kepler, Newton, Darwin and, yes, Adam Smith, the spread of money was not only worldwide, but European businessmen were keeping double-entry books, writing bills of exchange, issuing letters of credit and speculating in futures.

The problem with money is that it measures the unmeasurable, i.e., value. But human beings are willing to overlook this contradiction because money can be expressed in numbers—the second degree of abstraction—a form of thinking that provides a degree of certainty found with no other tool of reason. As Brian Arthur, the real-life hero of M. Mitchell Waldrop's *Complexity,* put it, "Used correctly mathematics can give your ideas a tremendous clarity."[16]

THE WANDERING ECONOMISTS

One of the effects of the widespread illusion that money is an accurate reflection of value was to send economists on a futile search to express economic insights in the language of mathematics, with the certainty of mathematics. Read a book published for professional economists in the first half of the 20th Century and you will find it filled with algebraic-looking formulae. Mancur Olson, who published his *Logic of Collective Action* in 1965, obscured his incredibly perceptive insights (on why the economies of established governments stagnate while those of new governments thrive) by attempts to prove his theory mathematically, and the majority of economists did not take his theory seriously because they were dissatisfied with the mathematics. In the 1980s, when economist Brian Arthur proposed his theory of "increasing returns," he attributed the hostile reaction of American economists to "their well-known fondness for mathematics."[17]

Max Weber's reputation rests largely on his attempt to bridge the gap between the empirical nature of the social sciences and the mathematical nature of the physical sciences, but as Talcott Parsons says in his introduction to *The Theory of Social and Economic Organization,* Weber "failed to complete the process, and the nature of the half-way point at which he stopped helps to account for many of the difficulties of his position."[18] In the aforementioned *Complexity,* Waldrop gives an amusing description of a meeting of physicists and economists to compare their respective disciplines. He writes:

> Unfortunately, the economists' standard solution to the problem of expectations—perfect rationality—drove the physicists nuts. Perfectly rational agents do have the virtue of being perfectly predictable. That is, they know everything that can be known about the choices they will face infinitely far into the future, and they use flawless reasoning to foresee all the possible implications of their

actions. So you can safely say that they will always take the most advantageous action in any given situation, based on the available information. Of course, they may sometimes be caught short by oil shocks, technological revolutions, political decisions about interest rates, and other noneconomic surprises. But they are so smart and so fast in their adjustments that they will always keep the economy in a kind of rolling equilibrium, with supply precisely equal to demand.

The only problem, of course, is that real human beings are neither perfectly rational nor perfectly predictable—as the physicists pointed out at great length. Furthermore, as several of them also pointed out, there are real theoretical pitfalls in assuming perfect predictions, even if you do assume that people are perfectly rational. In nonlinear systems—and the economy is most certainly nonlinear—chaos theory tells you that the slightest uncertainty in your knowledge of the initial conditions will often grow inexorably. After a while, your predictions are nonsense.[19]

As many politicians have learned to their dismay, economists are not very good at making predictions. In the 1960s, the followers of John Maynard Keynes thought they could end recessions by fine-tuning taxes and spending. In the 1970s, the monetarists tried to stabilize the economy by controlling the money supply. In the 1980s, supply-siders proposed lowering tax rates to increase tax revenue. None of these plans worked, but economists keep on trying. They have a compulsion that theirs is not a science unless they can predict what will happen. Prediction is a good test of theory in astronomy. But humans, who determine the course of economic events, do not perform with the constancy of heavenly bodies. Darwin's theory of natural selection is not considered unscientific because it cannot predict the future course of evolution. Nor did Darwin try to prove his theory mathematically. But then money, with its numerical accountability, is not the grease that makes biology work as it is in economics.

There has been a significant shift, however, among more recent economists. *Newsweek* called it *psychonomics*, and reported that "after failing to find answers with brute computing power, economics is now seeking help from psychology. Known as behavioral economics, this controversial combination of psychological insights and economic methods is moving fast into the mainstream.[20]" More significant, the 1996 Nobel Prize in economics went to two scholars for studies on how the disequilibrium of information affects economic negotiations.[21]

MISUSING THE TOOL

Albeit a fiction, money is a useful tool. It facilitates the exchange of objects and services. I can work for one man and use the money he gives me to buy food from another. It makes it easy to save for the future. I can sell the yearling before it gets old and put aside the money to buy a young horse years later.

But a useful tool can also be dangerous. Inflation is the best example of how money can turn on us. The money I put aside for a future horse may not even buy a cat. In the beginning something of widely recognized value was used for money, such as gold or silver. But since even that was an attempt to standardize value artificially, it was easy to slip into using paper money—first as certificates representing gold in vaults, and eventually with nothing to secure the paper symbols but the creditworthiness of the government.

But money's most important—and perilous—function was to facilitate social insurance, which is the basis of all society. Although love and the need for companionship was undoubtedly fundamental in the formation of communities, an important and universal factor from the start was insurance. Community, even when it consisted only of those who shared a cave, was founded on the realization that the uneven and unpredictable risks of living could be managed more easily when shared by a group.

As communities grew, money became a government facilitator, a tool for more easily sharing risk. Instead of all the inhabitants joining to build walls to protect the community, citizens gave money to the government which used it to pay the stone masons. As time went on, individuals started to share risks privately. By the 14th Century insurance for ships' voyages was common. London's professional underwriters began meeting regularly at Lloyd's Coffee House in 1688.

Both public insurance, through government, and private insurance, through business underwriting, were created to protect individuals against the unknown, the unpredictable. Hence it should be no surprise that advances in information cause problems for both government and the insurance business. As knowledge increases, both the insurers and the insured develop new ways

6. Adam Smith's Arthritic Invisible Hand

to exploit the system. The insurers look for ways to control risk and exclude the risk-prone. The insured look for lower premiums, agree to the exclusion of the more risk prone than themselves, and study ways to milk the system.

The more either party learns about how the system functions, the more expensive it becomes to operate a government or insurance system. Insurance experts speak of two problems in insurance: *adverse selection* (those who want insurance most pose the worst risk for the insurer) and *moral hazard* (people tend to take greater risks once they are insured).

This is a major problem for government. The expense of rescuing the savings and loan industry was much greater because federal insurance covered risky loans. Yet farmers, manufacturers, shippers and thousands of other special interests run to the government for protection, for security against risk. The more risk protection the government assumes, the more taxes are required—and the more citizens learn about how to claim the goodies and avoid the taxes.

Nor have private insurers been able to overcome these problems. Insure people's health and people incur more health expenses. Cover automobile accidents, and suddenly there are more accidents. Millions are paid each year to cover fraudulent claims, because doctors have learned the fine art of turning symptoms into claims and lawyers have divined the maximum insurers will pay rather than go to court.

Finally, the growth of knowledge has magnified the risks themselves. Advances in medical science have driven up the cost of healthcare. Cars covered by collision insurance are more complex and expensive than they used to be. A catastrophe like Florida's Hurricane Andrew or the San Francisco earthquake costs both government and private insurers much more than it would have a century ago because our growth in knowledge has made homes and infrastructure more elaborate and costly.

LEDGER LEGERDEMAIN

Just as the growth in knowledge threatens government and insurance, the information deluge is sweeping away the stability of our financial world by increasing the uses and availability of credit to the point where individuals, corporations and the federal government handle debt as if it were an asset. Since the early 1980s major lenders have been securitizing receivables, and bundling loans to turn them into assets.[22] Credit has invalidated the economist's definition of standard of living as the quantity of goods and services which can be purchased by average national income and killed the bourgeois idea that a human is worth what he is worth in good hard cash.

While information about money was encouraging credit, it facilitated another trick: speculation. Money enables us to traffic in futures, to buy the farmer's crop before he grows it, to invest in a piece of land with the hope it will be worth considerably more several years from now. There is, of course, nothing wrong with investing in reasonable hopes. Every human being who plans for the future does it. Every business does it. Speculation only becomes dangerous when it gets out of hand, as in 1995, when Brazil, Colombia and the Central American nations held an emergency meeting on plummeting coffee prices due to speculators "eliminating any sense of reality from the market by negotiating more coffee in futures contracts than actually existed."[23]

There are two reasons why speculation tends to get out of hand. One is that there are always con men who will take advantage of other people's hopes. The other is that the deeper you get into working with money the more you get to thinking of it entirely in terms of numbers. And numbers are like mirrors, no two reflect the same aspect of reality. Hence over-reliance on numbers is like walking through a funhouse. The more we multiply the mirrors, the further we get from reality.

In 1991, an established publishing company called Family Media died. The company owned six magazines: *Health, 1,001 Home Ideas, Homeowner, Discover, Tennis Illustrated* and *Golf Illustrated,* none of them leaders in their fields, but all of them pretty good properties that had just gone through a tough year for the advertising industry with only one of them declining in advertising income. I was personally acquainted with Bob Riordan, the man who ran the company. He was a great manager, with extensive experience in publishing and a reputation for running a tight ship. Five years earlier, he sold *Ladies' Home Journal* to Meredith Publishing for an estimated $84 million profit. Four years later, with less than $60 million in ad revenue, Family Media was carrying more than $60 million in debt, the result of wild borrowing to finance even wilder projects.

6. Adam Smith's Arthritic Invisible Hand

Somehow this very savvy publisher got lost in the hall of mirrors. The problem with reliance on numbers is not that it makes managers calculating and cold, but that it makes them mesmerized and confused.

WHEN MANIPULATION OVERSHADOWS PRODUCTION

We have all read stories about misers, miserable people who become so obsessed with money that they can think of little else; the symbol of value becomes their only value. Something similar takes place in "advanced" economies. Business managers become so obsessed with money that they become more interested in corporate dollars than corporate sense. Manipulation gradually becomes a more important economic activity than production. This trend came to a head in the 1980s, as financial raiders ruined entire companies in their mad rush for quick killings in paper profits. Their obsession gravely injured innumerable people from the workers who lost their jobs at Philip Morris to my friend, Bob Edgell, chief executive of Edgell Communications, who got lost in the hall of mirrors and ended in suicide.[24]

Because money can be moved about so easily, it easily becomes separated from the real, but slower-moving, world of producing and trading goods and services. This rupture has become particularly acute with the rapidity of electronic communication. It takes milliseconds to transfer money from New York to Tokyo, while one still needs days to ship products.

The trend to favor playing with money over creating real wealth does more lasting damage than a one-time loss of jobs or even someone's death. It distorts the whole structure of society by forcing more and more people into non-productive activity. Thousands of American lawyers, accountants, bookkeepers, bankers, clerks and government employees now devote their entire working lives to managing the manipulation of money. We now have an entire industry, for instance, built on making profits from the fluctuating value of different currencies.

As information proliferates on how to milk the weakness in the global monetary system, governments respond with regulations to control abuse and protect the value of their currencies. This requires more employees to enforce the regulations, which means higher taxes and prompts all these non-productive activities to hire more lawyers and accountants. And the vicious spiral goes on and on.

WHY GOVERNMENT INTERFERES

Adam Smith saw no contradiction in the basic duties of government and his economic theory. I doubt, however, that he foresaw how much the government's obligatory functions would ultimately subsume. If government must protect its citizens from outside invasion, then tariffs and immigration restrictions may be essential. If government must prevent injustices among citizens, anti-trust laws, the Federal Trade Commission, the Securities and Exchange Commission and the Food and Drug Administration may be necessary. If government must establish and maintain institutions the private sector cannot provide, there may be a justification for Social Security, Medicare, public education, public transportation, etc.

Hence the argument between liberal and conservative is not one of principle or dogma, but always one of interpretation. In their zeal for discouraging excessive government, organizations like the Cato Institute tend to oversimplify the issue. Arguments that anything run by government tends to be ineffective beg the question. Private efforts can be just as ineffective, though seldom as noticeable.

Once we recognize a social need, we have to make the decision as to whether we can (1) afford to ignore it, (2) somehow turn it over to private enterprise, or (3) create a government department to handle it.

Beyond these basic problems, such decisions have been greatly complicated by the growth of knowledge about what economists call *externalities*, the consequences of business activity that are not factored in as costs. We know a lot more about pollution, over-harvesting, resource depletion and the consequences of waste than we used to. The first impulse is to have the government make laws against such abuses. But we are finding out this solution can be both costly and ineffective.

Some years before he became President Johnson's Director of the Bureau of the Budget and later chairman of the President's Council of Economic Advisers, Charles Schultze gave a series of lectures which were turned into a book, *The Public Use of Private Interests*.

The book argues that government should use techniques that appeal to private interests (i.e., marketing techniques) to get people and businesses to do the right thing in activities that affect society as a whole. It is very realistic in explaining why our democratic system favors command and control (legislat-

6. Adam Smith's Arthritic Invisible Hand

ing what should be done) rather than creating a system of incentives similar to those of the marketplace so as to make private choice consonant with public virtue.

Once we recognize that the community must establish institutions—whether armies, courts, police departments, school systems, Medicare or the Postal Service—we are allowing a new form of competition with free enterprise. These government organizations will compete with private business by purchasing goods, hiring people and borrowing money on the open market. What is doubly troublesome is that government has an unfair advantage in the open market. It makes the rules. In borrowing money it can offer guarantees no private business can offer.

The result is that the entire society becomes much more complicated, and the more business adapts to cope, and government legislates to prevent abuse, the more information has to be known to navigate the shoals. Since this knowledge maze is so complicated, more and more specialized pilots are required to navigate it: lawyers, accountants, and consultants. And they in turn, because it is natural to foster the need for one's own services, generate more complications with greater and greater need for their special kinds of services.

WHAT IS WRONG

The information deluge has not only left us all in over our heads, swimming in a storm-tossed sea. Knowledge—and with it, change—is multiplying faster and faster, creating new problems, each harder to solve than its predecessor. Almost everyone agrees that we are in the midst of major social and economic revolution. The two most popular explanations of this phenomenon are future shock (the term invented by Alvin Toffler) and the knowledge economy (if not invented, certainly popularized by Peter Drucker).[25]

Both analyses mislead.

Future shock is a genuine psychological phenomenon, but it is a symptom, not a cause. At the close of *Future Shock,* Toffler, like King Canute, stands on the shore and orders the waves of change to stop.[26] They won't. As long as information multiplies, change will accelerate. The challenge lies in managing information, not in controlling change.

The widely accepted explanation that we have moved into a knowledge economy is misleading because every economy the world has ever witnessed has been a knowledge economy—created, sustained and advanced by the state of human knowledge at the time. It is true, as Lewis Mumford observed in 1934, that science moved invention from mechanical ingenuity in the workshop to theoretical engineering on paper.[27] But every manufacturing process, no matter how primitive, has always required knowledge.

Every worker had to know what he was doing. Whether throwing a spear in the hunt or tightening a bolt on the assembly line, man had to know how to recognize the game and aim the spear or find the bolt and turn the wrench. It is true that today we have and are using more knowledge, but we also have and are using more products, more services and more methods of distribution.

The changes that make an economy essentially different lie not in how we manufacture but in how we distribute what is manufactured. I see six such economic eras in human history, depending on whether commerce was dominated by self supply, barter, shopkeeping, retailing, mass marketing or interactive marketing.

In lock step with each of these periods marches the evolution of communications, for it was communications that made each of them work. Barter was promoted largely by word of mouth. Shopkeepers used signboards to attract customers for the things they made. Retailers, since they offered products manufactured by others, perfected personal salesmanship. Mass marketing developed media advertising. And interactive marketing, where buyer and seller develop the product together, is made possible by the advance of two-way, largely electronic communication.

The problem is information, multiplying at a rate beyond any individual's mental powers. Business has developed interactive marketing to manage the effect of the surfeit of information on the distribution of products and services. But we are not applying the same kind of thinking to solving the larger social problems created by the information flood. Charles Schultze has shown the advantages of using marketing techniques to govern, but no one has proposed, or even looked for, a genuine substitute for command and control.

That, I believe, is what is wrong.

WHAT IS RIGHT

I have great faith in the ingenuity and resiliency of business people, much more faith than I have in economists and social scientists, who tend to dis-

6. Adam Smith's Arthritic Invisible Hand

cover solutions only after individual entrepreneurs are using them. Since most people recognize that we have a problem, many people propose and attempt solutions. A lot of changes are taking place in the way we try to run the government. But even more are found in the way business people are beginning to do business.

In Part Two, we shall examine how these solutions are developing, why the most successful are new ways to manage information, and the evidence that similar techniques are beginning to transform the way humans organize communities to govern themselves. But, first, we must take a look at the changes that have taken place in communication, particularly in our single greatest cultural catalyst, what we now call the media.

7

THE MEDIA: FORMED, FED AND FOILED BY INFORMATION

"I think media are so powerful they swallow cultures. I think of them as invisible environments which surround and destroy old environments"
— Edmund Carpenter, 1973[1]

The media both reflect and influence culture. Information flow fostered the free press but made it impossible to keep journalists' opinions out of the news. Government has always worried about the Fourth Estate's power, which can affect individuals, politicians and society even in ways unintended by journalists. Although the information deluge has damaged the media through erosion of public confidence and attention, loss of financial independence, and pressure from outside communication professionals, most of us still look to the media to pilot us through the chaos of cultural confusion and to help us create communities of shared interests.

CULTURE CREATOR AND REFLECTOR

It is important to realize that American democracy—and every other widely accepted way of looking at the world—is always as much a product of the media as it is reflected by the media.

Culture, in the sense of the conglomeration of memes common to a group, develops and changes largely under media influence. Every communication—from words and gestures to movies and books—not only reflects the culture in which it was born, but always alters it. Each message's reflection of the culture always includes some distortion, an interpretation that itself becomes part of the culture. Hence culture is constantly changing and the media play crucial roles as initiators and transmitters (and sometimes resisters) of the changes.

Cultures studied by historians or anthropologists have an artificial stasis with arbitrary boundaries in time and place, whereas real cultures are like running rivers, consisting of many different streams continually merging into and transforming each other. We can scoop up a glass of the water and analyze it. But the next glass will be different. Today, the culture stream has become a rapids, making it extremely difficult, probably impossible, to accurately define or even describe cultures separately. Consider the ever-evolving life of just one important meme at our culture's heart: "Freedom of the press is essential to democracy."

FREEDOM FOR PRINT JOURNALISM

From the nation's earliest days, thoughtful Americans qualified what they meant by freedom of the press. Thus Benjamin Franklin wrote about the newspaper he published some four decades before the Revolution:

> In the conduct of my newspaper, I carefully excluded all libeling and personal abuse, which is of late years become so disgraceful in our country. Whenever I was solicited to insert any thing of that kind, and the writers pleaded, as they generally did, the liberty of the press, and that a newspaper was like a stage-coach, in which any one who would pay had a right to a place, my answer was, that I would print the piece separately if desired, and the author might have as many copies as he pleased to distribute himself, but that I would not take upon me to spread his detraction; and that, having contracted with my subscribers to furnish them with what might be either useful or entertaining, I could not fill their papers with private altercation, in which they had no concern, without doing them manifest injustice.[2]

Note that Franklin's qualms were about including the material in his newspaper, not about printing it separately. His argument for not accepting the material was based more on keeping the readers interested than on moral obligation. This pragmatic (cynics might say, "business-oriented") approach to freedom of the press was (and is) typical of American culture.

When England passed the Sugar Act, merchants in the Colonies grumbled. When England passed the Stamp Act decreeing that stamps be affixed to newspapers and pamphlets, there was an uproar, which grew into attacks on the nature of British government and calls for economic boycott and civil disobedience. So, even then, journalists screamed louder when you stepped on their toes than when you stepped on the toes of others. We shall return to this subject, but the media's biggest bias is always its natural inclination to favor what is good for the media.

Franklin left us another lesson on press freedom in connection with a pamphlet he wrote arguing that the Pennsylvannia colony should print paper money. *The Nature and Necessity of a Paper Currency* was, in his own words,

> ...well received by the common people in general; but the rich men dislik'd it, for it increas'd and strengthen'd the clamor for more money, and they happening to have no writers among them that were able to answer it, their opposition slacken'd, and the point was carried by a majority in the House.[3]

Press freedom is not equally advantageous to everyone. It does not help those who "have no writers among them."

REGULATION OF BROADCAST JOURNALISM

As media grew, it became more evident and more worrisome that the power of the press could be exercised by the few against the many. Nothing bears more evidence to this than the history of government-broadcasting relations in the United States.

Because the number of frequencies for broadcasting were limited some sort of government regulation was inevitable. There were more than a thousand amateur and disaster radio stations operating before the Radio Act of 1912 made it against the law to send radio signals without a license from the Secretary of Commerce, but that law did not assign frequencies. There were more than 10,000 broadcasters, including 571 commercial stations, before the Radio Act of 1927 set up the Federal Radio Commission (changed to the Federal Communications Commission in 1934) to assign frequencies, and license station operators for three years at a time.

The 1927 Radio Act also specified that "Nothing in this Act shall be understood or construed to give the licensing authority the power of censorship over the radio communications or signals transmitted by any radio station, and no regulation or condition shall be promulgated or fixed by the licensing authority which shall interfere with the right of free speech by means of radio communication."[4] At the same time, the government borrowed phraseology from the licensing of public utilities and prescribed that the stations serve public interest, convenience and necessity, and specified that legally qualified candidates for public office should be given equal opportunity to use the broadcast station.

Undoubtedly the concern about freedom of expression and avoidance of censorship was one reason why the government made the rather shortsighted decision to "award" radio licenses to qualifying applicants for three-year periods rather than sell temporary licenses every three years to the highest bidder. It was not until 1994 that Congress told the FCC to auction certain types of airwave licenses.

The result was that early broadcasters were extremely careful about public service, fairness and objectivity. Remember the CBS memorandum, quoted in Chapter 3,[5] stating that Columbia had a policy of having no editorial views and that its radio commentators "must not express their own feelings?" That may have been good theory, but it was extremely difficult to practice. Early on, commentators like H. V. Kaltenborn and Cecil Brown got in trouble with their bosses for allowing personal opinion to color their comments.[6]

POWER FOR INDIVIDUAL JOURNALISTS

Gradually personal opinion crept into broadcast news, and eventually it became an asset. In the CBS-TV March 9, 1954, "See It Now" program, Edward R. Murrow attacked the techniques of Senator Joseph McCarthy, illustrating his remarks with selected video clips showing the senator in action—a revealing example of how the mere selection and arrangement of pictures can be as much of an editorial and carry as much opinion, as spoken or written words. As Ben Franklin would have pointed out, McCarthy had no communication expert to do on his behalf what Morrow had done against him, as was amply shown by the amateur production of McCarthy's response on April 6.[7]

Although certain print editors and by-line columnists had huge followings, it was broadcasting, especially television, that transferred mass loyalty from the medium to the individual newsperson or commentator. Unlike the anonymous print reporter, the individual newscaster was heard and seen, which led people to transfer their confidence and trust from the institution to the personality—and eventually enabled the newscaster to get involved in making news as well as reporting it.

Over time, personalities promoted by broadcasters as authorities were accepted as authorities by the public and began to act like authorities. By 1968, no one thought it outrageous or even incongruous that Walter Cronkite would pass judgment on the Vietnam conflict by declaring on the air: "But it is increasingly clear to this reporter that the only rational way out then will be to negotiate, not as victors, but as honorable people who lived up to their pledge to defend democracy and did the best they could."[8]

This brings us to press freedom's final frontier: the news reporter as news maker. Nine years after his public pronouncement on Vietnam, the same Walter Cronkite arranged, during a broadcast interview, the initial meeting of Anwar Sadat and Menachem Begin that opened the way for the peace treaty between Egypt and Israel.[9]

THE FORMIDABLE FOURTH ESTATE

America's freedom of the press has helped the media become a political and cultural force with more muscle than any other group in society. In the 18th Century, British statesman Edmund Burke said the reporters' gallery in the English Parliament was "a Fourth Estate more important by far" than Parliament's other estates: the peers, bishops and commons. In the 20th Century former Texas governor John Connally said that the press "constitutes the fourth member of our institutional giants, which are big government, big business, big labor and big media."[10]

The very freedom of today's press in the face of the information avalanche and the multiplication of media may trigger a movement to curb press freedom. According to a 1994 Freedom House report, the press is completely free in only 68 of the 186 countries surveyed.[11] And many governments, particularly those of third-world countries, feel that the world press (dominated by the American press) is unfair. In fact, the United States and Great Britain withdrew from the United Nations Educational, Scientific and Cultural Organization (UNESCO) because other countries wanted a "new world information order" which affirmed "freedom of the press" but gave UNESCO the right to regulate news organizations. Even Britain, our ally against the resolution, still has its Official Secrets Acts, which makes it a crime to disclose government documents without permission.

There is growing doubt, in the words of *The Economist,* whether "the first amendment has been used to extend free expression beyond the limits tolerated in the most advanced societies."[12] Since 1990, U.S. juries have awarded more than $250 million in libel damages against the media.[13] Many Americans feel the press freedom was a major reason why we "lost" the Vietnam War. There were unaccustomed press restrictions and military censorship during the initial invasion of Grenada and throughout the Persian Gulf War. Meanwhile the courts seem to be leaning more and more in the direction of curtailing press freedom, including a number of decisions jailing reporters for refusing to identify sources. The 1994 Freedom House report rated the U.S. press as less free than that of eight other countries.

I shall try to show in this and later chapters that managing the information torrent requires more freedom, not less—and less government, not more. As we saw in Chapter 3,[14] all communication is manipulative. That is as true of the media as it is of the used-car salesman or your next-door gossip monger. Like all communication, professional communication is subject to the wiles and weaknesses of both speaker and listener, both medium and audience. This is equally true of orators, journalists, broadcasters, movie-makers, book writers, advertisers, publicists and any other communicator, including the person sending messages to a bulletin board on the Internet. In each case, the recipient has as much to do with the final impact of the message as its creator. That is both the glory and frustration of communication.

THE POWER IN COMMUNICATION

There are three important characteristics that every communication has in common: (1) it has a purpose, (2) it fights for attention and (3) it adds to both the quantity and noise level of information in the world. These three elements affect the nature of the communication and its impact whether or not the information is important or true. Since communication always has a purpose (even if only to entertain or call attention to the communicator), it is always an instrument of power, intent on influencing others.

As an instrument of power, communication has always been eyed with fear and jealousy. In 1671, Sir William Berkeley, Virginia's longtime colonial governor, wrote:

But, I thank God, we have not free schools nor printing; and I hope we shall not have these for a hundred years. For learning has brought disobedience and heresy and sects into the world; and printing has divulged them and libels against the government. God keep us from both.[15]

That attitude atrophied as democracy grew. In fact, there is no better argument for the inborn nature of democracy than that all human beings are born with the ability to communicate, with the potential power to influence others. That power increases with knowledge, which is why, I believe, democracy has spread and will continue to spread across the world in the wake of flooding information.

In 1644, John Milton argued in his *Areopagitica* for a free marketplace of ideas, since "Who ever knew Truth put to the worse, in a free and open encounter?"[16] The argument was echoed by Oliver Wendell Holmes, Jr.: "The best test of truth is the power of the thought to get itself accepted in the competition of the market."[17]

That was the theory, but there was a problem. More than a century after Milton and a century before Holmes, Thomas Jefferson spoke of "the artillery of the press" and described his presidency as the subject of an experiment "fairly and fully made, whether freedom of discussion, unaided by power, is not sufficient for the propagation and protection of truth."[18] In the eyes of its critics, the trouble with a free press, with this group of professional communicators, is that it amplifies the power we accept in individuals and too easily becomes a loose cannon rolling uncontrollably around the ship of state. The harshest criticism of the Fourth Estate is that it undermines orderly government.

MEDIA VS. MESSAGE

The media can be a legitimate source of worry because they can have unexpected and unintended impact on the affairs of men. A number of highly respected commentators believe that Richard M. Nixon lost the 1960 election to John F. Kennedy not because of what he said but because of how he looked in the preelection television debates. Much later, after he had become president and been forced to resign, Nixon himself attributed his downfall not to the Watergate hearings as such, but to the fact that the hearings were televised, for, as he said, "the American people don't believe anything until they see it on television."[19]

7. The Media: Formed, Fed and Foiled by Information

In the 1940s, Harold Adam Innis from the University of Chicago and, later, his disciple Herbert Marshall McLuhan from McGill University in Montreal, studied and popularized the idea that media forms had major effects on the process of communication. McLuhan's famous summary of this "discovery" was that "the medium is the message." Although both Innis and McLuhan were so enamored with form that they slighted the importance of content, they did open up a new field of inquiry on how the nature of the media influences the way humans think, act and evolve their cultures.

One does not have to grasp all the subtleties of McLuhan's distinction between linear and circular, cold and hot media to see that print is best for logical communication, radio for rhetorical communication and television for aesthetic communication (as defined in Chapter 3[20]). The aesthetic bias of television explains why its news is so frequently more drama than significance, more about politicians' peccadillos than about their policy proposals. Some two decades ago, NBC News president Reuven Frank dictated that "every news story should, without any sacrifice of probity or responsibility, display the attributes of fiction, or drama."[21]

But form has further uncontrollable effects in that some forms are more available to senders or receivers than others. Radio talk shows offer the airwaves to anyone with a phone and have made President Clinton, according to *Talkers Magazine* editor Michael Harrison, "the most bashed individual in talk-radio history."[22] Technology is opening up mass communication to people and groups with fewer resources (and frequently with less responsibility). A justifiable criticism of CNN, the first "worldwide" television network, is that, because its access to the world has been more technical than editorial, its principal contribution, in the words of Tom Rosenstiel in *The New Republic*, has been "to accelerate the pace with which international events would turn, and to give voice to political leaders who otherwise lacked political standing."[23]

There is little doubt that the very existence of television coverage has increased the frequency of public demonstrations and even riots. Television has not only increased the cost of political campaigns, but it is largely responsible for public passivity with regards to politics. As McLuhan observed over 30 years ago, "As a cool medium TV has, some feel, introduced a kind of rigor mortis into the body politic. It is the extraordinary degree of audience participation in the TV medium that explains its failure to tackle hot issues."[24] On the other hand, as Joshua Meyrowitz observes in *No Sense of Place*,[25] the "ability of electronic media to 'capture' personal attributes," reveals the human side of politicians and other public figures, abetting public disrespect and distracting from the importance of their ideas.

Recent leaps in communication technology have also weakened the control of media by giving more power to the audience. Up to now, as Nicholas Negroponte has pointed out,[26] what was communicated and when it was communicated depended on the medium's convenience. With the new digital communications, e.g., video recorders, and the Internet, what and when will be decided by the convenience of each individual in the audience.

PROFESSIONAL VS. AMATEUR

Some people communicate more effectively than others, and the people who communicate most effectively have the most power. Naturally, those who devote their lives to communicating or make their living by communicating are more likely to be better at it. When they organize into businesses, where practitioners are hired because of their skill in communicating, and technology is purchased and developed for effective communication, these businesses will have more power than the great majority of individual amateur communicators.

In Chapter 5 we saw how the rising flood of information involved the federal government more and more in the concerns of its citizens. Something similar happened in the early history of the media. As the public realized how much more there was to know, people began to depend increasingly on professionals to tell them what was happening. At the same time, professionals were teaching the public how much more there was to know. This natural development fed on itself, making the public increasingly dependent on the media and the media more and more powerful.

Power is a part of life. It can be used for good or evil. It becomes dangerous to society only when it is unlimited and uncontrollable—when, to use Galbraith's term, there is no countervailing power. A curious phenomenon in the history of American media is the frequency with which critics, worried about media power, credit the media with a cohesion and singleness of purpose that seems totally absurd to most media practitioners. It began with a number of books portraying a press enslaved to business: Upton Sinclair's *The Brass Check* (1919), Oswald Garrison Villard's *Some Newspapers and*

7. The Media: Formed, Fed and Foiled by Information   137

Newspaper-Men (1923), George Seldes' *Lords of the Press* (1938) and Harold L. Ickes' *America's House of Lords* (1939).

Today no one is surprised by expressions like media monopoly, press lords, the Eastern establishment, media conspiracy or the New York/Washington communications elite. Nixon, Bush, and Clinton have all joined the parade of presidents going back to Jefferson who saw the press as a united force dedicated to causing them problems. Michael Novak, perhaps the most perceptive and prolific media analyst of our generation, writes about the national media's unified voice or single point of view, which he calls "the national news culture."[27]

SCHIZOPHRENIC HOMOGENEITY

There are five reasons why the media are frequently envisioned as an organized power cabal, a single-minded threat. If we look at all five together, however, we find sufficient countervailing pressures to dissipate worries about uncontrollable media power.

1. The media are a professional group. Like any group of people working in the same business, media people have similar interests and concerns. Above all, they are unanimous in thinking that what they do is very important. This bonding of kindred souls has been tightened by the information deluge. However, the media profession is made up of a multitude of sub-professions. Newspapers are different from magazines. Radio differs from television. The world of business-paper editors and reporters is distinct from that of the producers of consumer magazines. There are a number of lobbying groups representing media in Washington, but no one group represents all media.

2. Media people tend to be more liberal than conservative. Perhaps nothing feeds the media conspiracy theory in America more than warnings about "the Eastern liberal elite." House Speaker Newt Gingrich accused reporters of being disseminators of liberal propaganda and editorial writers of being socialists.[28] Yet there is a good deal of justification for the belief that media people are more likely to be liberal than conservative. People who fear change do so because change threatens their possessions or their power. Those who love change do so either because it gives them hope or because they find it stimulating. Hence the prosperous and established tend to be conservative, while liberalism prospers among the underprivileged, the young and especially those who earn their living by observing rather than preserving (reporters and historians). As Richard Nixon once told a group of *Newsweek* editors, "Historians are liberal—like you." He then added that conservatives "went into business."[29]

3. The media tend to be overly critical of business and government. "Anytime a bunch of executives gets together these days you can be sure somebody will start talking about what's wrong with the news media," said Bethlehem Steel vice chairman Frederick West Jr. in 1977.[30] Business people are still doing it today. Although this complaint flies in the face of those who believe the media are controlled by big business, it is a frequent criticism. The media do emphasize stories about shortcomings in big business and government because readers like such stories. The problems of the powerful have always delighted the powerless, and news accounts that attack the elite have at least the appearance of defending the common people. As Ben H. Bagdikian observed in *The Media Monopoly*, the success of Pulitzer, Hearst and Scripps in the heyday of the daily newspaper was due less to "yellow journalism" than to their defense of labor and the poor against big corporations and the rich.[31]

4. There has been a significant consolidation of media ownership and control. The American media scene is dominated by giants: Time-Warner, the Newhouse empire, Hearst Corp., Gannett, Disney-Capital Cities/ABC, Westinghouse-CBS, General Electric-NBC—all of which own multiple media, including many newspapers, magazines, television and radio stations. Actually this trend is due more to weakness than power. What looks like consolidation is actually the result of fragmentation.

Individual media have lost readers and advertisers. Although audience decline began long before, what has happened in the last dozen years is significant. In 1982 the 24 top newspaper markets in the U.S. had 37 daily papers with a total 15.3 million paying readers. By 1995 the number of papers had dropped to 30 and the paid circulation to 13.2 million.[32] In the same 13 years, America's 20 largest magazines lost 17 percent of their paid circulation, a loss of 20 million paying readers.[33] Something similar was happening in television. In 1981 the three major networks had 15 prime-time programs that were watched in more than one out of five U.S. televison households. In 1995, only two programs, "E.R." and "Seinfeld," attracted the same 20 percent audience share.[34] In fact, from September 1996 to May 1997 the three big networks together attracted only 49 percent of prime-time television viewers, the first time the combined share of ABC, CBS and NBC has fallen below 50 percent.[35] The giant owners of media may be hungry, but they are too frightened to throw their weight around in the political arena.

I am not saying the media have no influence in Washington. Media companies do have lobbies and do contribute to politicians' campaign funds, but almost always for the purpose of influencing legislation that affects profits. Newspapers have won exemptions from child-labor and monopoly laws, have preserved favorable postal rates and have blocked attempts to put taxes on media or tariffs on newsprint. Broadcasters have managed to slow the growth of cable television, to win the deregulation of radio and curb the fairness doctrine for television. Magazines have forced the Postal Service to temper the advance of second-class-rate hikes.

But these victories were all in battles to protect profits. The power of the media in rallying the electorate to support specific policies or politicians has almost reached the vanishing point. Of course, even when newspapers and other media took sides in presidential elections, media might was not very impressive. Franklin Roosevelt defeated Herbert Hoover when nearly 60 percent of the nation's daily newspapers were for Hoover. He did even better with 75 percent of the dailies backing Wendell Wilkie. As Frank Luther Mott wrote in *American Journalism*: "There has never been any considerable correlation, positive or negative, between majorities of papers bearing a given party's label editorially and success at the polls."[36]

5. Power and profit do interfere with media objectivity. Outside of the runaway egos of some journalists, nothing interferes with objectivity in American journalism more than the fact that the media are businesses and have to make money. America's early newspapers were launched to keep printing presses profitable. Pulitzer and Hearst waged campaigns as much to sell papers as to do good. In pursuit of profits, some newspapers rely on wire-service copy rather than original reporting, magazines substitute inexpensive free-lancers for experienced editors, television determines news coverage by camera-crew location rather than significance, and both publishers and broadcasters think twice before offending major advertisers.

On the other hand, the triumph of commercialism in the media is not necessarily a bad thing. Unlike the press under communism or fascism, in fact unlike much of the press in other countries, the U.S. media have great value to democracy precisely because they are published for profit rather than for politics. But the virtue of marrying news media with advertising media goes deeper than that. No one has described it better than Marshall McLuhan in *Understanding Media*:

> The book-oriented man has the illusion that the press would be better without ads and without the pressure from the advertiser. Reader surveys have astonished even publishers with the revelation that the roving eyes of newspaper readers take equal satisfaction in ads and news copy.... The ads are by far the best part of any magazine or newspaper. More pains and thought, more wit and art go into the making of an ad than into any prose feature of press or magazine. Ads are news. What is wrong with them is that they are always good news. In order to balance off the effect and to sell good news, it is necessary to have a lot of bad news. Moreover, the newspaper is a hot medium. It has to have bad news for the sake of intensity and reader participation. Real news is bad news.... Ads, in contrast, have to shrill their happy message loud and clear in order to match the penetrating power of bad news.[37]

LOSS OF POPULAR TRUST

Professional cohesion, liberal leanings, elite baiting, cross ownership and the profit motive have always influenced media. But all of them together have not had an impact equal to the crisis created by the information deluge. One of the seven side-effects of information overdose is distrust. Government, religion and other institutions have lost the widespread respect they used to enjoy before the public knew so much about them. The media are among those institutions as well.

In an *Adweek* survey,[38] only 16 percent of respondents described the media in pursuit of a story as "neutral observers." More than 50 percent called them "vultures circling for the kill," and another 25 percent, "a pack of wild dogs." Some say the media's descent into the abyss of distrust began with the 1959 revelation that TV's "The $64,000 Question" was rigged. But that was only one incident in the public's growing realization that the media was no more worthy of trust than any of the other major institutions in our society.

In the preface to *Ethics and the Press,* the book's editors speculated that journalists may consider many ethical questions unimportant "because they realize that they are a part of an intrinsically unsystematic craft and that the public generally realizes this and tolerates a tremendous amount of error and

7. The Media: Formed, Fed and Foiled by Information 141

sloppiness (technical and ethical) on the part of the press."[39] Journalists may think their craft unsystematic but, if the public was so tolerant in 1975, when that was written (which I doubt), it was due either to a lack of awareness or pure ignorance. Today there is very little tolerance in the public's growing realization of just how sloppy and unethical the media can be.

The incredible information expansion hurt the media in two ways. First, it made the media's job of controlling information quality and content nearly impossible. At the same time, it made the public more conscious of the media's humanness (self-interest) and fallibility (tendency to error). The problem grew as technological advances in printing, typesetting, photography, electronic reproduction and transmission launched an avalanche of new media. Increased competition among information sources meant that the public was seeing many more, and frequently contradictory, points of view.

LOSS OF FINANCIAL SECURITY

The media taught business how to advertise, and as business grew, largely through advertising, it became the principal financial support of the media. By the 1750s, newspapers in the colonies were carrying three to five pages of paid announcements of sales, services, lotteries, entertainment and runaway slaves. In the late 19th Century, Cyrus Curtis' *Ladies' Home Journal,* Samuel Sydney McClure's *McClure's Magazine* and Frank Munsey's *Argosy* proved that selling magazines at low prices, even less than cost, could build huge audiences for which advertisers were willing to pay. Eventually all the major media lived on advertising revenue.

Despite some shameful examples among lesser media, the great majority of publishers and broadcasters did not have to prostitute their media to obtain this support. American media served the needs of business and were supported by business as an honorable home maker helps and is supported by the family breadwinner. Smart publishers and broadcasters learned early that the way to an advertiser's pocketbook is through the loyalty of their audience. Success was achieved by serving readers, listeners and viewers.

Trouble began when the media became less useful to advertisers and business began to withdraw its support. As the lubricant for mass marketing, advertising increased sales, but it also increased the flood of information. In the second half of the 20th Century advertising reached a noise level that undermined its effectiveness. In addition, advertising also fell under the shadow of public distrust. According to a Yankelovich Partners survey,[40] in the early '90s only 5 percent of the public said they trusted advertising. The result was that attention to individual ads was going down, while prices for advertising space and time continued to go up. Desperately trying to find more cost-effective marketing techniques, advertisers redirected more and more of their advertising budgets into promotion, direct mail and other forms of communication outside the major media.

AN INVASION OF ACCOUNTANTS

All this might have been more bearable if financial people had not moved into the business side of media. Here, again, the information deluge brought about major changes in the economy and these changes brought new influences to bear upon media management.

Years ago, when the economy was dominated by manufacturing, money was lent to business for investment in tangible assets, like machinery and buildings, and these became security for the loan. In those days it was very difficult to borrow money to launch or purchase a media property, particularly if it did not own its printing presses or transmission tower. A company without tangible assets was considered a poor risk. Audience and advertiser loyalty, editorial and programming talent were too intangible to serve as security.

But, as the nation moved into an information/service economy, more and more businesses became knowledge-intensive, with ideas as their inventory and their principal assets going down on the elevator every night. Bankers and securities marketers had to either change their attitudes or go out of business. So they changed, and business was increasingly done on the basis of intangible rather than tangible assets.

Suddenly media did not need tangible assets to raise money for expansion or to sell for high prices. In 1985, Ziff Davis sold its consumer publications to CBS for $362.5 million, at that time an incredible sum for 12 special-interest magazines. The 1980s brought financiers into the media business, increasing the pressure on editorial departments to realize that profits must come first.

Ten years later, Bill Ziff, who negotiated the 1985 sale and since built a second successful publishing company, warned fellow publishers about what was happening:

7. The Media: Formed, Fed and Foiled by Information 143

I think there's a growing tendency for all too many companies to be managed not just for short-term financial purposes, but also by accountants at the expense of those who are absorbed by journalism and markets. How could such companies fail to become mediocre over the course of time? Power gradually gets delegated to people who don't know operations, don't know publishing, don't know editing, don't know advertising and generally don't know media. These are people who do budgets. That's a terrible way to manage a company.[41]

This new concern for media as financial investments, coupled with the loss of advertising and rising production costs, forced many publishers and station operators into a steroids approach to management—building an impressive physique at the cost of long-range health. To boost Wall Street's evaluation of the company, money was spent to bloat circulation and ratings, advertising space and time were sold below published rates, and editorial consistency was sacrificed to big-splash features.

Meanwhile, to save money, reporters let on-line services like American Enterprise Institutes' *Presidential Campaign Hotline,* do their research. Print media cut back on page size and paper quality, while demanding more money from readers. The networks reduced the quality of programming, introduced more "magazine" programs and increased the frequency of reruns. Entire blocks of space or time were sold to advertisers for advertorials, infomercials or advertainments.

LOSS OF COMMUNICATION CONTROL

Another development that was part of the increase in information and that weakened the influence of the media was what the Tofflers call "the vast multiplicity of channels through which both information and misinformation may pour."[42] As the monopoly of the monks who transcribed books by hand was broken by printing technology, so today's media monopoly on public dissemination of information has been broken by electronic technology, which is arming an incredible number of communicators with the power to transmit news and ideas all over the world independently of traditional media.

Yet, even more important than the impact of these amateurs, was the multiplication of communications experts outside the media. This first developed in a big way with the rise of advertising agencies. The original advertising agents were free-lance representatives of the media. They persuaded businesses to advertise and the media paid them a commission. The agents soon found that they had more success when they showed the advertisers how to create successful ads, and before long there was a whole new industry of advertising agencies that created ads for business and were paid by the media.

Meanwhile another communications business was growing, and it was much less dependent on the media: publicists and public relations practitioners. Although this new profession worked closely with the media, it did not depend on the media for financial support and it frequently worked at cross purposes. These experts sold their services to individuals and, more frequently, to businesses, for whom they promised to obtain favorable media coverage. So now the communications experts in the media had to worry about whole battalions of media experts trying to subvert their objectivity.

In the 19th Century President Andrew Jackson brought newspaper editors into the White House. In the 20th Century, instead of hiring editors, politicians hire communication experts to influence editors. By 1959, according to journalism analyst Douglas Cater, the 1,200 reporters assigned to Washington had to deal with more than 3,000 federally employed public-information officers.[43] Today the proportion of almost three media-handlers to each reporter still stands.

Paul Weaver, author of *News and the Culture of Lying*, argues that many of the problems in government are caused by politicians trying to satisfy the media's thirst for crises.[44] But the media have always looked for crises. That is their business. What has changed is that media experts have taught the politicans how to "translate themselves and their projects into the language of crisis"[45] to get media attention.

The principal ally of media manipulators is sloth. They bank heavily on providing reporters and producers with information that will make their jobs easier. On occasion they supply the medium with the central idea, background information, artwork, photos and even the interviewees and promotion to make the "story" successful. And, with the current pressures on media editors, a ready-made package with lots of superficial audience appeal can be very hard to resist.

THE FOURTH ESTATE AS VICTIM

In 1995, in a little coffee shop in Stonington, Connecticut, I had breakfast with Osborn Elliott, who, in the 15 years from 1961 to 1976, rose from editor to president of *Newsweek*. As we talked about this book, Oz told me about a speech he had given at the Harvard Club some weeks earlier. He called it, "My Failed Romance With Journalism." I quote a very small part:

> I believe that journalism, in its more cynical mode, is also in part responsible for a default of the national spirit that recently has allowed a meanness to spread throughout the land. What caused journalism to abdicate its responsibility in the Eighties? Exhaustion? After the turmoil of the Sixties, after the strains of Vietnam, after the shock of assassinations, after the tensions of the Cold War and the treacheries of Watergate, who wouldn't be tired? Fear? As readership began to shrink, and audiences splintered, and advertising dollars evanesced, who wouldn't be afraid to challenge Reagan—the most popular President in memory? Distraction? Plenty of that, as well. A kind of Murdoch's law saw bad journalism chasing out the good in the scramble for ratings and readership....
>
> Having pretty much withdrawn from the field of combat in the Eighties, it appears that journalists have returned to the fray in the Nineties—with a vengeance, and with a chip on the shoulder. In this new journalism it seems there is an unkind cut for almost anyone in public office, and little sense that any public policy is much worth pursuing.[46]

In 1994, looking back at the '70s, former Nixon aide John Ehrlichman, wrote:

> When I think back over those ten years it's a shift in power that stands out. We started out the '70s with the power pretty much as it had been—in the presidency and the business community. In the first five years of the decade that power shifted to the media and the noncommercial elements of society.[47]

What Elliott saw as exhaustion and fear and what Ehrlichman saw as a shift of power was actually the collapse of power under the onrush of the information deluge. Nixon tried and failed to control the flow of information, even out of his own office. The Fourth Estate became exhausted, afraid, distracted and too often dependent on belligerence to attract attention.

VICTIMS OF ALL SEVEN SIDE EFFECTS

Having lost public trust, financial security and much of their control of the communications process, the journalistic profession is suffering from all seven side effects of information overdose. (See Chapter 2.)

Modern journalists are paralyzed by *uncertainty*. Today's news pours into their offices with bewildering volume and speed. They have more facts to check and less time to check them. Meanwhile the quality of average news staffs had declined in size and quality due to financial pressures and increased competition for talent.

Editors, reporters, publishers, television and radio writers and producers live in *fear* of advertisers, vigilante groups, their bosses, but most of all the legal department. Today's journalists work under the constant shadow of possible lawsuits. There are exceptional editors who will defy the threat of legal action, but the great majority prefer to quietly kill the story that means trouble, whether from lawyers, advertisers, management or another group of militant citizens.

While journalists have become victims of public *distrust*, they themselves have become more and more cynical, distrustful of everyone. No government official or even religious leader can expect media respect. Although President Franklin Roosevelt spent most of his presidency in a wheelchair, his infirmity was hardly ever mentioned in the press and the wheelchair was judiciously kept out of photographs. Today, not Supreme Court justices, not United States presidents, not even His Holiness the Pope can expect such consideration. As Elliott said about the current attitudes of journalists, "There is an unkind cut for almost anyone in public office, and little sense that any public policy is much worth pursuing."

The information flood promotes *knowledge warp* by forcing journalists into pigeonholes: financial reporters, science reporters, medical reporters, education reporters. Politics are covered by the White House press corps, the Congressional press and occasionally experts on the content of the legislation. The information has become so complex that print loses the meaning of what is happening between specialization and oversimplification, while broadcast loses it between visualization and dramatization.

The saddest side-effect of information overdose is editorial *tuneout*, an abdication of journalistic reponsibility. In 1985, when *Time* was defending it-

7. The Media: Formed, Fed and Foiled by Information   147

self against Israeli general Ariel Sharon's libel suit, the editors issued a press release charging that "the jury completely misread what *Time* said,"[48] as if the audience, rather than the editor, had primary responsibility for the success of communication. More and more of the nation's newspaper and magazine pages, and radio and television hours are being padded with trivia, either pure entertainment, or pseudo-news edited to entertain.

Groupthink has been forced upon the media by the vicious struggle for audience attention. Years ago editors of major newspapers and magazines were very upset when a competitor featured the same story they were headlining. Today, they seem to go out of their way to copy one another. Editors of newspapers throughout the country scan *The New York Times* every morning to learn what they should consider important. If you see an exceptional story on one of ABC's news-magazine shows, it will probably be *Newsweek's* cover story that week. And now local newscasts report network interviews and other features as national news.

When I started researching this chapter, *alienation* was the one serious side-effect that I did not think applied to the media. I was wrong. With all this uncertainty, fear and distrust, media people are becoming more and more paranoid. If media people have a common conviction, it is that they are a misunderstood and persecuted minority, which explains Oz Elliott's observation that they approach their work "with a chip on the shoulder."

TRAFFIC COPS FOR A WORLD OF CULTURAL CONFUSION

The old cliche that the media are a mirror of the civilization in which they operate is a surprisingly meaningful metaphor, nor does it contradict the quote at the head of this chapter. Mirrors do surround and destroy what they reflect. No mirror gives a perfect reflection and every mirror reverses the image. Like mirrors, the media change or evolve culture by enabling society to see itself in action and to react to that sight. As the public reacts, the media reflect it back again and the public reacts to the media's somewhat distorted reflection of the public's reaction.

Just as there are all kinds of mirrors, some better reflectors than others, so there are all kinds of media. Today, however, there are more media sending out more reflections than ever before, continually accelerating the feedback process. This is one reason why today's culture changes so rapidly.

Commentators point out again and again that the confusion in our culture can only be untangled by a return to community. Unfortunately the designs for community advocated by politicians like Newt Gingrich and Bob Dole and authors like Amitai Etzioni and John Nirenberg are too shaped by nostalgia to be practical.

The community of space and time, whether defined by neighborhoods, workplaces, cities, states or nations, has been undermined by modern technology. Although media are used to promote and defend tribal cultures, as Lester Thurow once wrote, "the world is probably past the point of no return when it comes to limiting the importation of the global electronic culture in which everyone lives."[49] At CNN, correspondents are forbidden to use the word "foreign."[50] Rupert Murdoch told a 1994 gathering in Melbourne, Australia, that television was succeeding where the government of India had failed. Community language barriers were finally breached by common use of Hindi, because all the best TV programs were in Hindi.[51]

Our new way of life leaves no time to put down roots. Since the 1970s there have been a large number of new city magazines. Almost all started with articles on local politics and government. But the articles, even some outstanding exposes, did not catch sufficient community interest. Most of these same magazines now rely on service articles, such as where to find the best pizza. Even the family, for centuries considered the basic cell of community life, no longer has the unity, longevity or uniformity it once had. Today's alienation and ethnic "cleansing" are traceable, at least in part, to panic of people desperate to restore community where it has become too splintered to survive.

A NEW FORM OF COMMUNITY

I see a new society based on communities of interests rather than communities of locality. In its essentials the community of interest functions like the community of time and space, except that it no longer is tied to either time or space. Human beings are social by nature, and they will always congregate and interact wherever and whenever they share common interests. But now, due to modern technology, neither time nor space constrains most interests. We have communities of scientists, communities of chess players, communities of Martha Stewart devotees, communities of jet setters, communities of

7. The Media: Formed, Fed and Foiled by Information   149

opera enthusiasts. We also have communities of neo-Nazis, White suprematists, anarchists, vivisectionists and ultra-right militants.

Regardless of its value or virtue, a shared interest defines each of these communities. Though some of their members may congregate in specific places at specific times, none of these communities are defined by space or time. So, in yet another area, the multiplication of information has breached traditional boundaries only to restructure new ones. For each such group, sometimes called a virtual community, is essentially an apparatus for filtering and applying information.

The old societies were constructed like the pyramids. A number of families lived in an area; upon these families was built the neighborhood community. Multiple neighborhoods supported the town community; many towns, the county; several counties, the state; and 50 states, the community we call the United States of America.

The new society is becoming more like a tapestry. Every interest is a thread, and the threads are long or short, thick or thin, strong or weak and run in all directions. The durability of the pyramid resulted from the weight and stability of its parts. The durability of the tapestry comes not from the weight or stability of the threads but from their number and the tightness with which they interweave.

This new society, not yet fully formed, is being created with the help of the media, which have always fostered alliances of minds, and which now make it possible to do so across huge distances and long periods of time. But everything is so new, even the media are not sure of what is happening. As Marvin Kalb put it,

> However one comes down on the emerging issue of "community-connectedness," it's become blindingly clear that journalists have never been so centrally important to the political process, and at the same time never so confused about their role.[52]

In the next chapters we will see how the mechanism for the application and administration of these information-management alliances is already being developed—especially in the business world.

Part Two

The Rise of Partnership Networks

The most thrilling part of researching this book was discovering how many people and institutions were working on solutions to the problem described in Part One. The more desperate the problem, the more human ingenuity and creativity seems to rise to the occasion. The five chapters of Part Two analyze these new solutions and how they work, and explain why they will transform our economy and the way business operates.

8

MANAGING INFORMATION IN THE WORKPLACE

"In the new knowledge environment we have to rethink the very nature of rule, power, and authority. A revolution in the technology of organization—the twilight of hierarchy —is already well under way."
— *Harlan Cleveland, 1985*[1]

New ways to manage information are appearing in the workplace. History shows that communication advances to meet the degree of knowledge workers have and need. Before the Industrial Revolution instruction was the predominant form of work-related communication. Direction dominated work communication when bureaucracy was developed to run factories and other projects requiring organized manpower. Today conference is becoming the dominant way: communication that pools the information-processing abilities of many workers through partnering and networking.

THE ADOLESCENT SOCIETY

All of us want enough knowledge to feel we are in control of matters that are important to us. Either we have that knowledge ourselves, or we depend on others whose knowledge we trust to make decisions for us. Children live a secure childhood so long as they trust the wisdom of their parents. As they grow older and learn that their parents are not all-wise, they move into that terrifying period of insecurity called adolescence, where the trauma lies less in physical change than in the loss of the "parental-wisdom" security blanket.

In a sense, we are living in an era of social adolescence. The flood of information has risen to the point that most people now realize the institutions that have been "parenting" them are not all-wise. We no longer have unquestioning confidence in governments, corporations, religions, or school systems—the social structures that have been making decisions for us. Hence our growing sense of insecurity, the feeling that things are out of control. All the social, political and business organizations developed since the industrial revolution have been designed on the premise that leaders know more than followers, that politicians know more than voters, that bosses know more than workers. And the leaders, politicians and bosses are now having the same problems with followers, voters and workers that parents have with a house full of teenagers.

Nowhere is this more evident than in the workplace, where more and more employees are challenging the wisdom of their employers and more and more bosses are having difficulty trying to manage their "adolescent" employees because they still want to treat them as children. As John Star, formerly an Alcoa division president, described it:

> Since the dawn of time, parents have had an irrepressible instinct to protect their young. It may sound a bit strange, but those of us who are corporate managers often suffer from this same instinct. We carefully insulate our "babies"—the various departments that support any organization—from the harsh realities of the outside world.[2]

INSTRUCTING, DIRECTING, CONFERRING

As individuals develop more knowledge and become more independent in using it, their communication with each other moves more and more from instruction, to direction, to conferring—the three ways people manage information when working together. In **instruction**, one person transmits information to another, knowledge that the first person has and the other person needs. In **direction**, one person orders or prompts the other to do something. In **conference**, two or more people exchange, compare and evaluate information for the purpose of arriving at a mutual judgment.

Note that all three forms of information exchange involve at least a minimum of decision-making. The instructor must decide what instruction is needed and the person receiving the instruction must decide to pay attention and use the information. The director must decide that giving the order or suggestion is required and the directed must make the decision to obey, i.e., follow directions. In conference, all parties have to decide to cooperate and, if the conference succeeds, it will give rise to a new decision. In all three instances the parties involved share the same objective. They want to get the same job done. Instruction conveys the means, direction delivers the motive and conference creates the method—but all three aim at the same target.

As on previous occasions, I ask the reader to accept my precise definitions for purposes of understanding what follows. In ordinary speech the verbs "instruct," "direct" and "confer" can have much broader meanings and sometimes even be used interchangeably.

WHEN THE FAMILY WAS THE WORK UNIT

It is no coincidence that the institutions that have been "parenting" us for the last century grew out of the family. The first bosses were fathers and mothers.

So far as we know, when early human beings lived by hunting and gathering, fathers or some other experienced hunter instructed the boys on how to find and kill game, while the mother or an experienced female taught the girls where to find berries and other wild produce. In either case, when the job required cooperation, the senior gave directions and the juniors obeyed. Later, when mankind moved up to herding and horticulture, a maximum of instruction and a minimum of direction was still required in the workplace. Occasionally, in both eras, conferences did occur to make decisions on the spot, particularly when people of equal expertise worked together.

As society became more complex with people living in towns and villages and work divided according to needs and skills, instruction became more specialized, the importance of direction grew, and there developed more frequent need for conferences. Whether one agrees with social theorist Emile Durkheim that proximity led to more conflict and specialization of work was introduced to reduce competition, or whether one believes that people began to live closer together precisely because they found specialization more efficient, we do know that the more elaborate social structures both required and facilitated sharing information for the purpose of work.

An example of such a structure was the system used to pass craft expertise from one generation to the next, with craftsmen starting as apprentices, learning enough to become journeymen and eventually becoming masters with apprentices working for them. But whether it was a farmhand moving up to farmer, or a squire becoming a knight, or a pupil rising to scholar and then teacher, the basic system of sharing information required for work remained more or less the same: person-to-person communication, with instructing, directing and even conferring almost always conducted one to one.

THE RISE OF BUREAUCRACY

There were exceptions to one-to-one management, particularly when large-scale cooperation was required. A Greek army invented the phalanx, with soldiers moving and fighting in formation. The Roman navy used the trireme with three banks of cooperating oarsmen. These were among the earliest bureaucracies, for they operated by segregating information. The soldier had to be instructed how to hold shield and spear; the oarsman, how to row. But the soldier did not know where the phalanx was going or why, and the oarsman rowed with his back to the prow below deck where he could not even see the enemy. In both operations someone else was in charge of the whole job. Although primitive bureaucracies were used for peaceful purposes such as building the pyramids of Egypt and the Hanging Gardens of Babylon, it was the evolution of military strategy that perfected the bureaucratic system and, as Warren Bennis and others have observed,

> Modern industrial organization has been based roughly on the antiquated system of the military. Relics of the military system of thought can still be found in the clumsy terminology used, such as "line and staff," "standard operating procedure," and "table of organization."[3]

Early bureaucracy was most often used with slaves, who were presumed to be more important for their muscles than for their minds. The beauty of bureaucracy is that it is the perfect system for creating cooperation among workers who lack the information for creative conferring. These early systems set the information-flow pattern for every bureaucracy. They rationed instruction, depended very much on directives and tended to resist conferences.

8. Managing Information in the Workplace

When man's ingenuity learned to harness power and build machines, bureaucracy became the most efficient system for managing factories. The owner or manager of a complex operation, like a ship, mine or factory, knew all he needed to know to do what he wanted to do but, having only two hands, he could not do everything himself. So he used hired hands, workers who, with a minimum of knowledge, could shovel the coal, tend the looms or do whatever else was necessary to run individual parts of a complex operation.

Henry Ford did not have to teach all his employees to design cars or even how to set up an assembly line. All each worker had to learn was his specific job on the line. Information was rationed so that supervisors learned more than line employees. But only the boss had to know it all.

As always, once a system gets started it is subject to constant improvement. Innovators develop better ways of doing things and the information spreads. Henry Ford's assembly line was soon adapted to all kinds of manufacturing. Analysis of the mechanical side of bureaucracy reached its acme with the time and motion studies of Frederick Winslow Taylor, the turn-of-the-century industrial engineer whose time and motion studies earned him the title, Father of Scientific Management.

PHASES IN THE USE OF TECHNOLOGY

In *Technics and Civilization*, Lewis Mumford traces the effects of technology on society through three phases, which overlap and interpenetrate. The eotechnic phase or dawn of machine creation covers the years before 1760. The paleotechnic phase, the Industrial Revolution that consolidated machine use, ran from 1750 to 1850. Mumford published his master work in 1934 and saw his own time as part of what he called the neotechnic phase, in which business was dominated by a scientific approach to manufacture. I think his neotechnic period began to fade into a post-neotechnic phase around 1950 when the electronic phase started to take over and business became dominated by computerization and electronic communication.

Mumford argues that each of his three periods was supported by a principal energy source: renewable firewood, wind and water in eotechnic times; mined coal and oil in the paleotechnic period; and generated electricity in the neotechnic world. I add that the principal energy source for the electronic age is digital circuitry. These four periods were also characterized by different ways of managing the information required to use the technology. There is a significant parallel between the management of people and the management of power.

During the eotechnic age, power (wood, wind and water) was localized and not easily transferable. The transfer of workplace information, too, tended to be local. One-to-one communication usually remained in the family or neighborhood.

In the paleotechnic period, the dominant power sources were coal and oil, which could be transported from where they were mined to where they were stored as fuel to power machinery. Correspondingly, workers were gathered from the countryside and packed into cities to work in the factories. The emphasis with both fuel and people was on bulk consumption for raw power. This was the era of company towns, child labor and sweatshops. The management system was what I call primitive bureaucracy, with instruction minimal, directives dictatorial and conferences almost unknown.

In the neotechnic phase, electricity became the principal source of power, and electricity was clean, more easily controlled than coal or oil and, above all, easily transportable. Instead of clustering around the power plant, manufacturing could be located nearer to raw materials, manpower and markets. This was the period of enlightened bureaucracy. Instruction, though still rationed, was more thorough and considerate. Directives were less demanding, depending on persuasion more often than coercion. Conferences were more frequent as bosses learned the value of at least listening to employees.

As the flood of information rose, bureaucracy adjusted. There were two major management innovations during the period of enlightened bureaucracy. Both involved workplace information. The first introduced scientific methods for motivating personnel. The second tried to graft professionalism onto the bureaucratic structure.

CODDLING THE COGS

If you are dependent on cogs to keep your machine running, sooner or later you become concerned about the material out of which those cogs are made. So, enlightened bureaucracies began to pay more attention to employees and their human needs. Turnover became unbearably expensive in the years before World War One. In one twelve-month period the Ford Motor

8. Managing Information in the Workplace 159

plant in Highland Park, Michigan, had to hire 54,000 workers to maintain a workforce of 13,000.[4]

Although the formation of trade unions forced capitalists to pay attention to what laborers wanted, the labor movement was not a revolt against bureaucracy. The unions demanded that the human machine be oiled more often, but their objective was to improve the comfort of the cogs, not to change the machine. In fact, most labor unions mirrored the bureaucracies with which they battled. Specifications in union contracts sounded as if they had been written by union enemy Frederick Winslow Taylor. The United Steel Workers 1946 contract with U.S. Steel specified that sand shovelers were expected to shovel twelve and a half fifteen-pound shovelfuls per minute.[5] The principal problem for modern labor unions is that they have been traditionally organized to deal with bureaucracy, to balance the power of numbers (the workers) against the power of knowledge (the bosses).

The same problem eventually killed Communism, the most extreme philosophy in defense of the laboring class. Communism was enslaved to and ultimately strangled by bureaucracy. Affinity to bureaucracy is also suffocating American unionism. Since 1945, when close to 36 percent of the U.S. nonagricultural workforce was unionized, union membership has dropped to less than 16 percent, despite major gains in public-sector unions.[6]

While labor was fighting for shorter hours, better pay and more benefits, management consultants were teaching the bosses how humane treatment of employees could improve productivity. "Toward the end of the 1920s and the beginning of the 1930s," writes Guy Benveniste in *The Twenty-First Century Organization*, "we became aware that the well-designed organizational machine was made of people, and that people are not motivated by economic incentives alone."[7]

Social psychologists like Kurt Lewin and Carl Rogers promoted sensitivity training for management.[8] Douglas McGregor's 1960 book, *The Human Side of Enterprise*,[9] preached that business, too long handcuffed by Taylor's Theory X, needed McGregor's Theory Y that workers would be more productive if managers presumed their employees enjoyed being productive and wanted to participate in workplace governance. Peter Drucker prescribed "management by objectives": the boss should explain the immediate objective and allow the employee to make his own decisions on how to achieve it.[10]

After a study of work practices in the Yorkshire coal mines, British researchers proposed "sociotechnical systems" to coordinate technological systems with human systems.[11]

Behind all these improvements was a double trend that would ultimately undermine even the most benevolent bureaucracy. Workers were learning more and more about what they were doing and why they were doing it, and workers were discovering with increasing frequency that they knew as much or more than their bosses.

THE GRAFT THAT WOULDN'T TAKE

Behavioral science did not advance in isolation. All the other sciences were also advancing at an accelerating rate. In Chapter 6 we saw how marketers recruited specialists from academia to better understand and motivate consumers; in Chapter 7, how communication specialists were developed and used outside the media. Similarly, other branches of business began to realize they needed specialists, and specialists meant professionals, people whose working status depended more on what they knew than on what they did. Hiring professionals was business' first major response to the rising information deluge.

It resulted in the first serious crack in the superstructure of benevolent bureaucracy. Professionals were recruited and inserted in the bureaucratic organization, but they never quite fit.

More than 25 years ago, before I became a professional consultant, I had several intensive conferences with a publisher who was launching a business publication on how to manage scientists and other professionals employed by corporations. My friend's marketing instincts were on target, for almost every large corporation was looking for the answer to that question. Yet the magazine failed. I cannot remember whether it was due to a lack of investors or insufficient advertising, but I do remember that I felt then, as I feel now, that my friend's underlying problem, recognized by both investors and advertisers, was that he was promising to answer a question for which there was no answer. There is no way for a bureaucracy to manage professionals.

Bureaucracy works so long as the person at the top commands and controls all the necessary information for the enterprise. The chief executive officer has to make the final decisions and he can do that only so long as he can obtain and apply the necessary information.

The CEO can leave many of the details to employees so long as he receives adequate summaries, but he cannot afford to be completely ignorant of how and why his employees compile those summaries. The problem with hiring a professional was that, unless the CEO was also an expert in the professional's discipline, he could never really understand what the professional was doing.

Even in that exceptional case, bureaucratic management does not work when an employee's value depends more on his or her knowledge than on what he or she does. How, for instance, do you supervise and compensate a chemist working in basic research? Do you pay him for thinking? How do you know he is really thinking? Paying him by the hour makes no sense. Nor can you pay him on piecework.

Some companies solved the problem by engaging specialists only as consultants, letting the scientist decide both working schedules and compensation. Others felt they had to lock in the allegiance of these experts, so they gave them handsome salaries, expensive facilities and huge operating budgets—and then prayed.

Another problem was that specialists could not remain specialists and climb the bureaucratic ladder. In bureaucracies the only way to get ahead is to move into managerial positions, and managing was not why most specialists were hired. To solve this problem, more than three decades ago, General Electric introduced a new advancement track which offered its professional employees "parallel opportunities," newly created nonmanagerial positions with managerial pay. As Drucker observes, in *The New Realities*, the professional specialists have "largely rejected" the solution.[12] Most of them saw through the pretense, for rising through management is the only meaningful opportunity in a bureaucracy.

BUREAUCRATIC SOLUTIONS TO COMPLEXITY

Of course, as bureaucracies became more complex and required more and more information, managers tried to develop techniques to compensate. Some companies set up an office of the president, a sort of team that ran the company. This worked, but only to a point, for sooner or later the bureaucratic system demanded that one individual be responsible for the whole.

The conglomerate was another "solution," a network of separate bureaucracies tied together by top management's supervision of profit and loss statements to protect corporate investment, or by sharing select centralized services like accounting, purchasing, insurance or pension plans.

Still another technique of dealing with the growing complexity in information distribution and administration was to set up special divisions to handle individual aspects of bureaucratic management. Big companies developed administrative divisions for special management concerns such as personnel (human resources), finance, accounting, legal matters and public relations. Each of these departments (and some required hundreds of employees) made no direct contribution to the company's productivity. When not processing administrative paperwork, they served as a special-interest police force (*Gestapo* in the eyes of some employees) to defend the corporation from external threats and internal disorder.

Most of these administrative departments echoed the growth of non-productive government departments described in Chapters 5 and 6. They were caused by the same problem and they had the same kind of effect. Outside the organization they fostered a cloud of non-productive suppliers: lawyers, accounting firms, consultants. Inside the organization they created a wall of intermediaries that distorted communications between line workers and top management. And, most disastrous of all, they made it difficult, sometimes impossible, to promote innovation or change management procedures.

THE PROBLEM IS TOO MANY PEERS

The essential technique for dealing with complexity in bureaucracy is delegation, and the problem in delegation lies in deciding how much autonomy you can afford to give the delegate. If the delegate is just an agent, he is restricted to operating between the information he receives from his boss and the information he gathers for the boss. Once the boss gives him authority to make decisions on the basis of what he knows rather than what the boss knows, he becomes a professional. He has cut the transmission belt that powers the bureaucratic system.

8. Managing Information in the Workplace

What enlightened bosses are beginning to realize is that they themselves are professionals. Their value is more in what they know than in what they do. The principal problem they face today is having too many peers. The information deluge is creating a workforce of professionals, people whose essential value lies in knowledge.

I am aware that there was one type of knowledge worker that existed before the Industrial Revolution and remained necessary to it throughout its history: the craftsman. In the world of machines, as Lewis Mumford pointed out, "the diffusion of handicraft knowledge and skill as a mode of education is necessary, both as a safety device and as a means to further insight, discovery, and invention."[13] But bureaucracy was able to reduce most of these repair or maintenance people to stand-by line workers by limiting their knowledge and responsibility to one kind of machine. There were exceptions, but few of these factory craftsmen became inventors, and most functioned very much as line foremen, with responsibility for machines rather than men.

LOOKING FOR A SOLUTION

The thesis of this book is that the social and personal problems outlined in Chapters 1 and 2 as well as the government, economic and media problems outlined in Chapters 5, 6 and 7 are caused by trying to manage the flood of information with systems that were created to survive in a world with far less information. These systems, including the business bureaucracy just described, are no longer adequate, first because they are all based, more or less, on the presumption that there are individuals who can personally process all the knowledge required for vital decisions, and second because information is too widespread to presume leaders always know more than followers.

Because of the dependence on such obsolete systems, in the previously quoted words of Alvin Toffler, "The quality of our decision-making is deteriorating across the board. Not because the people in charge are stupid. But because they're all running too fast, making too many decisions, too fast, about too many things they know too little about."[14] The solution, then, is to create new systems, new ways of processing information to replace forcing single individuals to deal with more information than they can manage.

I am convinced that the solution lies in pooling people's ability to process information. Such systems are not only possible and practical, but they are already being used, though many of them are still tentative and leave much room for improvement.

As with most of humankind's useful inventions, these systems are being developed first in the business world, the social environment that provides, better than any place else, the motivation, opportunity and freedom to innovate. Versions of these systems have been described in dozens of books and hundreds of lectures under names like *matrix management, skunk works, quality circles, continuous improvement, kaizen, self-directed teams, partnerships, alliances, networks, linkage, autocracy, outsourcing, collaboration, virtual corporations, learning organizations, teamnets, creative compartments, participation, internal markets, intrapreneuring, power mosaic, intelligent organizations, empowerment, entrepreneurial management, post-entrepreneurial management,* and on and on.

Not all these techniques have been widely adopted. When they are, it is because they seem to work better. The one thing all these management systems or variants thereof have in common is that they facilitate the sharing of information. I believe that is the key to solving our problem: enabling a number of individuals to pool their expertise in different but complementary areas of information. The growing popularity of managing by sharing information explains why we are witnessing a major movement in business and society from competition to cooperation, from secrecy to information-sharing.

PARTNERING VS. NETWORKING

To explain what follows I again assign very specific definitions, this time to two words widely used in books on modern management: *partnering* and *networking*. Although other writers use these words in many different ways, sometimes even as synonyms, I will give them distinct meanings to distinguish between two very different types of cooperating alliances for sharing information.

I define *partnering* as an operating alliance wherein participants agree to contribute their individual expertise to a joint application. I define *networking* as an operating alliance for the purpose of exchanging information. The essential difference is that partners pool information to achieve the same objective, while networkers transmit information which the networking parties use separately, each for its own ends. As Michael Schrage insists in *Shared Minds*, there is a tremendous difference in language used for transac-

8. Managing Information in the Workplace 165

tions (what I call networking) and language used for collaboration (what I call partnering), for collaborative language is used "as a medium to create meaning and shared understanding rather than simply to exchange information."[15]

In partnerships, the information exchange is applied by conferring to generate synergism. In networks, the information exchange is either by instruction or by direction. In partnering, participants operate as equals and have the same objective. In networking, participants operate as supplier and supplied (when they instruct) or delegator and agent (when they direct), and each has a distinct objective. Thus, when IBM and Apple Computer set up a joint venture to produce a new form of programming, they are partnering. When IBM signs an agreement with Intel to purchase microprocessors, or arranges to have its PCs sold in Computerland stores, it is networking, as are Intel and Computerland.

The distinction between partnering and networking is based on how information is transmitted and applied. Partners work in tandem. All the parties contribute as well as receive. They pool their information to collaborate in solving a single problem or set of problems. What results is the creation of multiple minds — as in sexual reproduction where the partners mix their genes to produce something no one partner could do alone. Networkers work in sequence. One party gives and the other receives. No new ideas are generated. It is more like cloning than sexual reproduction. To partner you must collaborate. To network it is enough to communicate.

In practice, allies may frequently partner and network at the same time. Thus when my wife visits the butcher they usually network. He instructs her on the price of the meat, and she directs him to wrap it up. On occasion, however, when she needs a special roast for a party, for a brief moment they will partner. She will share her menu plans and what she knows about the tastes of the guests, he will share his knowledge of meat and how it responds to cooking, and out of that conference will come a decision on a cut of meat and how it will be prepared.

Although most partnering relationships last longer than most network connections, their essential difference has nothing to do with longevity—or proximity. Both partnering and networking may be consummated in a single phone call. In fact, advances in electronic communication have breached the barriers of distance and, to a great extent, the barriers of time, in partnering and networking. Successful network alliances frequently involve temporary partnerships. Editors and their printers often pool their respective expertise to come up with a creative solution to layout problems. For many sophisticated marketers selling requires a technical team to partner with the customer's staff before the purchase is completed. Such mixed alliances are increasing daily with the growth of interactive marketing and product customization.

NOT NEW, JUST MORE PREVALENT

Neither partnerships nor networks are new. People have been partnering since Adam and Eve got together in the Garden of Eden, and, unfortunately, Eve got into networking with the Serpent. We are talking about basic forms of human communication, which have been used from the very beginning to get things done for personal and social advantage.

What is new is the realization that the rising flood of knowledge is forcing us to use these two communication techniques differently. We have seen how the growth of knowledge changed the way human beings got things done. Initially they depended predominantly on instruction. When life became more complicated and projects more elaborate, the emphasis shifted to direction, and bureaucracy was designed to organize human beings for maximum power by directives. Today the extent of human knowledge—in both depth and breadth—has risen to a level where conferring must predominate.

KNOWLEDGE VS. INFORMATION

In 1995, Oxford University Press published a study by Ikujiro Nonaka and Hirotaka Takeuchi of Japan's Hitotsubashi University.[16] In *The Knowledge-Creating Company: How Japanese Companies Create the Dynamo of Innovation*, they claim that western companies put a great deal of emphasis on "explicit knowledge" or hard data, numbers and words, while the Japanese are more interested in "tacit knowledge" or the hunches, ideas and skills of their employees. The way to create the "dynamo of innovation," according to the two scholars, is to encourage employees to make their tacit knowledge explicit.

In Chapter 3 of this book, I defined information as "anything a mind has perceived whether from observation or communication," and knowledge as "the mind's translation and retention of information as an idea." I then defined wisdom as "a mind's accumulation of judgments and designs that have been

8. Managing Information in the Workplace 167

tested by practical use." It is important to note that information has no real value until it becomes knowledge, and that, in the workplace, an individual's value is being judged more and more by his or her wisdom.

What the Japanese study describes as the tacit knowledge of their employees, I call the employees' wisdom.

In the new workplace culture, as we shall see, it will become very important to have respect for each other's wisdom—the accumulation of judgments and designs that each of us has tested in practical use. There has been much discussion in recent years about the widening gap between the learned and the ignorant, whether between the literate and the illiterate or between those who know how to use computers and those who do not. That gap has frequently been cited as the primary cause of the widening gap between the rich and the poor.

I believe this relationship is based on a misconception. Not only is there no inherent relationship between wealth and wisdom, but you can have considerable wisdom without literacy or computers. One of the major problems in our world today, exacerbated by the information deluge, is a lack of respect for other people's wisdom.

There are too many Americans working for a minimum wage (or not working at all) because managers ignore the wisdom they may have and value them only by what they can do with a minimum of instruction and a maximum of direction. In fact, a major lacuna in most of the books on how our work world is changing is the total absence of comment on the less-educated worker and how the new systems may apply to the postman and the cleaning lady, the delivery boy and the file clerk, the truck driver and the garbage collector.

I promised myself that I would not preach in this book. But that does not stop me from hoping. One of my strongest hopes is that we will eventually learn to treat all our fellow workers as professionals, appreciating the accumulation of judgments and designs that have been tested in practical use by cleaning ladies, postmen, garbage collectors and all the undervalued entrepreneurs who help to make our lives livable. Significantly, the man who said, "There is nothing that can replace the special intelligence that a worker has about the workplace," was Ronald Contino, former deputy commissioner of the New York City Sanitation Department.[17]

Everybody has some special wisdom, and no one wisdom is superior to another. I agree entirely with Peter Drucker when he writes, "There is no higher or lower knowledge.... The knowledge of the knowledge society, precisely because it is knowledge only when applied in action, derives its rank and standing from the situation."[18]

In the next chapter I describe what I see as the most logical structure for organizing a world where every worker is considered a professional—for letting wisdom reign in the workplace.

9

NETWORKS OF PARTNERSHIPS

> *"All the experiments on enlightened management and humanistic supervision can be seen from this point of view, that in a brotherhood situation of this sort, every person is transformed into a partner rather than into an employee."*
> — Abraham H. Maslow, 1965[1]

To replace bureaucracy we must reconcile independence and cooperation. This can be done only by creating partnerships in which all the workers take risks as equals, pursue a single objective and share adequate knowledge. Some of these partnerships will be teams organized for a one-time objective; others will be firms running continuing projects. The partnerships will have no bosses, only clients. And, through networking, they will be able to handle any size project. Organizing the economy in partnership networks will improve business flexibility, reduce costs, foster motivation, eliminate labor conflicts, shrink overhead, decrease unfair competition and increase investment opportunities.

LOOKING INTO THE FUTURE

Business students at the Massachusetts Institute of Technology spend a lot of time looking for trends in management and projecting them into the future. Recently they designed two scenarios.[2] The first, in the words of MIT professor Thomas Malone, "imagined a world in which there were many, many firms with only one person, and many others with fewer than fifteen people. These firms would come together in temporary combinations for various projects." The second scenario postulated that the world's business would be conducted by immense global conglomerates with operating subsidiaries, strong alliances and cross-ownerships. These huge companies would be "virtual countries," uniting people by economic interests and providing cradle-to-grave care for employees and their families.

I could be wrong, but I cannot see any real possibility in the second scenario, certainly not if America maintains a major role in the business world. As Mike Harris, chief executive of Cable & Wireless Federal Developments, commented, the idea of a world ruled by massive conglomerates "goes against the grain of what's happening today."[3] Major mergers in the news do not gainsay Harris' conclusion. As many commentators have observed, and as we shall discuss in Chapter 12, today's mergers are more often a sign of weakness than of strength.

MIT's first scenario, however, makes a lot more sense. This chapter describes a somewhat similar picture. I, too, see a world of many, many firms, coming together in temporary combinations for various projects. But firms with only one person will be the exception. Most firms will be small groups of people working together as partners. They will be small to facilitate autonomy and independence. They will be partnerships because individuals will manage information by pooling their mental powers to solve specific problems.

TQM WORKED IN JAPAN BUT NOT IN THE U.S.

Marty Edelston, a former client and current friend, is the founder and chief executive of Boardroom Reports, a publishing firm that owes its success to Marty's expertise in direct marketing. In 1992, Marty published *"I" Power: The Secrets of Great Business in Bad Times.*[4] It is a short book, written in cooperation with Marion Buhagiar. Marty told me that he really did not intend to write a book, which is probably why, as you read it, you can feel salesman Marty and writer Marion struggling for control of the book's structure and tone. But the book is invaluable in that it sketches a method for tapping the wisdom of employees. The method is simple to the point of being self-evident. Businesses grow on ideas. Businesses are made up of people. And every person has ideas. Hence the first place to look for ideas is among your employees. Marty insists that, if you seriously look for ideas from your people and show them that you will use their ideas, the employees will respond by volunteering more ideas. When I last spoke with him, his 66 employees were volunteering more than 1,000 ideas each month.

Marty's system does in rudimentary fashion what Peter Senge advocates in much more complex and scientific ways in *The Fifth Discipline: the Art and Practice of the Learning Organization*. Both Edelston and Senge tell us how to encourage employees to cultivate constant improvement by deepening understanding to support better decisions. In fact, Edelston uses *kaizen*, the Japanese word for "continuous improvement" which has come to stand for the system of depending on every worker to look for and contribute ideas to improve performance. The methodology, often called Total Quality Management (TQM), was introduced to the Japanese during the post-war American occupation by W. Edwards Deming and other American business consultants.

I believe the system found fertile ground in Japan because it emphasized group thinking and required close group cooperation. This dovetailed beautifully with workplace attitudes of the Japanese, a people whose culture evolved from a civilization built on rice farming, a form of agriculture that requires community planning, community labor, and total and continuous community cooperation. Shintaro Ishihara, the prominent Japanese politician, saw continuing conflict between the "forest people" of the West and the "rice paddy people" of Asia.[5] This group orientation was reinforced in more recent times by the alienation of Japan Inc. described in Chapter 2.[6]

In the United States, selling TQM proved much more difficult, whether presented as "continuing improvement," "quality circles" or, as Maurice Hardaker and Bryan Ward called it in the *Harvard Business Review*, "process quality management."[7] American employees were too independent to take readily to this type of groupthink, not only because they were educated under the U.S. labor movement's radical dichotomy between labor and management, but also because of what Michael Harrington called this country's "egalitarian ideology and the lack of clearly defined limits to social mobility."[8] Most American workers were inclined to agree with the American employee who said: "TQM is about having us keep our mouths shut."[9]

American companies had been requesting, and rewarding, employee ideas for decades. More than 50 years ago General Motors was receiving some 115,000 employee suggestions a year.[10] But this was not the same as TQM. Not only were the ideas carefully sifted by management, but employees, whose jobs were not as secure as those in Japan, were careful not to make suggestions that might help the company at their expense.

What Edelston did in *"I" Power* was to take the basic idea of continuous improvement and reconcile it with the freedom and independence so precious to typical Americans. He shifts responsibility for *kaizen* from the group to the individual, from the "we" to the "I."

The advantage of "I" power is that, when the boss really listens to employees' ideas about their work, four things happen:

(1) Management attention to everyone's ideas convinces each employee that he or she is important.

(2) Each employee's approach to his or her job becomes active, rather than passive.

(3) Employee morale rises, not only because the importance of the individual increases, but because the system encourages all employees to look ahead rather than back.

(4) Resistance to change is weakened, for employees are looking for change and see themselves as initiators of change.

The shortcoming of "I" power is that emphasis on independent ideas ignores the amplification power of partnering, of producing new ideas by interweaving the wisdom of several people. Lester Thurow points out that American mythology extols only the individual, although "there is nothing antithetical in American history, culture, or traditions to teamwork."[11] Although I agree with Thurow that mythologies are often more important than reality, I believe the information deluge has swept away most of the prejudice against teamwork. It should now be possible to bridge the moat Americans have dug between independence and cooperation.

RECONCILING INDEPENDENCE AND COOPERATION

The solution to the problem of managing today's volume of information lies in creating working organizations that encourage every participant to apply his or her wisdom and partner with the wisdom of others.

How do people develop and apply their wisdom, the judgments and designs that their minds have accumulated and tested by practical use? Judgments, as I said in Chapter 3, form mental relationships between two or more ideas. When we interrelate a number of these judgments we construct a design. When people make judgments and construct designs, they are being creative. They have taken raw information and welded it into something new and usable. Psychologists describe this as the ability to abstract a pattern of relationships from factual contexts. Thus, according to legend, the fall of an apple was the factual context in which Sir Isaac Newton saw the design we now call the laws of gravity.

But making the judgment and forming the design is not enough. I am sure Newton dropped a lot of apples to test his theories, for it is only after they have tested the designs they have created that people have the confidence that comes from knowing that their designs are really useful. We call such people experienced. They have wisdom.

Everyone who has rational ability develops wisdom about the areas in which he or she has experience. Even the mentally retarded can and do develop wisdom regarding the areas of living they are able to master. That wisdom, like the wisdom of every individual, is unique and, therefore, precious not only to the possessor but also to others with whom it can be shared. This is why parents learn constantly from their children, why the senior executive can learn from the junior mail-room clerk, and why many different individuals, with wide differences in both education and experience, can be valuable partners.

NOURISHING WISDOM

The creative processes that lead to wisdom are restricted to no area of activity. The tested design may be a way to carve a statue or write a novel or build a house or cook a dinner, but it can also be a way to handle people or diagnose a disease or raise money or sweep the floor. Wisdom is used to solve problems. Judgments and designs are the mind's answers to questions occasioned by our constant struggle to deal with reality.

The building of wisdom is a continuing thing. People do not come to a project with their store of wisdom forever frozen. Their most valuable contributions will come from the wisdom they develop in working on the project, by the judgments and designs occasioned by the task and integrated with those previously tested. Deming, called these preliminary judgments and designs "theories," insisting that where there is no theory there is no learning.[12]

But, before a theory can lead to wisdom, these new judgments and designs have to be tested. Thus wisdom cannot be developed without taking risks. Some of the risk can be tempered by testing under controlled conditions. The Saturn division of General Motors has a "learning laboratory" so workers can test new ideas before full implementation.[13] But testing is always necessary. We progress only by applying judgments and designs that have never been applied before. If the theory does not work, we discard or reconstruct it. When it works, it is added to our store of wisdom. Hence the only way to encourage wisdom is by allowing every worker to take risks on his or her own terms.

Years ago, John Shuttleworth, publisher of *Mother Earth News*, started a search for editorial talent with this help-wanted ad:

> Name your own salary, pick your own assignments, design your own office, head up your own special projects, travel when and where you choose, and oversee your own research facilities and personnel.[14]

Several of the editors who answered the ad later quit because Shuttleworth was the boss and ultimately did not really let them do their thing. So long as creative people have to answer to a boss, they cannot take risks entirely on their own terms.

NO BOSSES, MANY LEADERS.

Without a boss, who will provide the vision and management direction required to make teamwork effective? Eliminating bosses does not eliminate leadership; it fosters it. When every member of the team has equal authority, leadership naturally gravitates to the partner best fit to show the way, i.e., the teammate with superior wisdom regarding the task at hand.

A father does not have to be master of the house to be a leader in the partnership we call family. In fact, he becomes a more effective father precisely because he willingly follows the leadership of his wife in matters where she is wiser. Both parents will encourage the children to lead in areas where their knowledge is superior.

To develop such leadership in the workplace, it is necessary that the team:

9. Networks of Partnerships

(1) encourages every worker to take risks on his or her own terms.
(2) is held together by a unified purpose.
(3) has mustered sufficient knowledge to get the job done.

1. ENCOURAGE RISK TAKING

If we really want everybody to contribute their wisdom to an enterprise, all participants must be free to take risks on their own terms. In an incredibly prescient essay, published in 1965,[15] Jay W. Forrester proposed "elimination of the superior-subordinate relationship" as a key requirement for a new, more effective form of business organization. Forrester realized that the boss-worker dichotomy had a "stultifying effect" on initiative and innovation, and therefore had to go. The only way to do that is to make everybody the boss.The only workplace situation in which individuals can work together without an employer-employee relationship is a partnership.

For most human beings the risk involved in partnering is much more dreadful than the risk of applying a new idea to inanimate objects. Our ideas are at the core of who we are and it requires great courage to expose them to the judgment of others before we have tested them ourselves. Yet such exposure is of the essence of true partnering. Out of the sharing of preliminary judgments and designs arise new judgments and designs—a complicated validation of the adage: two heads are better than one.

To take the risk of exposing our mental self, of testing our thinking against the thinking of others, we must be equally confident in the value of our thoughts and the value of the other's thinking. In a word, true sharing of thinking processes requires that the sharers are partners, i.e., working as equals in the endeavor. To foster and apply as much wisdom as possible, everyone in our new workplace must be a partner—which is the first requirement of our new basic working unit.

When I say everyone should be a partner, I mean everyone, including secretaries, file clerks and the people who clean the premises. The decision as to whether a worker should be part owner of the work unit depends on whether his or her principal contribution to the project is through partnering or through networking. When cleaning the office is routine and can be done adequately by a cleaning service, networking suffices. If managing the physical premises is a complex task, involving conferences with the people working there, the environmental maintainer should be a partner.

2. FOCUS THE OBJECTIVE

In the last chapter we spoke of partnering as an operating alliance in which the participants agree to contribute their individual expertises to a joint application. The idea is to combine the wisdom of more than one mind, not just randomly, but channeled toward a joint endeavor. What we want to achieve is a very special form of partnership, not the traditional legal partnership where the principal synergism comes from investment, but a partnership in which ownership arises entirely from sharing knowledge and wisdom.

The catalyst that enables minds to interact so that they create new wisdom is unity of purpose. The partnering minds must be working on the same problem. As Michael Schrage says, "Unlike romance, a collaboration is supposed to produce something. Collaboration is a purposive relationship."[16] Hence the second requirement for our basic working unit is that it should have a single objective or purpose.

The single objective is not identical to "shared vision," discussed in Peter Senge's *The Fifth Discipline*,[17] although shared vision can be the objective's rational foundation. Senge writes that shared vision designs and nurtures the governing ideas of the enterprise, including its purpose and core values. The objective or purpose of a partnership is the hard fact that gives it direction and holds it together. The shared vision is the psychological ambience that can facilitate collaboration and make it incredibly exciting.

Since the partnership or team requires a single purpose, its longevity will depend on the duration of the purpose. Teams formed to complete a single project will dissolve when the project concludes. When a partnership is formed to build a bridge, it will have no reason for being once the bridge is built. When a partnership is formed to paint, clean and otherwise maintain the bridge, it will continue to exist so long as there is a bridge to be maintained, or until some other firm takes over the job of maintaining the structure.

Defining singleness of purpose will probably be the biggest stumbling block in forming partnerships for network organization. If the purpose of a partnership goes beyond a core competence and begins to reach out to provide unrelated services because they will produce added revenue, there is a danger that individual partners will start to run distinct departments until the partnership falls apart (if the partners remain equal) or slides into bureaucratic management (if one of the partners is stronger and more successful than the others).

A well-defined purpose directs every effort and all plans toward a single objective. Pursuing multiple goals dissipates attention and generates conflict. Two or more individuals can partner successfully for several distinct projects, but only if they see their relationship as more than one alliance, a separate partnership for each project.

3. ENGAGE ENOUGH MINDS TO DO THE JOB

This business organization may involve only two people, but usually if the objective is in any way complex, more than two partners will be needed to bring together as much relevant wisdom as possible. To be effective the work unit should have sufficient partners to cover all the information areas required, but not so numerous that collaboration will be difficult or that the goal will not justify the payroll.

Thus a partnership brought together to design a house may consist of a partner who is an expert in the mechanics of construction, a partner who is an expert on what interests modern homeowners, and an architectural student with expertise in drawing blueprints and constructing models. These three people can work together as partners, and each will be boss in his field of expertise. Will they own the partnership equally? No, they will negotiate proportional ownership when the partnership is established. It could be a 40-50-10 ratio, depending not only on the nature of the project and each partner's experience but also on many other factors, including reputation, time promised to the project, involvement with the client and, yes, personal need and negotiating ability.

How many partners can a team or firm have? Theoretically there is no limit, but practically, as Mancur Olson observed years ago, partnerships are "generally unsuccessful when the number of partners is very large."[18] There has been much talk recently of how large efficient working groups can be. In 1995,[19] Tom Peters cited a large range of opinion, from 55 monkeys to 600 railroad workers, and decided that "150, give or take, may be the answer," although three years earlier, in *Liberation Management*,[20] he preferred 50 or 60. But he was talking about working communities, not partnering nor true collaboration. No one would dream of a successful partnership as large as Gerard Fairtlough's "creative compartments."[21] Fairtlough's basic size limitation is that all the members know each other personally, which he speculates might work with as many as a thousand people.

Some 40 years ago, Professor A. Paul Hare studied groups of five and 12 boys and found that groups of five were usually more effective for "interaction and consensus."[22] Around the same time, Professor John James studied group performance in a large banking company and found "that committees should be small [average 6.5 members] when you expect action and relatively large [average 14] when you are looking for points of view, reactions, etc."[23]

Since most partnerships are created for action, in practice I believe the effective number will be determined by the project relevance of the varied wisdoms: a small number for partners contributing primary or essential wisdom; a larger number for partners contributing secondary or facilitating wisdom.

In the end, as Olson reasoned, "when the number of partners increases, the incentive for each partner to work for the welfare of the enterprise lessens."[24] My guess is that, when a partnership consists of more than 25 people, its purpose is probably too broad and should be divided into two or more objectives with as many partnerships.

In fact, there will occasionally be partnerships within partnerships. Say the A Team hits a particular problem and wants temporary assistance. It may decide to do some short-term partnering with an outside consultant, the B Team. The A Team would consider this a running expense. The B Team would partner with one or all of the A Team partners, but this temporary partnership would have an objective distinct from the A Team's final goal. The purpose and time frame for the A-B partnership would be set at the beginning and dissolved when attained.

So the third requirement for our basic working unit is that it incorporates enough partners to assure the expertise required to get the job done.

COLLABORATION IN THE HIGHEST SENSE

We can review our three conditions for partnering in the light of Michael Schrage's 13 "ingredients" for successful cooperation, as described in his book *Shared Minds*.[25] Although, as Schrage says, "there is no recipe for a suc-

9. Networks of Partnerships

cessful collaboration any more than there is a recipe for successful friendship," these themes appear again and again in productive collaborations.

Three of the 13 are basic to the structure of the partnerships we are discussing. (I retain his numbering.)

    1. **Competence.** The object is to bring together as much relevant wisdom as possible.

    2. **A shared, understood goal.** Every partnership has to be created for and sustained by a single objective or purpose.

    13. **Collaboration ends.** Schrage agrees with what I said above, "once the purpose is achieved, the need for the collaboration usually evaporates," except that I would change his "usually" to always.

Four of his ingredients describe attitudes that make collaboration (and partnering) possible:

    3. **Mutual respect, tolerance, and trust.** It is impossible to voluntarily agree to partner without respect, tolerance and trust.

    9. **Clear lines of responsibility but no restrictive boundaries.** Since the partners originally came together because of their varied wisdoms, each will be recognized as "boss" or leader in the area of his or her expertise. Since they are partners, each will be free to question, comment on or add to the expert's suggestions.

    10. **Decisions do not have to be made by consensus.** This is an interesting point that deserves more space than Schrage gives it. As he observes, "If collaborators consistently diverge, the collaboration ultimately dissolves." So there is always tacit consensus in so far as all the partners want to get the job done and are willing to defer to the leader or majority when a decision is necessary. On the other hand, there would be no true collaboration if everybody always thought the same way. The spark of creativity requires that the steel of one opinion strikes the flint of another.

    12. **Selective use of outsiders for complementary insights and information.** Partnerships cannot operate meaningfully except in networks, and networks will often occasion momentary partnerships with outsiders that will nourish the core partnership.

The remaining six ingredients pertain to the way collaboration (or partnering) operates:

4. **Creation and manipulation of shared spaces.** Schrage is speaking about "the collaborative tools that people wield to make sure that the whole of the relationship is greater than the sum of the individuals' expertise." True partnering requires mutual communication, whether over coffee table, desk, phone or Internet.

5. **Multiple forms of representation.** "Since collaboration inherently fuses multiple perspectives to address a task, it must use multiple representations to manage those perspectives." Even when partners are in different countries, communication has to be frequent and informal, or it will become mere networking.

6. **Playing with the representations.** Sometimes this is called brainstorming, sometimes "what if?" Often it is unconscious, since partners presume no idea is ready to be tested until it is processed by the other partners' minds.

7. **Continuous but not continual communication.** "Successful collaborators create patterns of communication appropriate to their relationship and their task." The use of words is borrowed from Francis Crick, one of the collaborating biologists who discovered DNA's double helix. It means that continuity of communication does not require constant communications. Hence it is possible for an individual to be a partner in several teams or firms at the same time.

8. **Formal and informal environments.** There will be occasions when the partners appear formally as a team, in sales presentations, for instance. But partnering will always extend to informal contact.

11. **Physical presence is not necessary.** Communication is essential, and today communication can be profuse and instantaneous without physical presence.

SOME PRACTICAL CONSIDERATIONS

What about remuneration? The partners must own the unit to make sure that they have the independence to create. Since they own the unit, each partner will be remunerated according to his or her contribution. In most cases, this will be part of the agreement, approved unanimously, when partners agree to launch the project, and will take the form of agreed-on salaries with proportionate division of profits when the project is finished. This system applies equally to the example of the A-B partnership. Since that short-term consulting partnership would involve a contingent fee, there would even be a division of profits at the end.

Profit distribution only at the end of the partnership keeps purpose on target. Although he was still talking about traditional corporations, in his 1993 review of his original essay,[26] Forrester pointed out the folly in basing rewards on current operations, since "such rewards favor short-term decisions for immediate personal advantage instead of long-term success of the organization." Hence he recommended that "all rewards should be based on final accounting," with "program termination built into the accounting."

In any system there will be people who prefer to operate alone, or individuals who do not need partners to provide a specific service. There is no reason that individual entrepreneurs should not be able to sell their service to others. In practice, a one-person business will operate just like the partnerships, for it will have no employees and will prosper only if clients think it has the singleness of purpose and adequate wisdom for the assignment. Hence networking will include individuals as well as partnerships, although partnerships are likely to become the norm as business operations continue to become more complex and services require more knowledge.

DISTINGUISHING BETWEEN TEAMS AND FIRMS

The objective or purpose of a partnership is always a service paid for by one or more customers. (In today's marketplace customization is fast destroying the distinction between "product" and "service," so I shall speak of service whether I am referring to such things as shining the customer's shoes or providing him with a stick of gum.) There must always be a single purpose, but that single purpose may be for many customers or so unique that only one customer is willing to pay for it. For convenience, I refer to partnerships that do a unique job for a single client as "teams," and partnerships that provide repetitive services for multiple clients as "firms."

In 1989, Elliott Jacques proposed an interesting distinction for management requirements based on decision horizons.[27] He divided work or projects into four domains:

(1) **Direct work:** hands-on work that has a decision horizon of one day to several months,

(2) **Operation:** management which can have a decision horizon of several months to two years,

(3) **General:** unit management that can cover two to ten years,

(4) **Strategic:** corporate planning involving multiple units requiring more than 10 years.

I shall borrow his concept of decision horizons but apply them, not by unit size or complexity, but by the nature of the partnership's purpose or goal. To set up a partnership, the partners must decide, from the beginning, what their partnering is supposed to achieve. But that singleness of purpose can involve vastly different decision horizons.

When the bridge is one of a kind, the bridge-building team will include a completion date in the contract it negotiates. That date sets the decision horizon, influencing everything the partnership decides to do. When the bridge is finished, the team will divide the profit and disband.

A firm that is partnering to do a series of similar bridges and hopes to sell them to many clients will have a very different horizon, and must plan accordingly. Now the goal is no longer set by one client. The partners must decide precisely what they want to achieve as a bridge-building firm. Do they feel comfortable with a five-year goal, or would a 10-year goal be more realistic? Basically the decision horizon will be set by the date they set for closing down the operation and dividing the profits.

It is possible, even likely, that firms will also set time frames for reassessing the decision horizon. After five years of operation, the firm might decide that the planned 10-year horizon is not worth the wait and that the partners will disband at the end of the sixth year; or they might extend the horizon from 10 to 20 years. The essential thing is that singleness of purpose is preserved by dividing profits only after the goal is reached. Meanwhile, of course, all the partners will receive their agreed-upon salaries and may even, by common consent, agree to raise—or cut—their salaries.

CLIENTS ARE NOT BOSSES

If the partnering team works for a client, is it really autonomous, genuinely independent? It is as autonomous and independent as anyone can be in this life. Clients are customers. It is true that the customer is king, but not in the sense that the bureaucratic boss is king. The essential distinction between a boss and a customer is that the boss' power is direct while the customer's is indirect. The customer can prescribe the nature of the product or service he wants and negotiate the price, but he cannot dictate the way the product or service should be created, overrule the decisions of the partners, or confiscate a portion of their profit. To put it simply, customers control the terms of sale; bosses control the terms of work.

WHO WOULD DO THE FINANCING?

When a project needs up-front money, it can either be borrowed at going interest rates or it can be provided by investors in return for a share of the profits. Investors can be silent partners, sharing profits as they do today in limited partnerships. There is no need to incorporate. Future limited partners would have no say in the management of the partnership except for veto power if the partnership wants to change its dissolution date. Unlike primary partnerships, silent partner's shares can be sold, so there will be a limited market in partnership securities.

Banks, of course, will no longer be large multi-purpose institutions. Small, separate partnerships will organize and administer individual functions. Today most banks not only have networks of regional offices but have put separate teams in charge of distinct functions, even locating them at different addresses. There will be partnerships, for instance, that do nothing but lend money, processing borrowers and collecting payments.

Venture capital partnerships will operate very much like mutual funds, which have already proved that a small team can handle billions of dollars for millions of investors. Venture capital firms will network with partnerships needing money, and they will succeed by selecting the right borrowers.

In *Intrapreneuring*, Gifford Pinchot observed:

> Over the last fifty years the venture-capital community has evolved a pattern for controlling investments that meets both their fiduciary responsibility to investors and their entrepreneurs' need for freedom. One of the most important parts of the venture-capital control system is selection of the right entrepreneurs, ones who are capable of self-control.[28]

Even when venture capital is provided along with loans to increase accountability, with default on loan payments entitling the lender to a larger share of ownership, it is part of the original agreement, not an exercise of hierarchy. As Pinchot concludes, "In the Innovation Age, control systems will be based primarily on selecting and empowering the right people to manage resources, not on building elaborate controls to make sure inadequate people do what they are supposed to."[29]

WHAT ABOUT BIG BUSINESSES?

Can teams manufacture thousands of cars like General Motors, sell computers and other products worldwide like IBM, deliver millions of packages like UPS? The evidence suggests it's possible. In fact, the MIT students sketched a plan for manufacturing automobiles with a network of autonomous teams. Japan is already fairly advanced in using manufacturing networks. According to Kuniyasu Sakai, head of several small companies in Osaka,

> industrial companies are not what they appear to be. They do not develop their own product line, nor do they manufacture it. In reality these huge businesses are more like "trading companies." That is, rather than design and manufacture their own goods, they actually co-ordinate a complex design and manufacturing process that involves thousands of small companies.[30]

Major U.S. companies are already using teams to do most of what they are doing, though they are not genuinely autonomous teams—which, in my opinion, is precisely why General Motors, IBM and UPS are riddled with problems, as are so many corporations today.

Consider the kind of project undertaken by a company like American Homes, which builds multiple-housing projects. Suppose a firm decides to compete with American Homes, but with a network of independent units. I will call this imaginary firm Continental Homes.

As a network-initiating team of five partners, Continental Homes' purpose is to build a 1,000-unit retirement complex. The partners buy the designs for the buildings and layout from an architectural team, borrow the money needed from a banking firm, hire one construction partnership to clear the land, another to put in roads and still another to construct the buildings. Each of these teams or firms buys services and supplies from other teams or firms, which in turn network with still others. By the time the 1,000 units are completed and sold, over 100 independent partnerships are involved, some extensively, some tangentially, some for only a single transaction. But in every case the partners on each team or firm had a precise mission, charged a specific amount for their contribution, and used that income to pay their salaries,

9. Networks of Partnerships

to buy products and services from other teams and to provide a profit to be shared proportionately when their partnership dissolved.

Thus in place of the old-fashioned bureaucratic monster held together by regulation and supervision, we have a network of autonomous partnerships held together by networking needs, achieving everything a bureaucratic corporation could achieve but without the extensive, restrictive and unnecessary report and command structure.

Does this spontaneously formed lattice of relationships seem confusing? In *The TeamNet Factor*,[31] Jessica Lipnack and Jeffrey Stamps describe Team-Nets as "lumpy, clustered, and multileveled," and argue that "this cross-level multiple-role feature of networks is one source of its power." Most important, it is a structure simultaneously created by and fostering communication. In a word, it is information managed by purpose—the holy grail this book has been seeking.

PRIMARY ADVANTAGES

What advantages does such a network of partnerships have over the bureaucracies that rule the business world today?

1. There is no conflict between purpose and structure. These partnerships exist only so long as they have purpose. The partners' pay stops and profits are distributed when the job is completed, the goal reached. The more efficient the group is in reaching that goal, the larger everybody's share of the profits.

Today's corporation has enormous problems defining its purpose because, as Professor Mark Warner of James Madison University wrote recently, "there's no congruity among statements at different levels within the organization, since they are formed for individual units and presented independently of the others." He proposes a "nested mission statement" to relate the company's institutional purpose to the more precise objectives of its divisions, departments and individuals.[32]

Mission statements tend to be abstract and, at best, indirectly pertinent to work that has to be done, for in bureaucracy the unifying structure is rigid and more or less permanent, which gives the corporation, its divisions, their departments, and even individual employees a working life distinct from the actual work done.

There is evidence of this in the vernacular use of "job" and "position" as synonyms, even though the first dictionary meaning of "job" is a small piece of work, while "position" refers to one's status. In a bureaucracy one's position is presumed to continue even after the completion of the project or job on which one is working, and frequently people are hired for positions before they or their supervisors know exactly what they will do. The result is a continuous conflict of interest between getting the job done and preserving or improving the position. That conflict radiates through the entire organization, which is why bureaucracies tend to become bloated and stocked with deadwood.

2. Personnel motivation and quality control take care of themselves. One of the biggest problems in business today is the alienation of employees, even sales representatives. I once had a Dodge dealer shrug his shoulders in frustration and tell me that Chrysler was "no longer making cars like they used to." When was the last time you heard an employee use "we" when speaking for his or her company? When something goes wrong in the supermarket, at the bank, or on the train, the clerk, teller or conductor usually responds as if he or she were as mystified or horrified with the situation as the customer.

That has to change in a world of partnerships, because as David Osborne and Ted Gaebler say in *Reinventing Government*, "Teams hold employees to high standards, acting as a more acceptable quality control mechanism than evaluations and orders from the top."[33] Not only is every person on each team involved in setting objectives and negotiating remuneration but peer pressure reinforces desire to get the job done as quickly and efficiently as possible. Partners also realize that their working future depends on the reputations they establish as productive partners.

In bureaucracies quality and effort have to be induced from above either by fear or persuasion. In either case, workers feel that their effort is more for the benefit of the bosses than for themselves. Peer pressure often works against the organization, for peers frequently see themselves as sharing a common lot against the hierarchy.

The principal control mechanism at most modern corporations is financial—setting budgets and reviewing compliance. Chief executives pride themselves on their tight financial controls. Teams will also have tight financial controls, but they will be set by the partners themselves. In a bureaucracy the team can suggest, but not decide. The essential difference is that true autonomy requires the ability to say, "We can't and won't do it at that cost."

3. There is no need to worry about unprofitable divisions, whether to preserve a working unit for the future, to act as a loss leader, to ride out external misfortune or to recover from management mistakes. Since profits will be available only when the partnership ends, there will be no opportunity to sacrifice long-term benefits for short-term gains.

Teams and firms, of course, will fail. Some will not make the profit they planned. Others may even collapse before their project is finished, forcing their client to swallow a loss and network another supplier. But these will be one-time losses, the normal risks of doing business, and will not be embedded into the organization's structure, which too often turns a temporary puddle of red ink into an indefinitely running river.

In recent years there has been much talk about and some experimentation with virtual teams, virtual divisions and even virtual companies. These experiments show that bureaucratic, i.e., structured management, is not necessary for getting things done. Actually, the kind of network I have described can be called a virtual corporation.

4. Management-vs.-labor problems are eliminated. Since everybody is management, the entire concept of labor in both the sociological and Marxian sense disappears. For the same reason there is no need to worry about fringe benefits and the other impediments that bureaucracies have invented to pacify the proletariat.

There will undoubtedly be pensions, but these will be managed by the individual, free from the jeopardy of being managed by a corporation over which the pensioner has no control. They will be something like today's IRAs, individual retirement accounts in which partners deposit part of their salaries and profits to provide for their old age. Insurance, whether health, disability or life, will be available. To compensate for the burden on society caused by individual lack of foresight or responsibility, both deposits into pensions and insurance may even be compulsory. (More about that later.)

5. There is no need for overhead departments. Although teams will network with accounting and employment firms, bookkeeping, personnel and purchasing functions will be integral to the work of each team of partners, thus avoiding the conflicts and confusion common in bureaucracies because people at headquarters seldom understand the precise needs of people on the line.

In *Reinventing Government*, David Osborne and Ted Gaebler make a big point of separating steering from rowing, by which they mean that the government should make policy but outsource administration or services.[34] As anyone who has ever rowed a boat or paddled a canoe knows, it is a lousy metaphor, for the way you row the boat has a lot to do with its steering. One of the principal problems of bureaucracy is that it tries to separate rowing (the workers) from steering (the bosses). It seldom works, because the people at the oars can, and often do, make the steering look ridiculous. Osborne and Gaebler want to free "policy managers to shop around for the most effective and efficient service providers,"[35] but that itself is a "rowing" function. What Paul Cook, the founder and chief executive of Raychem Corporation, said about innovation is equally true about policy: What separates the winners and losers is who masters the drudgery, the real work of propelling the idea to practice.[36]

The virtue of partnering lies precisely in that it tightly integrates steering and rowing. Years ago, Buckminster Fuller railed against the modern practice of training our best minds to be specialists vs. what he called "comprehensivists."[37] Specialists, as I pointed out in Chapter 2, easily slip into knowledge warp. Fuller saw the advantage of intellects that could see the complete picture. One of the advantages of the partnership is that it, in Gifford Pinchot's words, "solves problems holistically."[38] Every partner is forced to learn about and give attention to the multiple aspects of an autonomous enterprise: marketing, sales, purchasing, administration and finances as well as the core business.

6. The business system becomes much more flexible, with more agility to adapt to new challenges. When Capital Cities first took over ABC, it appointed John Sias president of the television network. When I asked him how he found his new job, he grinned and said, "It's as easy as turning around the Queen Mary." The strongest force in bureaucracy is not top management power. It is inertia. The greatest value of a network is its flexibility. Network connections are too tenuous to solidify into inertial structures.

When a large, bureaucratic corporation sees a new business opportunity it must consider a number of factors that have nothing to do with the opportunity itself. Does the new business fit the public image of our company? Will it hurt any of our current businesses? Will the required investment affect the price of our stock or siphon money from other endeavors? If we attempt this new venture and it fails, will it hurt our corporate credibility, depress our stock, make it harder to borrow money, interfere with the marketing of other new products? Since in partnership networks new ventures will affect only the reputation of the partners, all these encumbrances to innovation disappear.

7. Monopoly and oligopoly become almost impossible and unfair competition less likely. Monopoly and oligopoly are abuses that grow out of concentrated power. The courts deprived Ma Bell of her children because they gave her the power to maintain inappropriately high long-distance rates and control equipment sales. It is because countries like Japan have the power to corner a market by selling below cost that we have laws against dumping. It will be extremely difficult for either networks or partnerships to amass that kind of power, since the existence of both depends on temporary contracts between free agents. Not only will unfair competition be less likely but, as partnership networks increase, all competition will decline.

A common error of business commentators is to equate risk with competition. In *Head to Head*, Lester Thurow points out that former Soviet economies will have great difficulty converting to free markets. The reason he gives is that managers in these countries do not understand capitalism; they are used to cooperation, while competition makes them very uncomfortable.[39]

Since competition requires winning and losing, it involves risk. But that is not the kind of risk we are talking about in testing ideas or trying new ventures. In fact, competition is frequently an obstacle to innovation. It was Deming who pointed out that nothing is more destructive to the spontaneity and creativity of a children's costume party than offering a prize for the best costume.[40] When two inventors compete in testing a new idea, they need twice the money that would be necessary if they tested the idea cooperatively. In addition, they increase the risk for the investors by putting the investment in double jeopardy—failure of the idea and failure in competition. Cooperation eliminates the distraction of competition and shares the risk.

8. Partnership networks restore the fluidity of financial markets. In the last three decades the growth and power of pension funds, mutual funds and other institutional investors so warped the financial marketplace that it is no longer primarily devoted to serving individuals, whether as a source of entrepreneurial capital or as a market for personal investment. If the trend continues, institutional investors will soon control half of the country's publicly traded common stock. Pension funds also hold more than 40 percent of the mid-term and long-term debt of major corporations.[41]

Like the giant handicapped by his size, institutional investors find they have lost the maneuverability needed to best serve the pensioners and mutual-fund holders who employ them. Nor has the situation helped large-company employees and corporate managers victimized by corporate takeovers. As Peter Drucker observes, "Without the concentration of voting power in a few pension funds and the funds' willingness to endorse hostile takeovers, most of the raiders' attacks would never have been launched."[42]

In a world of partnerships, funds would invest their money in hundreds or thousands of small endeavors. This would give them the advantages of a genuinely diverse portfolio. Rather than wagering large chunks of money on companies whose management might change tomorrow, they would be investing in selected individuals and specific projects. Finally, they would have the opportunity to advise and guide the partnership in whom they invest. And with so many partners unencumbered with corporate caution, there will probably be more places to invest.

What Rochester University professor of finance Clifford Smith says of initial public offerings will be even more true of partnership financing. It will make us all richer by allowing "the economy to tap into entrepreneurial zeal," which is "a big part of what makes the whole capital market process possible."[43]

THE BIG PROBLEM

What I have just described is not meant to be science fiction. I believe we are headed for a world where business—and all the other institutions in our society—will take the form of networks of partnerships. The question, of course, is: Can this really happen? And if so, how?

9. Networks of Partnerships

I believe it can. There are good reasons to believe it is already happening. The purpose of the next two chapters is to deduce the changes we can expect from what is going on today. No one can predict how quickly society will be transformed into networks of partnerships. But if we realized that it can be done, and how advisable it is, it will undeniably happen more quickly than if we do not.

10

ORGANIC NETWORKS: COMPLEX ADAPTIVE SYSTEMS

"There are few workers in the United States today who cannot do their jobs better than their bosses. This implies that supervision is a decreasingly appropriate function of management."

— *Russell L. Ackoff, 1993*[1]

Other writers have proposed solutions less radical than partnership networks, usually in order to retain the corporate structure while overcoming bureaucracy's most bothersome problems. The best of such solutions is the concept of "internal markets." But there is an essential contradiction in trying to eliminate bureaucratic disfunctions while preserving corporate functions. It is impossible to change attitudes, for hierarchy requires competition. Nor is a corporate shell necessary for structure and direction, since both are attained by the synchronization of purpose, payment and knowledge required for networking. The essential difference between partnership networks and bureaucracy lies in managing information organically rather than mechanically.

LET'S BE PRACTICAL

How practical is the scenario presented in the last chapter? Has anyone tried to apply it? If so, did it work? Are there other scenarios that might work just as well—and, even more important, are there scenarios that could be introduced within the structure of current corporations without drastic surgery?

10. Organic Networks: Complex Adaptive Systems

As I shall show in Chapter 11, partnership networks are very practical and have worked. In this chapter I want to answer the second question. Are there other scenarios that might work just as well? There certainly have been many proposals. Very few suggest an entirely new system. Most presume that large corporations will continue to dominate the business world, and design their solutions to fit within the corporate structure. This is not surprising, since most of the solutions are proposed by consultants who sell their advice to major coporations.

Though many of these proposals curb the problems of bureaucracy, I do not believe any of them provide a permanent solution. The purpose of this chapter is to show that there is an internal contradiction in trying to resolve the problems of bureaucracy while preserving corporate power. The reluctance of top executives—and most business consultants—to accept this fact explains why it will take considerable time before partnership networks dominate the business world even though they have been tried, been proven to work and are a growing business phenomenon.

INTERNAL MARKETS

The proposal that comes closest to resolving the problems of bureaucracy within the corporate structure is described in *Internal Markets,* a compilation of essays published in 1993. The book explains how a company can be operated so that each division or team is given the autonomy to act as an independent business serving markets within the company (and occasionally outside as well). The various essays provide a number of examples of applying this innovation in major companies and explain how it overcomes many of the problems of bureaucracy. In their chapter, "Corporate Integrity and Internal Market Economies," Julio R. Bartol and Ali Geranmayeh give a succinct definition of the concept:

> The internal market approach brings the principles of the free-market system inside what is traditionally thought of as a single indivisible firm. In an internal market system, every organizational unit is a business in its own right, having its own customers, suppliers, competitors, and responsibility for the profitability of its operations. Success or failure of the unit will depend on how well it serves its customers' needs.[2]

Note that everything in this definition applies to the partnership network—with one exception. The partnership network is not "inside what is traditionally thought of as a single indivisible firm." And that, in my opinion, is the critical flaw in the proposal. The trouble with internal markets is that the markets *are* internal. Theirs is an incestuous relationship, for the internal customer and the internal supplier have the same corporate parent.

THE FUNCTION OF CORPORATE MANAGEMENT

Advocates of the internal markets idea, in the words of their prophet, Jay W. Forrester, want to "combine the stability and strength of the large, diversified business organization with the challenge and opportunity that the small company offers to its founder-managers."[3] Thus, in the introduction to *Internal Markets*, we are told that:

> Rather than managing operations through the chain of command, corporate executives design and regulate the infrastructure of their "organizational economy" just as federal governments manage national economies: establishing common systems for accounting, communications, financial incentives, education, governing policies, and the like.[4]

My first reaction on reading this was that any system is in major trouble if it models itself on the way federal governments regulate national economies. As was spelled out in Chapter 6, government's inability to regulate national economies is one of the major problems caused by the information deluge. But my objection to the internal-markets theory is more fundamental.

As we have seen, the spread of information forced primitive bureaucracy to become benevolent and, over the years, persuaded managers to be increasingly considerate of the needs, independence and wisdom of their employees. This has resulted in a gradual shift of targets in bureaucratic direction. When Taylor's theories ruled, the goal was to direct each physical movement of the employee. Under McGregor's Theory Y[5] (and Drucker's "management by objectives"), direction was shifted from the worker's movements to the worker as an individual, giving him some freedom in how he did the job. With internal markets, the hierarchy is still giving direction, but this time it has shifted from the individual to the group, which is free to decide how it will do the job as a group. A precursor to *Internal Markets* was called *Theory Z*, published by William Ouchi in 1981.

In a partnership network, the group that conceives and plans the project (the initiating partnership) exercises control over the project externally by net-

10. Organic Networks: Complex Adaptive Systems

working with groups willing to assume responsibility for parts of the project. In a corporation, the chief executive exercises control over the project internally by ordering (or persuading) groups to assume responsibility for parts of the project. What is the difference? Whether it exercises it or not, a corporation has the power to force a group to do something it is unwilling to do,[6] whereas a partnership network does not have that power.

Advocates of internal markets propose several devices to control or moderate top management's power to force or override. One is that corporate management can forbid a unit from selling its service to an external customer, but must remunerate the unit for any loss. Another prescribes that corporate management make general rules of things the units cannot do, just as the government makes laws banning certain types of economic activity.

In their version of internal markets (*The End of Bureaucracy and The Rise of the Intelligent Organization*), Gifford and Elizabeth Pinchot speak of

> the right of intrapreneurial individuals and teams, without leaving their employment in the larger organization, to leave their jobs working for the bureaucratic chain of command and instead create an intraprise of their own, which then pays their salaries.[7]

The authors immediately add that these "intrapreneurs" must give reasonable notice and complete their commitments to their old jobs and must not violate the laws and policies of the organization.

To facilitate this ruling from above while granting freedom below, proponents of internal markets seem to favor Jay W. Forrester's suggestion that every company should adopt a "constitution," analogous to the U.S. Constitution.[8] Since nothing is said about procedures for amending corporate constitutions or a judicial system to interpret them, we can only imagine the complications involved in enforcing these limitations on hierarchical authority.

But my principal objection to retaining any form of hierarchy is its effect on the attitudes of corporate managers and workers, and how that destroys worker autonomy.

STRUCTURE SUPPORTS ATTITUDE

A common blunder in addressing management difficulties is to apply normative solutions to structural problems. If we can change the attitude of both boss and employee everything will work fine. Tell the manager that he is still the boss and still has his power, but that he should apply it sweetly, exhort rather than order, call his employees "associates" and listen to what they have to say. Tell the workers their pay depends on the company and their loyalty is expected, but they are part of a family and should enjoy working in this one big happy home. This could possibly work, if all managers were saints and geniuses, and all employees were selfless and idiots.

There are cultural conditions under which bureaucracy functions more smoothly because people live in a highly homogeneous society accustomed to close relationships and shared responsibility. According to some scholars, that explains why Max Weber thought so highly of bureaucracy. In the Prussia of Weber's day, each business or government organization employed only a few hundred people, all from the same small community, and all bound together by strong family and religious ties.[9]

An even better example is Japan, where industrialization succeeded by imbedding bureaucracy in a culture of collective responsibility and communal interdependence. Read William Ouchi's 1981 treatise, *Theory Z, How American Business Can Meet the Japanese Challenge*, or Imai Masaaki's 1986 book, *Kaizen, The Key to Japan's Competitive Success*.

But Weber's Prussia is long gone and Japan's insular cultural homogeneity is fast fading. Hence *Internal Markets* prescribes that, in the internal-markets company...

> the role of executives is to create a superstructural framework of performance controls, incentives, and communications, and then to provide encouragement, support, and other forms of leadership to assist the internal market in allocating resources spontaneously instead of by administrative fiat.[10]

But, in the real world, employees quickly recognize the incongruity of acting spontaneously under a superstructural framework of performance controls. To quote the book again, "providing a sharp, sound focus on controlling the performance of operating units while minimizing intrusions on their autonomy poses a difficult challenge."[11] It sure does.

10. Organic Networks: Complex Adaptive Systems

This is probably why Professor Ouchi comes to the conclusion that "a concentrated form of ownership or control may be a necessary condition" for the development of the kind of corporate culture he recommends.[12] A single leader with the right attitude and the charisma to inspire his workers can sustain a remarkable coherent spirit, because, as Ouchi points out:

> When the firm is effectively controlled by its founder, that person need not justify decisions to anyone. If some of the critical long-run decisions are subtle, then the owner may base decisions on "intuition" or an inherent but inexpressible sense of the long-run.

But Ouchi immediately adds:

> If, on the other hand, the firm is owned by a large number of shareholders, each of whom owns stock in many firms, then quite a different situation occurs. In such a case, none of the owners of the firm is close enough to it to have a sensitive awareness of the intricacies of the business. Lacking intimacy, the owners fail to appreciate subtlety and thus have no basis for trusting the judgment of their professional managers. The managers, knowing that their job security and future advancement will be based on the outcomes of decisions with clear-cut, short-term outcomes, shy away from tenuous, long-term decisions.[13]

Most business reformers agree that bureaucracies suffer from bad attitude, certainly among workers and even among managers. Their first suggestion, in many cases, is to propose psychological devices that improve attitude. What they overlook is that in management, as in most of life, attitudes are less successful in ameliorating structures than structures are in fostering attitudes. Many of the psychological suggestions make sense and should be adopted. But the ultimate problem lies in the structure of the bureaucratic organization which engenders bad attitude. Most of today's workers know enough about their capabilities and their work to want to get out into the sunlight of self-determination and away from the shadow of that superstructural framework of performance controls.

An extreme example of the normative approach is found in *Framebreak: The Radical Redesign of American Business*, a brief but interesting book by Ian I. Mitroff, Richard O. Mason and Christine M. Pearson. The authors recommend what I consider the ultimate ambition of bureaucratic insolence: let the corporation direct not only the employees' bodies but also their souls. The authors want to apply what psychologists are learning about group therapy to large organizations. Their cure for the problems of modern corporations is to introduce six "new key functions": issues management, crisis management, total quality management, environmentalism, globalism and ethics. They would do this through a "total systems approach" of audits and structures under "the four dimensions of a new organizational structure," namely (1) knowledge and learning, (2) recovery and development, (3) world service and spirituality and (4) world-class operations.

Since companies are expected to establish a center for each of these four dimensions with someone in charge, one has to smile when the authors write that "the intent is not to add another bureaucratic mechanism, to exercise dictatorial control over every business function or unit of an organization, or to collect paralyzing mountains of data."[14] Every road to bureaucratic hell is paved with such good intentions.

There is a strong temptation to amend bureaucracy by finding individual cures for its most evident failings, to suggest ways to alleviate the pressure of the yoke of hierarchy. Even the proponents of internal markets fall into this trap, for they argue that a major benefit in their system is that it fosters internal competition. The "autonomous" work units will compete with each other improving motivation and enforcing quality control.

COMPETITION IS AN INEFFECTIVE MOTIVATOR

In discussing the attempt to introduce internal markets at Control Data Corporation, David M. Noer, former president of Control Data Business Advisors, speaks of "the difficulty of changing a collaborative culture into a competitive one."[15] The extent to which bureaucracy demands competition can be seen in a 1989 *Harvard Business Review* article written by Yves Doz, Gary Hamel and C. K. Prahalad. It was titled "Collaborate With Your Competitors and Win." The authors seemed totally oblivious that in collaboration both paricipants should win. They speak of "competitive collaboration" and conclude that "the point is for a company to emerge from an alliance more competitive than when it entered it." They even recommend such partnerships as "a way of getting close enough to rivals to predict how they will behave when the alliance unravels or runs its course."[16]

For years, I have been telling executives that competition is a self-defeating device for improving performance. Although competitive motives can bring out the best in people, they can also bring out the worst, particularly

10. Organic Networks: Complex Adaptive Systems

where cooperation is required to attain management goals. Who has not heard of the destructive, demoralizing effect of office politics—a direct consequence of internal competition? Competition is divisive. For every winner in employee competition, the company creates at least one, usually more, losers. Some will leave. Others will accept a consolation prize or reconcile themselves to being considered second-rate. In either case, the organization has lost or discouraged valuable talent.

Its built-in need for competition is one of the major weaknesses of bureaucracy. Bureaucratic structures are always pyramids. The higher the job, the fewer the openings. Yet success in bureaucracies is synonymous with promotion, even though promotion depends as much on the number of openings as on the performance of the candidates. The result is corrosive competition for all and guaranteed frustration for most.

COOPERATION FREES THE MARKET

Competition between units in the same company or even between different firms in the same industry frequently backfires.

Years ago, when I was editor of a newsletter for magazine publishers, I waged a lengthy and largely futile campaign to discourage competitive backbiting in selling advertising space in business publications. Instead of promoting the value of the publication they represented, most of the sales people would devote a large part of their presentations to belittling their competitors. I knew, from conversations with advertisers, that the practice was hurting the entire industry. Advertisers were coming away from these sales calls with enough misgivings about the business press to shift their advertising dollars into other media. Smart retailers concentrate on satisfying the customer, not on winning her away from some other firm. I have known shopkeepers who gladly sent customers to competitors when they felt the customer would do better.

The effect of competition on one's business should be treated as an externality, an outside condition like the weather or the state of the economy—something you cannot control though its impact should be considered in planning. A genuinely free market is one in which people are free to cooperate. Businesses succeed by cooperation much more than by competition. Working with others, for mutual benefit, is essential to every successful venture, whether the others happen to be suppliers, customers or government officials. The merchant who offers me the best deal is cooperating with me. The merchant who is trying to keep me from buying from someone else is working to restrict not only the other merchant's business but my right to get the best deal. There is only one form of competition that contributes to success: competition with oneself, the desire to outdo one's own previous performance.

THE POWER OF PARTNERING

In a partnership-network economy there will be competition in so far as more than one partnership may pursue the same assignment. But because of the service element in both networking and partnering, most choices of suppliers or agents will be based more on continuing congeniality and confidence than on point-of-sale persuasion and price.

Because of the expanding influence of technology almost all network connections will prompt some partnering. The need to pool knowledge will become greater not only in networking with agents but also in networking with suppliers. The more partnering becomes an auxiliary in networking, the more congeniality will become a key factor and the more stable and less competitive networks will become.

In his 1965 essay, Forrester said that "moving away from authoritarian control in an organization can greatly increase motivation, innovation, and individual human growth and satisfaction."[17] I add that we have now reached a state in civilization that administration, or the power to get things done, not only does not need authoritarian control but that the concept of control must be replaced by cooperation, by equals willingly working together.

Administration will eventually shed all the accoutrements of bureaucracy and be reduced to its two essential elements: planning and persuading:

• To do anything that requires the cooperation of others one must plan how the necessary work (and consequent responsibility) will be allocated, whether the project requires one working unit or hundreds of working units.

• Then one must convince those units, directly or indirectly, to do the work (i.e., take responsibility for completing their part of the project).

Can administration be effected that way in an internal-markets organization? Probably, but there will always be a danger that the shadow of the control framework will contaminate top management's persuading or inhibit the working unit's response.

It is impossible to predict the future with any accuracy, but my guess is that much of the business turmoil in the next few decades will be caused by large companies experimenting with forms of internal markets until the corporate shell atrophies and the work is turned over to more efficient partnership networks.

A NEW WAY OF OPERATING

In a 1992 article in *Fortune,* Thomas A. Stewart wrote that a new "post-hierarchical organization" was arising at the confluence of three streams:

1. The "high-involvement work place," meaning operations with self-managing teams and other devices for empowering employees.

2. A new emphasis on managing business processes rather than functional departments like purchasing and manufacturing.

3. The evolution of information technology to the point where knowledge, accountability, and results can be distributed rapidly anywhere in the organization.

"The trick," the article continues, "is to put them together into a coherent, practical design." Once more we find an author and his sources trying to jam an anti-bureaucratic system into the corporate structure. McKinsey & Company developed a ten-point plan for installing such a system inside corporations. The article describes several successful small-scale applications of "high-involvement" management but adds that the concept has not really spread. To explain the difficulty Stewart quotes McKinsey management consultant Frank Ostroff's wry observation: "Senior managers need to be able to say 'empowerment' and 'accountability' in the same sentence."

Eliminating the problems of bureaucracy requires eliminating functional and hierarchical walls. But, as the article points out, one trouble with breaking down walls is that "in most companies functional and hierarchical walls are load bearing. Remove them and the roof caves in."[18] To take down the walls you must first remove the roof.

PURPOSE IS THE ULTIMATE POWER

Because they assume the corporation is the source of all power, most advocates of networking make the process more complicated than it is. Some consultants speak about a flat vs. vertical organization; others make the network three dimensional. The power in any network is its objective or purpose. Hence all networks begin at a single point, where the purpose is initiated, and spread from that point in as many directions as required to fulfill the purpose.

If my wife and I decide to throw a party, we start with a little planning. We will need guests, a time, a place, food and music. Once the plan is clear and the date set, we begin networking. My wife engages a caterer and tells the housekeeper when she will be needed. I tell my secretary to send out the invitations and ask a friend to play the piano and bring audio tapes.

The original purpose has now been divided into four subsidiary purposes, which have been networked to our caterer, housekeeper, secretary and musician friend. Each of these in turn will plan to effect their new responsibility. The caterer will network with food suppliers, liquor shops, and personnel agencies. The housekeeper may buy cleaning materials and hire someone to sit with her little boy. The secretary will deal with the printer and buy stamps. My pianist friend might buy sheet music or borrow a tape or two. In each case a subordinate purpose has been passed on from the larger purpose, and in each case the subordinate purpose has created its own subordinate purposes for further networking.

Networks are always genealogies of purposes, with an ancestral purpose from which all the other purposes descend, as partnerships give birth to new but related purposes. In life, of course, caterers will supply food for many parties, our cleaning lady buys from many stores and uses several baby sitters. But those relationships have to do with other projects and, therefore, other networks. Each network is defined by its purpose.

Can things go wrong in networks? Of course, but it will always be because the purpose was lost somewhere, and it will always be clear that correction must be made by restoring purpose on the level it went astray either by the unit responsible or by calling in another unit. If the housekeeper cannot keep her promise because her baby sitter got sick, either she gets another baby sitter or I get someone to take her place. If the caterer puts more liquor on my account than I need for the party, she can make a correction or I can fire her. If my secretary forgets to buy stamps, he can make another trip to the post office or I can send someone else. Of course, the mistake might also be in the original planning. My wife and I could select a date on which few of the guests would be free, or forget to call the caterer. But always the purpose will define what are mistakes, where they are made, and how they can be corrected.

Finally, payment should pursue purpose. At each step in the network, the partnership that sets the purpose offers pay to match the purpose, and the partnership that accepts the purpose does so with the understanding that the pay covers expenses, salaries, profit and the money needed to network others. I make this point in detail, because one of the major advantages networks have over bureaucracies is that bureaucracies create nooks and crannies for hiding costs or making them seem unrelated to benefits, while networks relate costs and benefits much more directly.

This is an important consideration in every management situation, but it will become colossally significant when we consider, in Chapter 13, what is wrong in government.

THE ARGUMENTS FOR CORPORATE STRUCTURE

Does top management retain any necessary function once we take away its power to supervise and control? Since E. F. Schumacher wrote in 1973 that "as soon as great size has been created there is often a strenuous attempt to attain smallness within bigness,"[19] more and more business analysts have decided, with William Bergquist, that there is new emphasis "on the value of being small—or at least flexible in one's attitude about appropriate size."[20] However there are still four reasons beyond size that are most frequently given for keeping the corporate shell:

1. The corporation can supply capital, the money to seed new ventures and keep small enterprises growing.

2. A large company can realize economies of scale, especially in manufacturing.

3. The company has resources—personnel, machines, departments—that the entrepreneurial team can use.

4. The corporation can share some of the risk.

None of these reasons is supported by experience, especially today. An independent business, no matter how small, can raise all the money it needs without being part of a larger company. In fact, it is frequently easier to convince independent investors or venture capitalists to supply required capital than it is to persuade corporate managers, who must answer to other divisions in the company as well as to board members and stockholders. Once the members of a company group are turned down by the chief executive, where can they go?

Similarly, resources, including manufacturing facilities, are always available to those willing to pay for them. Anyone who relies on other departments in a company to provide free help for someone else's project is living in a dream world. As Peter Senge points out, when several divisions share a free facility, such as a research team, sales force or secretarial pool, each division tries to get as much free help as possible until the common resource rebels or becomes inefficient.[21]

As to risk-sharing, operating in a large company does not share risk, it increases it. Every magazine founder I have queried, including Bob Anderson of *Runner's World*, Bernie Goldhirsh of *Inc.*, Jim Crockett of *Guitar Player* and Norman Glenn of *Media & Marketing Decisions*, has insisted that starting a new magazine as part of a major publishing company is more risky than doing it independently.

Corporate size magnifies fear of failure as well as the cost of personnel, overhead and management systems. Besides, as each of these entrepreneurs added, it is impossible to share risk without sharing control.

In *Intrapreneuring*,[22] Gifford Pinchot admits that the advantages companies provide for their intrapreneurs change. Financial clout and the size needed to manufacture cost-effectively have become less important. But he insists that marketing clout and access to proprietary information are as important as ever.

By marketing clout Pinchot means access to the company's distribution channels, and especially use of the company name. There is no doubt that these are advantages, but they are advantages that many independent companies have enjoyed through alliances, franchises and other cooperative arrangements.

10. Organic Networks: Complex Adaptive Systems

Nor does type of ownership affect the way consumers or distribution channels value a reputation. The impact of the Coca-Cola and McDonald's names are not diluted by the fact that most of Coca-Cola's bottlers and McDonald's restaurants are independently owned. There is no reason why our imaginary Continental Homes could not develop a marketworthy name for its housing developments even though it operates through a network of partnerships rather than a traditional corporation.

By proprietary information Pinchot means the large firm's technology base. He does not argue, as John Kenneth Galbraith once did (see Chapter 4),[23] that research and development requires large corporations with extensive capital resources. His argument is that "large companies can expect a greater return on fundamental research than small ones because one never knows for sure in which business area the results of research will lead."

Yet even Pinchot admits that most large firms "rarely implement more than a tiny fraction of the good opportunities created by new internally developed technology," and that employees responsible for such innovations frequently "leave, taking the new technologies with them."[24]

As we shall see later, corporate secrets, from patents to customer lists, are becoming harder and harder to protect at the same time that the accelerating pace of change makes it less and less important to protect them. But, even if the technology base remained as important as it has ever been, many corporations have found hogging technological innovations far less profitable than sharing them with other companies through licensing, franchising or joint ventures.

Although I believe the legal corporate structure is not only useless but harmful, as I shall argue at length in Chapter 20, all we need to realize here is that it is possible to operate the business world in networks of partnerships without the traditional corporate organization.

HOMOGENEOUS VS. HETEROGENEOUS HUMAN BEINGS

Japanese commentators and politicians have said repeatedly that America's weakness is due to its heterogeneous society, while Japan's strength lies in its homogeneous society. And they are right. What most of them do not seem to realize is that the heterogeneous nature of society is the inevitable consequence of the information deluge, and that one day Japanese society will become as heterogeneous as our own.

Back in 1981, when William Ouchi published his *Theory Z*, which tries to develop a Japanese-like social structure within corporations, he took a cue from sociologist Emile Durkheim for his final argument:

> In a mobile society, it is one's occupation alone which can remain constant throughout life—even as all else changes. If this occupation takes place entirely within one organization (as in Type Z companies), then the hope of moral integration with the larger social order and of solidarity without one's community can be more fully realized. Paradoxically, however, most bureaucracies respond to increasing mobility not with Theory Z, but in just the opposite fashion. As mobility increases, individuals tend to regard their current employer in a very short-run fashion, and such a person will be distant, uncommitted, often hostile, and even litigious.[25]

What Ouchi did not seem to recognize is that the mobility of our society is not just physical. It is mental. We know too many things, get information from too many sources and confront too many points of view to coordinate our interests by a single lodestar. Today's thinking human beings live by heterogeneous rather than homogeneous thought processes. The foci of their interests are so diverse and so widespread that exclusive membership in and dependence on a single community is impossible.

In Chapter 3, I defined community as "the interrelation of a number of individuals brought about by sharing one or more common interests."[26] The spread of knowledge, abetted by advances in communications technology and our freedom of movement, has greatly increased both our interests and the number of people with whom we can share them.

In simpler times, both one's interests and the people who shared those interests were pretty much concentrated in a single geographical area. A seamstress interested in chess, child-raising and education exchanged ideas with the people in her neighborhood who played chess, had children, served on the school board or were involved in sewing. The geographic community and the interest communities shared the same boundaries.

In more recent times, an individual can join an international chess club, exchange child-raising ideas with readers of *Parents* Magazine, go to education conferences in Washington, and discuss sewing projects on the Internet.

10. Organic Networks: Complex Adaptive Systems

Today the average person's interests are not only widely dispersed but so are the people with whom they are shared.

In fact, in today's America we are apt to consider anyone who puts all his or her interests in one basket a fanatic and, maybe, even dangerous. To be well adjusted in today's society we have to learn how to coordinate or blend our many interests so that they not only do not conflict but actually reinforce each other. A well-rounded human being will have many interests and belong to many communities.

ORGANIC VS. MECHANICAL MODELS

As has been said many times, Isaac Newton's interpretation of natural phenomena in mechanistic terms had a great influence on the thinkers of his time. Both businessmen and economists began to look at management and the economy as machine-like procedures. The development of more and more machines and their impact on commercial life confirmed this way of thinking. At first factories housed machines. Eventually the factory became a plant, i.e., a big machine of which workers were an integral part.

As Daniel Bell observes in *The Coming of Post-Industrial Society*, the business corporation was a new social invention, "an instrument which coordinates men, materials, and markets for the production of goods and services."[27] Bureaucracy was the logical outcome of applying the mechanical model to operating a social endeavor.

Since Isaac Newton's time a number of scientists have tried to learn from organisms as their forebears learned from mechanisms. Among the more recent is Margaret J. Wheatley who argues that

> Our concept of organizations is moving away from the mechanistic creations that flourished in the age of bureaucracy. We have begun to speak in earnest of more fluid, organic structures, even of boundaryless organizations. We are beginning to recognize organizations as systems, construing them as "learning organizations" and crediting them with some type of self-renewing capacity. These are our first, tentative forays into a new appreciation for organizations. My own experience suggests that we can forgo the despair created by such common organizational events as change, chaos, information overload, and cyclical behaviors if we recognize

that organizations are conscious entities, possessing many of the properties of living systems.[28]

Of course, as Wheatley admits, we are still speaking in metaphors. But the switch of metaphors is enlightening, for the difference between a machine and an organism is that the first is rigid while the second is adaptable. An organism differs from a machine in that it is made up of parts with the ability to create, grow and repair themselves while still advancing the function of the whole.

There is much we still have to learn about how organisms operate. But we do know that each part of an organism has purpose built into it, that the parts of an organism work together to provide nourishment for the whole, that these various cooperating parts, while they live, multiply and die independently, operate as a single entity by communicating with each other in multiple ways (chemically, electrically, mechanically).

About a decade ago, John H. Holland, an economist at the University of Michigan, developed an analysis of what he called "complex adaptive systems."[29] He studied examples of organic systems, from the human brain to ant colonies, and applied what he learned to economic systems. Every such system, he argued, has four important qualities:

1. It consists of a network of agents acting independently yet in constant interaction with other agents in the system.

2. These agents are organized in many different ways, with each constantly revising itself in response to serving other agents.

3. The whole system depends on anticipating the future, so that foresight or planning dominates every level.

4. The system has many niches requiring a great variety of agents.

His conclusion was that all organisms, and most social and economic systems have these characteristics, and that they all are, therefore, subject to what he called "perpetual novelty." They are always changing, never in equilibrium, which is why traditional mathematics is not a practical tool for analyzing them.

Holland's analysis of complex adaptive systems is a perfect description of how partnership networks operate. His four characteristics describe a sophisticated, ever-changing way of knowledge management: constant independent

10. Organic Networks: Complex Adaptive Systems

response to information from other agents through planning the application of unique expertise.

While the machine was a model for the bureaucratic organization, the organism, or complex adaptive system, is the model for networks of partnerships, with both networks and partnerships constantly forming and reforming in response to changing objectives or purpose—an economic system flexible enough to navigate the ever-accelerating flow of information.

11

SUPERPARTNERING:
OPERATIONS AND KNOWLEDGE NETWORKS

"Only when the increase of gifts moves with the gift may the accumulated wealth of our spirit continue to grow among us, so that each of us may enter, and be revived by, a vitality beyond his or her solitary powers."

— *Lewis Hyde, 1979*[1]

The operations network described in Chapter 9 requires a knowledge network, a tool for superpartnering by every business involved. The histories of three firms illustrate how networks have been used for years, how bureaucracy interferes with networking and how the new sophisticated knowledge network makes possible a $16 billion business while preserving partnership autonomy. Knowledge networks require deliberate management, complete cooperation, a ban on secrecy and fundamental changes in thinking as we move from a market economy to a gift economy.

TWO TYPES OF NETWORKS

We have seen how management of information can be improved by partnering and how, through networking, products can be made and services rendered without hierarchy. What this chapter strives to show is that every business-network transaction presumes two different information networks, distinct in purpose and performance yet correlated like body and soul.

The life force that binds autonomous partnerships into organic networks is communication. But communication takes two forms:

11. Superpartnering: Operations & Knowledge Networks

(1) The basic transmission of information through the contracts that organize the network. I call this primary network of agreements as to what each partnership will do and how it will be compensated an *operations network*.

(2) The ever-evolving pool of ideas and information through which individual links in the network share what they learn as they operate. I call this sharing of knowledge for mutual assistance a *knowledge network*.

Businesses are not only setting up operations networks, but they are developing communications systems that go beyond operations to create a symbiosis of information that nourishes all the network nodes as it is nourished by them. They must do this because, as Lewis J. Perelman observed in 1992, "...expertise itself is rapidly becoming less an attribute of individual persons and more a property of systems and networks."[2]

The word network, like so many terms in this book, is used elsewhere with many meanings—from *Merriam-Webster's* "a fabric or structure of cords or wires that cross at regular intervals and are knotted or secured at the crossings," to Robert K. Mueller's in *Corporate Networking*:

> The term "network" is the communications analog to the sociological concept of group; but the "network" is distinct from the "group" in that it refers to a number of individuals (or other units) who persistently interact with one another in accordance with established patterns. Networks can be measured sociometrically, but they are otherwise not visually obvious.[3]

Mueller is describing the networks that are the principal subject of his book: the informal communication and negotiation that rises spontaneously among people who work together. His book was written to help managers understand that phenomenon and how it can help or hinder corporate objectives. Although such networks do affect the management of information (and the management of companies), they are externalities, like the weather or the health of employees. They must be considered, prepared for and sometimes even moderated, but they are not a directly controllable element of business strategy.

The two networks that concern us here are both controllable and are, in my opinion, essential elements in building the new, non-hierarchical, antibureaucratic organization. The first is the operations network described in

Chapter 9—the body in our body/soul analogy. The second, the soul of the relationship and the subject of this chapter, is the knowledge network.

Both these networks are communication networks powered by purpose. The goal of the operations network is to get something done. The goal of the knowledge network is to provide a learning environment that facilitates the performance of the operations network.

These two distinct systems are already in use in many companies. To better understand how knowledge networks propel and improve operations networks, I analyze three companies. B&O, the firm that built my home, exemplifies both types of networking in their simplest unsophisticated forms. Apple Computer, an early leader in the digital revolution, illustrates the impossibility of trying to marry operations and knowledge networks with business bureaucracy. ABB Asea Brown Boveri, a European conglomerate, has developed prototypes of the sophisticated operations and knowledge networks we can expect in the 21st Century.

PRIMITIVE NETWORKING AT ITS BEST

Bill Ballestrini and Jim Onorato met in the early 1950s, while they were apprentices at a state-sponsored trade school for construction workers in Connecticut. Jim was one class behind Bill, and each was at the head of his class. Graduation made them journeymen in Local 30, the New London branch of the Connecticut Carpenters Union, and they found themselves employed by the same contractors on a number of jobs. Then, still in their twenties, they decided to start their own business. They called their partnership B&O, and built their first two houses on speculation. For financing Bill sold a house he owned and Jim borrowed money from his mother.

For a while their principal customer was a contractor, who told them that the house that was easiest to sell was a raised ranch. Eventually they designed a raised ranch themselves, and that became their "bread and butter" house, which they built and sold hundreds of times in the following years. When I bought a new house from them in 1980, B&O was a well-established firm with a good reputation, but it still operated as a two-man partnership.

B&O is just one example of thousands of partnership businesses all over the United States. For close to 25 years Bill and Jim had no employees. It was not until the 1980s that they began hiring help, principally Bill's three sons,

11. Superpartnering: Operations & Knowledge Networks

and Jim's two. But, in the early years they worked hard, doing most of the carpentry and whatever else they could do themselves.

Of course, they had neither the skills nor the time to do everything. So they set up an operations network. They did not call it that, but they ran their business through a web of other independent businesses. A lumber company provided the blueprints for the first house they built. Realtor Anne McBride sold the houses. Chelsea Savings Bank gave them their first line of credit. They relied on separate independent contractors, all specialists in what they did, to clear the land, excavate the foundation, pour footings, frame walls, put in plumbing, install electricity, shingle the roof, brick-lay fireplace and chimney, put up drywall, tape ceilings, lay floors, paint rooms, put in insulation, build cabinets and supply appliances.

The individual teams in that network were almost all one-person operations or partnerships. A few, like the company that supplied the fiberglass insulation, were large firms. But even the insulation provider paid the installers on piecework (about 1.5 cents per square foot), so the insulators worked like independent contractors. "Specialization," Jim explains, "allowed them to make more money and cost us less."

B&O depended on these suppliers not only for labor, expertise and materials but for reliability and availability. Hence the network became relatively stable with links dropped only, in Jim's words, "if work or products did not come up to our standards or they didn't take care of their people."

One reason for B&O's success was that Bill and Jim believed in continuous learning. My house was built with many refinements that did not exist when they started their business. Their knowledge network was largely the informal flow of information that came from talking to and negotiating with suppliers and subcontractors.

The nearest thing to a conscious knowledge network was their membership in The National Association of Home Builders. They considered dues and involvement worth the expense, not only because NAHB represented the interests of residential builders in Washington, but chiefly because NAHB sponsored publications and trade shows that enabled them to keep up with innovations and new products in their field.

Bill and Jim retired at the end of 1995. At least three of their children have joined the ranks of American entrepreneurs, managing independent operations sustained by networking. One of Bill's sons has his own home-building firm. One of Jim's sons is a realtor; the other has his own landscaping business.

A CLASH OF TITANS

There are few better examples of what can happen when bureaucracy is superimposed on entrepreneurial networking than the strange, short-lived partnership of Steve Jobs and John Sculley at Apple Computer.

Jobs, a giant in creative partnering, invented the Apple computer with Steve Wozniak. Sculley, a giant in bureaucratic management, was president of Pepsi-Cola and a prime prospect to succeed Don Kendall as chief executive of Pepsico, the parent company. I take most of the details of this story from Sculley's autobiography, *Odyssey* (written with Robert F. Byrne in 1987). Naturally Sculley tells his tale to defend himself, but all the facts are there—and what happened after the book was published gives us the advantage of hindsight.

The people who ran Apple, particularly Jobs, went out of their way to persuade Sculley to leave PepsiCo and become president of their company. When Sculley finally decided to take the leap, he did so with great enthusiasm, fostered by deep admiration for Jobs. Yet within two years Apple Computer—up to then a phenomenally successful company—was in deep trouble. Jobs had a complete break with Sculley and was eventually forced to resign. Sculley had to restructure the company along more traditional bureaucratic lines to "save" it from bankruptcy.

Although the book overdramatizes many of the emotional aspects of what happened, it exposes an unusually perceptive management mind. Sculley is an extraordinary executive, not only an experienced administrator and creative marketer but an unusual management theoretician. He fills his book with perceptive observations on what works in business and, more interestingly, what he sees as necessary for "third wave" companies (a term he adopts from Alvin Toffler): "the emerging form," to use Sculley's own words, "not only for high-tech companies, but for all institutions."[4]

But Sculley was a colossus with one foot in the hierarchical world of the traditional package-goods business and the other in the antibureaucratic world

11. Superpartnering: Operations & Knowledge Networks   215

of Silicon Valley. Despite his enthusiastic theorizing about third-wave business freedom, he could not hold his balance without keeping that one foot firmly planted in hierarchical management.

FOUR MISTAKES

Sculley made four major mistakes. Judging from the book, he fully recognized only the first two.

(1) **Sculley tried to turn Steve Jobs into a bureaucratic manager.** Of course, Jobs and the other leaders at Apple made the primary blunder. The founders of Apple were not as creative in management as they were in technology. When their first computer became an incredible success and money started pouring in, they presumed the financial side of the company had to be managed like that of any other large corporation. They sold stock to the public and went looking for a traditional big-company manager. Jobs asked Sculley to teach him how to manage, and Sculley responded. Soon Jobs was running an entire division with more than a thousand people reporting to him. It was an unnatural situation for a man who had created Apple as an operations network nourished by the knowledge network of Silicon Valley.[5] Unsurprisingly Jobs failed as a bureaucrat.

(2) **To sell computers, Sculley invested millions of dollars in television advertising.** As Sculley had once created the Pepsi Generation, he now tried to create an Apple Generation. Mass advertising is the key communication invention of industrial bureaucracy. It worked wonderfully with products that could be mass manufactured and sold with a long-lived market image. Pepsi-Cola was such a product, unchanging and mass-priced. But Apple's computers were constantly being changed and required a substantial customer investment. Sales slid disastrously, forcing Sculley to realize that the more the company improved a computer the less of a consumer product it became. Only then did he switch to newspaper advertising targeted at business, a decision he would have made in the beginning had he built and used a real knowledge network with Apple's developers, suppliers, retailers and customers.

(3) **Sculley applied package-goods marketing strategies to the computer business.** In the book he explains at length the value of share of market and especially share of mind, techniques that work only with strong centralized marketing. He realized that computers change too quickly and clones are

created too easily to establish a share of market (or share of mind) for the product. His solution was to try to win a significant share of mind for the company, not realizing that the marketing penalty rising from rapid change also applies to companies, as it certainly did to Apple.

(4) **Sculley could not shake off the competitive instinct so important to industrial bureaucracy.** At PepsiCo he rallied his troops against Coca-Cola; at Apple, against IBM. Although he exulted in Jobs' dream of transforming the world by enabling every human to use a computer, it never occurred to him that a partnership with IBM might further that goal better than competition. To the very end Sculley was saying that Apple's advantage was that, due to its proprietary software technology, "nobody can clone the Macintosh as they can IBM's PC."[6] Yet the clones were to do more to make computers widely available than either the "real" Macintosh or the IBM PC.

Most important of all, Sculley could not visualize a business enterprise without hierarchy. Sculley kept Apple Computer from foundering and brought it back to profitability by dismissing 12,000 employees, closing two plants, and making the company much more bureaucratic than it had been. Of the key people he promoted to heads of departments, the majority had formerly worked in traditional companies.

A GLIMPSE OF THE FUTURE

What might have happened if Sculley had taken a completely different, much more revolutionary course? What if he had restructured the company by dividing it up into autonomous units each owned by its operating team, joined only by the spirit of Apple and a willingness to cooperate? Jobs suggested something like that,[7] though both he and Sculley were thinking too traditionally to see how it might work.

Yet, within a couple of years the unthinkable became company policy. Toward the end of his book Sculley wrote:

> Because we believe that interdependencies—networks of smaller companies—are a major source of strength, we are spinning out from the Apple mothership new ideas, new business directions in the form of new companies. While many former Apple employees have gone off to create companies that evolve around us, Apple has for the first time created one of its own, and more are likely to follow.[8]

11. Superpartnering: Operations & Knowledge Networks 217

The first spinout was Claris,[9] a software company staffed with Apple volunteers and headed by Bill Campbell, who thereby resigned as Apple's executive vice president for sales and marketing. Other spinouts followed. Sculley wrote that he encouraged spinouts because outside software companies would resent direct competition from Apple. (He does not explain why they should find competition from satellite companies partly owned by Apple more agreeable.) The book's last word on spinouts and networks:

> The ultimate aim is to expand the network further than it has gone. In the future we envision a federation of companies spun out of the mothership in such fields as systems products and in markets like engineering or industrial training.
>
> We are networking out of opportunity. We think we can become stronger, faster, more flexible, and hold on to more creative people by creating a federation. Its ties to the mothership should be similar to our ties with our third-party companies, offering clear direction to where we are going so the spinouts have a place in our future, not just in our present. The difference with the independent companies is that we can more directly influence the spinout's course. The mothership manages the federation through the bonds of interdependency.[10]

The book ends with Apple Computer once more in the black and Sculley's promise of a glorious future.

But although Sculley had seen the future, he was still trying to tie it to a bureaucratic mother ship. After the book was published, Apple again ran into serious trouble. Sculley even worked out an ill-fated joint venture with IBM called Kaleida Labs, which was launched in 1991 to create a software language to enable PCs, video games and other machines to play the same multimedia programs. It never got off the ground and disbanded in 1995.[11]

In 1993 the Apple board fired Sculley. Afterwards, the company experimented with allowing production of clones by competitors and sharing software. Attempts were made to sell the company (to IBM among others!), but the board eventually fired Sculley's successor as well.

In July 1996, Gilbert F. Amelio, who would be chief executive for five months, had just assembled his new five-person executive staff, all trained in other large companies and none with any experience in manufacturing or marketing personal computers.[12] At this writing Amelio is out and none other than Steve Jobs has returned as "interim" chief executive. Apple posted a healthy $101 million profit in the third quarter of 1998 and its chances of survival are much better. It is very unlikely that it will ever recapture its former glory.[13] Even so, the key point in this story is how back in 1987 Sculley, with all his blind spots, recognized the need for networking.

THE BEST NETWORK YET

ABB Asea Brown Boveri seems to be every recent management book's number-one example of the new network-and-team structure that is revolutionizing business management.

ABB was formed in 1988 by the merger of two mammoth electrical engineering competitors, Sweden's Asea AB and Switzerland's BBC Brown Boveri. Today this industrial giant has annual revenues of more than $33 billion in businesses ranging from power generation and transmission to transportation and financial services. Although legally ABB consists of more than 1,000 interrelated corporations, operationally it is a network of more than 5,000 autonomous profit centers averaging 50 people each and usually organized into much smaller teams.

Chairman Percy Barnevik, who was ABB's first president, created the network largely by purchasing and reorganizing traditional smaller companies. For eight years he ran the company out of Zurich with a six-member executive committee, until he turned over the CEO job to Goran Lindahl in 1996. Lindahl said he "sees no reason to change strategy."[14]

The Zurich committee keeps in touch with more than 200 senior executives, who are coordinators, some for all the profit centers in a particular country, others for the profit centers in a particular industry. The overlap is intentional, for ABB operates in at least 140 countries and is involved in 36 different businesses. In many cases the national or business coordinator also heads one of the profit centers.

Tom Peters, who devoted a chapter in *Liberation Management* to ABB, described this unique organization as a "matrix structure, with countries and industries in the two dimensions," and then commented:

> I've railed against the matrix organization structure for years. Matrices become hopelessly complex bureaucracies and gut the emotional energy and "ownership" of those closest to the mar-

11. Superpartnering: Operations & Knowledge Networks

ketplace. I still believe that. Yet Barnevik's unique format passes my high-energy/accountability test, though I'm not confident that an ABB without Barnevik wouldn't deteriorate—his abiding hatred of bureaucracy is critical to making the ABB structure work.[15]

It was an insightful and very significant observation. Presuming that the 5,000 profit centers are as autonomous as everyone, including Barnevik, says they are, what is the role of the Zurich committee? Its members supervise top personnel in that they appoint and can fire the senior executives. They arbitrate disputes among senior executives, although Barnevik once said that senior executives who cannot resolve their own disputes are soon replaced. They supervise finances by watching the relationship of each profit center's performance to budget and making decisions on ABB investments and acquisitions.

MANAGING THE KNOWLEDGE NETWORK

Most important, the Zurich committee, through the 200 senior executives, supervises and facilitates one of the most sophisticated knowledge networks in the world, a network which reports in detail the performance of every profit center not just to the executive committee and the senior executives but to every other profit center.

Note how little is left of traditional bureaucracy in this enormous organization. The sole vestige of hierarchy is the Zurich committee's power to appoint or dismiss and to settle disputes, and Barnevik, at least, preferred these functions to be exercised by mutual agreement rather than by headquarters authority. The financial function is not much different than it would be if the Zurich committee were an investment-banking or venture-capital partnership supervising money invested in a network of small companies.

In other words, ABB could continue to operate if all the profit centers were completely independent and united only in voluntary participation in a knowledge network. The only really essential function of the Zurich committee is the management of the company's information system, the knowledge network that is the soul of ABB.

This complete and constantly interactive communication enables 5,000 individual profit centers to recognize possibilities for cooperation, to share opportunities for new business and, most of all, to learn from each others' insights and experiences in buying, selling and managing. Even when two profit centers are in the same business and compete for the same customers, ABB preserves the duplication on the theory that having two units facing identical problems increases the potential for originating and testing new ideas.

It is true that Barnevik's vision and leadership made the whole thing work, but I would be surprised to find a single ABB executive who wants to change what Barnevik had wrought. What if, Tom Peters asked, something happens to Barnevik?[16] Now Barnevik has left, and time will test the longevity of his creation.

But one cannot help wonder whether he would not have done ABB a favor by eliminating the remaining chains of financial and legal hierarchy.

But my point is not to tell ABB what to do, but to suggest that it is not only possible but very likely that knowledge networks will one day become the norm with no vestiges of hierarchy at all.

SUPERPARTNERING

The knowledge network as developed by ABB is far more than the traditional Management Information System (MIS) that was bureaucracy's response to data processing and computer communications. By supplying instantaneous information on what every unit is doing to all the units, ABB takes partnering to a new level.

This unlimited sharing of information between autonomous units to facilitate creative thinking on every level of management is the most—and maybe the only—promising solution to solving the problem of the social and business management in today's deluge of information. As in partnering, a knowledge network pools the power of multiple minds. What results is not just the sum of all the information but a symbiosis, a higher form of partnering than can be achieved by a group small enough for face to face collaboration.

Of course, the knowledge network was not invented by ABB. As a social force it has an ancestry that goes back to when humans began to live in communities. Ad hoc consultation, get-togethers, powwows, town meetings, jamborees, conventions are all networking tools that frequently share information among enough people to create a synergy that results in new ideas useful to the group. Peter Drucker has written that permanent organizations were developed to provide environments for knowledge work.[12]

11. Superpartnering: Operations & Knowledge Networks

In his 1979 book, *The Gift*, Lewis Hyde spoke of "a community of scholars, one in which each individual thinker can be awash in the ideas of his comrades so that a sort of 'group mind' develops, one that is capable of cognitive tasks beyond the powers of any single person."[17] What has now happened is that organizations like ABB are learning to organize and manage such groups to keep them focused for pertinent problem-solving capability.

In many industries the germ of knowledge networks exists in trade associations, although few such groups see that as their primary function. Media, particularly trade papers, perform some of the knowledge network function although clumsily due to serious limitations on how much "inside" information they can cover. A real knowledge network requires complete openness, a willingness to share everything, and confidence that both parties in every communication will give as willingly as they receive.

Electronic communications, both external and internal electronic networks, make the gathering and rapid transmission of such information much easier. Every ABB executive has a portable computer and uses Lotus Notes. But, no matter how indispensable, computers and electronic networks are just tools that facilitate a knowledge network.

Just as a convention without rules of order and a chair will become a babbling chaos, so knowledge networks require discipline in gathering, sifting, organizing, directing and transmitting information. This is the function of ABB's senior executives, and why some of them are in charge of a particular country while others are concerned with a specific type of business. The senior executives also are knowledge leaders in that they serve as consultants, constantly evaluating the information and bringing what they consider significant to the attention of the profit-center managers. This does not restrict the local managers in any way, for they frequently communicate directly with other profit-center managers to pursue ideas or opportunities. Look for the management of knowledge networks to become a major career opportunity by the early years of the new century.

THE DEATH OF SECRECY

It may seem preposterous that two independent profit centers, going after the same business, should be completely open in sharing information. But that is how they do it at ABB, and that is how a knowledge network must do it to work. The two essential—and related—principles for operating a knowledge network are total cooperation among participants and complete openness regarding relevant information.

Many executives, because of their bureaucratic training, find it difficult even to imagine running a business with complete candor. Remember the puzzlement, even suspicion, during the Cold War when people heard that American scientists were exchanging information with their Soviet counterparts—an exchange the scholars found perfectly natural and desirable.

But attitudes change. Today many American companies invite executives from other corporations to visit their plants and offices to learn how they are managed. At least one organization, Productivity Inc., has made a business out of organizing these industrial visits. According to *Business Week,* "The visits usually represent a serious effort to absorb what works at the best companies in the hope of applying those precepts back at home."[18]

When cooperation is the goal, secrecy makes little sense, for secrecy is a weapon from the competitive arsenal of bureaucracy employed to:

(1) protect bureaucrats from negative opinion whether of customers, employees, suppliers, the public, or even stockholders and—far too often—their bosses.

(2) give bureaucrats an advantage over others (competitors inside and outside the company, subordinates, even suppliers who might act differently if they knew what the buyer knows).

(3) suppress information supposedly harmful to morale (e.g., salaries of coworkers, threat of a layoff).

I do not intend to become entangled in the longstanding debate among moralists as to when secrecy becomes deception. But it should be evident that none of the above advantages will hold up in a truly cooperative situation. There can be no real partnering when either of the partners hides information relevant to the collaboration. Withholding information undermines trust, the foundation of partnering and knowledge networking. It is also shortsighted, for the more that is shared, the greater the likelihood that new and mutually beneficial ideas will evolve.

NETWORKS OF NETWORKS

The advantage of networks over bureaucracies is that they are freeform and flexible. How far should the openness, the willingness to share information extend outside the knowledge network? Actually it never extends outside, for any source of usable information becomes part of the network. When ABB organized a consortium to build a $1.2 billion hydroelectric plant in Iran, the other members of the group became an ABB operational network and part of ABB's knowledge network.

Although each knowledge network will tend to concentrate around the members who use it most, there will be many occasions when knowledge from other industries is needed and used. The boundaries between businesses are already being bridged more and more often as the world of businesses becomes a tapestry of interrelated knowledge networks, the links strengthening, weakening, joining and parting as knowledge is needed.

This will generate a new role for the media, particularly the business media, which will become knowledge-network beacons, alerting network managers and individual businesses as to what knowledge they need and where they can find it.

A GIFT ECONOMY

In his book, *The Gift*, Lewis Hyde expanded on a concept he attributed to Marcel Mauss, a French scholar who published *Essai sur le don* in 1924, and whose ideas were further developed by Marshall Sahlins, a University of Chicago economic anthropologist in his 1972 book, *Stone Age Economics*.

Hyde described two antagonistic economies that have existed side by side since primitive times and have a marked influence on the basic psychological and physical currencies of society. He called one the gift economy, the other, the commodity (or market) economy.

Hyde, a student of the arts, wrote beautifully about poets and poetry. The basic argument of his book was that art and literature are gifts and "that there is an irreconcilable conflict between gift exchange and the market."[19] To explore the social ramifications and community-building impact of gift economies, he went into great detail regarding ancient stories and tribal customs from all over the world.

The attitude of the American Indians toward peace pipe and potlatch and the South Pacific Massim toward necklaces and armshells indicates that these items were treasured for their symbolism. Their value came entirely from being given and received as a gift. They were a means for indicating and perpetuating community. They could not be bought or sold. Hyde saw the residue of the gift economy in many current customs, including the wedding practice of the father's giving his daughter to the groom.

Much as I enjoyed his analysis, Hyde's emphasis on the symbolism and emotional aura of gifts obscured what I think is the most important element in the contrast between gift and market economies: human beings exchange certain things that have a value the market economy cannot handle. It is not the object's tangible value that the market economy cannot handle; it is its symbolic value. Economists sometimes talk of "communal values," sociologists of "sacred values." To trend researcher Daniel Yankelovich they were "sacred/expressive" values.[20]

What interests us here is that Hyde applies the concept to things that are not necessarily instruments of community or religion in the traditional sense. He argues that literature, works of art, and even creative ideas are gifts, and concludes that this is why most writers, artists and scholars do not prosper in the market economy.

I do not agree with Hyde entirely, but what interests me, and is important to this book, is that there are things which of their very nature cannot be bought or sold, valuables that cannot be handled by the market economy and so require a gift economy. The most important of those things is knowledge.

Many commentators have remarked that the knowledge economy is different because knowledge is not a depreciable resource. When I have an idea and pass it on to someone else, I do not lose the idea. The market economy, even when money is used, is founded on barter, surrendering one item of value in order to obtain another. We cannot barter ideas, because knowledge, like love, grows rather than diminishes when it is shared.

There are four distinctive qualities that give knowledge its peculiar value and put it out of the reach of the market economy:

(1) You do not lose knowledge by giving it to another. In fact, you usually gain because communication both clarifies and develops thought.

(2) Knowledge inspires a compulsion to be shared. Though possible, it is unnatural for human beings to hoard knowledge.

(3) Knowledge changes in the transmission, as we saw in Chapter 3.

(4) Knowledge is fertile. Transmitted ideas create new ideas.

I shall say more about the significance of the gift economy in later chapters. The key point here is that if, as all the recent commentators seem to agree, we are really in a knowledge economy, it has to be a gift economy, something very different from the market economy now ruling the world.

Unfortunately there are not as many scholars who have studied gift economies as there are students of market economies. But we do know the gift economy's major difference from the market economy, for a gift economy requires cooperation rather than competition and thrives on openness and trust rather than secrecy and suspicion.

These two traits alone can make a tremendous difference in 21st-Century society.

12

THREE ECONOMIES

> "As we struggle with the designs that will replace bureaucracy, we must invent organizations where process is allowed its varied-tempo dance, where structures come and go as they support the process that needs to occur, and where form arises to support the necessary relationships."
> — Margaret J. Wheatley, 1992[1]

The changeover to an economy of partnership networks will not happen overnight, but it will happen more quickly than we expect—first, because business has always used partnerships and networks; second, because business is becoming increasingly dependent on networks; third, because there is an affinity between the new economy and the economy of the informal; and finally because wisdom favors cooperation over competition. There will be many experiments, many setbacks but eventually a new attitude will emerge regarding competition, cooperation and sharing information.

INERTIA AND FEAR OF CHANGE

I expect the business world to move into partnership networks inevitably but gradually—not smoothly but by fits and starts as floods of entrepreneurial enthusiasm encounter backwaters of human inertia and fear of change. Among the principal obstacles to rapid change are four widespread attitudes:

1. The feeling that big companies are more credit-worthy than small firms. Even the U.S. government, despite its Small Business Administration, more readily risks millions of dollars to rescue a bankrupt Chrysler Corporation than thousands to sustain a small business. In Europe, the bias is even stronger. The governments of Europe, according to *Business Week*, have...

> wasted tens of billions of dollars over the last fifteen years pumping up big national corporate champions that stumbled badly. They did little to cultivate smaller, nimbler companies with better products. European business culture is also profoundly anti-entrepreneur. Banks don't loan to small, promising companies, and industry won't buy from them.[2]

Significantly, almost 10 months later, the same magazine declared that startups and small companies were rescuing the European economy.[3]

2. The conviction that outsourcing, downsizing and spin-offs increase unemployment. When Chrysler decided to sell its outdated Detroit glass factory and buy windshields for its minivans and pickup trucks, the United Auto Workers went on strike until the company agreed to save the plant and invest $70 million to bring it up to date. The UAW is on the defensive because, on a cost basis, 55 percent of the average vehicle at General Motors, 62 percent at Ford and 66 percent at Chrysler are already outsourced, according to a study by the Michigan Industrial Technology Institute.[4]

Quite naturally labor unions are not mollified by the number of union members who may go into business for themselves or become partners in small firms.

3. The worry that small firms are unable to provide health insurance and other benefits on which most employees depend. Chapter 16 will discuss how the knowledge economy is likely to meet this need. Here it is sufficient to say that thousands of small-business owners now manage to provide health insurance for themselves, and with partnership networks every worker will be an owner.

4. The fear that comes from abandoning one's sense-of-security framework. This is a crucial problem in Russia, where no one under 70 can remember living without a government-guaranteed job and paycheck. It may not be as bad here, with our long tradition of independence and free enterprise, but it is still the major obstacle to change in the corporate world—not only among employees, but also among managers, suppliers, investors and customers, as well as the lawmakers and bankers.

MORE EVOLUTION THAN REVOLUTION

These same factors will nourish efforts to preserve as much of the old when forced to accept the new. Hence the tendency in the business world, discussed in Chapter 10, to retain the corporate shell, to try to fuse the new concepts of teams and networks with the old concepts of centralized control and bureaucratic dominion. But the struggle, painful as it may be for many individuals, will not, in my opinion, result in outright war.

Four facts make it likely that the move to partnership networks will be evolutionary rather than revolutionary:

(1) In the Western world, at least, partnerships and networks are not radical innovations. We have a long tradition of using both in doing business.

(2) Big business is becoming increasingly dependent on sophisticated networking.

(3) Partnership networks can bridge the economic gap between developed and undeveloped countries (and localities), the world's most threatening problem.

(4) There is increasing evidence that Americans, and leading business people throughout the world, have decided that cooperation is a distinct business advantage.

OUR LONG PARTNERSHIP-NETWORK TRADITION

As we saw in the previous chapter, B&O is just one example of approximately 1 million partnerships now running businesses in the United States. Of the 13 million nonpartnership businesses in our country, 11 million are proprietorships. Only 2 million are corporations (with a mere 40,000 of these publicly owned).[5] It is useful to remember that an estimated 5 million businesses in our country are operated out of the owners' homes, and that most of them were home-based long before computers.[6]

B&O was not unusual in 1995, nor was it unusual when it was launched almost 45 years ago. A substantial segment of the American economy has always been run by small, independent business people, as were the earlier economies of Great Britain and the European continent.

Benjamin Franklin not only was a small businessman himself, but he became partner with a number of former apprentices who ran other print shops. Interestingly, after the death of the printer he set up in Charleston, South Carolina, the widow turned out to be a much better business partner than her husband, information that Franklin passed on "for the sake of recommending that branch of education for our young females, as likely to be of more use to them and their children, in the case of widowhood, than either music or dancing."[7]

What changed over the years was not the usefulness of individual enterprise and partnering but the growth of complex projects at a time when the great majority of available workers had little education or relevant knowledge. Bureaucracy was invented to apply the knowledge of the few to work that had to be done by many. Bureaucracy is effective for big jobs where all the basic thinking can be done by one person even though the physical labor cannot. But the rising tide of information has brought about three major changes:

(1) Most important projects have become so complex and detailed that no one person can mastermind the necessary information alone.

(2) Most workers have more than enough information to do their part of the job without direction from above.

(3) Machinery has eliminated most of the need for purely physical human labor.

What is new, therefore, is not the existence and usefulness of partnerships and networks but their universal applicability. In the past the jobs were limited that could be done effectively by small, independent work units supported by networks. Today advanced technology and widespread education make it possible to use partnership networks to run our entire society.

NETWORKS BECOME MORE SOPHISTICATED

Networking in business is not new. In 1976, the U.S. Justice Department compiled a list of top companies with networks of board members. The largest companies shared directors with 70 percent of other large companies. In the oil business alone, Exxon shared directors with Atlantic Richfield, Mobil, Standard Oil of California, Standard Oil of Indiana and Texaco.[8]

But there were thousands of other business networks that did not even concern the justice department. A marketer's relationship with the retailers and wholesalers in his distribution chain is very much a network, as are those of a franchiser with her franchisees or a manufacturer with his suppliers. VISA and Master Card operate worldwide service networks uniting thousands of independent banks run by many nationalities with different currencies and different banking laws.

What has changed considerably since 1976 is the importance of information in these relationships. To facilitate two-way, on-the-spot communication industrial suppliers now dispatch teams of experts to work with corporate customers' engineers and other users of what is purchased. The growth of franchising in recent years is directly proportionate to the individual units' dependence on franchise headquarters for information concerning everything from real-estate location and quality standards to business operation and hiring practices.

CORPORATE ALLIANCES

As traditional networks were becoming more information-directed, another species of networking was growing: corporate alliances, both domestic and international. In the United States corporate alliances were somewhat inhibited by antitrust laws, although today's Justice Department is interpreting the laws more and more liberally. European and Asian governments have always been more tolerant of cooperation among manufacturers, financial institutions and, usually, local, regional and national government bodies.

Corporate alliances or networks played a very important role in the rise of Japan as a major power in international trade. While Japan's Ministry for International Trade and Industry (MITI) promoted competition among the country's companies and group of companies, it also sanctioned the *keiretsus,* established networks consisting usually of a central bank, a trading company to import raw materials and export the group's products, and a number of independent companies related by cross-ownership of each other's stock.

Although membership and coordination within the *keiretsu* are voluntary, the financial ties assure that each member looks out for the welfare of the others. Toyota is tied to the Mitsui group, Nissan to the Fuji group and Mazda to the Sumitomo group.[9] At the same time each manufacturer has developed a second network of suppliers by sharing technical information and guaranteeing exclusivity.[10]

Japanese companies have profited immensely from shared technology and cooperative research and development. To overcome the advantage of Japanese networking, foreign firms have been forced to partner with Japanese companies, and MITI is now accepting foreign firms as junior partners in its regulatory network.[11] America's TRW is a junior member in both the group headed by Toyota and the group led by Nissan.[12] General Motors' Delphi Automotive Systems even attends the Toyota *keiretsu* strategy meetings.[13]

Partly influenced by Japan's success, the European Union is creating its own networks to share technology even across national borders, and the United States is becoming much more lenient regarding corporate alliances. Kenichi Ohmae, McKinsey's man in Tokyo, speaks of trilateral consortia of Japanese, U.S. and European firms "being formed in nearly every area of leading-edge industry including biotechnology, computers, robots, semiconductors, jet engines, nuclear power, carbon fibers, and other materials."[14]

IBM and Toshiba are jointly pooling $1 billion to build a facility to produce advanced memory chips. Hewlett-Packard and Canon share laser-printer engine technology. General Electric supplies the equipment and technology, while the Mitsui bank supplies the financing and contacts to win power-plant contracts in Asia. Caterpillar's principal manufacturing source in Asia is a joint venture with Mitsubishi Heavy Industries.[15]

Boeing exchanges engineers with Deutsche Aerospace[16] and has linked its design operations with those of five Japanese aerospace firms.[17] Kodak and worldwide rival Fuji Photo Film collaborate in joint research on an advanced photo system.[18] Microsoft works with Sony.[19] So does rival Apple. General Motors has manufacturing partnerships with Japan's Toyota,[20] Suzuki and Isuzu as well as Sweden's Saab. Ford works with Japan's Mazda and Nissan, Germany's Volkswagen and Italy's Fiat.[21] Olivetti in Italy and Corning in the U.S. have such arrangements with dozens of companies.[22]

Large corporations like General Motors, still slaves to bureaucratic thinking, presume they need an ownership position to establish a significant alliance. But alliances do not require ownership or even a dominant partner. Small companies have found they can design, manufacture and market products as a network without any cross-ownership. The Philadelphia Guild in

Pennsylvania (furniture), TEC-NET in Florida (laser printing), and Team Nashua in New Hampshire (prepackaged electronic components) are examples.[23] Other independents cooperate in purchasing (Southeastern Massachusetts Sewn Products Network), in training (Center for Quality Management), and in promotion (Belmont Arts Black American Artists).[24]

TOWARD COMPLETE BUSINESS KNOWLEDGE

What is happening is that the more sophisticated networks become, the more their ultimate purpose is sharing information, rather than pooling financial resources or eliminating competition. Benetton is able to realize more than $1.2 billion in clothing sales in some 50,000 stores in 80 countries because its information network provides supplier mills, retail outlets and headquarters with real-time order and sales data including details on fabrics, colors and styles. It costs Benetton $13 million a year to run the system, but the network saves that and more by controlling paperwork, inventories and market response.[25] A similar though simpler inventory-control system connecting all its stores and suppliers is the principal reason for WalMart's success in the U.S.

The next step beyond Benetton's and WalMart's networking data on products and transactions is to share ideas that affect management and morale, as the Union of Japanese Scientists & Engineers (JUSE) tries to do with the 170,000 quality circles on its register. Most of JUSE's networking is conducted through meetings of quality circle representatives, a dozen or so national conferences supplemented by some hundred regional meetings.[26]

The more networks graduate from mere data to complete business knowledge, the more the chief executives using them will begin to think like ABB's Percy Barnevik and the sooner they will realize that the system works better when freed from the restraints of bureaucracy. At the same time, as suppliers and retailers become accustomed to networking, they will realize that networks give them all the advantages they could get by belonging to a bureaucratic organization while leaving intact their independence and self-reliance.

CORPORATE SHELLS AS TRANSITION MECHANISMS

Companies like ABB, Benetton and Wal-Mart can be expected to retain their corporate structure for some time for practical reasons. During the transition period from the hierarchical world to the partnership-network world it will be necessary for established companies to retain at least the appearance of being large, hierarchical institutions.

Not only will it take some time before most employees and managers are ready to abandon the security blanket of working for a sizeable company, it may take even more time before the marketplace (customers) and the financial world (bankers, brokers and money managers) will adapt to dealing with many small partnerships in place of much larger publicly held corporations. I shall not hazard a guess as to how long that transition period might be. But I am certain it will not go on forever, and I am confident it will happen in the coming century. Although human perceptions usually lag far behind specific changes, they always eventually catch up with reality.

In many instances, financial motives will hasten the first cracks in the corporate shell. Major companies are finding that value to their stockholders can be multiplied by splitting into two or more corporations and issuing separate stock for each of the pieces. The French conglomerate Chargeurs recently became Pathe (movies, television) and Chargeurs International (textiles) resulting in a 22 percent increase of value to stockholders.[27] In England the total stock market value of chemical producer ICI and drug-manufacturer Zeneca is far above the worth of the former parent company.[28]

Of course, U.S. companies have been using the technique for years. PepsiCo has spun off Kentucky Fried Chicken, Pizza Hut and Taco Bell as an independent restaurant business.[29] AT&T learned how much investors could profit from its government-forced divestiture of the Baby Bells in 1984. Now it is using the same technique on its own. As chairman Robert Allen put it,

> We have focused for a hundred years on integration as a strength. We have changed our strategy.... In recent months it has become clear to me that for AT&T to take advantage of all these business opportunities we have to split into smaller business groups.[30]

Allen's first step was the spinoff of Lucent Technologies and NCR as separate companies.

THE ECONOMY OF THE INFORMAL

Chapter 4[31] of Serge Latouche's *In The Wake of the Affluent Society* is titled, "The Archipelago of the Informal." Latouch is writing about what has been called "the informal economy." He calls it an archipelago because islands of this economy of the poor are scattered throughout the world in both developed and undeveloped countries.

The informal economy includes all the economic activity that takes place outside the formal economy. It covers the illegal, alegal or just nonregistered transactions from money-laundering by drug lords to barter by ordinary folk to the "shadow work" discussed by Ivan Illich. As an example, Latouche describes the informal economy studied by a research team funded by an organization called Environment & Development in the Third World. The team found the informal economy in the greater Yoff district, one of the poorest sections of Dakar, the capital of Senegal. Latouche summarizes their report:

> The "networking" structure makes it possible for families averaging twelve people to have access to a money income around seven times larger than the "official" figures show. The informal "economy"' is at the origin of this. It is not a matter directly of *products* of the informal activity which explains the difference. The direct source of the supplementary income is the accumulation of "drawing rights" on the various networks in which the family members participate, not the sale of goods and services as such. There is an intense circulation of gifts, money, investments, loans and advances, reimbursements, contributions, rotative credit associations (*tontines*), and so on, which in turn relates back to a very substantial activity of goods production, furnishing of services, delivery of goods. All these materials, money, goods and services enter into complicated social circuits: gifts for births or marriages, presents, voluntary or forced loans, and so on.[32]

To show how the gift economy persists among the poor in many of our own cities, Lewis Hyde[33] tells the story of a poor couple in an American ghetto who went through an unexpected $14,000 inheritance in six weeks due to their obligations to return favors and extend help to families and friends—a perfect parallel to Dakar's complicated social circuit of gifts, presents and voluntary loans.

BRIDGING THE CHASM BETWEEN RICH AND POOR

The fact that the new knowledge economy as described in the previous chapter and the informal economy that sustains so many of the world's poorest communities are both gift-economies has tremendous significance for the development of society in the 21st Century.

As economists and historians have pointed out repeatedly, it is extremely difficult to bring an undeveloped country into the world of business bureaucracy and industrial development. Almost 40 years ago, in *Passing of Traditional Society*,[34] Daniel Lerner suggested that the pattern for modernizing backward economies should involve four phases:

(1) urbanization and industrialization,

(2) education and literacy,

(3) mass-media exposure,

(4) politicalization or mobilization.

For economists, at least, the sequence seemed logical. Cities and factories were required before schools could be organized and financed. Education had to precede the media. And good government was not possible without revenue, education and communication. But, in the first half of the 20th Century it never worked out that way. Politicalization and mobilization always seemed to come first; education and literacy, last.

In those days modernization always meant bureaucracy, and no country could build bureaucracy (and an industrial base) without centralization and mobilization, without herding people into cities to work in factories. That is why so many attempts at economic modernization in undeveloped countries ended up in dictatorship, dependence on foreign financial aid, exploitation by the West for cheap labor and raw materials, and severe cultural shock for a citizenry lured from life on the land into factory and sweat-shop slavery.

But western economies are changing and so is the idea of modernization. Where the 20th Century burdened poor countries with debt, dictators and false hopes, the 21st Century promises access to knowledge, inexpensive technology and a gift economy analogous to their own.

Latouche claims that recent developments have put the formal economy (strictly an invention of Western culture) in jeopardy and that there is a trend to rediscover the informal economy and use it "to plug the holes, plaster over the cracks."[35] Since the formal economy has so much influence on Western values (e.g., the work ethic, economic self-interest, cost/benefit analysis, importance of profit), the informal economy is being studied to understand on the one hand the contrarian values that have arisen in our society, and on the other the values of Eastern cultures with which we must do business.

This leads to a worry that attempts to understand and integrate the informal economy will kill it by cutting it off from its social roots because, Latouche argues, "the normalization of the informal tends to destroy the social ties existing at infra-national levels, on which the informal's dynamism rests."[36] But his fear, I think, rises entirely from his presumption that bureaucratic attitudes will always dominate economic thinking. He makes no provision for the rise of the knowledge economy as a gift economy.

MARRYING THE NEW INFORMALITY TO THE OLD INFORMALITY

How easy will it be to merge the knowledge economy of our highly technological society with the informal economy of American ghettos and African slums? There is no possible answer, of course. Far too much depends on how many people in both camps have vision, creativity and good will. All this book can do is point out that the likely business environment of the 21st Century is right for such a marriage.

The word "informality" keeps popping up in books on modern management and how the most advanced executives operate. In *Leadership and the New Science,* Margaret J. Wheatley writes about the kind of team experiences she cherishes most:

> In the interest of getting things done, our roles and tasks moved with such speed that the lines between structure and task blurred to nothing. When we speak of informal leadership, we describe a similar experience—the capacity of the organization to create the leadership that best suits its need at the time. We may fail to honor these leaders more formally, trapped as we are in a hierarchical structure that is non-adaptive; but at the level of the living, where the people are, we know who the leader is and why he or she needs to be there.[37]

Bill Gore, the chief executive of W. L. Gore & Associates, is cited again and again as a "new" manager. He calls his company "a lattice organization," and no one who works for him has a job title. Compensation includes salary, profit sharing and a stock-ownership program. If a worker thinks she deserves a raise, she selects a sponsor who researches her performance and presents her case before a compensation team drawn from her co-workers in the plant. Although employees frequently work in teams, the organization of such teams is entirely informal.[38] To keep the informality natural Gore divides his factories into two plants before the number of employees reaches two hundred.[39]

Gifford Pinchot, describing Gore's teachings as "Zen-like," explains:

> What Bill Gore has done is to invert the normal system of a corporation. He has taken the informal network of voluntary associations which exists in every company and turned it into the formal system. The hierarchy still exists, but it has gone underground.[40]

In May 1996, I was traveling in China. One evening after dark, as our bus turned onto a very busy Beijing street, we drove through what looked to me like a highly organized and very busy bazaar. All the booths were small and most were selling food. I asked our guide whether there was a celebration. "Oh, no," she said, "the stands are here every night. People work at government jobs during the day, and at night they run these little independent businesses to make extra money."

The street was adequately lit, the booths orderly placed and there were no police or soldiers in sight. Here was Asia's informal economy in action. With no strain I could imagine these same people feeling right at home working in a Bill Gore factory.

AMERICA'S INFORMAL ECONOMIES

One of the unfortunate circumstances of the civil rights movement is that it happened at a time when bureaucracy held all the power in the United States. Hence the equality goal of both black and white civil rights leaders was recognition by and access to the ruling bureaucracies.

Before the destruction of Jim Crow there was a strong, even thriving, informal black economy. Black ghettos all over the country were busy with black-owned businesses serving black customers. Harlem had a distinct and very successful black entertainment business separate from Broadway's white theaters. In 1956, according to an African-American Los Angeles resident, "Central Avenue was alive, Avalon was alive, and there were strongholds of black entertainment, restaurants and hotels. Now that's all gone."[41]

This informal economy, like every informal economy, was a gift economy founded on family concerns and extended family relationships. The civil rights movement drew black leaders out of that gift economy and into the commercial economy of the white world. It left behind the less enterprising and less able, to rely on government jobs or government welfare.

Today Latinos and Asians have moved into the ghettos and established their own informal economies. Danny Villanueva, who finances small businesses in the Los Angeles ghetto, says that most Latinos have rejected the politics-based strategy of African Americans. There are, of course, Asians and especially Latinos who have gone into politics. But the great majority, especially those isolated by language, are building a typical informal economy, dominated by family businesses. In California 27 percent of African Americans work for the government vs. only 10 percent of Latinos.[42]

IT'S ALREADY HAPPENING

If it seems farfetched to graft the informal economy of the poor onto the big-business economy of the technological society, consider what is happening in Bangladesh. A group organized to lend small amounts of money to poor people who want to start their own businesses (mostly women asking for loans averaging $60 to $70) has become the full-fledged Grameen Bank, the largest nongovernment organization in the country. The bank still operates with its original purpose and owes its success (over 2 million members with a default rate under 2 percent) by organizing borrowers into small groups with each member responsible for the loans of the others.[43]

In fact, the informal economy of backward countries governs the economies of Hong Kong, Taiwan and other business centers of the Pacific Rim. As Peter Drucker[44] and others have pointed out, the Chinese, who dominate the Pacific Rim economy, run their companies first for the welfare of their extended families and only secondarily for profit. The Chinese diaspora's success in business rests on a vast network of family loyalties and obligations.

Richard Madsen, professor of sociology at the University of California in San Diego, asked an interesting question in a 1996 article: "After Liberalism: What If Confucianism Becomes the Hegemonic Ethic of the 21st Century World Community?"[45] He argues that East Asian economies are likely to be the dominant global economies for much of the next century,[46] and that these economies are ruled by the Asian ethic that always puts society above the individual and bases social relationships "not simply on voluntary contracts between individuals, but upon *responsibilities* defined by the network of one's social relationships."[47]

A *Business Week* editorial described how American companies are baffled by what the writer called Asia's "crony capitalism":

> U.S. corporations are discovering that doing business in Asia increasingly requires a major rethink of classical market economics. Who you know often overshadows what you sell, and personal connections can matter far more than price or quality.[48]

The editorial ends by urging Washington "to insist that those nations who enjoy the fruits of the open, free trading system also play by its rules." Some day, and I hope it will be soon, American executives, *Business Week* editors, and even our people in Washington will recognize that what they have been calling crony capitalism is really the gift economy that has risen from successfully grafting the technology of the West onto the informal tribal economy of the East or, if you prefer Madsen's description, onto the Confucian ethic.

If anyone has to learn to play by new rules, it is the West, whose commercial economy of industrial bureaucracy is being replaced by the gift economy of knowledge partnering and networking.

IS COMPETITION DEAD?

The competitive spirit is built into human nature. The growing interest in cooperation will not kill it.

Partnerships will compete for business assignments, and individuals will compete for positions in partnerships. Human beings will continue to be incredibly excited by competition in spectator sports, even though there is a growing interest in noncompetitive sports such as long-distance running, mountain climbing, hang-gliding, and surf and sail boarding. What has changed is the emphasis.

The business world we are leaving was dominated by competition, even though there were numerous instances of cooperation. The business world we are moving into will be dominated by cooperation, even though there will be numerous instances of competition. In the past business people cooperated to put themselves in a better position to compete. In the future they will compete to win a better opportunity to cooperate.

In 1992, the Canadian Institute on Research for Public Policy printed a report on the two-year round table conducted by senior Canadian officials on

Governing in an Information Society. One of the participants made an observation very relevant here:

> In a sense, what we are seeing is an inversion of the old dictum that "knowledge is power." Today, by contrast, it seems that the propensity is to get out and share the knowledge as a basis for building coalitions for action. And that is quite a reversal of past practices that used to be followed in government and, indeed, in most human organizations, where the husbanding of information was used to give people bargaining or other power.[49]

I shall have more to say about this remarkable study in later chapters where I track how government is changing under the pressure of partnering and networking. But there is little doubt that government is realizing the importance of business cooperation.

One sign is the way governments are surrendering policies that were based on the importance of competition. In the U.S. the Justice Department is giving major corporations much more leeway on antitrust matters than it had in the past. It recently took steps to release IBM from its 1956 antitrust consent decree on computer sales.[50]

In Japan, overseas investments have reached the point where the Japanese must choose between business success and the country's traditional ethnic chauvinism, and the choice, of the government at least, has favored business. In 1996, after years of enmity, representatives from Japan and Korea sat at the same table to consider solutions to mutual problems in international trade. In the European Union, there is agitation from without and within to lower tariff barriers and work more openly with businesses outside the EU.

KNOWLEDGE VS. COMPETITION

The reason for the new attitude is the growing importance of knowledge. As knowledge becomes the principal currency in doing business, competition gets in the way. To quote McKinsey's Kenichi Ohmae:

> In the past, for example, you tried to build sustainable competitive advantage by establishing dominance in all of your business systems's critical areas. You created barriers to entry where you could lock away market shares wherever possible, and used every bit of proprietary expertise, every collection of nonreplicable assets to shore up the wall separating you from competitors. The name of the game in most industries was simply beating the com-

petition. If you discovered an ounce of advantage, you strengthened it with a pound of proprietary skill or knowledge. Then you used it to support the defensive wall you were building against competitors.[51]

Ohmae went on to show that information technology has breached those walls. Rapid fluctuations in market demand, technical ability to quickly analyze and copy innovation, and continuous challenge with new ideas from smaller, more nimble companies make it a distinct liability to be a closed system devoted to the preservation of information monopoly.[52]

The ultimate result, in the words of Tom Peters, is that:

> Outsiders *must* become privy to virtually all of the firm's information — this includes suppliers, suppliers' suppliers, distributors, franchises and other middle persons, customers and customers' customers. So must *all* the people on the company's own payroll.[53]

Or, as I would say, everybody in the operations network.

Since knowledge comes chiefly from sharing, wisdom always favors cooperation over competition.

TECHNOLOGY HELPS AND HINDERS

So far I have said relatively little about the significance of the new information technology to partnering and networking. It is evident that it can help, for it enables us to partner with people all over the world, and to set up knowledge networks that can work in real time. As Percy Barnevik has said, the network that connects ABB's 5,000 profit centers would be impossible without computers and electronic communication. But, as it helps, information technology will also be a stumbling block.

Technology frequently outraces application, and it certainly is doing so today. Its glamour entices people to invest in it before they know what to do with it. In the 1980s, American business put computers on almost every office desk, spending billions of dollars on hardware, software and training. Yet, in 1989, *Newsweek* economist Robert J. Samuelson complained that, while "productivity in the manufacturing sector is rising at the fastest rates in decades,...productivity in the non-manufacturing sector (where white-collar workers are concentrated) has risen only 0.7 percent annually."[54]

The problem was that tools had changed but the systems had not. That was nine years ago and corporate managers are now beginning to see the computer's potential for systems innovation.

Such management myopia regarding the communication potential of information technology can be expected to continue. Currently, for instance, the Internet is, in almost everyone's mind, the supreme achievement of information technology. Yet, for almost everybody, Internet browsing is a total waste of time. It is like wandering through a junkyard. You may possibly stumble upon a treasure, but you will have to sift through incredible heaps of garbage before you find anything.

The Internet may be an information network, but it is not a knowledge network. The reason is that its content and form are by design not determined by a single operations network. Before ease of access opened the Internet up to nearly everybody with a modem in the past five years or so, it existed for over two decades mainly as a communications tool for scientists and academics. This mainstreaming of the Internet has made it even more decentralized. In 1969, the first four Internet servers went online at the University of California at Los Angeles, University of California at Santa Barbara, Stanford University and the University of Utah respectively. These networked computers were capable of sending and receiving a very primitive form of electronic mail, and little else. Today there are over 29 million servers in no fewer than 75 countries, most of which can effortlessly transmit pictures and sounds as well as words in a matter of milliseconds.

Parts of the Internet, such as bulletin board systems or special interest sites, approach knowledge networks in so far as they serve a group that has a special purpose, particularly when that purpose happens to be organized to work on a specific project. A growing number of companies, such as AT&T, Federal Express, 3M, Levi Strauss,[55] McGraw-Hill,[56] as well as virtually every firm in the information technology industry, are using Internet technology to facilitate intranets, or self-contained computer networks accessible only within the company. Many companies are also creating extranets, which enable customers and suppliers to transmit secure data, such as purchase orders, quotes or payment information, directly to the company through a web site. These intranets and extranets, created to make communication easier and more direct both to the company and within the company, are a first step toward creating something like a knowledge network.

CONTROLLING KNOWLEDGE NETWORKS

Because a knowledge network serves an operations network, there is a natural current that governs its flow. ABB's knowledge network may seem disorganized, with many bits of information that are of no practical use to its many users, but the knowledge it transmits is limited to the information-generated by the operations network. At the same time, there is no single mind or team in the operations network that controls the size and flow of the knowledge network. At ABB, senior executives spend much of their time coaching individuals on how to use the network. They help to keep the network's floodgates wide open. But they are not allowed to limit the flow or direct where it goes.

Information has to be plucked from the stream, analyzed and organized before it can be applied, but the only one who can do that is the ultimate user, the decision maker. Over the last 20 years I have been approached by at least a dozen publishers or prospective publishers with the idea of creating a newsletter that will screen the press and other sources of business reportage and opinion and *summarize all that is relevant* to the reader in a single weekly or biweekly publication.

Some of these "incredible executive timesavers" were published. None of them succeeded. The competent decision-maker cannot rely on someone else to control the information flow that helps him or her make decisions. Learning and deciding are as closely related as inhaling and breathing. An effective knowledge network has to bring necessary and useful information to every decision-maker in the entire operations network, supply all the information that might possibly be useful and provide it in the freeform mode that encourages creative thinking (remember brainstorming?).

In other words, knowledge networks have to be selective without selecting, controlled without controlling, limited without limiting. If that seems confusing, it is—which is why our move into the new era will take considerable time and involve many false starts and frustrating setbacks.

UNDERSTANDING THE FORMLESS FORM

I have said repeatedly that what holds a network together—both operations and knowledge networks—is purpose. Purpose also gives the network its form.

Business analysts have gone out of their way to describe the new management's lack of structure. Alvin Toffler speaks of checkerboard and pulsating organizations; Peter Drucker, an orchestra; Charles Savage, a jazz combo; Karl Weick, improvisational theater; Tom Peters, a carnival; Richard Crawford, adhocracy and the collapsible corporation. Most of these analyses make two mistakes. First, they are still viewing what is happening from the top. Second, they describe its "form" by contrasting it with the structure of traditional organizations. Thus an article in the Winter 1990 issue of *Sloan Management Review*[57] speaks of the "hollow corporation," a company that outsources almost all its operations. In *Liberation Management* Tom Peters commented:

> With so much outsourced, what's left of the firm? Answer: A lot. But something new. Company chiefs become "managers of intellectual systems," moving away from "functional" management and toward "coordination and conceptual" management. At Apple, which the authors label an "intellectual holding company," managers learn to focus their efforts on "dominating those services crucial to [their] strategy"—e.g., design and marketing.[58]

You can have a financial holding company because you can hold, supply or withdraw money, enabling the company to control other companies because it owns part of or all their tangible assets. But an intellectual holding company is an oxymoron. Ideas and knowledge cannot be controlled like money. Our laws allow corporations to own property, and money. Although our laws do authorize a certain limited ownership of ideas, which I shall discuss at length in Chapter 21, no law can authorize a company to have or own an intellect.

The difference lies in the distinction between ownership and leadership. Leaders can conceive ends, recognize means, inspire and teach cooperators, but they cannot own them or operate through them as a driver drives a car or a pianist plays a piano. At best leaders are coaches, never kings.

MAKING KNOWLEDGE NETWORKS EFFICIENT

We must not confuse either operations or knowledge networks with mechanical or electronic networks like telephone systems or the Internet. Since both operations and knowledge networks are made up of human beings, neither can be controlled mechanically or electronically. It is especially important to realize that knowledge networks are distinct from their facilitating electronic or mechanical networks.

The content and form of each knowledge network is determined by the needs and activities of its corresponding operations network. It may appear that one project is using the same information banks and human contacts as another, but that is never entirely true. No matter how similar the purpose of two operations networks may seem, time, place, externalities and people will make their knowledge needs unique.

Both operations and knowledge networks will be more or less efficient according to the way the humans involved adhere to or wander from the network's specified purpose. Detours or distractions in the performance of the network can come from weakness of will, as when an individual or team surrenders to the temptation to let an alien purpose interfere with the specified purpose. They can come from weakness of intellect, as when an individual or team does not realize the most efficient way to achieve their part of the purpose. And, of course, they can arise from externalities that interfere with the link's promise to perform.

It is easy to understand how operations networks are kept efficient. Each link is established with remuneration contingent on project fulfillment. The efficiency of a knowledge network, however, depends less on how it is set up than on how it is used, and that is controlled by the efficiency of the operations network. The more determined and intelligent the teams and individuals, the better they will use the knowledge network.

As we shall see in the next chapter, the problem with government—the biggest management project of all—is that its enormous resources for collecting and channeling information cannot be used as knowledge networks until operations networks replace the current bureaucracy.

Part Three

The Application of Partnership Networks To Social Structures

Part Two showed us how business is espousing partnership networks. Part Three describes how our more conservative social structures are being prepared for a new form of democracy, and governance by partnership networks. The following five chapters explore why bureaucratic government no longer works, how self-rule and individualism can be achieved without rupturing the social fabric, and the impact of a world of partnership networks on society's three basic concerns: governance, commonweal and education.

13

REDISCOVERING GOVERNMENT

"I am certainly not an advocate for frequent and untried changes in laws and constitutions . . . but I know also, that laws and institutions must go hand in hand with the progress of the human mind."
— *Thomas Jefferson*[1]

The public is revolting against the present government structure. To find a less burdensome, more efficient form of governance we must abandon four presumptions of bureaucratic government: (1) that social order requires centralized sovereignty, (2) that communities are defined by geography, (3) that government requires general taxation, (4) that laws can be used to engineer social reform. Only by distributing self-governing authority among communities of common interests can we achieve the kind of democratic governance required by the information age.

THE TROUBLED WORLD OF GOVERNMENT

We have seen how partnering and networks can enable the business world to survive the information deluge. Is there a similar solution for the troubled world of government? I believe there is, and it can reduce the chaos we now find in government—whether local, regional, national or the global government in exile we call the United Nations.

Today governments are almost exclusively bureaucracies. To my knowledge, the only exceptions are the governing arrangements of a few primitive tribes and small volunteer associations. *Merriam-Webster* defines government as "the act or process of governing; specifically: an authoritative direction or control." Can we have "authoritative direction or control" without bureaucracy, without hierarchy?

Democracy in its simplest form does not require hierarchy. Yet, to date, no one has figured out a way to govern anything bigger than a village or a Greek city state without bureaucracy. The most widely admired modern democratic system, that of the United States, solves the problem of making the hierarchy answerable to the people by representative government: the people elect representatives who are thereby authorized to rule. This authority, though limited in time and extent of jurisdiction, is truly transmitted. The citizenry has no way to directly exercise its authority once it is delegated, which may explain why so many citizens feel that their responsibility for government ends when the polls close. Allowing voters to approve or reject a proposition offers a very limited expansion of citizen authority, but hardly solves the problem.

The U.S. Constitution established a refinement of simple representative government called federalism. It grew out of the fact that the United States was formed when the 13 former British colonies agreed to surrender specified, and therefore limited, governing powers to a central government.

As we saw in Chapter 5, over the years the flow of information stretched the limits of these powers with new interpretations and applications. Sometimes the changes favored the federal government; at other times, the state governments. At the present time the pendulum is swinging toward the states. In 1936, a Gallup poll asked Americans whether they thought power should be concentrated in the federal government or in the states. The response was 56 percent for the federal government. In 1995 the response to the identical question was only 26 percent for the federal government.[2]

To the perpetual tug of war between Washington and the states add the cacophony of concerns released by the multiplication of information and it is easy to see why federal, state and even local governments had become incredibly more complex by 1998 than they were in 1787, and why self-government today may not operate as the founding fathers expected it to operate when they wrote the U.S. Constitution. In the words of William Ophuls,

> The idea of representative government assumes that both the voters and their chosen leaders can comprehend their world well enough to control it (and that it is actually amenable to control by

the latter). This assumption now lies shattered by the sheer size and scope of a complex, differentiated global civilization driven by market forces that annihilate borders and dominated by multinational corporations that foster a continuous technological and social revolution.[3]

Representative government, as understood by the Founding Fathers, compensated for the average voter's ignorance of government affairs by empowering him to delegate someone he knew and trusted to make his judgments for him. Representative government, as understood by today's politicians and the public, presumes that average voters have boundless time and ability not only to know and trust more local, state and federal representatives than they can ever meet, but also to influence the judgments of these numerous representatives after they are elected. Yet polls indicate that most Americans cannot name even one of their congressmen.[4] As social science educator Martin Tarcher put it in *Escape From Avarice:*

> Neither the means to the knowledge required for good citizenship nor the opportunity to use such knowledge in a democratic, responsible manner is available in our daily activities. We do not experience it in our schools, on the job, through the mass media, or in the political mechanism itself.[5]

APATHY IS A SYMPTOM, NOT THE CAUSE

It is *au courant* for Americans to criticize our democracy and the way it is run. The easiest and therefore most frequent criticism blames the politicians. But, since the public elects these politicians, more thoughtful critics blame public apathy.

A few critics see a conspiracy of the rich and powerful to distort our democratic system for their selfish ends. Noam Chomsky has made a career of describing a worldwide alliance of the rich against the poor and portraying our government on the wrong side.[6] Chomsky cries out against, but offers no solution for an unavoidable problem in democratic government.

No matter how democratic the government, there will always be leaders who believe (often with good reason) that they know better than the public. Since they usually are more able at attaining and using power, they are often successful in manipulating the structures of a democratic society to achieve their goals. Since self-interest inevitably colors thought and action, their way usually benefits them.

What should we do about these power manipulators? Echoing the 1955 complaint of Walter Lippmann, Canadian political scientist Anthony King[7] argues that the United States is too democratic. The desire of Americans to influence the decisions of their representatives forces those representatives to run scared, continually campaigning instead of governing. King wants citizens to leave their representatives alone once they are elected. *Economist* contributor Brian Beedham,[8] on the other hand, would restrict the power of elected representatives. He wants more referenda to give citizens the opportunity to vote on every major government decision.

The realistic vs. the ideal approach to social systems is one reason why Asian attitudes differ so much from those of the West. In *Looking at the Sun*, James Fallows observes, "The Western approach, most of all the American, views concentrated power as an evil; the Asian approach, most of all the Japanese, works with it as a natural phenomenon of society, like hierarchy and inequality."[9] Asians cannot see why completely free markets are ideal. (Neither can westerners, in reality, for there are none.) But our history has made us fearful of central authority and, since we have managed without absolute central authority for so long, we do not have the attitude of Asians who accept it as a way of life precisely because they have known no other. Today, for most Asians, central authority has become a symbol of holding on to tradition and morality, while we in the West see it as a threat to freedom.

The disagreement is an unfortunate distraction from the central problem: how to balance individual freedoms and community needs in a democratic society. Corporate greed and public apathy are not so much causes of government ineffectiveness as they are its results. We are trying to govern our society with a bureaucratic apparatus whose underpinnings have been swept away by the information deluge. Hence I agree totally with Alvin and Heidi Toffler that "over the months and decades ahead, the entire 'global law machine'—from the United Nations at one end to the local city or town council at the other—will eventually face a mounting, ultimately irresistible demand for restructuring."[10]

I also agree with Chomsky that the U.S. is a "defective democracy,"[11] with William Greider that there is "a systemic breakdown of the shared civic values we call democracy,"[12] with the Center for Communities of the Future that "American citizens across the country feel alienated from the decision making processes which impact their lives,"[13] with Beedham and the League

13. Rediscovering Government

of Women Voters that greater citizen participation is essential, and with the Tofflers that politics is divided between those committed to second-wave industrial civilization and those ready to move to new, third-wave civilization.[14] But I believe that these problems require solutions more specific than Chomsky's dismantling of wealth-perpetuating structures by grass-root and labor-union pressure, Greider's local popular control of political parties, the Center's Consensus Democracy, the League's Citizens' Juries,[15] or the Tofflers' Semidirect Democracy.[16]

This chapter analyzes the key concepts of bureaucratic government that have been voided by the information deluge. Chapters 14, 15 and 16 will describe a system of governing through partnering and networking, a system that requires major changes not only in the way we govern our society but also in the ways we think about government.

DISILLUSION WITH BUREAUCRATIC GOVERNMENT

On November 15, 1994, the Associated Press sent an interesting essay to its subscriber newspapers. Since the 1980s, the AP writer argued, there has been a significant increase in the number of Americans who question the benefits of big government and the way it intrudes on their lives. The cause of their questioning in 1980:

> Government was everywhere, and for all its benefits, everyone was tripping over it. A federal government that spent $1.7 billion in 1902 spent $942 billion in 1980. Per capita taxes that were $18 in 1902 were $3,286 in 1980. The number of federal employees numbered 3.2 million in 1929, but 17 million in 1980. There were positive impacts, on poverty, housing, equality, environment, safety, the workplace and much more, but increasingly, negative ones too: laws, regulations, mandates, rules and limitations on behavior. And waste. Doubts continued to rise about the benefits of activist government, with increasing references to the intentions of the founding fathers, and prominent among the citations were the words of James Madison, to wit: "I believe there are more instances of the abridgement of the freedom of the people by gradual and silent encroachments of those in power than by violent and sudden usurpation." According to many people, government was a burden on their back.[17]

Two weeks earlier, the Federal Reserve Board's Lawrence Lindsey told a bankers' housing conference that "the chief obstacle to economic development in distressed neighborhoods is often the government itself,... maybe we should try getting government out of the way of the private sector."[18]

Even America's state governors are tired of federal interference. In 1995, under the heading, "Release Us From Federal Nonsense," Massachusetts Governor William Weld told *Wall Street Journal* readers, "America is well on the road to block-granting welfare, Medicaid, and job training, and allowing the states to shape these programs to fit their own ends. And most of the nation's governors say a mighty hurrah."[19]

"Get government out of the way!" is a cry heard with increasing frequency in every advanced country of the world. In Canada public unrest occasioned a two-year study by senior government officials on how governing should change in today's society. The results were published in 1992 by the Canadian Institute on Research for Public Policy under the title, *Governing in an Information Society*. Among the study's findings:

> As society becomes more interconnected, complex and turbulent, more traditional ways of organizing and governing are being overwhelmed. In a more educated, interconnected, information-rich environment, government systems predicated on a limited flow of information, including both bureaucracy and representative democracy itself, lose their credibility and authority.[20]

There is no way to know if the 1992 study had anything to do with Canada's next election. But in 1993 balloting, the governing party, which held 153 seats in Parliament before the election, became a minority party with two seats.

IT WOULD BE FUNNY, IF IT WEREN'T SO SAD

At every level of our federalist system, government bureaucracy, erected nobly on a foundation of limited information, now leads to ludicrous law.

- Antipollution regulations obliged companies like Amoco Oil to spend millions ($31 million in Amoco's case) to capture minuscule amounts of benzene at their smokestacks while large amounts of benzene escaped at their loading docks.[21]

13. Rediscovering Government

- The tax code gave tax credits and exemptions to companies producing ethanol, when there was only one important company that qualified (Archer Daniels Midland, coincidentally a major contributor to congressional campaigns).[22]
- The Federal Highway Administration had to cancel a highway desperately needed by the Choctaw Indians because an endangered species of beetle lived on the right of way.[23]
- Of the $30 billion the federal Superfund law spent over 13 years to assign liability for cleaning up toxic wastes and spills almost $10 billion went to lawyers, while less than $10 billion was spent on actually cleaning up.[24]
- State and city ordinances required removal of lead paint to protect children even when the removal process did more harm than the paint.[25]
- An executive who spends a day presenting his company's interests before the New York City Council must register with the City Clerk as a lobbyist and issue a quarterly report if he earns more than $2,000 that day.[26]
- In Kansas City a federal agency ordered a bank to put a Braille keypad on a drive-through cash machine.[27]

If you wonder precisely how the information deluge distorts the legislative process, consider the 293-page 1991 Intermodal Surface Transportation Efficiency Act, which replaced the 28-page 1956 Federal Aid Highway Act. In addition to building highways and aiding mass transit, the new law mandated:

> that the secretary of transportation relieve congestion, improve air quality, preserve historic sites, encourage the use of auto seat belts and motorcycle helmets, control erosion and storm water runoff, monitor traffic and collect data on speeding, reduce drunk driving, require environmental impact studies, control outdoor advertising, develop standards for high-occupancy vehicles, require metropolitan area and statewide planning, use recycled rubber in making asphalt, set aside ten percent of construction monies for small businesses owned by disadvantaged individuals, define women as disadvantaged individuals, buy iron and steel from U.S. suppliers, establish new rules for renting equipment, give preferential employment to Native Americans if a highway is to be built

near a reservation, and control the use of calcium magnesium acetate in performing seismic retrofits for bridges.

To this *partial* list of objectives Congress added extensive criteria to be used in planning. Transportation plans should be designed to relieve congestion and preserve existing facilities, be based on life-cycle costs, evaluate impacts on land use, encourage bicycle paths and pedestrian walkways, control water and air pollution, and take into account "all" social and economic effects. In addition, the law designates scores of specific projects—bridges, tunnels, roads, studies, experiments—that must be funded in specific states or cities or through specific organizations.[28]

The above description comes from *Deregulating the Public Service* and its author, James Q. Wilson, concludes by saying,

> There was, of course, nothing in the act suggesting how the secretary ought to weigh these competing goals and constraints or manage the inevitable tradeoffs among them, nor any indication how anyone other than God might foresee "all" the social and economic effects of a transportation plan.[29]

Our presidents have recognized that something is wrong, but seem to have no idea what should be done about it. Hence the procession of futile gestures: President Eisenhower's Goals for Americans,[30] President Johnson's Planning-Programming-Budgeting-System,[31] President Nixon's National Goals Research Staff,[32] President Reagan's New Federalism,[33] and most recently President Clinton's National Performance Review[34] followed by his ricochet from wanting the federal government to adopt his health plan to surrendering responsibility for welfare to the states.

1. THE DEATH OF CENTRAL SOVEREIGNTY

In a 1996 interview, former Citibank chief executive Walter Wriston said, "The nation-state is not about to disappear. But the old concept of sovereignty, as governmental acts that cannot be reviewed by any other authority, is no longer valid." He based his conclusion on the spread of information through modern technology whereby television and other news sources acted "as a global plebiscite conducted on the behavior of nations."[35]

INABILITY TO KEEP UP

What really killed central sovereignty was the inability of government to keep up with the flood of information. The systems used by today's government were created to manage knowledge long before information had reached its present flood level. Today, as Richard B. McKenzie and Dwight R. Lee conclude in *Quicksilver Capital*, "Government leaders *cannot* know all that their constituents know and, therefore, *cannot* know all that they need to know in order to manage their societies—from the center." Their conclusion: "Today the economic and political decision-making locus must, as never before, reside with individuals."[36]

I contend that governing bureaucracies cannot work because their structure assumes that there is someone at the top—secretary general, prime minister, president, governor, mayor, city manager, borough president—who has sufficient grasp of the knowledge necessary to be the final authority in running his or her community. If, as mentioned in Chapter 1, 90 percent of our legislators in Washington cannot read 90 percent of the bills they pass, one has to wonder how the President of the United States finds time to read the bills he signs. In *Birth of a New World*, Harlan Cleveland wrote:

> The evidence is now overwhelming that every national government is beyond its depth. This is certainly true of the industrial democracies plagued by inflation, unemployment, pollution, urban congestion, insecurity, drug addiction, and youthful crime. It was fatally true of the Soviet system, unable to feed its people and afraid to let them escape. It is true of the "China model," whose leaders used to speak openly about "ten lost years" of cultural revolution and political infighting, and after the Tiananmen crackdown opted to lose more years in fear of that explosive mix, young people and education. It is also true in most developing nations, unable to meet basic human needs or avoid the worst mistakes of the early Industrial Revolution.
>
> Political leaders keep up a brave front, but their incapacity for decision making becomes more and more visible.[37]

DECISION DIVISION

Recognizing the same problem in their 1995 book, *Creating a New Civilization*, Alvin and Heidi Toffler proposed what they call "decision division":

> To cure today's decision logjam, resulting from institutional overload, we need to divide up the decisions and reallocate them—sharing them more widely and switching the site of decision-making as the problems themselves require.
>
> Today's political arrangements violate this principle wildly. The problems have shifted, but the decision power hasn't. Thus, too many decisions are still concentrated, and the institutional architecture is most elaborate at the national level. By contrast, not enough decisions are being made at the transnational level, and the structures needed there are radically underdeveloped. In addition, too few decisions are left for the subnational level—regions, states, provinces and localities, or non-geographical social groupings.[38]

Unfortunately the book carefully avoids describing how such a system might work. Although I shall be less cautious in Chapter 14, all I want to do here is make the point that whatever solution the future will bring, it has to get rid of the idea that real government requires an ultimate centralized authority with direct or indirect sovereign jurisdiction over everything.

The information deluge has forced us to realize that authority, because it requires knowledge, must be distributed according to expertise. Each community should have the right and duty to govern itself.

2. THE FUTILITY OF TERRITORIAL GOVERNMENT

But what is a community? Can we identify it with civil society? In *The Coming of Post-Industrial Society*, Daniel Bell defines "a particular society" as "a territorial unit bound by a common past and ethos, and organized in a political sovereignty."[39] *Merriam-Webster* defines society as "a community, or nation, or broad grouping of people having common traditions, institutions and collective activities and interests." Both Bell and the dictionary, however, tend to use the word more broadly than they define it. Certainly Bell does not expect his entire post-industrial society to be organized in a single political sovereignty. And, if the United States is a distinct society, how much room does the melting pot or rainbow coalition leave for a common past and ethos?

GEOGRAPHIC COMMUNITIES ARE OBSOLETE

In 1888, the German sociologist Ferdinand Toennies distinguished between communities and societies. The first, he said, were organic institutions decided by fate; the second were structured institutions under social control. Peter Drucker[40] points out that neither Toennies nor his contemporaries spoke of organizations, institutions that you do not join by fate and are not by definition under social control. Yet, as Drucker concludes, modern society is made up of organizations, institutions defined not by territory but by purpose,[41] and "the knowledge society is a society of organizations in which practically every single social task is being performed in and through an organization."[42]

If almost all society's tasks are being performed by organizations that are not bound by geography, and if global concerns are meshing more and more with national, regional and local concerns, geographic boundaries have become irrelevant to governing. Consider some well-known facts:

- Washington D.C., less than 10 square miles by order of the U.S. Constitution, is the political center of our country, swarming during working hours with government elite. But the majority of its 578,000 full-time residents are slum dwellers whose elected mayor did time for drug possession.[43]

- New York City is America's major business center, where a large number of very influential people exercise power and make their livings. Much of what they do depends on how the city is run, and their salaries are taxed to help support the city. But most of them cannot vote in New York City, for their homes are outside city borders.

- There are some 83,000 state, county, city and other government subdivisions in the United States[44] and most of them have overlapping federal, state and local programs. (In Kansas, for example, there are at least seven state and federal agencies running rural-area loan programs.[45]) So difficult is it to decide which agency to deal with that citizens and local officials hire experts to help them.

- More and more city, county and state governments are forming alliances that cross government jurisdictions to solve social and economic problems. The Port Authority of New York and New Jersey, the Third Regional Plan for the New York-New Jersey-Connecticut Metropolitan Area,[46] the Economic Development Council of Northeastern Pennsylvania, the Appalachian Regional Commission, and the Illinois-Indiana Crescent Corridor Project[47] are a few examples.

POROUS BORDERS

Now consider the increasingly porous borders of sovereign nation states. According to Jonas Widgren, head of the International Center for Migration Policy Development, an estimated 300,000 illegal immigrants from Eastern Europe, Africa and Asia were smuggled into Western Europe in 1995.[48] Germany, already harboring 3 million immigrants and refugees,[49] is so worried about illegal immigration that it gave $72 million to Poland to improve border security[50] and $142 million to Vietnam to repatriate some 40,000 Vietnamese deported for smuggling cigarettes into Germany.[51]

Although the United States granted amnesty to 2.7 million illegal aliens in 1986, by 1996 Congress found it necessary to double its 2,500 Border Patrol guards and added 9,000 new detention cells for intercepted border violators.[52] The federal government is having as much difficulty keeping jobs and money from leaving the country as it has keeping unwanted drugs and immigrants out of the country. As McKenzie and Lee explained in *Quicksilver Capital*, there are now entirely new ways to violate U.S. borders without swimming the Rio Grande:

> Workers from around the world can immigrate to this country via modern electronics. We noted that New York Life now has its insurance claims sent to a post office box at Kennedy Airport and then ships the claims by overnight courier to Ireland, where they are keyed into a computer and then, before the day is over, transmitted back to the States via satellite. In effect, the Irish workers have gotten American work permits without becoming citizens or landing on our shores.[53]

All over the world national governments, like provinces, states and cities, are acknowledging that there are projects they cannot handle within their borders, whether ad hoc like the SST, the London-Paris Chunnel and the World Ministerial Conference on Organized Crime,[54] or long-lasting like NATO and the EU in Europe, NAFTA in North America and Mercosur in South America,[55] or as basic as economic regulation for, to quote Lester Thurow, "a global economy gives rise to a world in which extranational geoeconomic forces dictate national economic policies."[56]

CITISTATES

In his 1993 book, *Citistates: How Urban America Can Succeed in a Competitive World*, urban affairs expert Neal Peirce presents a convincing case that large metropolitan regions have already replaced nation states as the key competitors in the global marketplace. This may sound like an argument for a new kind of territorial government. But Peirce himself writes,

> There is little to gain in trying to draw borders around a citistate. Dallas analyst James Crupi suggests the entire state of Georgia should be seen as the hinterland of the Atlanta citi-state, with Savannah as its port. Seventy percent of the investment in Guangzhou Province in the People's Republic of China comes from adjacent Hong Kong. Tijuana, although in Mexico, clearly falls under the orbit of the San Diego citistate, divided only by one of the world's busiest international crossing points.[57]

Peirce does not explain why San Diego does not fall under the orbit of Los Angeles or why we should not look at Savannah as a mini-citistate within the orbit of Atlanta or, for that matter, why Atlanta is not in the orbit of Washington, D.C. The reason, I think, is that all these things can be true at once, for every area is made up of interwoven communities of interest. This may be why he does not propose a metropolitan supergovernment to oversee or replace the government of each central city, but concludes that...

> in today's world, the challenge may not be so much to consolidate government or create new formal structures (though some surely are required) than to search for pragmatic arrangements, find ways to resolve conflicts, look toward a regional vision and capacity.[58]

Though politicians and statisticians still discuss, report on and compile data on their nations' economies, there are few, if any, national economies independent of the global economy. Peirce not only agrees, but emphasizes that the economy of each citistate is dependent on other citistates throughout the world. The question is whether a nation, or a citistate, without an independent economy, is truly an autonomous community.

My answer is that, like the economies, communities have also lost their independence and are taking on a new global character. Of course, this does not happen all at once. Just as many islands of economic segregation remain amidst the global economy, so islands of segregated community remain in the global community.

Just as the macro-economy is formed by all the interactive micro-economies, so the macro-community is formed by all the interrelated micro-communities. In economies, money is the binding factor; in communities, the binding factor is communication or, more accurately, the sharing of common concerns.

Determining jurisdiction entirely by region or locality worked beautifully so long as almost all significant social units and primary public concerns were confined by and, therefore, defined by territory. That is how the composers of the Constitution saw their new country, and why the U.S. federal system is based on geography, with units of jurisdiction traceable on a map.

But the world does not work that way anymore.

A NEW KIND OF COMMUNITY

Most of the dictionary definitions of community include a territorial element: "living in a particular area," "living together," "in a common location." All the definitions include common interest, for even the basic definition, "a unified body of individuals," implies more than a number of individuals unified by force or accident. The castaways on Gilligan's Island did not become a community (and the premise for a situation comedy) until they began to share common concerns.

Sharing physical geography almost always generates some common concerns. Hence geography is a very frequent basis for community. But geography is not enough, otherwise we would not have the modern urban phenomenon of community-less neighborhoods, where people can live on the same street, or even in the same building, without knowing or caring about each other.

In *The Great Good Place*, Ray Oldenburg insists that we cannot "create a satisfactory community apart from geography."[59] But, to me at least, he is defying reality. There are too many groups whose satisfactory communities have nothing to do with geography: e.g., the Jewish and Chinese diasporas, Apple Computer employees (at least in the early days), the U.S. Marines, the Jehovah's Witnesses, the Boy Scouts, and the World Future Society.

As I shall discuss at length in the next chapter, it is the community of shared concerns, not the community of shared territory, that must become the foundation for democratic government.

3. THE TRAGEDY OF THE FINANCIAL COMMONS

In 1968, the magazine *Science* published Garrett Hardin's "The Tragedy of the Commons."[60] Hardin used the example of the ancient custom of setting aside common land where all villagers could graze their cattle. Since there was no restriction on the number of cattle one could graze, every villager did his best to get as much use of the commons as possible. The result was that soon there was no grass left and everybody had to look elsewhere to feed their cattle. It is a mistake, Hardin concluded, to assume that decisions reached individually will always be in the best interests of an entire society.

THE TAX-POOL GRAB BAG

Hardin was discussing population control. But, with even greater validity, we can apply his tragedy-of-the-commons lesson to the practice of general taxation. So long as government has the right to collect taxes for a general fund every citizen will try to get as large a share as possible of the benefits from that money, and eventually any government that has an obligation to obey the will of its citizens will be immobilized between their natural desire for more benefits and services and their natural reluctance to pay more taxes.

America's tax laws supposedly ask more from the rich than the poor, but the fact that some citizens put more money into the pool does not make them less anxious to get more out of the pool. The U.S. system may be more equitable than that of many other countries. But the problem of the financial commons lies less in its inequities than in how it adds to what I described in Chapter 5,[61] and what Jonathan Rauch calls *Demosclerosis, the Silent Killer of American Government.*

GOVERNMENT BY PROGRAM

In *Reinventing Government*, David Osborne and Ted Gaebler list eight reasons why government by program does not work:[62]

1. Programs are driven by constituencies, not customers.
2. Programs are driven by politics, not policy.
3. Programs create "turf," which public agencies then defend at all costs.
4. Programs tend to create fragmented service delivery systems.
5. Programs are not self-correcting.

6. Programs rarely die.

7. Programs rarely achieve the scale necessary to make significant impact.

8. Programs normally use commands, not incentives.

The kind of programs Osborne and Gaebler are talking about are "administrative mechanisms: monopolistic organizations, normally of public employees, that spend appropriated money to deliver a service." "Appropriated money" is the key. It explains the constituencies, the politics, the turf, and the reason programs never die. Every pipeline inserted into the government funding pool is supported by a host of constituents and public employees whose primary interest is not to correct the program or perfect delivery systems but to keep the pipeline open—or, even better, to prove it must be opened wider before the program can "make significant impact."

In 1995, the Progressive Policy Institute's Robert Shapiro drew up a list of what he considered unnecessary federal government subsidies. The total for that year came to $265 billion equally divided between direct handouts and tax exemptions.[63] The two broadest pipelines into the U.S. Treasury are (1) the Reconstruction Finance Corporation, which has been borrowing money from the Treasury since 1932 to fund programs without the need for a congressional appropriation, and (2) "appropriated entitlements,"[64] which also work without specific appropriations and have become the preferred mechanism for giving congressional committees direct access to the general fund. Major entitlement programs dispensed close to $729 billion in 1992 and by 2002 the Congressional Budget Office estimates that figure will be $1.9 trillion.

LOCAL GOVERNMENT TOO

In *The Postmodern Organization*, William Bergquist provides a revealing example of how the financial commons works in local government:

> The cost of services in large cities is a result of an increasingly large proportion of the city's budget being devoted to indirect services and a decreasing proportion of the city's budget being allocated to direct services. Some of the indirect services support the direct services provided (such as the role of dispatchers in a fire department, transportation system, or emergency road service). However, a considerable amount of the indirect services are integrative functions that do nothing more (or less) than hold the

13. Rediscovering Government

organization together (such as accounting, management, interagency communication). A diminishing percentage of the total services relates directly to the mission of the department (for example, policing the streets, fighting fires, or driving buses).[65]

It has become an American tradition for presidential and congressional candidates to promise to cut taxes, balance the budget, and defend the inviolability of Social Security and Medicare. Yet even the most naïve voters no longer believe this can be done, which is why there is so much disillusionment in U.S. politics, and so little faith in politicians. As *Megatrends* author John Naisbitt put it, "The new political leader has not as yet been definitively described, but the old main-frame head of state is obsolete. The voters intuitively know what the pollsters and pundits are only beginning to grasp."[66]

WHAT ABOUT "INDIVISBLE BENEFITS"?

Sociologists and economists have argued at length on how government can have the right to *oblige* citizens to pay taxes and still be subject to the will of its citizens. The debate circles not around whether governments can and do impose taxes, but whether there are some benefits required by society that can only be filled by general taxation. Paul Samuelson, undoubtedly the most influential U.S. economist, argued that certain benefits are indivisible, i.e., they have to be available to everyone and without compulsory taxation some people will not pay their share.[67] Others argue that purely indivisible benefits are an abstraction, never realizable in practice.[68]

Whatever side is taken, the fact remains that there is no benefit, divisible or indivisible that cannot be provided without general taxation. The problem with the tax commons is not that taxation is compulsory but that money is collected for unspecified needs rather than specific purposes.

As we have decided to eliminate universal sovereignty and government by geography, so we must get rid of the tax-pool commons. In its place we must adopt a system whereby authorizing a benefit or service always generates a specific tax to cover its costs. Is it possible to govern a community under such a restriction? I think it is, and in Chapters 14 and 15 I shall show why and how it can be done. Nor shall I ignore the plight of the unfortunate citizens who need government help but cannot pay, who are the subject of Chapter 16.

4. THE LIABILITY OF MULTIPLE-PURPOSE LAW

If we eliminate centralized sovereignty, territorial government and general taxation, how can government run programs to solve the problems of society? It cannot. And maybe that is a good thing. Remember professor James Q. Wilson's quote in Chapter 5?[69] Legislation aimed at solving social or economic problems seldom works. It too frequently encourages unrealistic expectations that lead to disillusionment and disrespect for government.

PROGRAM OVERLOAD

The U.S. government has become overloaded with programs. John Herbers, correspondent for the *New York Times* and an expert on government, described the situation in 1996:

> At one time there were 492 federal programs covering everything from fire control to the resolution of individual disputes. Members of Congress perpetuated their careers through big campaign contributions from corporate and private interests who were given administrative control of some programs. The public did not know whom to hold responsible for what.
>
> Congress lost further credibility by piling up mandates on the states to partially fund programs that Congress originated, whether or not the states had the funds to fully finance them. Congress last year finally enacted legislation to curb unfunded mandates, but it is too early to tell whether that will be effective or disastrous.[70]

The principal problem with most socially oriented legislation is that it is almost always dual purpose. As any competent manager knows, there is a much better chance of people messing up if you give them two assignments rather than one. This is especially true when the primary directive is aimed at a clear-cut result while the goal of the secondary directive is difficult to measure.

It is easy to envision a conflict of goals when a small town sets up a speed trap because it needs more income. It is less obvious when federal or state governments raise a tax to discourage smoking, use tax exemption to help charitable and religious organizations, revise the administration of government contracts to assist minority businesses, construct public works to provide employment, change public-education standards to help the disadvantaged or impose trade restrictions to advance human rights.

13. Rediscovering Government 267

All these social goals are exemplary. But are we using the best method to advance them by coupling them with other governing objectives? How much of the cigarette tax is motivated by health worries and how much by income need? Would direct grants to charitable and religious organizations be more honest and easier to regulate than tax exemptions? Does preference for minority businesses undermine cost control of public works? Would retraining help the unemployed more and avoid burdening the community with long-range costs? Is the education of a majority of children being hurt to help a minority? Do trade restrictions damage American business while they are little more than political gestures in advancing human rights?

I do not have the final answers to these questions. But they are legitimate questions and sufficient reason to doubt the efficacy of a system that devotes so great a proportion of society's resources to these problems with so few successful solutions—which is why I believe that the idea that social reform is a duty of government is misleading, even dangerous.

AUTHORITY IS INFINITELY DIVISIBLE

One thing federalism has taught us is that government is divisible. The city, state and federal governments can each have their own lawmakers and law enforcers. They can even share responsibility for maintaining streets and highways. If this is possible, why not divide authority even further?

In fact. we are already doing that. We may not call them separate governments but there are numerous groups within our society governing themselves. Manufacturers adhere to requirements for the Universal Product Code and administer the system through the Uniform Code Council. Members of the Direct Marketing Association obey the decision to remove names of people who so request from their mailing lists. Physicians regulate standards for their profession and suspend doctors who violate them. Condominiums have boards of directors, screen new owners, authorize expenditures and draw up regulations. Trade unions have elected officials and rules. The American Association of Advertising Agencies has a president. The major baseball leagues have a commissioner. In fact, every organization in America, and there are tens of thousands, can be considered a community with a more or less democratic government.

A parallel development is taking place internationally. One thinks first of the United Nations, UNESCO and the World Court. But there are numerous governance bodies formed by cooperating nations: the Universal Postal Union, International Civil Aviation Organization, International Telecommunications Union, the World Bank, the Law of the Sea, the Ozone Treaty, and the Antarctic Treaty. In increasing numbers there are groups created by private initiative such as the World Meteorological Organization's World Weather Watch, the World Health Organization and the International Rice Institute.

On another front management guru Peter Drucker argues that the tremendous growth in a third sector of society—the nonprofit sector—is taking over many of the duties once considered the province of government, particularly in the areas of education, health and welfare.[71] I shall go further and say that I expect the distinctions separating public sector, private sector and nonprofit sector to fade away as individual groups take over more and more of the responsibility for governing themselves.

AUTHORITY MUST FOLLOW KNOWLEDGE

The problems caused by the information deluge can be solved only by returning responsibility to those with the knowledge needed to exercise it. We can no longer depend on educating administrators and legislators after they have been elected—no matter how long the hearings, how large the staffs and how many the lobbyists. We have to give the authority to those who already have the knowledge.

Since knowledge has become so extensive and the areas of knowledge are so splintered, authority too must be splintered according to interest groups, what Harlan Cleveland calls communities of the concerned.

In discussing this idea with colleagues, the most common objection is that to give an interest group authority over itself is to put the fox in charge of the chicken coop. This objection vanishes if you presume that the chickens have as much control over the fox as the fox has over the chickens. Consensus of the concerned has to give an equal vote to everybody concerned.

Community or industry self-regulation, which has grown over the years especially in the advertising, entertainment, appliance and food businesses, is usually initiated as a defense device: to keep government and other forces that "do not understand the business" from imposing rules that can damage an industry's interests. But that does not make these "policing" institutions less

13. Rediscovering Government

legitimate or less effective. Most organizations want to protect themselves from bad apples within and public outrage without.

There are good reasons to think that most self-regulation would be more effective if it were less defensive and not trying to keep just once step ahead of government regulation. The more responsibility one expects of people, the more responsibility they assume. I am willing to wager that the National Rifle Association's battle against any type of gun control would take on an entirely different complexion if they had the total responsibility to regulate the sale and ownership of guns. (I am not saying this is a good idea, though. Even without accepting members among concerned citizens who do not own guns, the NRA has too large a membership to be operated as a true democracy.)

In *The Twenty-First Century Organization*, Guy Benveniste advocated what he called "internalizing regulatory practice"[72] on the grounds that professional and business groups can do the job of regulation at less cost and with more effectiveness than a government agency since their knowledge or expertise on what they are doing has to be far superior.

The central problem of governance is similar to the problem of keeping order in a classroom. The choice is between imposing order through constant vigilance and exercise of authority or by allowing the students to assume responsibility for classroom order. There can be only one reason for considering the second way impractical, and that is a lack of faith in the students.

We cannot believe in democracy and lack faith in people's ability for self-rule at the same time.

How self-government by communities of the concerned may work will be explained at length in the following chapters. Here I just ask the reader to accept the possibility that a group of people with a common interest can govern their relationships in regards to that interest without a superior authority breathing down their necks.

14

RESTORING THE SUPREMACY OF THE INDIVIDUAL

"The hand that directs the social machine is invisible. Nevertheless ... all communities are obliged to secure their existence by submitting to a certain amount of authority, without which they fall into anarchy."
— *Alexis de Tocqueville, 1835*[1]

Amicable agreement is a more useful governing technique than majority rule, for it applies to governance the organic organization we have already applied to business. The objective is to develop regulation without dominion, to take power away from institutions and restore it to individuals. Partnership networks can do everything government does while limiting objectives, costs and authority.

AMICABLE AGREEMENT VERSUS MAJORITY RULE

In 1974, under the title *Amicable Agreement versus Majority Rule*, the University of North Carolina Press published a translation of a treatise by Jurg Steiner, a young German scholar who had devoted several years to studying the governing structure of Switzerland. Steiner was not the first sociologist to wonder why Switzerland works. With few natural resources except water and a population divided into no fewer than three ethnic groups, four languages and several religions, Switzerland has managed for more than a hundred years to avoid civil and foreign wars, and give its people a democratic government and a prosperous existence.

14. Restoring the Supremacy of the Individual

Steiner's study was aimed at discovering why the natural hostility between subcultures does not tear Switzerland apart. He quoted an earlier scholar's observation that "political stability can be maintained in culturally fragmented systems if the leaders of the subcultures engage in co-operative efforts to counteract the centrifugal tendencies of cultural fragmentation,"[2] and wanted to find out precisely why Switzerland's leaders succeed in their cooperative efforts. Borrowing the term "amicable agreement" from Gerhard Lehmbruch, Steiner wrote:

> I conceptualize amicable agreement as one of the two basic models of democratic decision-making, the other model being *majority rule*. In the Anglo-American tradition the *majoritarian model* is often considered the only democratic one....
>
> In the majoritarian model there is no concern for enlarging the agreement beyond the number required to win. Whenever a majority is reached, a vote is taken and the majority position wins. In the model of amicable agreement discussion goes on until a solution is found that is acceptable to all participants in the decision-making process. If a vote is taken, the purpose is only to ratify a commonly accepted decision. Amicable agreement corresponds in many ways to the method of palaver traditionally used by African tribes. The two types of decision-making patterns—majority rule and amicable agreement—should be considered as the two extreme points in a continuum.[3]

Note three significant points.

First, majority rule and amicable agreement are both methods for arriving at democratic decisions.

Second, the two methods do not exclude each other; they are extremes on a continuum, which means they can be combined in various degrees.

Third, Steiner saw amicable agreement as similar to the governing method used by African tribes, people who lived by a gift economy. Palaver, incidentally, was also the decision-making method used by American Indians, and I shall hazard a guess that it has always been the primary governing tool in gift economies. Interestingly, business discovered the power of palaver when learning how to manage teams. Charles Garfield explains:

> Smart teams focus not on achieving consensus but on what the Japanese call "harmonies of difference." They reconcile the diverse

opinions of group members and integrate them into a *common solution* that, most often, was not the original position of any individual or subgroup.[4]

My brief summary does not do justice to Steiner's book or the research that preceded it. But his thesis helps us understand how communities of interests can form networks of democratic governance. Steiner concluded, "In a political system with strong subcultural segmentation, the more often political decisions are made by amicable agreement, the more probable is a low level of intersubcultural hostility."[5]

THE SECRET IS SCRAMBLED ALLEGIANCES

But why do the Swiss so readily take to amicable agreement instead of settling their disagreements by majority vote? A principal reason Steiner discovered is that there were so many voluntary associations in Switzerland which cut across party, religious, and language groups. Thus average citizens had important allegiances not only to their political parties but also to a number of other organizations, whether ethnic group, church or synagogue, union, employer, business, canton, cause association or social club.

According to Steiner's report the Swiss are great joiners and have a large number of gymnastic, sports, motoring, travel and other special-interest societies. These clubs not only have a bearing on political attitudes but even make suggestions on how their members should vote. (In the 1967 election for the National Council, for example, the Sports Fishing Club of Berne recommended two Social Democrats, two candidates from the Swiss People's party, one Free Democrat and one Independent.[6])

At the time of Steiner's study there were 13 interparty groups in the federal parliament, ranging from the Group for Commerce and Industry and the Group of Artisans to the Group for Inland Navigation and the Group for Sports. He found that there was a very low level of party discipline in Parliament, because individuals members too often sympathized with nonparty groups.

This Swiss phenomenon occasioned Franz Lehner's 1983 critique of Mancur Olson's theory that stable governments stagnate because stability enables special-interest groups to form and fight against change. (See Chapter 5.[7]) Lehner points out that Switzerland's stability did not prevent growth, though it may have moderated it. He explains that in Switzerland...

14. Restoring the Supremacy of the Individual 273

both interest groups and parties are generally fragmented along cantonal borders and have strong cantonal sections with often heterogeneous interests. This fragmentation is often enforced by the cultural diversity of Switzerland.[8]

The more tangled a citizen's allegiances, the more likely that he or she cannot attack an opposing group without offending members of that group who are allies in other groups. Steiner concluded that "the crosscutting of political parties with other groups seems to keep the parties from differing strongly in their demands on the political system."[9] The more our concerns are interwoven, the more likely we are to prefer the careful patchwork of amicable agreement to a majority vote that might permanently rend the social fabric by which we live.

NETWORKS AS COMMUNITIES

In Chapter 13, I pointed out that, as soon as two or more people share a concern they become a community. They have a common interest and therefore a common allegiance in relation to that particular concern. By that defintion every partnership and every operations network is a community, for such communities share a common concern, the purpose that defines the partnership or network.

An operations network is a form of government. The purpose of the network sets off a pattern of engagement, cost and remuneration analagous to the citizenship, taxation and entitlements of traditional government. The network does everything a government does, but *only as it pertains to its purpose.*

All operations networks are democratic organizations. They are by their nature self-governing. Each link in the network participates voluntarily and controls the nature and extent of its participation. The result is a self-governing community so highly focused by its purpose that its power is extremely limited—even over the individuals that belong to that community, for it regulates them only in so far as they voluntarily participate in the purpose of the community and only with regards to activities that contribute to achieving that purpose.

ORGANIC GOVERNANCE

Note the difference between the exercise of democracy in a network compared with the the way democracy is exercised in representative government.

The network is organic: infinitely flexible, with complete internal control on every level. Each link in the network operates like a cell in the body. Representative government is mechanical: the individual's power is fixed and limited to a vote that culminates one chain reaction and sets off a second. The individual operates like a molecule of gasoline in a combustion engine.

Since humans have many concerns, they are always members of many different communities. As Harlan Cleveland observed in 1994,[10] the outward push of modern science and technology has widened our concerns and made us realize that we are members of a world community, adding to the multitude of communities in which every human being has always been involved: neighborhood, country; school, work, family, tribe, religion; shopping, finances, investment; self-improvement, health care, recreation, etc.

Because you and I have a multitude of concerns, we are constantly initiating operations networks. Since each network pursues a different concern, these networks can interfere with each other. If we are prudent, we learn to coordinate our various personal networks to minimize conflict and maximize coordination. I regulate my work so that it will provide both the means and the time for entertainment. If so complex a procedure can be managed by individuals, it should be manageable by society.

In marriage, the simplest and most fundamental society, a man and woman form a partnership to pursue life's goals together. The partnership has a multitude of concerns. It will be a successful and happy marriage if husband and wife learn how to balance and integrate the partnership concerns with their personal concerns. The partnership initiates many operations networks to achieve the many intermediate goals involved including earning a living, furnishing a home, raising children, and providing for retirement. Each of these networks creates a community of contributing individuals: fellow workers, sales people, doctors, teachers, bankers, brokers, etc. Depending on their purpose, some of these networks are short-lived; some involve very few people. Others are long-lived, or may involve hundreds of people.

Each of the many people in these networks is living his or her own life and is, therefore, initiating an incredible number of individual networks to achieve personal goals, partnership goals or network goals. This interweaving of zillions of operations networks creates the fabric of society, "in which," to use the words of Alvin and Heidi Toffler, "thousands of minorities, many of them temporary, swirl and form highly novel, transient patterns, seldom coalescing into a consensus on major issues."[11]

NEGOTIATION VS. FORCE

As we saw in Chapter 6,[12] according to Adam Smith one of the primary purposes of government is to protect individuals from injustice or oppression in their relations with other individuals. When one of my networks interferes with one of your networks there has to be some form of arbitration. You and I can negotiate and resolve the conflict together. Or we can ask government to interfere and use its authority to settle our dispute.

Clearly it is better to solve such difficulties ourselves. Outside interference is a last resort. My conclusion and the underlying conclusion of Steiner's book is that the more extensive the interrelation of our personal networks, the more disposed we are to settle disputes by palaver rather than by force. (I use the word force deliberately. Primitive societies depend on physical force as the last resort in settling disagreements. More advanced societies use legal force. But it is always force. Losers have to submit whether they want to or not.)

Since only one car was available and my wife had to go to the doctor while I had to go to the dentist, we could have had a hell of a fight. Instead we worked out a compromise where I drove her to the doctor on the way to the dentist and picked her up on my way home. Since we both had networks aimed at making each other happy, keeping peace in the family and economizing on gasoline, it was easy to avoid a fight by coordinating our networks.

One of the effects of the information deluge is that everyone has become more aware of the interdependence of their interests. Before humans had any knowledge of society it was easy for one primitive Neanderthal to kill another Neanderthal standing in the way of his meal. He did not know enough to worry that his opponent's cavemates might seek revenge or that he might need his opponent to help fortify his cave. But as society developed, the caveman became more aware of these more remote goals and that awareness made him less likely to kill and more likely to compromise.

I believe that society has become such a tangle of interests and so aware of that tangle that in the great majority of cases self-interest leads people to prefer compromise over conflict. The spread of knowledge creates a new invisible hand, persuading people to govern themselves more by amicable agreement than by legal restraints or majority rule.

RULES AND REGULATIONS

Am I suggesting a society without rules and regulations? Not at all. You cannot run a business venture, a school, a club, a family, even a game, without rules and regulations. Rules are nothing more than directives on how to achieve purpose, and, if the organization is democratic, they are arrived at by mutual agreement. Whenever regulations are required, the authority to formulate and enforce the rules comes into being because people have agreed to obey them.

Who has authority in a society of partnership networks? Everybody, since everyone has the power to initiate networks. When my neighbor's son agrees to mow my lawn for $20, I am exercising authority and he is accepting it. If he has to buy gas for the lawnmower, he is exercising authority and the gas station is accepting it. Just as purpose establishes the nature of the network, so purpose determines the right to and the exercise of authority.

We tend to think of business authority as fundamentally different from government authority, because in business agreements the goal or purpose is usually set by individuals, whereas in democratic government it is (or should be) set by the community. But in essence they are the same. Authority arises from the consent of the parties involved in pursuing the common purpose.

If all the residents on my street agree that we need street lights, we can authorize an individual or a committee to negotiate with the electric company to have them installed and collect the funds to pay for them. If the number of residents is small, they might make this decision by amicable agreement. If it is large, and palaver does not convert the minority who do not want to pay the tax, they might make the decision by majority vote.

EXERCISING COMMUNITY POWER

What can we do about the minority who will enjoy a well-lit neighborhood but refuse to pay for it? We can ignore their intransigence and go ahead without them, or we can punish them. How does a democratic community penalize or put pressure on members who do not cooperate? There are five possible methods.

14. Restoring the Supremacy of the Individual

1. Peer pressure. This is the most effective method in any community, and its strength depends largely on the extent of shared concerns among the members of that community. Peer pressure is usually the prime motive in settling disagreements by amicable agreement. It works particularly well when the minority is small.

2. Loss of benefits. If my neighbor does not care about the lights, but is very anxious for a garbage pickup, maybe we should couple these two goals. We can refuse to help pay for picking up his garbage, unless he helps to pay for the lights. Again, it is preferable to introduce this kind of bargaining in the amicable-agreement stage than to wait until it becomes punitive.

3. Exclusion. Sometimes the dissenters can voluntrily remove themselves from the plan. If they all live at one end of the block, the new lights can be placed so that they get no benefit from them. Since there will be fewer lights, the cost to the majority will be somewhat less. Should the holdouts refuse to exclude themselves, we can ostracize them from future neighborhood operations networks.

4. Boycott. The majority can decide to penalize the minority by having nothing to do with them. This is more extreme than involuntary exclusion because it affects the dissenters' participation in networks with purposes unrelated to improving the neighborhood.

5. Force. Theoretically (presuming there is no higher authority to stop them) the majority could use physical force to compel the minority to pay for the lights. Although the use of force is hard to imagine in the example I am using, there are instances in the most advanced societies where the use of force is the only solution. Present law permits citizen's arrests. Individuals as well as groups can legally use force to protect themselves from others, or even to keep others from hurting themselves or those around them.

These five methods of enforcement are available without traditional government and, as we shall see, can be exercised effectively in a society without a traditional government structure. I have listed the five in the order of preference, which, in practice, is also the order in which voluntary organizations tend to use them.

DETERMINING COMMUNITY MEMBERSHIP

But how do we set the extent of the authority? It is easy to say that authority arises from the consent of the community. But who decides who is in or out of the community? How can we have effective authority, if anyone who does not like a decision can drop out of the group?

Again we have to fall back on purpose. The purpose of the network set in motion will determine who has to be involved. In practice, this will result in three types of communities: *membership, geographic* and *ad hoc.*

Membership communities are made up of people who join, are recognized by the group and assume specific obligations, such as paying dues. You can drop out of a membership community, but not without losing its benefits. Labor unions are membership communities. So are organizations like the Boy Scouts and the Sierra Club.

Geographic communities involve everyone who lives in a designated area. The practical way to drop out of a geographic community is to move, unless you want to stay and be ostracized. As a landlord has the right to throw you out of his house if you break his rules, so the town can banish or even use force to protect the majority against a minority of lawbreakers. Your town is a geographic community. So was the network my neighbors and I set up to provide street lights.

Ad hoc communities have a one-time purpose and are usually short-lived networks. Membership is defined entirely by participation and is open to anyone who is concerned about or involved in making something happen. Americans who joined the 1986 campaign to refurbish the Statue of Liberty formed an ad hoc community. Users of the Internet belong to an ad hoc community. Today's political parties have become increasingly ad hoc, made up of anyone who helps the chosen candidate's election campaign.

THE PROFIT IN PURPOSE

If, as Drucker has written, "Society in all developed countries has become a society of organizations in which most, if not all, social tasks are being done in and by organizations,"[13] why not let organizations do the governing? But, as I am sure Drucker would point out, the government itself has become an organization, or a whole complex of organizations. And, like most permanent organizations, it has become an unwieldy bureaucracy.

14. Restoring the Supremacy of the Individual

The solution is the same as the solution for business. (See Chapter 9.[14]) Instead of the old-fashioned bureaucratic monster held together by regulation and supervision, I propose a network of autonomous partnerships held together by networking to achieve everything required to govern society, but without the illusion that central hierarchical authority can have all the information required to solve today's social problems.

Networks can do a better job for four fundamental reasons:

1. Networks always have a very specific purpose defined by someone who has specialized knowledge in the area of the problem to be solved.

2. Authority in the network is not only defined by (and, therefore, confined to) the purpose but it depends on the knowledge of each network subcontractor.

3. Costs are automatically controlled because no purpose is defined or authority transmitted without financial agreement between participants.

4. All authority ceases as soon as the network's purpose is achieved.

This bundling of knowledge, purpose, costs and authority should prevent the conflicts of interest and dissipation of resources so detrimental to government as we know it.

PUBLIC VS. PRIVATE

Can we suddenly eliminate the need for public dominion after centuries of depending on it? The dictionary defines dominion as "supreme authority: sovereignty." In the strict sense we have never had a supreme authority in the United States, for we have always believed that government gets its authority from the consent of the governed, and we have splintered government authority from the very beginning. Each of us submits in different respects to the authority of a city or town, a county or parish, and a state or commonwealth, as well as the authority of the federal government.

Moreover each of these governments makes and enforces laws, owns public land, provides public services, constructs and maintains public buildings and infrastructure, and has the right to collect taxes. But none of these governments has dominion over everything. In theory at least, we citizens give authority to many governments and limit that authority so that none of our many governments have final say about everything.

In other words, the powers exercised by our cities, states and federal government are created and *defined* by their citizens. The election that authorized your town to build a new school worked in exactly the same way as the vote that authorized my bridge club to buy a new table.

Traditional government authority is used to make laws, to enforce those laws, to provide services, to construct and maintain public facilities, to provide for the irresponsible and helpless, and to impose and collect taxes to cover the costs. As shown above, members give private associations similar authority. Private associations make and enforce rules, provide services, offer and maintain membership facilities, help less fortunate members and collect dues to finance these activities.

This is not pure theory. The best evidence that private partnerships and networks can do what government now does is the fact that private enterprise has already taken over many of government's traditional functions.

THEY CALL IT OUTSOURCING

In 1994, when William Bratton became New York City Police Commissioner, he was determined to run the police department as a business.[15] Most of the changes he instituted seemed based on the theories of business consultants, and they seemed to work. The city's recorded crimes dropped 12 percent in Bratton's first year. In many smaller cities, mayors have taken the idea of business-like police departments even further. They have let private businesses run their police departments. This was already true some 10 years ago, when Robert Deacon studied the costs of police and street maintenance in 64 Southern California cities. Not only had a substantial number of cities turned policing and maintenance over to private firms or other towns, but realized lowered costs—in policing by 42 percent, in street maintenance by 30 percent.[16]

A 1995 Roper Starch survey found that many Americans had accepted the idea of government hiring outsiders to collect garbage (55 percent), run the schools (36 percent), operate fire departments (26 percent) and police departments (25 percent). Public opinion tends to follow practice. In 1992 the International City/County Management Association reported that more than a third of its members use outside contractors for solid-waste collection, electric utility operation and legal services, more than half for gas utility operation and 83 percent for vehicle towing and storage.[17]

The trend to farm out functions is accelerating on every government level. During the Vietnam war the federal government departed from prior practice and had private companies manage the entire insurance program for military personnel. (Prudential was the prime contractor.)[18]

Private operation of federal prisons, forbidden by a 1925 law, was reintroduced in 1984, when the federal government contracted the Corrections Corporation of America to operate an immigration detention center in Texas.[19] Since then more than a hundred U.S. prisons have been turned over to private management. Federal authorities claim that the privately run facilities cost taxpayers from 9 to 15 percent less than government prisons. And, according to Roper Starch, 41 percent of the public think it is a good idea.[20]

In 1995 President Clinton signed a new law appropriating $13 million for the Internal Revenue Service to launch a program using private collection agencies and law firms to collect unpaid taxes.[21]

At least 10 states have passed new laws encouraging privately constructed and operated toll roads. A privately constructed 14-mile highway connecting Leesburg, Virginia, with Dulles airport was completed in 1995. The investors expected tolls to cover the $326-million initial investment as well as operating costs.[22] Washington state plans to privatize the entire 135 miles of freeway in Seattle's greater metropolitan area.[23]

For years, private universities and corporations have been given major grants or contracts to conduct research for the government. The Lincoln Laboratory at MIT and several departments at Columbia University get from 50 to 100 percent of their budgets from the federal government.[24] In *The Coming of Post-Industrial Society,* Daniel Bell describes a parallel development in which government sets up entirely separate businesses for the sole purpose of running specified government functions such as the Rand Corporation, the Battelle Institute, the New York Port and Triborough Bridge Authorities.[25] Both Amtrak and the U.S. Postal Service can be classified as more-or-less autonomous businesses providing public services.

There is one major problem with today's outsourcing of government functions. With the exception of some private roads paid for by tolls, and some privately run prisons that cover part of their costs by putting prisoners to work, most outsourced functions are financed from the common tax pool. If government functions were taken over by partnerships and networks, every function would have to finance itself.

This means that any public service would have to be paid for either by those who order the service or those who use the service. If my neighbors and I decide to buy a vacant piece of land and turn it into a public park, we can all agree to contribute enough money to buy the land and create the park and thereafter enough annually to maintain the park, or we can decide to impose an entrance fee for those using the park, or we can combine the two sources of revenue. Areas the size of our national parks could be created and maintained by subscription drives sponsored by networks of nature lovers.

FEAR OF FRAGMENTATION

Allowing networked teams and firms to assume all the responsibilities of government seems terrifying for it seems to fragment governance and, like a jig-saw puzzle dumped from its box, it is hard to realize that such a chaos of cutouts will be a beautiful picture when fitted together. We must realize that there are advantages in fragmentation, in splintering objectives into the many tasks required to reach it. The advantage of operations networks is that they provide a system for doing this—and, in doing so, facilitate the splintering of both responsibility and risk.

In *Reinventing Government,* Osborne and Gaebler tell the story of a city official who revolutionized the sanitation department's Bureau of Motor Equipment by empowering line employees.[26] A machinist handled all new equipment orders. Mechanics wrote specifications for new vehicles and tested them when they arrived. A staff unit was created to negotiate and enforce warranties. A group of mechanics became the research and development group to create design improvments.

There is no reason why each of these groups could not have operated as a separate partnership, as they would in an operations network. In fact, the research and development group was so successful it began earning royalties by licensing its inventions. The city executive's innovation succeeded because he divided responsibility among many individuals and groups.

14. Restoring the Supremacy of the Individual

Splintering responsibility for important matters triggers another fear. Who will assume the risk? Failure in matters of wide public concern can be costly. How many of a network's relatively tiny teams and firms can afford to take such risks? The public depends on the Nuclear Regulatory Commission, the Federal Deposit Insurance Corporation, the Food and Drug Administration, and even Amtrak. It depends on the resources of the federal government when an earthquake or hurricane creates a disaster area. Can we safely assume that such mammoth responsibilities can be left to a bunch of entrepreneurial teams or firms?

We can, if they are backed by a network.

Chapter 6[27] pointed out that insurance is the basis of society. We improve risk management by sharing it. I expect a huge flowering of insurance networks in the new economy. Since banks, for example, will be independent partnerships, they will have to buy insurance to protect depositors. The firm that insures them will, in turn, pay premiums to a partnership that underwrites bank insurers, and that insurer will be protected by an insurer further up the insuring network.

The concept is not new. There have always been insurers of business risk, and private insurers have always covered losses in natural disasters. At the present time major insurers are forming a network to insure individual firms against the impact of catastrophic natural disasters.[28] Parallel to these networks of insurers will be networks of venture capital investors as mentioned in Chapter 9.[29] After all, venture capitalist are insurers in reverse, offering to cover possible losses before they happen with their premiums coming later in the form of dividends and increased equity.

LET THE MARKET DO IT

Paying individual partnerships and firms for providing hundreds of our public needs may seem unbearably complex. Yet it is no more unmanageable than what we do now for all our other necessities. Just because we are continually buying food in all sorts of quantities and forms, does not mean it is a good idea to throw all our food money into a common pot and let someone else decide how to spend it.

Not only does the pay-as-we-go system eliminate the annual trauma of April 15, but it gives the individual more knowledge and better control of how his money is being used. Incidentally, information technology has already solved the logistics, since credit cards can consolidate public-service bills as easily as bills for food and clothing.

How will you and I find the time and energy to worry about crime prevention, traffic control, health care, schools, roads, libraries, public transit, the indigent, the armed forces, etc.? The free market will provide these services. Every one of them will be a business opportunity. Just as we do not have to worry about getting oranges and apples to the supermarket, but only as to whether we will buy oranges or apples, so all services now provided by government will be offered by entrepreneurs who will succeed or fail depending how the market—we citizens—accept them.

In *The Age of Discontinuity*,[30] Peter Drucker wrote of "reprivatization," whereby government would turn over to society's nongovernmental institutions the "performance, operations, execution" of its functions. His concept differs from mine, for he wants some sort of central government at the top "as society's resource for the determination of major objectives, and as the 'conductor' of social diversity." He uses the word "conductor" deliberately, for this government would function as an orchestra's conductor, knowing the capacity of each instrument, evoking optimal performance from each, but not playing any of them. Thus government would lead, but not do.

I do not think this will work, because the information deluge has made it impossible for the conductor to know all the necessary scores. As Alvin Toffler told *Wired* executive editor Kevin Kelly:

> What we're talking about is such a tremendous leap in the history of governance that there's no single architect, there's no brain that knows the answers to how to do it. We need to take advantage of millions of brains. We need the distributed intelligence in the system for this.[31]

The spread of information enables more people to think for themselves and leaves fewer people willing to let leaders make decisions for them. This is gradually undermining the efficiency not only of representative government but also of pressure groups. Hence the deterioration of political parties, the complaints that groups like AARP do not reflect the opinions of their members and their reliance on services to attract and retain members.

TRANSFORMING DEMOCRACY

The leaders of the future will recognize and use what Toffler calls "the distributed intelligence in the system,"[32] or what Citibank's Walter Wriston calls "the collective wisdom of people all around the world."[33] Many of these leaders will initiate networks to fulfill public needs. Some of these networks will be entirely nonprofit with all the links consisting of volunteers. But each of them will operate through the self-governing power of its participants.

This, I think, will be a transformation of democracy more practical than Drucker's reprivatization policy—and more effective and far reaching than grassroot organizations, workers' councils and vocal labor unions advocated by Professor Chomsky, revived political parties suggested by William Greider, consensus democracy promoted by The Center for Communities of the Future, citizens' juries run by the League of Women Voters, or anticipatory democracy as described by Mr. and Mrs. Toffler.

And, by the way, every four years we Americans will be spared billions of dollars in national presidential election campaign costs.[34]

15

THE DEATH STRUGGLE OF GOVERNMENT

"But nation-states show no signs of dying gracefully: rather, their power seems to be increasing."
— George C. Lodge, 1990[1]

The move from bureaucratic government to organic governance will not take place without a struggle. Yet its inevitability is evident in the devolution of national governments and the evolution of international relations, in the new uses of military force, in the growth of pay-as-you-go administration and in changes in the money system. As allegiances shift from geographic communities to communities of concern so must the power to enforce duties and protect rights.

DEATH THROES

Professor Lodge and I are in perfect agreement on the facts described in the quote that heads this chapter. But we disagree almost totally in interpreting those facts. The quote is from his 1990 book, *Perestroika for America,* in which he argues that the United States is at a disadvantage in competition with the rest of the world because U.S. economic policies are fragmented and incoherent while our competitors in Europe and Asia have developed formidable business-government coalitions. Since government always has a major influence on business, he concludes America would be better off if we redefined the roles of government and business and designed "new mechanisms and procedures for bringing them together."[2]

15. The Death Struggle of Government

I know that established governments will not surrender without a fight. As one writer observed,

> The group which is most exposed to the problems of rapid change is the *establishment* in general, and the political establishment in particular. What is worse, for all of us, is that its members represent the one group whose future is genuinely under *threat*—it is typically the establishment itself which is displaced (often violently) by any revolution—while simultaneously providing those who are in *charge* of the transition to the future. The result is, not surprisingly, a degree of panic—genuine fear of their *own* future that they have conveyed to the wider population. This too often leads to inappropriate measures that too frequently deny reality.[3]

Hence I see whatever increased power government manifests as the death throes of a dying animal. It is true that growing competition from foreign government-business coalitions have seriously hurt U.S. steel, automotive, electronic and other industries, but I believe such coalitions are relics of a former time that are doomed to die, just as Japan's advantage in its docile, homogenous work force is already dying.

Lodge himself recognizes the conflict between the goals of government and the goals of multinational corporations. He quotes NCR president Gilbert Williamson: "I was asked the other day about United States competitiveness, and I replied that I don't think about it at all. We at NCR think of ourselves as a globally competitive company that happens to be headquartered in the United States."[4] In today's world executives have an allegiance to their business that is distinct from their allegiance to their country. Since they share the goals of fellow workers all over the world, they belong to a community scattered throughout the world.

Professor Lodge distinguishes between two ideological paradigms on the role of government, which he calls "individualistic" and "communitarian."[5] Although the two attitudes are not exclusive, most national governments lean in one direction or the other in their relations with business. In predominantly communitarian governments, like Japan and Germany, the emphasis is on defining "the needs of the community over the long as well as the short term, and to see that those needs are met," whereas more individualistic countries, like the U.S. and Great Britain, tend to regulate business "only in order to achieve ends that the market cannot meet."[6]

In both cases he presumes that government is sovereign and in charge of all community interests, a presumption that does not coincide with reality. As the previous chapter discussed, nation-states have become increasingly ineffective as their citizens develop allegiances to many communities, many of which extend beyond government control.

LOOK FOR A LINGERING DEATH

But Professor Lodge is right in saying that government, whether local, regional or national, will not die easily. There are too many government-established systems in place and too many people dependent on them. It is not only the politicians themselves and the 17 percent of the work force on government payrolls, but there are millions of people outside government who look to government for sustenance, from individuals on welfare and families using food stamps to universities dependent on grants and corporations looking for contracts.

Whether we see government as a depressing shadow or a welcome shelter, we hesitate if someone asks us to get out from under it. Many Americans can see themselves leaving a corporation and starting their own business. Very few Americans can imagine doing anything completely free of government. The staunchest defenders of the present system of government will continue to be the large corporations, who are themselves facing extinction. This allegiance of the dying is one reason why the U.S. as well as the governments of Europe and Japan spend millions to save or succor huge corporations while doing relatively little to support entrepreneurs.

Multinational corporations headquartered in America, despite allegiances far beyond the 50 states, run to the U.S. government for help at the first sign of trouble, and seem to do it more frequently. Government help is so customary that chief executives, such as former Chrysler head Lee Iacocca, see no conflict in begging the U.S. government to shore up American automobile interests against Japanese competition while at the same time negotiating profitable alliances with that very same Japanese competition.

WITHERING AWAY

In the United States and most other advanced countries, the state will not be overthrown or abolished suddenly. It will, as Friedrich Engels predicted for the wrong reasons, slowly wither away. Unfortunately, unlike the decay rate

15. The Death Struggle of Government

of radioactive isotopes, the decay rate of human power is not predictable. No one can foretell how long it will take government as we know it to die. But anyone can recognize its power as being dissipated. There are six very evident trends which indicate a continuous, if erratic, dissolution of traditional government authority:

1. Outsourcing, sometimes called privatizing, where government relinquishes administrative power by turning over public services to private firms. In the United States this ranges all the way from Congress setting up an independent postal service to school boards asking private firms to run the schools. Chapter 14 provides other examples.

2. Growth of the private sector, where government allows, and frequently encourages, private initiative to serve a public need. Peter Drucker and others have commented on the significant growth of the private sector, from hospitals and schools to soup kitchens and flop houses. Government encouragement extends from exemption from taxes to direct subsidy, though many public-service efforts, some for profit, some nonprofit, manage without government assistance.

3. Global cooperation, where worldwide service agencies exercise power across national borders whether they have been created by private initiative or by international treaties. Supranational organizations, such as the churches, the international labor unions and the Red Cross, have existed for decades. But the number of such organizations and the areas in which they exercise power have multiplied exponentially in the last 50 years.

4. Devolution, where central or higher government turns power over to regional or lower governments. The U.S. has shifted responsibility for administering welfare from the federal government to the states. As *The Economist* has reported, "devolution...now increasingly means the shifting of power to cities and townships too."[7] France and Spain are creating regional tiers between central government and local authorities. Germany's federal system is allowing regional governments, like Bavaria and Saxony, to exercise increased independence.[8] Tony Blair, head of Great Britain's victorious Labor Party, advocates more autonomy for Scotland and Wales, and even for the city of London.[9] In undeveloped countries devolution is happening by default. In Africa, according to *The Economist,* "New centres of civilian power are growing up outside the state. Some are regional, some commercial; others are ethnically based or emerging from influential bodies such as the churches."[10]

5. Ad hoc administration, where a quasi-government body is set up to work on problems beyond the jurisdiction of existing governments. Some of these are trying to solve the problem of central cities that have lost their more affluent taxpayers to the suburbs, such as the Portland Metropolitan Area, Boston's Metropolitan Area Planning Council and the Minneapolis-St. Paul tax-sharing system. Others are set for regions with common problems that do not fit any existing jurisdiction, such as the Appalachian Regional Commission, the Economic Development Council of Northeastern Pennsylvania and the regional planning board for New York-New Jersey-Connecticut Metropolitan Area.

6. Subordination, where government surrenders some of its sovereignty to join an international union. As Jean-Claude Paye, secretary-general of the Organization for Economic Cooperation and Development, put it:

> The globalization of activities requires a rethinking of the rules which are needed....In a growing number of domains the possibility of having effective action by government no longer lies at the level of the state, but requires cooperation among governments and collective implementation of them.[11]

Formerly this was done primarily for military or defense advantage. Today it is more often done for economic advantage. The European Union and the North American Foreign Trade Agreement are examples.

Some of these changes may seem to increase rather than decrease bureaucracy, but each of them involves a surrender of authority and either fragments or decentralizes community decision making.

WORLD GOVERNMENT WON'T WORK

I did not use the United Nations as an example of subordination, because nations who join the U.N. relinquish very little of their power. The U.N. is more a forum than a union. As Hazel Henderson, head of the Center for Sustainable Development and Alternative World Futures, said in her speech at the World Future Society's 1995 conference in Atlanta, the U.N.'s principal functions are to act as a networker, a convener and a broker. Hence its only effective power is peer pressure, which is why efforts to enforce its resolutions have been so unsuccessful in matters insensitive to public opinion, such as local conflicts, outlaw governments or the internal affairs of totalitarian regimes.

In 1993, at the request of Secretary-General Boutros Boutros-Ghali, the Ford Foundation convened the Independent Working Group on the Future of the United Nations, consisting of 12 notables from as many countries co-chaired by former Pakistan prime minister Moeen Qureshi and former Federal Republic of Germany president Richard von Weizsacker. The group concluded their work in 1995 with recommendations for "new institutional mechanisms...to prevent or resolve intrastate as well as interstate conflicts, and to promote sustainable economic and social progress."[12]

The proposed institutional mechanisms were an enhanced Security Council and two "new" councils: an Economic Council and a Social Council of 23 members each to replace the present 54-member Economic and Social Council. Other suggestions included three proposals for significant change:

(1) The veto power of the Security Council's permanent members should be limited to decisions on the use of military personnel.

(2) A standing U.N. Rapid Reaction Force should be established to facilitate quick implementation of decisions on military action.

(3) An expert group should be appointed to examine the possibility of developing public sources of U.N. funding beyond assessments of member states.

None of the Independent Working Group's proposals indicated any intention of moving the U.N. in the direction of world government. The Rapid Reaction Force might facilitate its military power, but it would be harder than ever to make decisions on deploying it, for the working group would double the chances of a veto by adding up to five new permanent members to the Security Council, while increasing total membership from 15 to a possible 23. Though the group recognized the U.N.'s income problem (member states, including the U.S., may and do withhold payment of their assessment without penalty), they offered no specific solution beyond suggesting a committee to consider some system of international taxation, "such as designated levies on the global commons."

In other words, these leaders from 12 different countries seem to agree that the U.N. should remain a discussion forum and make no attempt to become a world government. Subordination is expected but only if it is restricted to very specific goals. They also recognize "the rapidly-growing importance and power of non-state actors such as the media, religious groups, business communities, and people everywhere."[13]

In 1995, *The New Republic* carried a two-part article by Michael Lind[14] arguing that the U.N. not only was misconceived at its birth but also has proven totally irrelevant in world affairs. Lind even denied its value as a forum on the grounds that the General Assembly had been a platform "for ritualized denunciation of the West and its allies." I do not believe that the U.N. is totally useless, but I do believe its bureaucracy is totally obsolete and that it would be more effective if broken up into a number of independent agencies.

SALVAGING THE UNITED NATIONS

The General Assembly, with the Security Council as a management committee, can amply fulfill the U.N.'s function as a forum. The Secretariat is needed only to arrange meetings and serve as an interim contact point. The Trusteeship Council has outlived its usefulness, for the only trusteeship left is the U.S. administered Micronesian islands. The functions of the Economic and Social Council are either covered by or should be covered by various U.N. agencies. And the International Court of Justice should be as independent as possible, even though the General Assembly may continue to elect its judges.

Most of the U.N.'s more than 20 agencies have proved their usefulness, but each of these could function independently, financed either by their own fund-raising efforts, by the nations that need them, or by the organizations or companies they benefit.

In his *New Republic* article, Lind made a distinction between two non-isolationist schools of thought on American foreign policy: *globalist* and *realist*. Globalists believed conflict between sovereign states will eventually disappear "as humanity progresses to a higher level of social organization and even morality." President Woodrow Wilson and former Secretary of State Cordell Hull are his examples. Realists "view organized violence as the foundation for both world order and domestic political order." His examples are Franklin Delano Roosevelt, Winston Churchill, George Kennan and Walter Lippmann, since they advocated a balance of power to maintain world order.

It does not seem to occur to Lind that one might be a realist while being a globalist, that some of his realists might have believed that the use of power was necessary on the way to a higher level of social organization. For my part, I believe organized violence was necessary in the past, but that now we are moving to a new kind of social organization which, fortunately, does not have to wait for the human race to reach a higher level of morality.

There was a time when some very respected thinkers advocated world government, but few of them are left. Today most champions of international cooperation agree with Yale professor emeritus Wendell Bell: "Democratic global unification, if and when it comes, may correspond more to a loose confederation than a strong unitary state."[15] Most scholars and politicians are against total centralization. As Charles S. Maier concluded in the July-August 1994 issue of *Foreign Affairs,* "It is time for confederalism, cantonization and overlapping citizenship to receive more creative attention."[16] Even the leaders of the European Union are not talking about a superstate. As *The Economist* pointed out in 1996, the EU's top promoter, German Chancellor Helmut Kohl, "leans increasingly towards decentralization in all but foreign policy, defense, money, commerce, immigration and crime."[17]

FROM MILITARY MIGHT TO POLICE PROTECTION

One of the recommendations to strengthen the U.N. involves creation of a Rapid Reaction Force. In the past, troops were volunteered from national armies when the U.N. needed a military force. But a Rapid Reaction Force has to be permanent and specially trained, which could create problems if the soldiers were borrowed. To avoid such problems I suggest the U.N. hire a private police force.

Soldiers for hire used to be called mercenaries. A number of governments have hired soldiers of fortune and graduates from the military schools of other nations to train troops and even direct field operations. A growing number of private companies provide security personnel for corporations and individuals and even operate police departments for local governments. Today, in the U.S., for every law enforcement officer paid by a government there are three on private payrolls.[18] There is no reason that the kind of police work necessary both locally and internationally cannot be done by private firms. There is every reason to believe that private policing would be done less expensively and more effectively if it were a competitive market.

Private policing would encourage specialization, which is greatly needed in a world where expert information and advanced communication are as available for criminal activity as they are for law enforcement. There are major opportunities for private enterprise in the control of drugs, illegal immigration and computer crime.

TAXATION WITH REPRESENTATION

The Independent Working Group mentioned that the income of the U.N. might be supplemented by having the International Monetary Fund create special drawing rights that would be equivalent to a levy on the world commons.[19] Hazel Henderson has proposed issuing U.N. bonds, charging fees or commissions on international fund transfers, operating a currency exchange and taxing operations that harm the environment.[20]

The trouble with all these proposals, beyond the difficulties in implementing them, is that they bolster the U.N. bureaucracy by feeding its financial commons. The dissolution of government bureaucracy through outsourcing and devolution encourages public-service operations to become self-supporting. If semi-autonomous public-service organizations like the Tennessee Valley Authority and the New York Port Authority can pay their way, there is no reason why the Postal Service, Amtrak and the National Park Service cannot be supported directly by those they benefit. The goal is not so much to lower taxes, which it will probably do, but to restore control to the individuals who pay for public services.

As these public-service firms become partnerships, they will tend to be smaller and more specialized. In assignments like traffic management and policing public places, as well as drug control and illegal immigration, they will become local. In matters like consumer protection, fraud and computer crime, they will concentrate on areas of expertise. Individuals will pay one firm to protect and insure personal belongings, while the insurer pays another to pursue the burglar and retrieve the stolen property.

I do not know how long it will take for this to happen, but when it does there will be an explosion of competitive marketing in the service sector, leading to a much-needed avalanche of innovation. The information deluge has been marked by a serious growth in white-collar crime. I believe the principal reason for that growth is the appeal of such crime to entrepreneurial minds. If

15. The Death Struggle of Government

so, perhaps the answer to such crime lies in assigning the solution to entrepreneurial minds.

ENTREPRENEURING IN THE MONEY SYSTEM

I also believe that the challenge for entrepreneurial minds is the principal reason for the growing tendency to favor speculating with money over creating real wealth. Since the abandonment of the Bretton Woods agreement, after President Nixon suspended the convertibility of the dollar to gold, the international money system has swung from fostering business enterprise to encouraging speculation. In the 25 years that followed, foreign-exchange transactions went from 90 percent business and 10 percent currency speculation to 10 percent business and 90 percent speculation.[21] There are multinational companies that now make (or lose) more money on fluctuating exchange rates than they do on their regular business transactions.

As Harvard University's Richard N. Cooper said in 1992, the solution to this problem is a single global currency, but "a single currency would, of course, require a single monetary authority, a bold, even radical step that governments and their publics are not yet ready to contemplate seriously, much less undertake."[22] Professor Cooper did not consider the possibility of a privately issued global currency.

Private money is not new. In the early 19th Century, many Americans relied on private money systems with banks issuing bank notes professedly backed by gold in their vaults. Even today, there are a private groups using script instead of U.S. dollars, such as the *Ithaca Hours,* traded in Ithaca, New York.[23] Privately issued checks and credit cards have been in use for years, and now we have electronic funds transfer and digital currency. James A. Dorn of the Cato Institute suggested that "government fiat money may disappear as people choose to hold digital money issued by private firms rather than non-interest-bearing paper money issued by central banks."[24] Even though checks, cards and computers designate value in national currencies, they increase the fluidity of government-issued money far beyond government control.

Although the European Union plans to issue a common currency by January 1999, even its most optimistic promoters do not expect the *euro* to be accepted by all EU member states. There are European economists who argue that a single currency and the economic union it implies will create more problems than the EU faces now, since individual states will retain the power to make many decisions with unavoidable economic consequences. Nor have any of the member states done much to win popular support for the plan. Average Europeans seem highly skeptical about the whole idea.

PRIVATE ISSUE OF GLOBAL MONEY

A privately-issued global currency would not be burdened by most of the problems facing the *euro*. No one would have to use the *globa* (I give it a name to facilitate discussion). The *globa* would have to sell itself, and might even have competition from other privately-issued world currencies. The new money would probably be used first for international business deals, then for foreign deposits and long-range contracts. Consumer acceptance would follow as international firms discover savings in marketing products and services with a single global price structure.

The *globa* could be issued by a single bank, or a coalition of banks, or an organization such as VISA or MasterCard. Its value might be pegged to an average of the exchange rates of a list of representative currencies weighted by some measure of each currency's impact on the world economy (e.g., a validated measure of the issuer's gross national product or volume of international trade). To keep the value of the *globa* as stable as possible, the list would include every country with a reliable credit rating that is significantly involved in world trade.

Would firms and individuals have enough confidence in the *globa* to use it in business transactions? A similar question about electronic money was raised in May 1996 at the Cato Institute's Fourteenth Annual Monetary Conference on "The Future of Money in the Information Age."[25] After VISA executive vice president Rosalind Fisher argued that electronic money will not work "without the backing and involvement of regulated financial institutions," William Melton, founder and chief executive of CyberCash, pointed out that beyond guaranteed trust there is actuarial trust and that "we are moving and must move toward actuarial trust."

Guaranteed trust is based on a promise from government or other trustworthy source. Actuarial trust is based on experience, learning that the risk of the trust being violated is very small. We drive on the right side of the street, trusting that oncoming motorists will not drive on their left. We board a plane, trusting it will land safely at the proper airport. The insurance business is

15. The Death Struggle of Government

based entirely on actuarial trust. Life insurance relies on actuarial tables of average life spans.

Guaranteed trust itself is ultimately based on actuarial trust. We accept the government's guarantee because actuarial experience tells us that there is a very small risk of government failure. As Melton pointed out, "With the help of massive databases, sophisticated scoring techniques, and carefully delineated actuarial domains, banks issue billions of dollars of liquidity based solely on actuarial trust."

THE NEED FOR A STABLE CURRENCY

In the early 1960s, when exchange rates were fixed, Johnson Wax built a large plant in The Netherlands to cut transportation costs and make its products more competitive in European markets. The plan worked until the mid-1970s. By then European currencies were floating and the strength of the Dutch guilder made production costs too high for plants in The Netherlands to sell competitively in other parts of Europe.[26]

Unstable money makes long-range business planning impossible, which is why Argentina's finance minister, Domingo Cavallo, insists: "The only role of government in the economy should be to guarantee the integrity of market transactions" by making sure that money "will be worth as much tomorrow as today."[27]

But the impact of international business makes it impossible for individual governments to guarantee the integrity of market transactions, as was recognized some 60 years ago by the Viennese economist Friedrich Hayek. While the English economist John Maynard Keynes was advocating that each government operate its own monetary policy independent of international considerations, Hayek insisted that without a unified currency system currency fluctuations would result in inflation and other negative effects on individual national economies.[28]

Today, nation-states are even less the masters of their own economies than they were in Hayek's day. Two-thirds of net international capital now exists in a form that is neither government issued nor government controlled. The nation-state is no longer the guarantor of the integrity of market transactions, as Joel Kurtzman said in *The Death of Money*:

Rather than functioning as discrete nation-states, each isolated and buffered from the ups and downs of its neighbors, countries have now become increasingly irrelevant, economically speaking. Central banks, such as the Federal Reserve Board, while still powerful, have been downgraded. They are players, yes, but not as independent as before.[29]

What Hayek did not foresee is how the function of money would change. As financial commentator William Davidow wrote recently:

The money we all learned about in Economics 101 was defined by the agricultural and industrial ages. This "old money" was a store of value and a medium of exchange. The "new money" of the information age will be used less for these functions; instead, it will serve more and more as a measure of value. Money will be an information carrier that lets us compare the value of items, but it will become a very different commodity from the one we know today.[30]

The observations of Kurtzman and Davidow are confirmed in the October 1996 issue of *Wired*. Long-time Citicorp chief executive Walter Wriston told an interviewer that he is an advocate of floating exchange rates because money no longer gets its value from a government standard:

This huge pool of stateless money is destabilizing. It can move instantly, and it does. It's also annoying to governments because the market isn't in any one place, geographically. It resides in cyberspace....

What annoys governments about stateless money is that it functions as a plebiscite on your policy. There are 300,000 screens out there, lit up with all the news traders need to make value judgments on how well you're running your economy...a referendum reflecting the collective wisdom of people all around the world on what they think of our economic policies.[31]

This was not a spur-of-the-moment idea. Almost a year earlier Wriston had written in another publication:

The new source of wealth is not material—it is information, knowledge applied to work to create value .... The changing perception of what constitutes an asset poses huge problems in expanding or even maintaining the power of government. Unlike land or industrial plants, information resources are not bound to a particular geography, nor easily taxed and con-

15. The Death Struggle of Government

trolled by governments. In an economy dominated by products that consist largely of information, this power erodes rapidly.[32]

Since international business cannot be enslaved to money whose value expands or contracts with every political breeze, most major transactions are now conducted in the stronger currencies: dollars, marks, yens or pounds. The *globa* could be more stable than any of these—until one day, far in the future, when national currencies have fallen into disuse, global money will be pegged to some other actuarial table, perhaps the GWP (Gross World Product) or the total assets of the world's banking partnerships.

CULTURAL CONTRAST WITH ECONOMIC COHESION

Money is a form of communication. A global currency would mean that economically the whole world would be speaking one language. How is that possible when the world is sinking into what Senator Daniel Patrick Moynihan calls ethnic pandemonium? Informed and perceptive as was his 1993 book, *Pandaemonium: Ethnicity in International Politics,* it paid too little attention to the impact of economic interests on ethnic loyalties.

Humans do not live by bread alone, but having enough to eat is always their primary concern.

In the introduction to the 1950 edition of *Brave New World* (first published in 1932), Aldous Huxley wrote: "Without economic security, the love of servitude cannot possibly come into existence."[33] In the former USSR, the revolt against Communism and the resurgence of ethnicity were parallel consequences of economic collapse. So long as they are well fed, ordinary people do not become fanatical promotors of ethnic rights. But, like teenagers away from home, the moment financial security is threatened, they remember the importance of family.

One of the paradoxes described in John Naisbitt's *Global Paradox* (published a year after Moynihan's book) is "balancing tribal with universal." He goes on to explain:

> The bonding commonality of human beings is our distinctiveness. Also in this late 20th Century, each of us—absent a threat to our core identity—can identify with a number of tribal manifestations. One person can, with the freedom that comes with security, be simultaneously a Houstonian, a Texan, an American, an accountant,

and Chinese. But if you are a Muslim in dangerous Bosnia, you are overwhelmingly a Muslim.[34]

Naisbitt has seized a profound truth, but explained it poorly.

First, it is not the danger in Bosnia that makes one overwhelmingly a Muslim. It is the overwhelming importance of being a Serb, Bosnian or Muslim that makes Bosnia dangerous. The ethnic communities remained secondary so long as they were overshadowed by the economic community sustained by Yugoslavia's Communist government. As James G. Kellas explained in *The Politics of Nationalism and Ethnicity,* "Nationalism feeds on economic discontent and channels it into a nationalist perspective."[35]

Second, to call being a Texan or an accountant a "tribal manifestation" stretches the word "tribal" beyond recognition. I prefer to say the Houstonian accountant considers himself a member of a number of communities of concerns.

Finally, Naisbitt's "core identity" can be interpreted as ethnicity. If that is what he means, I disagree, for the core care for every human is to stay alive, eat enough and find shelter. I would say we can belong to many communities providing there is no threat to our basic well-being.

That is the answer to the question as to how economic cohesion can be reconciled with ethnic (or any other social) contrast. Humans can be simultaneously members of many communities without conflict, provided they are united in a community of economic security. What Mexican futurist Antonio Alonso Cocheiro said about his country, I say about every country: its salvation lies in the destruction of current political institutions and the rise of free-enterprise networks to replace them.[36] What Danish Ministry of Foreign Affairs state secretary J. Orstrom Moller said of Europe,[37] I say of the world: its future lies in economic internationalization with cultural decentralization and a soft security policy.

ORGANIC LAW AND ORDER

Moller defines soft security policy as "aiming at stabilizing adjacent regions by economic, commercial and cultural—human relations— instruments." In Chapter 14, we saw how every community creates its own law and order. The rules and regulations are made and enforced by mutual agreement. Since every operations network is a community, every network

15. The Death Struggle of Government

governs its own area of concern. We may no longer believe in government by divine right, but the great majority of us relate to the law as if it were established by an act of God. In a democracy, where power comes from the people, all laws are really contracts, agreements among citizens that they all have certain rights and obligations.

For a contract to be legitimate the parties to the agreement must understand what they are doing. Yet laws under bureaucratic government are no longer understood by most citizens. Since bureaucracy is based on the principle that those above have knowledge and those below do not, and that that the system works only if those above direct those below, it was natural that the people in charge felt they had to interpret the law for us below and therefore kept adding to its details. The 1936 *Federal Register* had 2,411 pages of proposed rules and regulations. Since 1975 there has never been a year when the *Federal Register* had less than 50,000 pages.

This avalanche of directives made most laws incomprehensible to ordinary citizens, required a growing army of bureaucrats to enforce the law and forced citizens to look for experts to interpret the law. In the early part of this century there was a lawyer for every 1300 U.S. citizens. Today there is one lawyer for every 300.[38] Experts estimate that the current tort system burdens our country with $300 billion a year in direct and indirect costs.[39] Runaway bureaucratic lawmaking also had another curious, and confusing effect. Just as the last defense of ineffectual individuals is to proclaim their good intentions, so the last defense of ineffective bureaucracy is to legislate principles. This may be why so many recent laws focus on rights rather than duties. It is easier to win popular support for laws proclaiming rights than for laws imposing obligations. But it is less effective. Suppose the tablets Moses brought down from the mountain had said, "Fathers and mothers have a right to be honored," instead of "Honor thy father and mother," or "People have the right not to be killed," instead of "Thou shalt not kill."

TARGETED, SHORT-LIVED LAWS

When the day comes that our only laws will be the contracts required to run each network, every "law" will be as targeted and short-lived as the purpose of the contract and fully understood by the people it binds. Occasionally, of course, there will be disputes and violations. But, as already exists in many fields today, there will be firms to arbitrate and associations to impose penalties. In his pathfinding book, *Simple Rules for a Complex World,* Chicago University law professor Richard A. Epstein wrote:

> The insistence on the autonomy of the person, and on the dominance of private over collective property, is an effort not to promote greed and selfish behavior but to create many small separate domains in which informal norms can take over, at far greater precisions and lower cost. A legal rule that calls for noninterference in the ordinary life of the family is one such rule. It recognizes that huge areas of personal behavior, from child raising, to sexual conduct, to financial affairs, are best regulated not by one collective response from the center, but by many smaller and autonomous groups pursuing their ends by means that they devise for themselves without popular or electoral approval. And similar rules can be developed for small groups. To the external world, the sign is "keep off." Within the membership, any number of different divisions of power and responsibility may be chosen by mutual agreement.[40]

Professor Epstein did not get into the situation of group overlap. Individuals belong to many groups. When one group does or wants to do something that impinges on the concerns of another group, the two groups share a concern thereby becoming a bridging community to resolve the conflict. In today's crowded world, autonomous settlements of conflicts have become common. Many are settled out of court, like the recent agreement of Schering-Plough and 12 other pharmaceutical companies in response to the class-action suit brought by retail pharmacists.[41] Many more conflicts are settled long before suits are filed.

The realization is growing that, no matter how complex the conflict, it creates a community that can resolve the dispute more effectively than the bureaucracy we now call government. This is organic governance, a system that automatically assigns both regulation and enforcement to those with the needed knowledge.

But what if the goals are not of direct concern? What if they are community needs that require the support of every member of the group even though some members do not see them as their concern? How organic governance will manage this problem is the subject of the next chapter.

16

SOLVING THE PROBLEM OF SOCIAL INSURANCE

"The right answer to the question 'Who takes care of the social challenges of the knowledge society?' is thus neither 'the government' nor 'the employing organization.' It is a separate and new social sector."
— Peter F. Drucker, 1995[1]

Social insurance is needed to protect individuals from weaknesses which may make them burdens on society. Though most networks will take care of noncontributing members out of self-interest, the larger share of the burden will be assumed by philanthropic partnerships specializing in specific problems. Though transition will take a long time, ultimately insurance will cover health and welfare, private firms will do policing, jurisdiction will reside with each community for its laws, with capital crime handled by regional branches of a World Court.

SOCIAL RESPONSIBILITY AND SELF-INTEREST

If Adam and Eve formed the first community, that community soon found itself burdened with the problem of the socially dependent. Cain and Abel were born and Adam and Eve had to take care of them. Thus began the most complex challenge of community governance: society's responsibility for the dependent, deciding when and how a community should deal with members who do not contribute to the community.

We define community as any group united by a common concern and presume that such groups are democratic, in the sense that each group's members decide what they want to do about the common concern. Those decisions form the rules or laws that govern the group. Complications arise when there are members of the community who will not or cannot observe the rules.

Lack of cooperation in the goals of the community can be deliberate or involuntary. To take care of the former every community needs a justice system; to take care of the latter, a welfare system. Though the two systems will differ in how they treat the exceptional members who occasioned them, the consequence for other members is the same. They have to pay the costs of both justice and welfare.

Is this fair?

It is as fair as any obstacle that stands in our way when we are trying to get something done. To reuse my street-lights example from Chapter 14,[2] if the weather, cost of materials or shortage of work crews complicates installation of the lights, we accept the situation as an unavoidable obstacle that must be overcome to get the job done. The problem of unwilling or unable members is such an obstacle. Hence communities make provisions both for the wicked and for the weak out of self-interest. Communities must take care of the lawbreaker, the malingerer, the poor and the ill because they have to if they want to reach their goals.

In *The Logic Of Collective Action*, Mancur Olson mentioned the conclusion of Anthony Downs' *An Economic Theory Of Democracy:* that when services for everyone in a group are unsuited to market mechanisms, they can be supplied "only if everyone is forced to pay his assigned share." I mentioned this problem of "indivisible benefits" in Chapter 13.[3] Such government decisions, Olson concluded, are collective decisions backed by force, and so restrict freedom.[4]

If Olson meant moral freedom, I disagree. No decision made democratically can restrict moral freedom. Olson pointed out in a footnote that "there would of course be no coercion if all decisions were unanimous."[5] I do not see obedience to the will of the majority as a loss of moral freedom. I draw this conclusion not just because dissenters in a democracy retain the right to try to change the ruling and usually are free to leave the community, but chiefly because human nature requires basic social obligations. Our need to live in society is as natural as our need to eat. Since obedience to the majority is a requirement for living in society, it no more restricts moral freedom than the need to breathe or the need to eat. Thus the costs of welfare and justice are freely accepted whether one becomes a member of a community by choice or by circumstance.

SOCIAL VS. INDIVIDUAL BENEFITS

In *The Coming of Post-Industrial Society* (first published in 1973), Daniel Bell warned against using the same norms for judging which costs should be borne by individuals and which costs by society as a whole:

> This is an atomistic view of society and reflects the utilitarian fallacy that the sum total of individual decisions is equivalent to a social decision. Yet the aggregate of individual decisions has collective effects far beyond the power of any individual to manage, and which often vitiate the individual's desires. Thus, every individual may value the freedom and mobility which a personal automobile provides, yet the aggregate effect of so many autos on the roads at once can lead to clogged transportation.[6]

Social decisions are usually more difficult to make than individual decisions, but they should not be considered essentially different. The process for making decisions on what is good for me, on what is good for my family, on what is good for my firm, on what is good for my neighborhood, on what is good for my country and on what is good for the human race does not change essentially no matter how broad or complex the application. The right choice must always be judged by its long-term consequences as well as immediate result, by its effects on other human beings as well as on the immediate beneficiary.

The butterfly effect applies here as well as in science. There is no individual decision that does not have social consequences just as every social decision has individual consequences. The aggregate of individual decisions has collective effects beyond the power of any individual to manage wherever people interact. The difficulty of managing such complex effects is precisely why men and women are developing partnerships and networks, and why friendly agreement works better than majority rule.

Ultimately every decision is a social decision in that there is no decision that concerns only one person. Many decisions that have nothing to do with government are made in the interest of large groups of people. Managers of supermarkets and owners of professional baseball teams make decisions that affect not only bag boys and ballplayers but thousands of food buyers and baseball fans.

These decisions involve not only who will benefit, but also who will bear the cost. There are very few enterprises, public or private, that are not burdened by freeloaders, beneficiaries who do not pay. Supermarkets have breakage and theft; baseball teams have fans who never buy tickets. Nor do customers always bear the costs equally. Some buy only sales items and bleachers seats, and many organizations base dues on ability to pay.

TAKING CARE OF ONE'S OWN

When most communities were defined by geography, the binding force of such communities arose less from location than from common culture, frequently identified with heredity, language, religion or shared history. Restricted by the difficulties of travel and communication between localities, it was rare for people to have serious concerns outside the locality. Physical, social, economic and spiritual goals and the means of attaining them were all within the community. For the same reason these communities were usually highly efficient in providing for dependents and disciplining members who violated community rules.

Although few communities are as isolated as they once were, there are still many groups whose concerns are so focused by ethnic background, religion or common history, that their members have few interests outside the group. This type of cultural cohesion, particularly when the group is a minority, can become very defensive. Not only do such communities punish or ostracize individuals who develop interests outside the group, but they tend to oppose, frequently to the point of violence, outsiders who invade their territory or seem to threaten their way of life.

This inability to get along with other communities, with groups whose concerns do not mesh with theirs, easily leads to violence, especially when it involves economic as well as cultural issues. This is the root of the terrible violence in former Yugoslavia, of discrimination against blacks in white neighborhoods and of attacks on Asians by blacks in Los Angeles' ghetto.

The information deluge provides the antidote to cultural strife not so much because it washes away cultural barriers but more because it exposes people to thousands of new interests, luring them into numerous communities of concerns they share with people outside their birth communities. As this allegiance to multiple and overlapping communities grows it makes unsolvable conflict between communities less likely, for, as explained in Chapter 14,[7] the more numerous and interwoven allegiances, the more likely conflict will be resolved through amicable agreement.

The multiplication of interests and overlapping of communities has turned our country, once called a melting pot, into a mixing bowl. Similar societal salads are rapidly spreading throughout the world—so much so that a growing number of leaders in the Americas, Europe and Asia believe that global interests have become so entangled that future military conflicts between major nations are unlikely and may even be impossible.

THE IRONY AND HONOR IN CULTURE PRESERVATION

One sign of the dissolution of cultural cohesion is the number of special communities that have risen to fight for fading cultures in the same way environmentalists battle to protect endangered species. Although they are doomed to fail (cultures, like species, are constantly evolving and cannot be preserved until they are dead), culture preservationists provide a useful link of understanding and good will between those who cling to the past in fear of the future and those who flee the past as a drag on the future.

How much should other communities contribute to preserving dying communities? When the costs of setting up a program to study a minority culture is out of proportion to the number of students taking the program, does it violate the rights of the other students? As Russell Hardin pointed out in a recent article in *The Good Society*, it is impossible to justify an obligation for outsiders to subsidize a minority community.[8] That does not mean that majorities will not support minority communities, whether to preserve the peace (e.g., the 16th Century Ottoman Millets allowed Christian, Armenian and Jewish communities limited self-rule[9]) or as a quaint and harmless antique (e.g., the Amish and Hasidic communities in the eyes of most Americans).

The one negative consequence of the fragmenting of communities is that it reduces the feeling that the community is responsible for every human problem. In the rising society of partnership networks it is far more likely that the needy will fall between the cracks, both because the needy, like everyone else, will belong to many communities and because individual communities will have such specific goals. Fortunately society has already evolved a new sector to pick up the burden.

COMMUNITIES OF COMPASSION

My emphasis on self-interest as the reason for community justice and welfare programs is not meant to slight the importance of compassion. On the contrary, I believe that both crime and disability are more effectively handled by charity than by governance. Compassion, happily, is a natural and self-rewarding virtue. There will always be people who want to comfort the prisoner, reform the sinner, instruct the ignorant, help the poor and nurse the sick. These high-minded individuals will create communities dedicated to those concerns.

It is natural and prudent that communities with non-charitable purposes should encourage charitable communities to take over some of the justice or welfare burdens. Of the 400,000 South Carolinians at risk from hunger or malnutrition only about 300,000 receive food stamps. The state relies on more than 240 volunteer-run pantries and soup kitchens to take care of the remainder.[10] The Florida state justice department paroles 25,000 first-time offenders into the custody of the Salvation Army, which runs a program that costs far less than imprisonment and is more efficient (80 percent are rehabilitated).[11]

Since charitable groups lighten the burden of noncharitable communities, the latter will frequently assist the former. The principal benefactors of educational and charitable organizations have always come from families or communities they have helped. The government funds many charitable organizations, as do foundations set up by business firms or private individuals. A 1987 federal matching grant enabled Oregon's White Bird Medical Clinic to provide free health care for the homeless,[12] and a $2.4 million grant from the federal Office of Substance Abuse Prevention helped five California volunteer agencies to develop the "Recover for East Bay Asian Youths" drug program.[13] A Prudential Insurance program distributes $1.2 million each year in grants to nonprofit organizations nominated by its agents.[14]

No one has more clearly recognized the growing importance of the "nonprofit sector" than Peter Drucker. Here is part of his explanation of the quote that leads this chapter:

16. Solving the Problem of Social Insurance

> In the last twenty years the United States has begun to talk of a "third sector," the "nonprofit sector": the organizations that take care of the social challenges of a modern society .... In the 1990s, about one million organizations were registered in the United States as nonprofit or charitable organizations doing social sector work. The overwhelming majority of these, some seventy percent, have come into existence in the last thirty years. And most are community services concerned with what goes on on this earth rather than with the Kingdom of Heaven .... We still talk of these organizations as "nonprofits." But this is a legal term. It means nothing except that under American law these organizations do not pay taxes.[15]

In Chapter 13 we concluded that government was ill-equipped to solve the problems of society. Then who will deal with social and economic problems? They will be addressed by groups of people who want to solve them, who will form networks to develop and apply solutions—and convert others to thinking as they do. A large number of such communities already exist. The Arms Control Association, the Cato Institute, the National Organization for Women, the Nature Conservancy, the Public Affairs Council, and the Sierra Club are examples.

WHO WILL PAY THE BILL?

But will there be enough such groups, and where will all the money come from to support them?

Christ said, "The poor you will always have with you." Though the need will likely remain several steps ahead of the providers, we have no reason to worry about a shortage of charitable organizations since compassion is a natural human instinct. People have reached out to those less fortunate than themselves even when their own lives are in danger—on the battlefield, in prison camps, during plagues and natural disasters. As the past century bears witness, once most individuals solve the basic problem of taking care of themselves, they feel compelled to help others. The number and effectiveness of such organizations seems to rise in direct proportion to the advance in our standard of living.

Today, when religion seems at its weakest and most divided, and immorality at its strongest and most prevalent, there are more institutions dedicated to good works and more volunteers anxious to help than there have ever been.

Research expert Daniel Yankelovich reports that 65 percent of Americans consider helping their community a personal value of top importance.[16] There are more than 800 voluntary institutions represented by the independent sector, and there are thousands of other such groups that are too small or too busy to register with that organization.

But can individual generosity make up for the loss of government largess that now pours from the tax commons? Will fund raising be affected when there are no tax deductions for charitable donations?

A perplexingly prevalent illusion about philanthropy is that tax deductions are a major motive for giving. Donations may be slightly larger when donors expect to get part back from the government, but sane people do not give away $10 to save $5. Americans were generous supporters of good causes long before the income tax, and there is every reason to believe they will remain so after income taxes disappear.

A study sponsored by The Independent Sector showed that household charitable contributions in the U.S. rose 8 percent in nominal terms and 2 percent in real terms between 1993 and 1995, despite high taxes and worry about the economy. The same study found that nine out of 10 families with more than $100,000 annual income donate to charity, with gifts averaging close to 3.5 percent of their income.[17] The very rich are no exception. In 1996, 16 Americans donated a total of more than $690 million to charity.[18]

There are six basic reasons why human beings help others:

1. Compassion. This is certainly the most laudable motive. In my opinion it is the most common motive, at least among the poor. Sympathy is love's half-sister, and like love she is both selfless and self-rewarding.

2. Shame. Others think highly of those who do good deeds and look down on those they consider selfish. Nothing boosts a fund-raising drive more than publishing a list of the donors with the amount they donated.

3. Self-esteem. Again we are ashamed not to give, but this time it is our own opinion that matters. Humans want to think highly of themselves. In a 1988 Gallup survey 43 percent of the respondents admitted feeling guilty when they ignored direct-mail requests for donations.[19]

4. Self-promotion. Giving makes the donor more important, not only to the receiver of the gift but to others who witness the giver's generosity. A study by Harvard sociologist Francie Ostrower indicated that the principal reason for giving among the wealthy is to reinforce social status.[20]

5. I-owe-you-one. Gifts are frequently given with the expectation that something will be given in return. June helps Mary because someday she hopes Mary will help June. Joe contributes to Mike's favorite fund drive so that Mike will contribute to Joe's favorite.

6. Self-fulfillment. This is infrequently a motive for monetary gifts, but it is often the primary motive when the donor contributes time and energy, particularly when the cause uses the donor's aptitudes and skills. Many a charitable project that was launched by compassion is propelled and sustained by self-fulfillment. Peter Drucker believes the "steady transformation of the volunteer from well-meaning amateur to trained, professional, unpaid staff member is the most significant development in the nonprofit sector."[21]

All of these motives are stronger than tax deductions, and all of them will be more powerful in a society where do-good communities are all around us involving either ourselves or friends and relatives. A 1977 survey shows one in every four American households with someone providing unpaid caregiving for an adult over 50 during the past 12 months, many at considerable financial sacrifice.[22] If such generosity exists while everybody has to contribute to the tax commons, we can expect much more when that money becomes available to be used as they see fit.

There is much evidence that charity is discouraged when government assumes responsibility for the needy. Whereas enormous sums are donated for education, the bulk of this largesse goes to universities and private schools. Practically nothing is given to public schools.[23]

A PASSION FOR PANACEAS

The objection may rise that, in a society as complex as ours, caring for the sick, the disadvantaged and the poor is a giant task. It is foolish to leave such an important job to hundreds of independent organizations running in all directions; it requires a coherent national policy.

In no area is the human hunger for cure-alls more evident than in social legislation. Again and again we hear the cry for a coherent national policy, whether it is for health care, foreign affairs, crime control, education, arts encouragement, military preparedness, environmental protection or workplace safety. And, of course, every attempt at coherent policy ends up in a mishmash of impenetrable rules and regulations that ultimately occasions a new cry for a coherent national policy.

One reason for this constant failure is that government too often sees a single overall problem when there are many disparate needs. The flood of knowledge has made us realize that sickness can be any one of a hundred diseases, each with multiple causes. The same is true of poverty and crime and drug abuse. The search for a coherent national policy in any of these fields is as foolish as the search for a single pill to cure the common cold.

Misery, whether physical, mental or moral, comes in too many forms to be cured by central solutions. The causes are innumerable and usually circumstantially specific. So solutions must be innumerable and ad hoc. There has been considerable progress in this direction in medicine. More doctors are specialists. Also clinics and hospitals have begun to specialize. The justice system has begun specializing as well, though, it still needs greater specialization in policing, in law enforcement, in the courts, in punishment and in jails.

That is why I believe a civilization made up of partnership networks will handle the problems of justice and welfare more efficiently and effectively than bureaucratic government. Let the community with the problem solve the problem.

DEMOCRATIC INSURANCE

Chapter 6 explained that a large part of government's function is to provide a form of insurance.[24] Overburdened with entitlements, governments are now studying ways to privatize social insurance. Chile since 1981 and Argentina since 1994 have proven that social security can be privatized easily and efficiently.[25] Mexico,[26] Columbia and Peru adopted similar plans, and a number of east European countries are studying them.[27] As explained in Chapter 15,[28] our better understanding of statistics and risk analysis has made it possible to replace government guarantees with actuarial trust. Actuarial science also encourages the development of policies to cover specific risks, a trend that will increase market choices and shift decisions on whom and what to cover from government and employers to the insured.[29]

16. Solving the Problem of Social Insurance

Privatization of government's security blanket will ignite an explosion of competitive activity in the insurance industry. Individuals will be able to choose among an incredible number of specialized policies to protect themselves against what they fear most, whether it be liability, theft, accident, fire, medical expenses or death of parents or spouses. Many marriage contracts will require divorce insurance to cover alimony and child support. Business partners will buy insurance against failure and lack of work. Annuities will replace pensions, and be used for specific future expenses like education or purchase of a home.

Although insurance will be voluntary, there will be considerable pressure to carry coverage. In some communities certain types of insurance will be a requirement for membership. Others will offer insurance as a motive for joining. Communities will buy insurance to protect themselves against the uninsured. Insurance to cover unpaid bills will be cheaper and more common as credit-rating databanks grow more sophisticated.[30]

Insurance partnerships will be able to keep costs down by using "asymmetric information" techniques developed by Nobel Prize winners William Vickrey and James A. Mirriees to counter fraud in claims and policy applications.[31] I expect that insurance will become the principal way of saving for most people, providing a new source of venture-capital formation as insurance partnerships look for places to invest.

DEMOCRATIC JUSTICE

Lawbreakers will be tried and punished by the community whose laws they break, just as today, doctors can be suspended by state medical boards and major league baseball players can be fined by the Baseball Commissioner. In many professions, the professional association or network will issue licenses for certain types of activity and withdraw or suspend the license when its rules are broken. The seriousness of expulsion will depend on how important the goal of the community is to the lawbreaker. In professional or business communities it could severely restrict livelihood, eliminating most clients or customers as well as possible partners.

Police surveillance and protection will be provided by private firms, as it is today in many private businesses and some towns. The community that makes the law will have jurisdiction to judge whether the law was broken and to impose penalties. Crimes that violate human rights, particularly crimes against the physical person (murder, assault, battery, rape) will be tried by courts authorized by everyone who agrees such acts are criminal. In the beginning, existing city, state and federal courts will handle such cases. Eventually a worldwide network will form to encode and enforce basic laws universally recognized. This network may be headed by a World Court, with regional and local branches in every population center.[32]

This will seem less complicated than it sounds, if one realizes that for every goal or purpose people will construct a specific network, even when the goal is universal. If the world as a community wants to punish the crime of murder or rape, the world as a community will not only decide what the punishment should be but set up the courts to judge cases and the prisons to punish crimes.

As to raising money to finance law enforcement, I suspect that penalties will more frequently take the form of fines, that criminals will be billed for the cost of their trials (as they now are in Virginia) and for the costs of imprisonment (prisons in 21 states now charge something).[33]

IT'S BOUND TO BE LONG IN COMING

Chapter 12 outlined the obstacles to the changeover from business as we now know it and business conducted entirely with partnership networks. Despite the fact that there are at least 21 Congressmen determined to shift the fight against poverty from government to private charities,[34] there will be tremendous resistance to eliminating welfare bureaucracies. Inertia is one of the most damaging characteristics of bureaucratic government and its greatest defender. It may well take the entire 21st Century to eliminate all traces of government as we know it.

When it does happen, how will it happen? Here is my guess.

As governments are forced to shed some of the entitlement burdens they can no longer afford, they will experiment with politically acceptable half measures. In most cases this will mean that they will privatize the administration of programs while promising to preserve basic funding. Private companies will see a profit opportunity and move in. Electronic Data Systems, IBM and Lockheed Information Services are already angling to take over the administration of welfare now that it has been turned over to the states. Kelly Services has recruiters stationed in a Detroit welfare office to offer free computer training and possible job placement. Plans for training welfare recipients are also being studied by Manpower and Olsten.[35]

The first cuts in funding will come partly from negotiating with administration providers, since private enterprise will compete for these jobs, and partly from a reduction in the welfare rolls, since the private firms can make money by training and placing welfare recipients in paying jobs.

The more money governments save through privatization, the more legislators will increase privatization. As individual public services are provided by private companies, it will become easier to assign costs, enabling politicians to reduce taxes by funding specific services by assessments, and eventually asking each service provider to bill service users direct. This will encourage even more private firms to go into public service, and create a political faction promoting the idea of complete privatization.

I will be very surprised if the United States does not lead the world in privatizing government services, for ours is one of the few major countries that has left many major public services in private hands, particularly in power generation, transportation and communication.

There is one major social concern now run by government I have not mentioned: public education. That is a big and special subject and deserves a chapter of its own.

17

TRANSFORMING EDUCATION

"For millennia ... children retraced the steps of their parents, were initiated into stable ways and ritualized routines, had a common book of knowledge and morality.... Today, not only does a child face a radical rupture with the past, but he must also be trained for an unknown future. And this task confronts the entire society as well."

— *Daniel Bell, 1976*[1]

Despite the money invested, public education fails because it tries to teach too much, it has lost unquestioning parental support, it is no longer the principal instructor of the young and it makes little provision for different intelligences. Education must concentrate on teaching children how to learn, how to use information and how to partner with their peers. These new objectives plus the need for lifelong learning will create a world in which everyone becomes both student and teacher.

BILL BENNETT'S LAMENT

In his *Index of Leading Cultural Indicators,* former U.S. Department of Education secretary Bill Bennett pointed out the dismal failure of the public school system. A mere 6 percent of 1992's high school seniors were competent enough in geometry, algebra and fractions to take college mathematics. Fewer than 13 percent of high school graduates reach the highest skill levels in reading and writing. In a geography test of citizens 18 to 24 in nine coun-

17. Transforming Education

tries, the U.S. group came in last. U.S. students also rated last in the 1988 International Assessment of Educational Progress exams in science.[2]

A Nation at Risk was the title of the government-sponsored 1983 report on the crisis in public education. Eight years later Marvin Cetron and Margaret Gayle published *Educational Renaissance,* a book on how "concerned parents and dedicated teachers, public-service organizations and major corporations are finding ways to revitalize their local schools."[3] Although their account is extremely upbeat, they begin by admitting "that educational reform will be a mammoth task" for authoritative studies have shown ...

> that only one high-school junior in five can write a comprehensible note to apply for a summer job; that fewer than one-third of seniors know to within fifty years when the Civil War was fought; that a majority of seventeen-year-olds cannot understand an average newspaper article; that barely more than half of high-school juniors know whether eighty-seven percent of ten is more than ten, or less, or equal to it. In one recent study, only a minority of junior-high-school students could find the United States on a world map!
>
> Our situation appears even worse when we compare this sorry record with those of other industrialized nations. Both in classes taken and in the degree to which pupils master the material laid before them, our students lag far behind. One American high-school student in five takes biology or chemistry, fewer will study physics, and only six percent take courses in calculus. By contrast, the typical Russian student studies—and *learns*—algebra and physics for five years, biology and chemistry for four, and calculus for two. In Japan, most high-school graduates know more than the average American with a B.A. Japanese companies setting up plants in the United States have found that it takes an American with a master's degree to learn the same statistical quality-control techniques routinely used by Japanese high-school graduates.[4]

Updating this sorry introduction to the extent of America's education problem, the Third International Maths and Science Study of 41 nations rated the schools of 16 countries superior to the United States in teaching science, while 27 countries do better in teaching mathematics.[5]

Such figures do not even consider the drop-out rates and violence of inner-city U.S. schools. To mention but one example, after six students and one teacher were killed and 10 students and four teachers wounded in separate incidents during the 1991-1992 school year, New York City allocated $28 million to fortify its schools with police officers and weapons detectors.[6]

MONEY AND EXPERTISE HAVEN'T HELPED

In the past three decades federal, state and local government investment in public education has more than doubled. It is now more than $250 billion a year or about $6,500 per student.[7] Teachers are getting more pay and better training. They know more about learning disabilities and the psychology of teaching. Many faculties now include specialists in social work. There has been a vast increase in teaching tools, from closed-circuit television to computers. Yet according to the official *National Assessment of Educational Progress,* between 1970 and 1980 the ability to understand written materials declined for all 17-year-olds, but especially in the top group, those able to read at an "advanced" level. This has been confirmed by Scholastic Aptitude Test scores, which declined sharply during the same period especially at the top.[8]

In the past decade many school districts throughout the nation have experimented with charter and magnet schools, greater school choice, a return to basics and other innovations in public education. There has been some improvement in test scores, but the overall picture is still bleak. So bleak that business leaders are alarmed. A Conference Board poll showed that two-thirds of American companies consider education their primary community-relations concern.[9] One out of every three companies employing 10,000 or more now offers remedial instruction for employees. According to the Business Roundtable, "As many as sixty percent of high school graduates are not prepared for entry-level jobs."[10] And the effects of poor schooling have reached middle-level executives, with many unable to convey ideas in speech or writing.

WHAT WENT WRONG?

Here are some of the reasons critics give to explain why public education does not turn out graduates with the skills they need:

1. Schools are run by boards of education, which too easily become local political franchises.

2. School accreditation is granted by evaluating means (subjects taught and facilities available), when the real measure should be results (graduates' knowledge and abilities).

3. Special interests have forced schools to introduce courses that detract from teaching the fundamentals. For example, high school students are allowed to spend up to 59 percent of class time on non-academic courses.[11]

4. School-budget pressures and teacher overload push students from one grade to the next regardless of actual achievement.

5. In their struggle to maximize acceptance and sales, textbook publishers excise anything that may be controversial, sacrificing educational value to political expediency.

6. Both the quality and number of teachers are lower than they should be, because talented people can make more money in other professions.

7. Unions make it difficult or impossible to evaluate or reward teachers on the basis of their competence or the performance of their students.

8. Deterioration of home life has left children without the basic attitudes, discipline and knowledge on which educational systems can build.

9. The schools have been forced to pay more and more attention to society's social and moral problems, leaving little time and energy for basic education.

10. Children are not spending enough time in school, because schools operate on a schedule that was created to accommodate farm families back in the days when children had to work in the fields.

11. Today's schools are swamped with pupils from totally different cultural backgrounds, including many who cannot understand English.

12. Since public schools depend on federal, state and local funding, each with strings attached, education suffers from "too many cooks in the kitchen."

13. Although the physically and mentally disadvantaged deserve equal education, assigning this obligation to the public school system draws money, time and attention away from the needs of the student majority.

14. The curriculum is too fragmented to give students the comprehensive view they need in today's world.

15. The schools no longer pay sufficient attention to developing student character, and without character knowledge is harder to grasp and impossible to use advantageously.

16. Educators seem unable to agree on the purpose of public-school education, and any project that lacks a definite purpose is doomed to fail.

That is a long list, but it could be longer. There are as many reasons given for the failure of our public schools as there are critics. The sad result, however, is not the extent of the criticism, but that so much of it leads dedicated educators, teachers, parents and politicians to mistake symptoms for the underlying disease. *Educational Renaissance,* to mention only one example, is replete with descriptions of ingenious and sometimes heroic programs to palliate consequences rather than the real problem. Yet five years after *Educational Renaissance* was published *Newsweek's* Jonathan Alter could write: "Whatever their individual talents, teachers' unions and educrats have failed as a group to save the public schools."[12]

Our school system, like our system of government and many of our business systems, is obsolete. It, too, has drowned in the information deluge.

HOW THE EDUCATION MONOPOLY DIED

Formal education, as we know it, was designed for a world in which the flow of information was much more limited than it is today. The mere fact that a man or woman was equipped to teach marked the teacher as someone special. Ordinary folk had high respect for learned people precisely because they had so little education themselves. But that is no longer the case. The information deluge has brought education to almost everyone, and in doing so has washed away this reverence for the teaching profession.

As pointed out in Chapter 2, a side effect of the information flood is distrust, the loss of respect for authority. Parents now see teachers as equals, and the change in attitude hobbles the power of the teaching profession. Parents critique what teachers do, censor textbooks, exert pressure for changes in the curriculum and are more liable to retaliate than cooperate when teachers discipline children. Since children's attitudes almost always reflect the attitudes of their parents, classrooms are less governable than they used to be.

Today parents are only one preschool influence. Television has access to most young minds years before school does. Elementary schooling is still organized as if it were the child's principal educational resource. That is no longer true, and it has not been true for years. Even when I was a child, long before television, print and radio were reaching the young. Newspaper comic strips, with a little help from my mother, taught me to read before I went to school.

In 1976, Edward Hall wrote in *Beyond Culture* that "how one learns is culturally determined, as is what one learns."[13] Today most educators feel that the influx of children from foreign cultures puts a serious strain on the school system. What they do not seem to consider is that the culture of the educational system itself may be foreign to every modern child. Today's children are drenched in information long before they are six years old. They arrive in school after several years of listening and watching television, a learning experience far more stimulating than kindergarten or first grade can ever be, and one that has taught them language and thought processes quite different from those in most textbooks.

As Lewis J. Perelman wrote in *School's Out,*

> In reality, the vast majority and most productive share of human learning takes place in real-world settings outside of schools. Moreover, the traditional design and practices of even "excellent" schools are either divorced from or contradictory to the natural learning abilities most people are born with.
>
> Cognitive research shows that learning *in context* is essential to acquiring knowledge and skills that are truly useful to working and living. Context turns out to be critical for understanding, and thus, for learning. The importance of context lies in the meaning that it gives to learning through the workings of the human's natural learning system. Human beings—even the small child—are quintessentially sense-making, problem-solving animals.[14]

One of the reasons that even the best courses fail to hold the student's interest is that when lessons do supply "context" to subject matter, it seldom is truly useful to the child at the time he or she is studying. To be in context, what is learned must make sense and solve problems in the student's world, not in the world of the teacher or other adults.

THE FUNDAMENTAL-FACTS FOLLY

But these oversights are overshadowed by the principal consequence of the information deluge. The incredible multiplication of information has voided the concept of elementary education as the imparting of fundamental facts, of information everybody should know.

Not long ago I watched a television documentary on the school's failure in teaching geography. Tests were cited and individuals interviewed to show how few young Americans know even where different countries are, to say nothing about naming their capitals, populations, products and climates. The program gave no hint that the champions of geography might be expecting too much, even though I, and I believe most adults, find it difficult to remember all the countries born or rechristened in the last three decades.

The following week I sat through another program on the lack of historical knowledge among grade-school graduates. A few days later I read an article on our schools' poor showing in science and mathematics, another protesting the failure to acquaint students with more of the West's classic literature and yet another deploring the short shrift curricula given to Asian and African culture. The final straw was a newspaper report on testimony to a congressional committee by the executive director of Bankcard Holders of America, who asked for "mandatory personal finance classes starting in Junior High, including credit education."[15] If we pool the demands of all these critics, I thought, the school year will have to be 12 months long and young people will have to remain in school at least until they are 25.

I decided that schools should concentrate on teaching children how to learn and let them pick up specific information as they need it.

THE THEORY OF CULTURAL LITERACY

Then I read E. D. Hirsch's 1987 book, *Cultural Literacy: What Every American Needs to Know*. Hirsch not only believed schools should provide young Americans with specific information, he ended his book with a list of words and names that he and two fellow scholars compiled to represent our "national literate vocabulary." Hirsch had a cogent argument for requiring specific information in general education. He reasoned that a knowledge of shared information is necessary for communication. He called this shared information cultural literacy and explained that its contents...

17. Transforming Education

can be identified explicitly, since they are identified implicitly by every writer or speaker who addresses the general public. If writers did not make tacit assumptions about the knowledge they could take for granted in their audiences, their writing would be so cumbersome as to defeat the aim of communication.

It is true that the specific content of the national literate vocabulary changes from year to year, even from day to day, as striking events catch national attention. But such changes are few when compared to the words and associations that stay the same. Of course, one literate person's sense of the shared national vocabulary is not precisely identical with another's; individual experiences produce different assumptions in different people about shared knowledge. But these differences are insignificant compared to what is common in the systems of associations that we acquire by daily experiences of literate culture.

It's also true that we adapt our conjectures about what others know to particular circumstances .... But when we address a general audience we must assume that we are addressing a "common reader," that is, a literate person who shares with us a common body of knowledge and associations.[16]

I agree that communicators must assume they are addressing people who share a common body of knowledge and associations, although I could write another book on our current communication difficulties because of the fragmentation of cultural literacy. But my fundamental disagreement with Hirsch is that I do not believe that formal education can provide cultural literacy. Hirsch attacked John Dewey, the father of modern American educational theory, for adopting the concepts of Jean Jacques Rousseau, "who thought that a child's intellectual and social skills would develop naturally without regard to the specific content of education." According to Hirsch, Dewey's "content-neutral conception of educational development has long been triumphant in American schools of education and has long dominated the 'developmental,' content-neutral curricula of our elementary schools."[17]

I do not know where Mr. Hirsch went to school, but the curricula in the schools I attended were not content-neutral nor do I believe they are today. If educators believe in content-neutral education, why does the National Assessment of Educational Progress make such a big thing of what children know in geography and history?[18]

Facts can be learned anywhere and are frequently better retained by accidental encounter than by formal instruction. How many adults today, 15 to 50 years later, could pass the same tests they passed in high school? Without regular use factual knowledge tends to evaporate. But learning to learn is different. Although we all learn how to use our minds willy nilly, learning is a skill that can be greatly augmented by formal training and repeated practice. And as Peter Drucker wrote in 1994, "Increasingly, an educated person will be somebody who has learned how to learn."[19] Or, in the practical words of Microsoft founder and president Bill Gates, everyone needs "an education that emphasizes general problem-solving skills."[20]

EVERYONE A SPECIALIST

A major consequence of the information deluge is that, while it has increased our need for skill in learning and problem solving, it has decreased the importance of remembering specific facts. Peter Drucker summed it up beautifully:

> In the knowledge society knowledge for the most part exists only in application....The central work force in the knowledge society will therefore consist of highly specialized people. In fact, it is a mistake to speak of "generalists." What we will increasingly mean by that term is people who have learned how to acquire additional specialties rapidly in order to move from one kind of job to another....But "generalists" in the sense in which we used to talk of them are coming to be seen as dilettantes rather than educated people.[21]

Every child is destined to grow up to be a specialist, to earn his or her living by mastering an area of learning different than any of the areas mastered by most of his or her neighbors. Today, more than at any time in human history, the body of knowledge most of us share with the majority of our friends, relatives and acquaintances has become much smaller than the body of knowledge we do not share.

Admittedly this causes problems in communication, and it is undoubtedly the reason why there are more difficulties in communication and less agreement in attitudes and opinions than there used to be. But it is a mistake to think that somehow the schools can solve those problems by adopting a syllabus of common content. All one has to do is to read through the list at the end of *Cultural Literacy* to realize the futility of trying to establish a uniform cultural idiom. Culture has always been a dynamic, ever-changing phenomenon, but never more so than today in a world of instant and constant worldwide communication. Undoubtedly the culture of each student will be influenced by teachers and classmates. But any attempt to mold every student to a predetermined "culture," no matter how basic or minimal, is both unfair and impossible. As educational psychologist Harold Gardner wrote:

> It may once have been true that a dedicated individual could master the world's extant knowledge or at least some significant part of it. So long as this was a tenable goal, it made some sense to offer a uniform curriculum. Now, however, no individual can master even a single body of knowledge completely, let alone the range of disciplines and competences. The period of the Renaissance Man or Woman is long past. Inasmuch as choices of emphasis and scope must be made, it becomes an issue only to choose which path an individual should follow.[22]

This does not mean that we can teach without content. No learning process can be content-neutral. To learn how to learn without absorbing information is like learning how to play golf without a golf ball. Not only do we need content to learn how to learn, but content is usually a stronger motivating force than the learning itself.

Young people find school boring precisely because there is so much content that had little relevance to what they consider important. This was true when I went to school, and is just as true today. Why not allow the students who love baseball to *read* about big-league games, *write* about little-league games, create and analyze baseball *statistics*. What kept teachers from letting children choose the content and motivate themselves to learn how to learn? The fetish for "fundamental facts."

Not only has the information deluge made it impossible for schools to supply a basic information package for every American, but it provides so many other sources of information that our schools must think of their task as supplementing and refining an educational base that already exists. As children grow and their interests widen, they should be encouraged to pursue whatever attracts their interest, and be shown how to learn more and do more with what they learn. A good teacher will dangle new interests before the student, but content should always remain a lure rather than a requirement.

EDUCATIONAL MASS PRODUCTION

The youngest child comes to school, even preschool, with a mass of impressions and miscellaneous information. If the school is to help the child, it must start with what is there and build on it. Children do not arrive with identical impressions or information. As early-education pioneer Jean Piaget has shown, there are wide differences in their attention spans, thought rhythms and learning paces. Hence it is folly to assign children by age to the same classroom and force them to undergo an identical curriculum. A number of authors have pointed out that today's school system was developed as a shadow-image of the industrial factory. Over 60 years ago, educational expert Elwood P. Cuberly wrote:

> Our schools are, in a sense, factories in which the raw materials are to be shaped and fashioned into products to meet the various demands of life. The specifications for manufacturing come from the demands of 20th Century civilization, and it is the business of the school to build its pupils to the specifications laid down.[23]

Schools were organized for the mass production of educated citizens. Of course, they never performed quite that way. Some youngsters got a lot out of school; others profited very little. The system itself was more efficient at teaching students to tolerate boredom and long-suffering than in developing a love of learning, the value and excitement of creativity or the satisfaction of understanding—which seems to confirm the theory of Jesuit scholar Walter J. Ong that secondary schools were really initiation rites created by 17th Century society to introduce young men to adulthood.[24] It also confirms the school memories of Nathaniel Branden, author of *The Six Pillars of Self-Esteem*:

> I vividly recall my own experiences in grade school and high school during the 1930s and 1940s. The two most important values conveyed to me in that world were the ability to remain silent and motionless for long periods of time and the ability to march with my fellow students in a neat row from one classroom to another. School was not a place to learn independent thinking, to have one's self-assertiveness encouraged, to have one's autonomy nourished and strengthened. It was a place to learn how to fit into some nameless system created by some nameless others and called "the world" or "society" or "the way life is." And "the way life is" was not to be questioned. Since I questioned everything

and found silence and stillness unbearable, I was quickly identified as a troublemaker.[25]

THE NEED FOR CUSTOMIZING

One reason educational mass production does not work is not only that every child comes to school with a unique package of ideas and impressions, but that many children do not have the linguistic and logical-mathematical intelligences the school is geared to train, which is why educator James Bryant Conant could say over half a century ago:

> We have a great deal of make-believe in our schools and colleges—too many feeble attempts at tasks which are proper only for a restricted type of individual; too many failures to explore talents which fall outside orthodox academic bounds.[26]

As Howard Gardner established in his revolutionary 1993 book, *Multiple Intelligences,* there are at least seven kinds of human intelligences and our schools concentrate on the linguistic and logical-mathematical but ignore the spatial, musical, bodily-kinesthetic, interpersonal and intrapersonal intelligences.[27] Gardner insisted, with ample evidence, that each of these intelligences can be extremely useful not only for the individual who has it, but also for those around him or her.

No one suggests that we should set up seven schools or courses. Nor can we label children by type of intelligence. What Gardner calls intelligences are ways of thinking, not distinct brains. Individuals use all these ways to an extent, and every individual has a unique blend. Others have suggested that there are as many as 14 intelligences.[28] (Gardner himself has added an eighth, naturalist intelligence, to his original seven.[29]) This is why Gardner and his collaborator Tina Blythe argued that the move to establish national standards to make our schools more uniform is a mistake. They want individual-centered schooling "to ensure that everyone receive an education that maximizes his or her own intellectual potential."[30]

AN EDUCATIONAL STANDARD

Is there, then, no standard foundation, no principles on which to base the educational system? Gardner and Blythe suggested that the theory of multiple intelligences can be used as a basis "on which to make suggestions and to choose electives."[31] To formalize individual-centered schooling they suggested three specialists be added to the faculty:

1. An assessment specialist: to provide a regular view of the particular strengths, inclinations and weakness of each child.

2. A student-curriculum broker: to assist each student in choosing courses and teachers to fit his or her abilities and manner of learning.

3. A school-community broker: to help each student find a vocational or avocational role that matches his or her profile of intelligences.

The authors stressed that "none of these roles is designed in any way to minimize or circumvent the role of the individual teacher,"[32] although I find it difficult to imagine how teachers could meet the considerable differences in how individual students learn without considerably altering their traditional role. There is only one way to customize elementary education and apply all we now know about children's minds and educational goals. We must replace classrooms and courses with collaboration and coaching.

AN IMAGINARY CURRICULUM

After studying the way many major companies do their hiring, Harvard economist Richard Murnane and MIT economist Frank Levy (in *Teaching the New Basic Skills*) concluded that the ability to use English and math in solving practical problems, initiative, flexibility and teamwork are more important than literacy, mathematics and an acquaintance with civilization's classics.[33] Peter Drucker complained that

> no educational institution—not even the graduate school of management—tries to equip students with the elementary skills that would make them effective as members of an organization: the ability to present ideas orally and in writing; the ability to work with people; the ability to shape and direct one's own work, contribution and career.[34]

To prepare children to survive and succeed in the world created by the information deluge, a society dependent on networking, partnering and specialization, we must help them learn:

1. How to use the basic tools of communication: speaking, reading, writing and arithmetic, without which networking is impossible.

2. How to work with others, since ability to cooperate is essential to partnering. According to the authors of *The Collaborative Dimensions of*

Learning, a collaborative approach "helps develop academic skills while promoting understanding and self-esteem," and helps students adjust to the demands of today's workplace and civic culture by tapping students' social nature.[35]

3. How to develop and have confidence in their intuition. Schooling today tries to manage the accelerated flow of information by slowing it down to fit the traditional learning process. What it should be doing is developing methods to sharpen intuition, which is nature's tool for handling information too swift for standard processing. Play helps develop intuition, and play in school—from sports to chess—should be an integral part of the curriculum not a respite from it.

4. How to evaluate and exploit their personal talents and interests, which will determine their future value as partners.

What follows is my visualization of how such an educational system might work in practice. Experts in pedagogy may have a more effective vision. My "curriculum" is imagined merely to help us understand how an educational system might prepare our children to survive the information deluge and succeed in the knowledge economy.

As I see it, elementary school should give children facility in communication, enumeration, collaboration and self-direction. High school should help them select their careers. The final years, what we now call college, should provide the training or learning required for their chosen careers. Of course, education should not end there, for the knowledge economy demands continuous education throughout life. (More about that later.)

Following these objectives, I see five phases in preadult education. I designate them by age, but ages should be understood as averages, for children mature at different rates.

1. Primary development (ages 6 through 8), children learn how to talk, listen, write, read, count and interrelate with other children.

2. Intermediate development (ages 9 through 11), youngsters progress to more advanced reading, writing, mathematics and collaboration with their peers.

3. Middle development (ages 12 through 14), students learn problem solving and self-analysis or how to evaluate and exploit personal abilities to succeed in both personal and group activities.

4. Career exploration (ages 15 through 17), adolescents sample various fields of knowledge to help them decide what they want to do in life.

5. Career preparation (ages 18 to 22), young men and women concentrate on acquiring the specialized knowledge they need to work in the fields they have chosen.

In a 1994 article in *The Futurist,* George Washington University professors William E. Halal and Jay Liebowitz wrote about "Telelearning: The Multimedia Revolution in Education," and saw one result as the shift in the teacher's role "from lecturing to advising or coaching."[36] Technical tools may facilitate the switch to coaching, but I believe it will result not from tools but from a fundamental rethinking of the idea of education.

I propose that every elementary school teacher be trained as a coach with a specialty in one of the following areas: early-development, middle-development, graduate-development, career-exploration or general guidance counseling. In high school and college there will also be teachers who specialize in specific fields of knowledge. To avoid confusion I shall hereafter call them "professors," whether on the high school or college level. In other words, coaches are concerned with method; professors, with content.

COUNSELORS AND COACHES

Ideally, each youngster would have the same guidance counselor throughout his or her preadult education. The guidance counselor keeps a record of the student's progress, identifies unique abilities, difficulties and type of intelligence, assigns the student to proper coaches at each stage of development and occasionally holds back students who fail to progress as rapidly as their peers. A guidance counselor can handle as many as 50 students at a time, devoting an average one day every eight weeks to each student, half a day with the student and half with the student's current coach.

The average case load for coaches is 24 students, assigned to them for three years, usually eight new students a year.

17. Transforming Education

The primary-development coach supervises all 24 children during the entire school day, similar to current classrooms but without the formality and without separating the age groups. Older children help the coach in accustoming newcomers to the new environment and introducing them to skills like reading, writing, arithmetic and organized play. There are no "subjects" in the traditional sense. The coach pursues whatever topic interests the children. Listening, talking, reading, writing, using numbers and interrelating are skills developed more by practice than by instruction.

Much of these first three years are spent in games and small group projects that introduce the children to teamwork and require them to use the skills they should develop.

At the beginning of each school year, the guidance counselors and the early-development coaches use the knowledge learned about the children in the first three years to select middle-development teams, each with eight students with as great a variety of talent and types of intelligence as is practical. Each of these octets is then assigned to an appropriate middle-development coach.

Intermediate-development coaches supervise three eight-student teams. As they are assigned eight new students each year, they are always working with one new team, one in its second year, and one in its third. The principal teaching method during the intermediate years are team projects, each pursued as a team effort and followed by two written reports. The first is prepared cooperatively by the team and outlines what was achieved and how it was done. The second consists of each individual's confidential report on what he or she contributed to the project and how he or she thinks the whole team's performance might have been been improved.

Teams spend one to two days on each project in the first year, longer periods as they develop more experience and confidence and the projects become more complex. By the time they are in their third year of intermediate development, they are working on projects that require a week or longer. The coach assists each team to choose their projects, to design the strategy for executing them and to evaluate progress. The objective is to allow the students as much freedom as possible to develop initiative and learn what they do best, to develop communications skills in both speaking and writing, to manage the financial and accounting aspects of the project, and to learn how to use outside sources for information and assistance.

Coaches for the middle-development group will also monitor 24 students, in three age ranges. But this time they will mix and match the 24 to help the students evaluate their personal abilities and how others see them. During the course of the year, each of the 24 students, beginning with the oldest, will have the opportunity to propose a project (with the help and approval of the coach) and select four to seven volunteers to help. The volunteers are encouraged to sell themselves to the project leader by telling him or her what they can contribute. Those who have difficulty selling themselves get special counseling by the coach.

PROFESSORS AND CAREERS

Since career-exploration coaches spend less time with each student than the other coaches, they can supervise as many as 50 students. Their chief function is to launch each student into researching areas he or she chooses as well as areas the coach and guidance counselor believe match the student's abilities. In the first two years of this period, students are assigned to small teams (three or four partners) to research a subject together. In the final year, most of the research is done individually.

During career exploration students have their first contact with professors. Depending on the size of the "school," there will be a number of professors specializing in different information areas. In smaller schools professors may specialize in several fields. Professors function somewhat like coaches in that they assign projects (e.g., lists to compile, papers to write, experiments to conduct), suggest books, tapes and CD-ROMs and other sources for study and evaluate results. When an area of exploration is complete (which may be longer or shorter depending on the student's interest), professor, coach and student discuss the student's chance for success in that field.

At the end of the third year of career exploration, each student decides on the field he or she wishes to pursue with the help and counsel of a guidance counselor, career coach and career professor in that field. Students are counseled to think more about a field of knowledge than a specific type of job. The kind of work people do changes daily, and the student will be more useful as a partner if he or she has a wide grasp of a knowledge area.

In any case, the decision made here is not final. The student has three years of career preparation, in which he or she will be assigned to a professor as mentor, coach and instructor. If unhappy with the major chosen, a student can start over in a different area of specialization. A recent report showed that one in five graduates with degrees in engineering or the natural sciences end up in other fields.[37] My guess is that the number would be less in a system that gives more time to career exploration.

The ideal situation, of course, is to spend all three career-preparation years with one professor, studying a single area of knowledge. The professor will direct students to books, tapes and CD-ROMs, on-line services and the Internet in proper sequence, to interviews with practitioners in the field, to lectures by experts. Students will do as much of the work in teams as they do individually. By the third year each student will complete at least one major team project, an original dissertation, and a three-month apprenticeship with a working partnership in the field.

This bare-bones description of the system makes it sound more rigid than it would be in practice. In school, as in life, students not only must adapt to circumstances but also learn by so adapting.

CULTURAL CONSISTENCY AMID INFORMATION CHAOS

Would students who graduate from the system I have described be uncultured? They may not be acquainted with every single word on Hirsch's list for cultural literacy, but a knowledge of facts or words does not make a culture. According to every description I have read, culture covers moral as much as intellectual faculties and is defined by a person's behavior and taste as much as by what he or she knows.

In his 1995 book, *Commercial Culture,* newspaper expert Leo Bogart distinguished between popular and elite culture.[38] Popular culture "embraces the constantly changing figures, styles, and icons that, at any given moment, are generally familiar, attract wide audiences, and fill time and casual conversations." Elite culture, which has a more universal quality, does not exist naturally, but is "sustained, either as a matter of public policy, by educational institutions and public broadcasting systems, or by enlightened management of the privately owned mass media." Bogart was concerned about the commercial media's tendency "to manipulate social standards in the pursuit of its commercial interest." Our concern here is whether the school system should sustain elite culture as a matter of public policy.

Bogart made three important observation about elite culture. First, the American audience for elite culture "is remarkably small." Second, elite standards used by critics are frequently "totally at odds with those of the mass publics." Finally, "prevailing notions of good taste have undergone constant change throughout history, and indeed vary widely among different societies."

The curriculum I have imagined is not designed to promote elite culture largely because defining elite culture is so controversial. I agree with Robert Hughes, who wrote in *The Culture of Complaint,* that it is wrong to think "that one can construct a hierarchy of Timeless Values, and maintain it against the vicissitudes of the present,"[39] and I find totally unrealistic the nostalgic intellectual snobbery of Allan Bloom's *The Closing of the American Mind.*

Since coaches will be highly educated men and women, it can be presumed they will have a knowledge of and usually a taste for what they consider elite culture, that they will develop opportunities to expose students to civilization's master works, and that an appreciation of cultural achievements will rub off on their charges.

A CURRICULUM FOR BUILDING CHARACTER

But I am convinced that good taste is not as important to society as good character, and I believe that the curriculum's emphasis on cooperation and sharing goals will do more for the average student's character than the current educational system does. More than 50 years ago psychologist Erich Fromm wrote:

> In order that any society may function well, its members must acquire the kind of character which makes them *want* to act in the way they *have* to act as members of the society or of a special class within it. They have to *desire* what objectively is *necessary* for them to do. *Outer force* is replaced by *inner compulsion,* and by the particular kind of human energy which is channeled into character traits.[40]

The foundation of culture is character, and nothing builds character as effectively as teamwork, where children learn to want to do what is necessary for the objective of the group. Even when the group is at war with other groups, membership contributes to character. If we want to restore morality, we have to rebuild peer pressure by replacing vanishing communities of locale with communities of common purpose.

Individualism becomes selfishness when it is excised from a communal frame of reference. Even Henry David Thoreau's *Civil Disobedience* and *Walden* were built on the values of the 19th Century Transcendalist community. Without the opinion of others we lack norms against which to evaluate ourselves. In *Eupsychian Management,* psychologist Abraham Maslow argued:

> The trouble with education today, as with so many other American institutions, is that nobody is quite sure of what the goals and the ultimate ends of education are. Once the goals of democratic education are clearly set forth, then all the means questions will settle themselves overnight. Here we must be very bold; the goals of democratic education, once we leave aside the question of technological training, can be nothing else but development toward psychological health. That is, education must be eupsychian [i.e., in good psychological health] or else it is not democratic.[41]

Democratic society, certainly the democratic knowledge society, needs citizens who are psychologically healthy, people who understand and accept their strengths and weaknesses and are willing to work with others. So does every business. We cannot organize the information deluge, but we can organize ourselves and the people with whom we work and live. Again it is purpose that creates organization, which is why the central purpose of the educational system should be to teach children how to thrive in groups organized by purpose, to prepare them for a world in which everyone earns a living through partnering and networking.

I agree with Hirsch that a common language with common reference points is necessary for communication. But I think that language develops naturally in any group that works together. Culture is not the creation of regulations prescribed by government, school or religion. It is more like the weather, a perpetually changing condition resulting from billions of influences. A few of these influences may be momentous and traceable, but most are subtle and unnoticeable, and very few are controllable.

EDUCATIONAL PARTNERING

I have said nothing about school facilities, administration and funding. Here, too, I see education as a private enterprise offered and administered by partners working through networks and regulated by the educational community. If we look back in history, we see that that is how education began. Socrates had no government edict compelling students to attend his classes. The early American schools were all private enterprises. Our public school system itself grew out of the spontaneous agreement in small communities to erect a schoolhouse and support a teacher.

Returning education to the private sector will take the system away from administrators and give it back to educators. Parents will pay their children's guidance counselors, coaches or professors just as we pay auto mechanics, doctors, hair dressers and cable companies. Already today, in 1998, according to a *Newsweek* poll, 42 percent of Americans see "a great need for children to receive private outside tutoring."[42] As private tutors do now, in the future educational professionals will rent their own space and buy their own equipment. Charitable organizations and teachers themselves will help parents who cannot afford to educate their children, just as charities and suppliers help parents who cannot afford to feed their children.

EVERYONE A TEACHER; EVERYONE A PUPIL

Privatization of schooling will eliminate most of the bureaucracy in public elementary and middle schools. But colleges and universities, whether private or public, are also burdened with bureaucracy. As business and government partnership networks take over, I believe they will also become standard in higher education. Three factors will encourage this.

First, the constant multiplication of information, resulting in ever-changing fields of specialization, will make it impossible to maintain the established courses and specific departments that are the bedrock of educational bureaucracy. Future education is likely to be extremely particularized, conducted one-on-one or in very small groups. There will be less and less need for ivy-covered factories with huge lecture halls. When professors in wide demand have to communicate through lectures, the lectures will be provided on CD-ROM or videotape.

Second, most openings for young people seeking professorships will be as juniors in partnerships formed either to help youngsters explore a particular field of knowledge, or to educate those who have already chosen their field. What we now call colleges and universities will become extensions of the systems that provided their early education—with students working in small groups and professors coaching rather than lecturing. In *The Democratic Corporation,* Russell Ackoff describes his ideal business school: "Small groups of students (no more than ten) would be self-organized into learning cells in which they would share responsibility for teaching each other parts of the subject being 'taken'."[43]

Third, since the knowledge economy makes continuing education a universal necessity, adults will be constantly looking for professors who can customize courses to fit both their needs and their schedules. Today, with two out of every five adult Americans taking courses, students on part-time schedules include not only those in adult education but also half of college and university matriculants,[44] whose number has doubled in 25 years and should double again by the end of the century.

As education demands become more specialized, there will be increasing opportunities for individuals to supplement income during intervals between partnership assignments by instructing others. I see the average adult in the world of tomorrow alternating work, learning and teaching, with the proportion of teaching to learning increasing with age and experience.

DE-SCHOOLING SOCIETY

Some three decades ago Ivan Illich created a stir with his theories on "de-schooling society." He distinguished between schooling, which provided what he called a formal "knowledge stock," and education, which he defined as the "free determination by each learner of his own reason for living and learning—the part that his knowledge is to play in his life."

Illich felt that traditional schools created an inhibiting social hierarchy and should be abandoned in favor of "learning webs" consisting of skill-exchanges, peer-matching, educators-at-large, intellectual gurus and wandering scholars available when needed.[45]

He was far ahead of his time, and came very close to describing education as I expect it to be in the world of partnership networks.

Part Four

Toward New Paradigms

In Parts One, Two and Three I tried to stay close to what has happened in society and the resulting logical developments to help readers and myself understand what has taken place and what is likely to happen in the future. Throughout I tried to make observations without normative judgments. I asked readers to accept the organization of business and society in partnership networks, not as something I would like to happen, but as a logical outcome of what is already taking place.

Part Four is different. The following five chapters reflect hope as much as logic. They contain my personal opinions influenced by the conclusions of the preceding three parts, but not essential to them. To survive into the 21st Century, I believe society must break away from its present paradigms, principally in our way of thinking about the bottom line, the corporation and intellectual property.

To keep afloat in the information deluge, each of us must put the major problems of our time in perspective and develop new attitudes in self management. Because I am by nature an optimist, I am convinced the human race faces a great and overall beneficent future.

18

THE NEED FOR PARADIGM CHANGE

"Social structure changes, develops, adapts itself to an altered situation, only, ... in the last analysis, through a change in the habits of thought of the individuals which make up the community."
— *Thorstein Veblen, 1899*[1]

Human beings adopt many paradigms to facilitate social activity, but such paradigms can live beyond their usefulness and interfere with our management of reality. In my opinion, society would be better off if we abandoned three paradigms that have become outdated but still rule much of modern life.

A WAY OF THINKING

The quote that heads this chapter is from Thorstein Veblen's *The Theory of the Leisure Class*, first published in 1899. Veblen, a social analyst incredibly ahead of his time, argues that human institutions evolve by a process of natural selection brought about by the interplay of individual ideas and institutionally-formed attitudes, because

> ...institutions are not only themselves the result of a selective and adaptive process which shapes the prevailing or dominant types of spiritual attitude and aptitudes, they are at the same time special methods of life and of human relations, and are therefore in their turn efficient factors of selection....Institutions must change with changing circumstances, since they are of the nature of an habitual

method of responding to the stimuli which these changing circumstances afford. The development of these institutions is the development of society. The institutions are, in substance, prevalent habits of thought with respect to particular relations and particular functions of the individual and of the community; and the scheme of life, which is made up of the aggregate of institutions in force at a given time or at a given point in the development of any society, may, on the psychological side, be broadly characterized as a prevalent spiritual attitude or a prevalent theory of life.[2]

In Chapter 13 we examined three examples of institutions that have long been prevalent habits of thought with respect to particular relations and particular functions of the individual and of the community: central sovereignty, territorial government and the financial commons. All three are institutions which must change with changing circumstances, but which will not change without a change in the habits of thought.

CHANGING SCIENTIFIC PARADIGMS

More than 60 years after Veblen, Thomas Kuhn wrote his essay on *The Structure of Scientific Revolutions*. His basic argument was that in science "the decision to reject one paradigm is always simultaneously the decision to accept another, and the judgment leading to that decision involves the comparison of both paradigms with nature and with each other."[3]

In Kuhn's use the word *paradigm* means a way of thinking based on a theory that dominates scientific research for a significant period of time. Examples of paradigms which scientists once considered useful but were replaced by entirely new paradigms include Ptolemy's astronomy supplanted by that of Copernicus, Becher's phlogiston theory of combustion being outdated by Lavoisier's understanding of gasses and Newton's laws of gravity bowing before Einstein's theory of relativity. Relativity has changed our worldview, even though Newton's laws are still valid except for objects approaching the speed of light.

What Kuhn says of scientific thinking can be applied to popular thought. My examples of obsolete popular paradigms: the idea that the world was flat, that the sun revolved around the earth or that health and personality depended on how four "humors" were balanced in our bodies.

Kuhn is concerned exclusively with the physical sciences. In a postscript he mentions that readers have "read its main theses as applicable to many other fields,"[4] and warns that much of what he says is not applicable to non-scientific fields.

But he allows that "to the extent that the book portrays scientific development as a succession of tradition-bound periods punctuated by non-cumulative breaks, its theses are undoubtedly of wide applicability." Hence I feel free to use his definition of paradigm and to apply it to the field of socioeconomics.

CHANGING SOCIOECONOMIC PARADIGMS

A socioeconomic paradigm is a way of thinking based on a principle that dominates social, legal and economic life for a significant period of time, what Veblen calls institutions that are prevalent habits of thought, or what a more recent author, Charles Garfield in his 1992 book, *Second to None*, describes as "a story, or a set of stories, that we invent in order to make sense of the world around us. These stories provide us with a framework by which we create order out of chaos, a practical road map for making our way in the world."[5]

Like paradigms in science, widely accepted socioeconomic paradigms can be replaced by new paradigms when advances in knowledge make the old paradigm a source of too many unsolvable problems. The paradigm of the divine right of kings was replaced by the idea that government's power came from the consent of the governed. The primogeniture paradigm, that the firstborn had exclusive rights to a family's property and privileges, was displaced by the idea that all men are created equal.

We have seen that central sovereignty, territorial government and the financial commons are paradigms on the verge of being replaced. It is my contention that three other established paradigms in today's society should also be abandoned and replaced:

1. The bottom-line paradigm: profit is the purpose of business activity, and a way of measuring progress and success for both institutions and individuals.

2. The corporation paradigm: society can recognize an association or group of human beings as a legal person with responsibilities, ownership rights and liability distinct from members of the group. (Since I am talking about a socioeconomic paradigm and not the legal entities as such, I will ignore the differences in state laws, the distinction between general corporations. close corporations, professional corporations and limited liability companies.[6])

3. **The intellectual property paradigm:** ideas can be exclusively owned, bought and sold as if they were material things.

A MATTER OF PROPERTY

All three of these paradigms are related to and flow from the idea of property. The right of human beings to exclusive possession of things outside themselves has always been a sticky subject in both law and economics.

In the 17th Century two British philosophers, Thomas Hobbes and John Locke, disagreed radically about the origin of property. Hobbes held that there was no such thing in the state of nature, that ownership developed when people living in communities agreed to recognize each other's right to individual property. Locke held that ownership of property was a natural right because each individual's labor belonged exclusively to him, making the fruits of labor the exclusive property of the laborer.[7] Adam Smith more or less followed Locke, as did most economists after him.

If ownership flows exclusively from labor it becomes very difficult to explain how one person can be employed by another. Is the employer paying for the work or for the fruits of the work? And, if the latter, is piecework the only just form of compensation? Should the investor and the factory owner benefit from the products produced by the workers? Karl Marx's answer was communism and the dictatorship of the proletariat.

I believe that the basic right of ownership is natural, but that it flows from our ideas, not from our labor. The natural right to ownership rests on our inborn ability to create man-made things, to transform what we find in nature by informing it with our ideas. To borrow the conceptual distinction developed by Aristotle, the form is the human idea; the matter is nature's bounty.

I agree with Hobbes that natural things, such as stones, belong to everybody. I agree with Locke that when a sculptor takes a stone and carves it into a statue or an ax, the statue or ax becomes his property. But it is not the labor that made it his or her property, it is the imposition of the creator's idea on the stone. Thus the property owner who wants to build a house or put up a barn can hire laborers to realize his or her plan and still own the result.

Note that it is the creator's *imposition* of the idea, not the architectural plan or design, that makes the house or barn personal property. This is a very meaningful distinction, as we shall see, when we analyze the intellectual property paradigm.

Land, the most natural thing of all, becomes property when a man imposes his ideas upon it, no matter how humble the shelter built or the garden grown. In early American history a farmer or miner could put a claim on land that no individual owned. Since the U.S. government had bought the Louisiana territories from France in 1803, the Land Law of 1820 established a minimum price of $1.25 an acre. But the individual's claim hinged on a promise that the claimant would develop the land in some way.

Hobbes' theory of property by contract and Locke's theory of property by natural right have battled each other every time economists, ethicists or legal philosophers tried to reconcile the basic idea of ownership whether with the moral imperatives of sharing and caring, the legal restrictions against theft and booty, or the government requirements of public domain. The conflict is eliminated if we accept that the natural right of ownership can be applied and modified by social contract. It is precisely because humans have a natural right to own what they create that they can bargain away applications of that right to achieve or promote community.

A TRUER APPROACH TO OWNERSHIP

New paradigms are developed to meet human needs as they change with the growth of knowledge. They replace old paradigms because the old paradigms have been found to violate, contradict or obstruct new knowledge. When we study all the paradigms the information deluge is sweeping away, we find that most obsolete paradigms are replaced when influential leaders, followed by the public, realize one of three things:

1. The old paradigm no longer fills its purpose, because it oversimplifies the solution for a widespread problem. The idea that the world was flat became an obsolete paradigm when it no longer solved the problems of travel and transport. I believe the concept of the bottom-line as a business goal is an obsolete paradigm because it oversimplifies the purpose of business management and interferes with accountability.

2. The old paradigm has developed into an instrument for social abuse. The divine-right of kings became an obsolete paradigm because, once established to assure social order, it had become a tool of tyranny and social injustice. I believe the corporation has become an obsolete paradigm, because, once founded to facilitate group enterprise, it has become a shelter for exercising power without responsibility.

3. The old paradigm is no longer effective or applicable due to changes in the social environment. The right of primogeniture became an obsolete paradigm when it was no longer effective in regulating the new ways of distributing wealth and organizing industry. I believe intellectual property is becoming an obsolete paradigm, because it is no longer effective in regulating the new ways of transmitting information and applying innovation.

In the following three chapters I explain why I believe the bottom line, the corporation and intellectual property paradigms are not only obsolete but harmful.

19

THE BOTTOM LINE — A DECEPTION

"The practical value of the universe has never been stated in dollars."

— Henry Adams, 1907[1]

The idea of measuring success by the bottom line grew out of the use of money. Yet businesses do not need a profit to be healthy. While neither business planning nor business motivation require profits, a narrow concentration on the bottom line encourages social irresponsibility. We must replace the bottom-line paradigm with a paradigm of business balance.

Profit was not a concept intrinsic to barter. In a barter economy businessmen expected and looked for an equal exchange. The barterer who swapped something of less value for something of greater value was a cheat. This is probably why early cultures considered usury (loaning money at a profit) and engrossing (buying cheap in quantity to sell dear in small lots)[2] as immoral practices. Citizens of other early cultures applied the prohibition against usury and unequal barter only to trade with one's own people. Taking advantage of strangers was permitted.

BEHIND THE BOTTOM LINE

The idea of profit seems to have grown out of the invention of money. Chapter 6 showed how money, though a fictitious measure of value, became a useful paradigm, because it solved barter's problems arising from distance and time. Money made it easier to store wealth. Although investment existed under the barter system (trading sheep for seed to plant wheat, or wine for ewes who would bear lambs), the existence of money made it possible to invest in the labor and risk of others. A rich man could supply the money with which a sea captain could purchase a ship, pay a crew, and buy a cargo to swap for goods in foreign lands. If the trip was successful, the rich man would get his money back and more. That more was profit.

Of course, if the venture was successful the captain, and even the crew, would also profit. But for the captain, and certainly for most of the crew, the profit was a hand-to-mouth thing. If you were lucky, you lived through the trip and had some pocket money for grog, girls and games when safely home. It was the financier who saw the profit from the venture as the bottom line, the paradigm that was eventually applied to every serious business.

From the viewpoint of today's culture, the weaknesses in the paradigm were evident even then. Although the captain and crew invested a large chunk of their lives, and quite possibly life itself, in the venture, the bottom-line profit treated their contribution as an incidental cost. The success of the venture was measured entirely by what it brought the financier, totally ignoring the benefit it might bring the captain, the crew, or even the shipbuilders and tradesmen in the community from which it sailed.

This form of measuring accountability in business became an accepted paradigm primarily because it was easy to apply. Money could be counted with precision. Other values could not. More important, social attitudes at that time did not encourage a lot of soul-searching about the rights of seamen (who were frequently plied with drink and abducted into service). Social equality, as we know it, had not even occurred to most people. The thought-leaders of those days (as they usually are today) were the people of power and wealth. It was natural that the paradigm for measuring business would measure what interested them. No one was looking for a way to measure benefits or costs to workers, to the community, or to the environment.

Some readers will argue with justification that I make too big a thing of the bottom-line paradigm. As *Internal Markets* points out, "When evaluating the performance of a company, financial analysts do not look at profit by itself. They consider many variables including profitability."[3] True, but—beyond the fact that there would be little demand for financial analysts if all they looked at was the bottom line—we must remember that a primary reason for studying other variables is to predict tomorrow's bottom line.

WHY DOES A BUSINESS NEED A PROFIT?

Although I spent many years in school, I never took business courses. Hence early employment, especially in small businesses, gave me my first real experience with business management and accounting. What my schooling did provide were courses in philosophy which fed a natural tendency to question what others took for granted. One day, after my boss gave me a lecture on the need for profit, I asked myself (he would have given me up as hopeless had I said it aloud): "Why does a business need profit to be successful? If a business provides a product that satisfies customers, enables all its employees to make a comfortable living and pays its financial backers adequately for the use of their money, why does it also have to make a profit?" I could see why a business had to avoid a loss, but I could not understand why a business with a bottom line of zero was not a success.

I never found a satisfying answer to that question. I learned over the years that businesses need money for research and development, for growth, for slush funds to survive recessions and other setbacks. And, of course, the principal explanation was that profits were needed so that stockholders could be paid dividends. None of these answers satisfied me, for I saw all these expenses—including stockholder dividends—as costs of doing business. After all, the difference between a loan from a bank and an investment by a stockholder, is that the first charges a specific rate while the second charges a variable rate with the hope of greater return.

Businesses do not distribute their entire profits to their stockholders. In fact, some publicly owned companies do not distribute dividends at all. Nor is there any law, in this country at least, that forces a company that is not dissolving to share its profits with its stockholders. In today's economy, the only motive management has for distributing dividends is to make the stock more attractive on the stock market, which is important only because the company might want to issue more stock or, more often, because individual managers own stock.

PROFIT FOR PLANNING

Perhaps the most convincing argument for profits is that they are necessary for investment. John Kenneth Galbraith developed this thesis at length in *The New Industrial State,* arguing that long-range planning is the significant characteristic of the modern industrial economy. Large factories and machines require a commitment long before manufacturers can get a return on investment. This requires capital, i.e., savings.[4]

But ordinary people save relatively little. In fact, the industrial economy depends on the great majority's consuming rather than saving. The rich save more. Hence Galbraith argued that the great bulk of savings for investment come from the profits of large corporations, and concluded that the industrial economy depends on the ability of large corporations to invest profits in factories, machinery, research and development.

He also pointed out that modern governments also require savings to invest in our social future, and that they do this by taxation.

I do not agree that planning is a unique characteristic to the industrial economy. I believe planning is an essential part of any human life and intrinsic to even the most primitive economies. I agree with Galbraith, however, that the industrial economy he was studying in the '60s and '70s had become dominated by larger, more complex enterprises which required longer planning time and greater investment.

What Galbraith ignored was that business had greatly expanded the use of credit to accelerate consumption. The growth of credit is especially important, for it made planning possible without savings. Instead of saving to buy a new home, or even a new sofa, consumers could purchase a home with a mortgage or a sofa on time. Hence Galbraith was wrong in concluding that most Americans did not contribute to investment. The investment that had traditionally been done through saving was now being done by paying off one's debts.

The credit revolution did not stop with consumers. Businesses, too, began to depend more and more upon credit as a way to invest without saving. A large percentage of today's major corporations carry enormous loads of debt. The credit binge does not end at the corporate level. Today most national governments are also living on credit.

19. The Bottom Line--A Deception

There are two major consequences of the growth of credit. The first is that it makes it easier for the weak to get into trouble. In 1996, 1.6 million Americans filed for bankruptcy.[5] More portentously, bankruptcy, expedited by Chapter XI, has almost become a way of doing business for business bureaucracies. And, most fearful of all, the bankruptcy of nations, usually called currency devaluation, is no longer uncommon.

The second consequence is that the need to invest no longer justifies the bottom-line paradigm, since both payment of interest and repayment of debt are calculated before the bottom line.

PROFIT VS. THE PROFIT MOTIVE

The final argument for the bottom line is that the economy needs the profit motive. There is no doubt that money is a near-universal motive. But it is a means, not an end. Nearly everyone wants money, but people want it for many reasons. Not only do they want it differently, but they use it differently—from the man with a compulsion to spend whatever he happens to have in his wallet to the woman who puts every penny away "for a rainy day." These discrepancies wreak havoc with economic theory.

Individuals work to satisfy two classes of basic needs: material and psychological. Men and women devote labor and attention to business to supply the necessities of life and/or to achieve self-fulfillment, i.e., to make a living or to make a life. Hence, so far as individuals are concerned—whether entrepreneurs, managers or employees—businesses succeed only so far as they help provide a good living and a better life.

When we look at the social picture, businesses contribute to society also by satisfying society's material needs and/or by contributing to its desirable social life. One of the ways profit is supposed to do both is by encouraging growth, which tends to make the society richer. So long as the business manager has his eye on the bottom line, he wants his company to obtain a larger share of market, to invade more markets, and to find more people to buy its products.

This push for growth is supposed to help the whole of society. It is business' constant thirst for growth that raises everybody's standard of living. Because Henry Ford wanted to sell more cars, he doubled his workers' minimum wage so they could afford to buy his cars. However, the bottom line is neither a requirement for growth nor a basic motive. Growth requires both operational and capital investments, and both should be accounted for before the bottom line.

Today, most people consider concern for necessities and a better life as primary goals for both individual and society, which is why the bottom-line paradigm is obsolete, for it measures neither the material nor the spiritual values that a business can contribute to individuals and to society.

PROFITS VS. BUSINESS BENEFITS

On the contrary, businessmen who let the bottom line be their guide frequently end up hurting those values. Companies can and do improve the bottom line by:

1. Underpaying their employees.
2. Lowering the quality of the company's products or services.
3. Curbing investment in the company's future prosperity and growth.
4. Damaging the environment to save on costs.
5. Cheating or putting pressure on suppliers.
6. Avoiding the costs of safety measures to protect employees or customers.
7. Forcing employees to do work they hate or are ashamed of.

No less an authority than John Maynard Keynes argued that a market-driven society would lead to lasting underemployment, and recommended government suppression of the profit motive by what he called "euthanasia of the rentier" or a "somewhat comprehensive" socialization of investment.[6] Keynes' contemporary, Joseph Alios Schumpeter, saw the profit motive as eventually destroying capitalism:

> Capitalism creates a rational frame of mind which, having destroyed the moral authority of so many other institutions, in the end turns against its own: the bourgeois finds to his amazement that the rationalist attitude does not stop at the credentials of kings and popes, but goes on to attack private property and the whole scheme of bourgeois values.[7]

We still live by capitalism's bottom-line paradigm, although we do all we can to encourage companies to forget the bottom line in favor of "corporate

19. The Bottom Line--A Deception

responsibility," and give prizes and public applause to firms that help their communities, are rated "best places to work," or divert to charity money, time and effort that could have contributed to the bottom line.

Kent Nelson, president of United Parcel Service, once said: "The corporate mission at UPS has four areas: taking care of customers, taking care of employees, taking care of share owners, and taking care of community." But he immediately added, "All four are important to us, but we can't do any of them if we aren't profitable."[8] No one in the panel discussion from which this quote is taken asked him: "How profitable? Why can't you do all four if the bottom line reads zero?" Confusing profitability with avoiding red ink is a common example of double talk to protect the paradigm.

CHALLENGING THE PROFIT MOTIVE

Yet a few economists are beginning to challenge the profit motive. Peter Drucker acknowledges that economic performance is not the *only* responsibility of a business, but insists that it is "the *first* responsibility."[9] In *When Corporations Rule the World*, David C. Korten goes much further. He calls the "beliefs espoused by free-market ideologues" a "sanctification of greed."[10] Neva R. Goodwin of Tufts University is less dramatic but just as decisive. She writes:

> It is a mistake, for several reasons, to think that the concept of profit maximization adequately sums up the goal definition of firms. Empirical evidence against such a simple view has been produced by three groups: (a) theorists who emphasize the primacy of selfish individual goals over any firm goals (e.g., Oliver Williamson, James Buchanan and the public choice school); (b) institutionalists and others emphasizing the "behavioral theory of the firm" who suggest alternative firm goals, such as firm size, total sales, or market share; and (c) theorists of "social responsibility" such as Ralph Estes or Alisa Gravitz who affirm the obligation of firms to respond to society's needs.
>
> Neoclassical economic theory has been slow in adapting to these alternative possibilities because the primacy of the profit motive has been so strongly built in that it has taken on a normative force. What neoclassical economics most powerfully offers to social welfare is the promise that, if certain conditions are met, certain types of optima can be expected to be reached. Abandonment of

the central assumption of profit as the chief motive for firms undercuts some of the logic on which this promise is made.[11]

On the academic level, more scholars like Goodwin are critizing economic's refusal to incorporate human values. On the popular level, there are a growing number of attacks accusing major corporations or business in general of being greedy or inhuman. The problem on both levels is that no one has come up with a widely accepted method to measure economic and business success in human terms.

We need a new paradigm.

I believe the bottom-line paradigm will eventually be replaced by a paradigm of business balance, the conviction that the purpose of every commercial activity is to fill the needs of all the participants as completely as possible without harming others. Instead of thinking of business as a wealth-creator, we should think of it as a benefits-creator.

But business balance cannot become a paradigm so long as thinkers like Goodwin are a minority among thought leaders. The bottom-line paradigm is so established that there are still many businessmen (Scott Paper's Al Dunlap,[12] UPS's Kent Nelson[13]) and economists (Chicago University's Milton Friedman,[14] Northwestern University's Alfred Rappaport[15]) who insist that the primary, if not sole, goal of running a business is the interests of the stockholders. That is supposed to be the foundation of capitalism, under which, according to Noam Chomsky, "you're not supposed to care about anything except maximizing your own wealth."[16]

This is not surprising, for in business culture the bottom-line paradigm is a flying buttress supporting the gothic cathedral we call the corporation, the subject of the next chapter.

20

THE CORPORATION —
LEGALIZED IRRESPONSIBILITY

> *"Concentration of economic power in all-embracing corporations ... represents private enterprise become a kind of private government which is a power unto itself—a regimentation of other people's money and other people's lives."*
> — *Franklin D. Roosevelt, 1936*[1]

From its earliest beginnings the corporation was a form of government. Although corporations helped prepare for democracy, they have remained an undemocratic feudal system. As a legal person, the corporation is an invitation to abuse. As democracy has been gradually adopted by nations, so democracy must be adopted by business—by making every stakeholder a partner.

In 1973, Daniel Bell's *The Coming of Post-Industrial Society* observed that "the institution of property itself is undergoing a fundamental revision, in a significant way.... Individual property has become corporate, and property is no longer controlled by owners but by managers."[2]

THE MASTERWORK OF BERLE AND MEANS

Bell's observation was a remote echo of what Adolf A. Berle and Gardiner C. Means had explained four decades earlier in their classic text, *The Modern Corporation and Private Property* (first published in 1932, with a "revised" edition in 1968). Lawyer Berle and economist Means opened their study with the following paragraph:

> Corporations have ceased to be merely legal devices through which the private business transactions of individuals may be carried on. Though still much used for this purpose, the corporate form has acquired a larger significance. The corporation has, in fact, become both a method of property tenure and a means of organizing economic life. Grown to tremendous proportions, there may be said to have evolved a "corporate system"—as there was once a feudal system—which has attracted to itself a combination of attributes and powers, and has attained a degree of prominence entitling it to be dealt with as a major social institution.[3]

With considerable data and detailed legal reasoning Berle and Means concluded "that parallel with the growth in the size of the industrial unit has come a dispersion in its ownership such that an important part of the wealth of individuals consists of interest in great enterprises of which no one individual owns a major part."[4] The authors examined seven major changes in the basic concept of wealth and ownership. The corporate organization of economic life has:

1. changed ownership from active to passive. Stockholders who legally "own" the corporation do so with little control over its operation and no responsibility for its actions.

2. eliminated the spiritual values that formerly went with ownership. Stock ownership deprives the stockholder of the personal fulfillment one gets from direct ownership, such as the satisfaction humans get from putting their imprint on what they own, whether developing land, building a business or driving a car.

3. made the value of wealth dependent on forces over which the owner has little or no control. The price of the stock is determined by the company's management and the vagaries of the stock market.

4. increased the psychological stress of ownership. The constant fluctuation of the values of one's shares tends to affect both financial decisions and peace of mind.

20. The Corporation--Legalized Irresponsibility

5. provided extreme liquidity for wealth. This can be very convenient for buying and selling, but it destroys the owner's moral and mental ties to his or her property, since stock ownership has ...

6. deprived the owner of using wealth directly. The man who owns land can build a house or plant a garden on it. The woman who owns a car can run errands or take a trip. All the stockholder can do with shares of stock is store or sell them.

7. switched control of most of the nation's private wealth from its owners to a separate group. We call this group the corporation managers.[5]

As Berle summed it up in his preface to the 1968 edition:

> Evolution of the corporation has made stock-and-security ownership the dominant form by which individuals own wealth representing property devoted to production (as contrasted with property devoted to consumption). The last great bastion of individually owned productive property—agriculture—has been dramatically declining in proportion to the total production of the United States, and even in agriculture, corporations have been steadily making inroads.[5]

"In crude summation," Berle added, "most 'owners' own stock, insurance, savings and pension claims and the like, and do not manage; most managers (corporate administrators) do not own. The corporate collective holds legal title to the tangible productive wealth of the country—for the benefit of others."

How did this curious arrangement come about?

AN EXTENSION OF GOVERNMENT

The first corporations were agreements with medieval rulers allowing a certain amount of self-government to groups of citizens for specific purposes. Religious orders were made up of individuals who took a vow of poverty. Since no individual monk could own anything, the monastery and its monastic land were owned and operated by the group. Sometimes this ownership was a sort of delegation by the Church, which was considered the overall owner. At other times, depending on the political situation, the delegator and overall owner was the king. One of Henry VIII's earliest edicts, after declaring himself head of the English Church, was to declare that all monastic properties belonged to the king.

Medieval Europe was governed by landowners, noblemen who were strong enough to rule an area by the power of the sword. Just as modern corporations frequently grow by takeovers and mergers, medieval kingdoms and principalities grew out of conquests and agreements (often consummated by marriage) in which weaker nobles pledged fealty to stronger nobles.

At the same time, as knowledge spread, a new kind of citizen arose who earned his living by trade or artisanship. Since his livelihood was not connected to the soil, he was able to move out of the landowner's domain. Many of these freemen formed groups to protect themselves from rule by the sword, often in walled towns. It was natural that such groups took the road laid out by the monastic clergy. Thus the first formal corporations chartered by rulers were the towns and universities that changed the face of Europe in the 13th Century.

I stress all this because it is important to understand that corporations were extensions of government in both their formal and informal origins. The original corporate charters delegated the members of a group to govern a particular domain. Hence Berle's 1967 observation should not surprise us:

> There is increasing recognition of the fact that collective operations, and those predominantly conducted by large corporations, are like operations carried on by the state itself. Corporations are essentially political constructs. Their perpetual life, their capacity to accumulate tens of billions of assets, and to draw profit from their production and their sales, has made them part of the service of supply of the United States.[7]

TRANSFORMING THE CONCEPT OF DOMAIN

The original corporation was a very useful paradigm in humanity's painful progress toward individual freedom. The early corporation became the petri dish in which the seeds of democracy were cultivated.

1. It separated the power to govern from land ownership. Of course, religious orders, universities and towns built their monasteries, colleges and public buildings on land. But their power did not come from ownership of the land, but from the charter issued by the king or the agreement of the group.

The British East India Company, chartered in 1600, owned no land, although it developed enough commercial muscle to eventually rule a good part of India. But its principal purpose was trade and its principal power lay in the money it raised from investors and the business.

2. It replaced monarchy and rule by the sword with oligarchy and rule by agreement, a first step toward sharing authority and learning to rule by consensus. Since the corporation was established for specific purposes and had limited powers, it opened the way to government without absolute sovereignty.

3. It created a way to transfer wealth outside the family. Most corporations were chartered with rights of ownership, whether direct or indirect. When members of the corporation died, corporate property (and debts) remained with the corporation instead of being inherited by the heirs of the deceased.

4. Most important of all, it facilitated the raising of huge amounts of capital that became necessary when the Industrial Revolution swung human production from farm to factory. In fact, as we shall see, the ability to raise the capital required by industry is the principal argument for justifying the corporate system today.

As Berle and Means recognized back in 1932, the stock market's importance in providing liquidity for people's assets soon overshadowed its function of raising investment capital. Since successful companies generated most of their investment capital out of earnings, new issues became a very small part of the market. Soon a large part of that small part was devoted to turning founder-ownership into ready cash.

In *The Modern Corporation and Private Property* Berle and Means provided enormous detail on how managers weakened stockholder control through legal and nonlegal maneuvers, and gradually won the right to manipulate a stock's value by altering charters of incorporation and limiting distribution of profits.

ECONOMIC FEUDALISM

Berle and Means were incredibly prescient. They foresaw how the corporate system would dominate the entire U.S. economy, although they did not seem to realize the importance of transnational corporations and how they would eventually transcend national boundaries and create a unified global economy.

Most significantly for my argument, they realized that the corporation was a form of government, a specialized ministate. They quoted the German scholar Walther Rathenau who ten years earlier called the corporation "an institution which resembles the state in character."[8]

It seems more than coincidence that they compared the gradual evolution of the "corporate system" to the evolution of the feudal system, for there are remarkable similarities in the governance of medieval society and that of today's major corporations.

In the Middle Ages, the power to govern was undemocratic. Although legally transmitted by inheritance, in practice power was usually exercised by a small coterie of top people who advised or manipulated the sovereign. When the sovereign wanted to expand or protect the realm, he relied on his knights and retainers to finance the project and lend their arms.

The productive people of this society were serfs. They had nothing to say about the government of the realm, and their loyalty as well as the first pick of what they produced belonged to the sovereign.

In the corporate world, the power to govern is also undemocratic. Although it is legally bestowed by the votes of stockholders, in practice it is almost always exercised by a small coterie of top people who advise or manipulate the chief executive. When the chief executive wants to expand the company or protect it against raiders, he relies on banks and consultants to finance the project and contribute their expertise.

The productive people of this society are employees. They have nothing to say about the government of the company, and their loyalty as well as the profits they generate are controlled by top management.

Just as feudalism served to preserve social order in the period between the barbarian invasions that gave the coup de grace to the dying Roman Empire and the building of the modern state, so the modern corporation served to preserve economic order in the period between the dawn of the Industrial Revolution and today's knowledge economy.

AN INVITATION TO ABUSE

If bureaucracy is on the way out, as argued in Chapter 10, then so are large corporations, for they cannot operate without bureaucracy. But the corporate paradigm does not apply only to large companies. There are many more small and medium-sized corporations, and quite a few of them are controlled by their owners and are flexible enough to overcome the problems of bureaucracy. Is it bigness and an excess of power that creates the problem, or is it the concept of the corporation itself?

A charter of incorporation gives any business, regardless of size, the status of a "persona" in the eyes of the law. This fact (or, more accurately, fiction) gives the corporation—according to a 1886 decision of the United States Supreme Court—all the rights, privileges and obligations of a natural person, including those defined by the U.S. Constitution and the Bill of Rights. This means that:

1. A corporation can own property and other assets, independently of its shareholders. This has the advantage of freeing the "owners" of direct personal responsibility for what the company owns. A company's "owners" can be so numerous that direct involvement in company operations will be impossible for most of them.

2. A corporation assumes liability for company actions, freeing owners and operators from direct responsibility for debts incurred by the company or corporate acts harmful to individuals or the general public. This enables the company to assume risks that would be prohibitive for most individuals.

3. A corporation does not automatically dissolve when one of the partners or the proprietor dies. An incorporated company can live forever, giving it far greater potential to build wealth and power, since it can pursue goals far beyond an individual lifetime.

Like Mary Shelley's Dr. Frankenstein, the well-meaning law created a monster, a creature with much greater potential for power than any human but without a human's ability to think for itself or develop an internal sense of morality. Like Charlie McCarthy, the fictional legal persona can think, act and make moral judgments only to the extent that it is manipulated by real human beings, the corporation's managers.

While the stock market separated ownership from control, the legal fiction separated control from human responsibility.

The law holds the managers of a corporation responsible for protecting the interests of the stockholders. If the managers make decisions that hurt the environment, their employees, their customers or the public, the law fines the company, not the managers. The result is that, for corporate managers, the bottom line has become the moral code.

WHY GOVERNMENT CONTROLS FAILED

Government had not always given corporations such free reign. Early charters of incorporation were much more restrictive, often bestowed for a limited time, and frequently demanded that specific individuals accept direct responsibility for how the corporation was run. Corporations reached their present status due to a lengthy tug of war between businessmen anxious to protect themselves while making money and the government trying to protect the public without hobbling commerce. Throughout the last half of the 19th Century and the first half of the 20th, business interests won more and more rights for the corporation and government introduced more and more curbs on what corporations could do.

This might have kept the paradigm on course except for one major mistake. A runaway car was endangering public safety, but instead of fixing the car, the government spent all its time directing traffic. Not one piece of the corrective legislation designed to protect the public or any decision penalizing corporations for misbehavior ever considered dismembering the monster that was causing the problem. Both the defenders and attackers of corporations accepted the historic misconception that corporations belonged to the stockholders, to those who put money into them, and that obligations as well as legal rights and privileges had to be based on that supposition.

As Galbraith explained in *The New Industrial State,* what he called mature corporations are not run by or for the "owners." Stockholders have very little power in mammoth corporations. Mature corporations are run by and for the "technostructure."[9] (Galbraith defined the technostructure as the knowledge workers who make the corporate organization possible. But he used the term as a synonym for corporate management, which almost always refers to top management.) Hence the principal concern of mature corporations is not

20. The Corporation--Legalized Irresponsibility 363

so much profit as it is growth and, when growth is difficult, survival. As with any mature political organization, the central purpose is power.

In the semi-final chapter of their 1932 book, Berle and Means argued that the traditional theory of the corporation was "inadequate," and in the final chapter they proposed that the community was now in a position to legally demand that corporations serve the entire society rather than only the interests of stockholders and managers. They based their argument on the fact that shareholder "owners" had in practice, if not in law, abdicatedownership control and thereby given the community the right to take over. They ended the book with this amazing prediction, which Galbraith saw as socialist,[10] though I judge socialism was the farthest thing from their minds:

> The future may see the economic organism, now typified by the corporation, not only on an equal plane with the state, but possibly even superseding it as the dominant form of social organization. The law of corporations, accordingly, might well be considered as a potential constitutional law for the new economic state, while business practice is increasingly assuming the aspect of economic statesmanship.[11]

Even these two advanced minds could not free their thinking from the presumption that ownership rights belonged to the stockholders. The stockholders had to somehow surrender their rights to provide legal justification for government dictation of corporate purpose and eventual "economic statesmanship."

But governments were unable to dictate corporate purpose and there was more economic politics than statesmanship. Instead, as David C. Korten summarized in *When Corporations Rule the World,*

> Corporations have emerged as the dominant governance institutions on the planet, with the largest among them reaching into virtually every country of the world and exceeding most governments in size and power. Increasingly, it is the corporate interest more than the human interest that defines the policy agendas of states and international bodies, although this reality and its implications have gone largely unnoticed and unaddressed.[12]

THE SOLUTION: DEMOCRACY

The recognition of the corporation as a mini state is important because it shows us both what is wrong and what must be done. The great triumph of the

20th Century was the hard-won, worldwide recognition that humans are destined to govern themselves. The transformation of national governments to democracies must be echoed in the mini-governments we call corporations.

Business organizations must become democracies. Their ownership and rule[13] must be wrested from stockholders and managers and given to each mini-government's real citizens, the people who do the work and make a living in the business. If a legal precedent is needed for an organization controlled by its members, we have one in the non-stock or nonprofit corporation, used by clubs and similar membership associations.

Every business is a community of concerns. Everyone engaged in that business is a member of that community and has a right to decide how it is run. That is why every business must become a partnership, with every employee a partner. Peter Drucker speaks of "the redefinition of the job as property right,"[14] a concept that might be useful in establishing the worker's rights in the employing company. But it is easier and more direct to recognize worker's rights by making every worker a partner.

Once founded to facilitate group enterprise, the corporation has become an obsolete paradigm because it has become a shelter for exercising power without responsibility. It must be replaced with a new paradigm: the ultimate form of business democracy, the partnership.

PROPERTY AND PARTNERSHIPS

We started Part Four with the problem of property. Without the corporation, how do partnerships handle ownership, particularly the ownership of business assets, not only cash and securities but land, machinery, factories, furniture and other tangibles? What happens when one of the partners dies?

Simple inheritance of property does not need the corporation. An individual can give what he owns to another, and since he can designate a date for the transfer, he can always decide that it will be the date of his death. When several people own property as partners, the simplest way to keep the property with the community is for each partner to agree to leave his share of the property to the other partners in case of death.

Can a partner leave his share of the partnership to someone else? It depends on the nature of the partnership. Consider the three types of cooperating groups I described at some length in Chapter 9.

1. True partnership or agreement to collaborate. Since this is based entirely on sharing knowledge or wisdom, it cannot be passed on to another person. You cannot will your brain or personality to another.

2. The network held together by purpose and a series of contracts. There is nothing here to pass on because each contract is a separate agreement. Networks, as such, do not own property.

3. Joint ownership. This is a form of cooperation, but it is not partnership as I define it (a true collaboration). Joint ownership can take several forms:

(a) *Invested property* (usually money, but not necessarily). If three people form a partnership and need money to finance their project, they can look for investors. These are not collaborating partners. They can be very influential, depending on what considerations they require to hand over the property. But since their contribution is merely property, not knowledge collaboration, they are silent or limited partners—i.e., their involvement is limited to contribution of property. Since they are limited partners, they also have limited liability (i.e., limited to the extent of their investment). For practical (and legal) purposes, they can be considered lenders who ask for a variable return based on the success of the enterprise.

(b) *Property purchased for business use* (as when the partners decide to buy a truck or factory). Such property is owned by the partners the same way they own the business, for it becomes part of the business's assets to be divided in agreed-on proportions when the partnership is dissolved.

(c) *Property purchased for joint ownership,* as when a partnership has been formed for the purpose of providing something for common use, as when three friends decide to buy a boat together or a thousand neighbors decide to buy a couple of acres for a public park.

Consider the boat first. Here again you have a union of collaboration and property. The three men collaborate on how to use the boat. But the boat, because it is property, is owned by them as limited partners. When this arrangement is discontinued, collaboration ends. However, the property remains. Hence each individual can sell his part ownership or give it to another. The three, of course, as in any ownership contract, may have limited their freedom in how they can dispose of the property. I see no difference in the ownership of the public park by a thousand neighbors. They collaborate in deciding how to use the land and that collaboration cannot be sold or bought or given away. But the park itself is property. Every one of those thousand neighbors owns a part of it.

When someone moves away from the community, what happens to his or her 1/1,000 share of the property? The park, of course, could have been financed by selling shares to the residents, and then he would be entitled to sell his share or shares to someone else, just as he sells his house. A more practical arrangement, however, would be to attach use of the park to home ownership, so that in selling his home he would also be selling his piece of the park. We see this type of thinking in the different arrangements in communities for the elderly, from fee simple to cooperative or condominium ownership.

What happens if someone gets hurt while playing in the park? Who is responsible? The individuals who own the park have total responsibility in so far as they operate the park as a collaborative venture. They have limited liability in so far as they own the property. Hence the person who sues can collect from the individuals (who are totally responsible to the tune of 1/1000 each), or from the value of the park as property (but only up to its total worth).

Proportional responsibility is not a new idea. California's first state constitution declared each shareholder in a corporation "individually and personally liable for his proportion of all debts and liabilities."[15]

PERSONAL VS. CORPORATE RESPONSIBILITY

The overall consequences of abandoning the corporate paradigm in favor of the partnership paradigm will, I believe, restore the integrity of responsibility in business, since every business will be operated primarily for the benefit of its participants rather than the benefit of investors.

When you work for investors, everything you do has to be focused on profitability. When you work for yourself, you are far more likely to consider all your needs, psychological as well as material. And this is as true of groups as it is of individuals. In fact, there is no situation where people are more likely to consider the wants and needs of others than when they are collaborating.

In the history of mankind no motive contributed more to the abuse of government than empire building. The Fourth Dynasty of Egypt's old kingdom, the campaigns of Alexander the Great, the wars of China's Emperor Wu, the conquests of Julius Caesar, the victories of the Emperor Charlemagne in Europe and the Caliph Mamun in Africa, the Christian Crusades, the age of exploration and colonization, the establishment of the British Empire, the Napoleonic wars, and the rise of Hitler were all purchased at the cost of death and desolation for multitudes of ordinary people.

Now, according to authors like Frank Adams,[16] Richard Barnet,[17] John Cavanaugh,[18] Noam Chomsky,[19] Lance E. Davis,[20] Richard Grossman,[21] Robert A. Huttenback[22] and David Korten,[23] the common people are again paying in oppressive and dreadful ways for the empires being built by transnational corporations. It is time to replace the corporation paradigm with a partnership paradigm that will establish democratic rule in business, make empire building less likely and restore human values to the world of commerce.

But corporations are not the only way to build empires. Cannot partnerships or networks become dangerously powerful via intellectual property, by monopolizing money-making ideas?

21

INTELLECTUAL PROPERTY — UNFAIR AND UNENFORCEABLE

"The greatest constraint on your true liberties may come not from government but from corporate legal departments laboring to protect by force what can no longer be protected by practical efficient or general social consent."
— *John Perry Barlow, 1994[1]*

Intellectual property is a legal, not a natural right. Such government-enforced protection no longer works. It is frequently unfair and it interferes with the common welfare. More important, it is unenforceable and unneeded.

The third paradigm that I am convinced should be replaced is the belief that ideas belong to individuals in the same way as material property and can consequently be bought, sold and monopolized. Developments in the many ways we transmit information and apply innovation have made the intellectual property paradigm obsolete. A freedom-of-information paradigm is rising to take its place, and it is time that we change or rescind the laws on patents and copyrights.

More than a decade ago, in *The Knowledge Executive,* Harlan Cleveland put his finger on the problem:

> The notion of information-as-property is built deep into our laws, our economy, and our political psyche—and into the expectations and tax returns and balance sheets of writers and artists and the companies, agencies, and academies that pay them to be creative.

But we had better continue to develop our own ways, compatible with our own traditions, of rewarding intellectual labor without depending on laws and prohibitions that are disintegrating fast, as the Volstead Act did in our earlier effort to enforce an unenforceable Prohibition.[2]

Some years ago I asked Gilbert Maurer, then president of Hearst Magazines, whether he worried that listening to outsiders with new magazine ideas might lead to lawsuits should the company later launch something similar. Maurer's answer was that "there are almost no really new ideas," and that "ultimately it's not the idea that's important; it's the execution."[3] It is the execution, the process by which an idea is realized, by which the idea becomes something outside the mind, that makes it property.

FREEDOM TO LISTEN

In guaranteeing freedom of speech the first amendment to the United States Constitution implicitly guarantees freedom to listen, and freedom to listen is meaningless if listeners cannot use what they have learned by listening. To be truly free every individual must have the right to use his or her ideas no matter where they came from, provided such use does not violate the rights of others.

I have said that the right of ownership flows from our ideas, from our ability to transform what we find in nature by informing or reforming it with our ideas, and that the imposition of our idea on matter makes the result personal property. It is the *imposition* of the idea, not the plan or design, that makes the result personal property.

Nor does it matter where or how we get the idea. So long as the idea is in our mind, its imposition on matter makes the result our property. When a caveman got the idea of attaching a stone to a stick to make a club, and made such a club, the club was his property. However, when his wife saw what he had done and decided to make a club for herself, the club she made was hers, not her husband's. Even though she got the idea from her husband, it became her idea when she learned it. She was imposing her idea on matter and that made her club her property.

We can argue further against the possibility of an intrinsic right to intellectual property from what we concluded in Chapter 3, the subjective nature of ideas and knowledge. Since all communication is manipulative and, therefore, imperfect, there is no way you or I can know how much of our ideas are the same as the ideas of others and how much are additions or subtractions unique to us. Hence, although you may get your idea from something I said or did, your idea is never identical with my idea. Thomas Jefferson explained it eloquently:

> If nature has made any one thing less susceptible than all others of exclusive property, it is the action of the thinking power called an idea, which an individual may exclusively possess as long as he keeps it to himself; but the moment it is divulged, it forces itself into the possession of everyone, and the receiver cannot dispossess himself of it. Its peculiar character, too, is that no one possesses the less, because every other possesses the whole of it. He who receives an idea from me, receives instruction himself without lessening mine; as he who lights his taper at mine, receives light without darkening me. That ideas should freely spread from one to another over the globe, for the moral and mutual instruction of man, and improvement of his condition, seems to have been peculiarly and benevolently designed by nature, when she made them, like fire, expansible over all space, without lessening their density in any point, and like the air in which we breathe, move, and have our physical being, incapable of confinement or exclusive appropriation. Inventions then cannot, in nature, be a subject of property. Society may give an exclusive right to the profits arising from them, as an encouragement to men to pursue ideas which may produce utility, but this may or may not be done, according to the will and convenience of the society, without claim or complaint from any body.[4]

As Jefferson says, the fact that the intellectual property paradigm is not a natural right does not, in itself, prove that society should not use the paradigm. We have the right to agree on laws we find communally beneficial. Patent and copyright regulations were instituted to encourage and reward inventors and authors, and that is a good thing. I contend, however, that the intellectual-property concept no longer works, for it is frequently unfair, invites abuse, cannot be enforced and interferes with the common welfare.

FREQUENTLY UNFAIR

A number of years ago, while I was editor of *The Gallagher Report,* I had lunch with the manager of New Jersey television station WOR-TV and suggested that a show interviewing a different mayor each week might make a good public-service program. Not long after, the station launched a new program called, "Meet the Mayors."

Over a year later, I visited the station manager and the producer of "Meet the Mayors" stopped by. When the manager introduced me as the person who had the original idea for his show, the producer's face changed color. I am sure the poor man thought the show was his idea, and it probably was. There is nothing unusual about two people having similar ideas. It happens all the time.

Is it fair to prohibit one person from using his own idea because another person happened to have a similar idea and managed to get it registered first? Life, of course, is full of inequalities and bad luck. Inventors will have to fight it out in the marketplace. But is the law really protecting inventors—all inventors, including those who do not get to the patent office on time? As Lewis Mumford wrote in *Technics and Civilization,* "most of the important inventions and discoveries ... were wind-blown seeds from other cultures."[5] Who protects the many minds behind the invention? Does the law help creativity as much as it helps patent attorneys?

The trouble with our system of protecting intellectual property is that no one has ever been able to come up with a good definition of what we are trying to protect. Gutenberg's idea for movable type changed the course of history, but he lost his business to a money lender. For Gutenberg personally, business knowhow, had he had it, would have been more valuable than his movable type. Yet, to this day, there are no laws protecting business knowhow. John Fitch designed his steamboat in 1786, 21 years before Robert Fulton launched the Clermont. But Fulton was a salesman and Fitch was not. Yet it is practically impossible to patent salesmanship or even sales ideas.

Every day thousands of people benefit themselves and others through the application of good ideas. Yet the law makes no effort to define those ideas as intellectual property even though many of them are considerably more valuable than some of the inventions buried in the U.S. Patent Office.

OPPORTUNITIES FOR ABUSE

In practice it is easier to swindle an inventor by purchasing his patent than it would be if there were no patent, since buying the patent assures the swindler that the inventor can no longer use his own idea. A similar situation arises when employees are bound by contract to give the employer ownership of anything invented at work, which was why Douglas Engelbart never got a cent of royalties from his invention of the electronic mouse.[6]

Patents have been used to kill good ideas. The bishop of Bluefields in Nicaragua once told me that he was building a church with a new kind of construction blocks, much lighter and much cheaper but just as strong as traditional cinder blocks. He added that "the industry won't let them sell them in the States." Patents for new products can be, and have been, bought and buried to protect more expensive or inferior goods already on the market.

Since names and trademarks are ideas protected by law, individuals have registered all sorts of names with the hope that they will be able to sell the rights to one or more of the names to companies that want to use them later. So many names are now "owned" that an entire industry exists to conduct title searches for proposed magazines and other properties. Although this abuse has existed for years, new technology and the multiplication of media has made it much worse. It is already a major headache for people who want to establish home pages on the Internet.

Another troublesome development is the patenting of genetic materials. A farmer who plants a crop with genetically engineered seed cannot sow his fields with seeds from last year's crop without paying royalties to the owner of the patented seed. Not only is it difficult to explain this obligation to poor third-world farmers who were supposed to be the principal beneficiaries, but it is even more difficult to enforce it. The patenting of natural medicinals has occasioned protests in India and other Asian countries, after people learned that natural remedies used by themselves now and their ancestors for centuries had suddenly become proprietary medicines.[7]

The growth in proprietary drugs has created a swamp of moral, social and frequently legal dilemmas. On one side major drug companies like Pfizer, Squibb and SmithKline Beecham claim that the income from proprietary drugs is necessary to support the research they require. On the other, federal and state governments, medical insurance companies and the public complain that proprietary drugs are too expensive.

The dispute goes beyond economics, involving moral issues that have not been fully faced. If my neighbor is in serious need and I know of a remedy that will help, have I the right to charge him for that knowledge? If I may charge him, when does my price cause such hardship that it is unjust to insist on it? Is it a criminal act to endanger the life of another by withholding information?

INTERFERING WITH THE COMMON WELFARE

In his theory of "increased returns," economist Brian Arthur has shown that the success of new products, their widespread use and acceptance is very often due more to chance than to the value of the idea or the skill with which it is marketed. In one of his earliest presentations, Arthur's example was the traditional clock. For hundreds of years when people looked at a clock, they expected its hands to run down the right side of the face and up the left. We do not know whose idea that was and we have no idea why that design succeeded while clocks running in the opposite direction never caught on. (The unsuccessful idea was not untried. One of Arthur's friends traveling in Europe ran across an antique clock that ran counterclockwise.)

Fortunately for the human race, most inventions were not monopolized by their inventors. We do not know who first used fire, constructed the wheel, planted seed or domesticated animals. We do know it would be a very sorry world if whoever it was had the power to monopolize these discoveries as intellectual property.

What was said in Chapter 4 about the free flow of information making democracy possible applies equally to democratizing business. If we are serious about developing the knowledge or gift economy, we cannot tolerate anything that restricts the flow of information. That is the fundamental thing wrong with the concept of intellectual property.

A *Business Week* editorial commented that "when companies care more about their patent portfolios than their factories, it's right for trust busters to ensure that market giants don't corner knowhow."[8] The time has come when no one should be allowed to corner any type of knowledge. Anything that restricts the transmission and use of ideas is a roadblock in mankind's advance to a better life.

TOO DIFFICULT TO ENFORCE

For the legally minded, there is an even more convincing reason why the intellectual-property paradigm is obsolete. Laws enforcing intellectual-property "rights" are becoming more and more difficult, some would say impossible, to enforce, and a law impossible to enforce is a bad law. Advanced technology has undermined the paradigm in four ways:

1. It has made copying of legally protected products so easy and available that copying has become, for practical purposes, a personal function. In response, the government has made several attempts to reform copyright laws, permitting limited copying for non-commercial purposes and suggesting indirect ways to compensate copyright holders (e.g., manufacturers of blank digital tapes and disks pay a "tax" to an artists and composers fund).[9] The solutions are far from effective, widely ignored and add to the burden of an overloaded justice system. What used to be basically a print problem has now hit the music business. For a modest charge, and sometimes for nothing, users of the Internet can download a music performance. As *Wired* magazine summed it up, "music copyright holders fear the Net, a place where they see a horrifying collusion of the information-wants-to-be-free attitude with rapidly improving audio transmission technologies."[10]

2. It has made it incredibly easy to secure the principal benefits of new ideas by making enough changes to avoid legally-prosecutable copying. People still argue as to how much Microsoft's Windows copied Apple's user-friendly graphics which, purportedly, had been copied from Xerox. It is no coincidence that four new stomach-acid remedies appeared in rapid succession: Pepcid AC from Johnson & Johnson Merck, Tagament HB from SmithKline Beecham, Zantac 75 from Glaxo Warner-Lambert and Axid AR from Eli Lilly.

3. It has blurred the boundaries between creating and informing. The National Basketball Association sued Motorola and America Online to stop them from "violating intellectual property" by transmitting sports scores in real time to subscribers' electronic pagers and computers. Who owns the photograph of an actor in action, the photographer or the actor? Who owns the videotape, the videotaper, the actor or the playwright? Can the politician protect off-the-record information as intellectual property? Is the new drug that comes out of the laboratory a creation or a discovery?

4. It has facilitated hit-and-run violation of intellectual-property laws. Bootleggers can make thousands of copies of audio or visual tapes, sell them and close down their operations before the copyright owners or police are aware the law has been broken. Illegal operators in China continue to repro-

duce American CDs and videotapes for the black market. Although the Chinese government, anxious to preserve its favored-nation trade status with the U.S., would like to stop it, it cannot. The violators are too numerous and the required equipment too easy to hide.

When I read estimates that U.S. firms lost "up to $17 billion last year because their intellectual property rights were not protected,"[11] I find it difficult to worry about an industry that can afford to lose $17 billion and still make loads of money. What I do worry about is the number of people in high places who believe that they can preserve the outdated intellectual-property paradigm by legislation.

Illegal copying continues in every one of the hundred countries that accepted the World Trade Organization's 1994 definition of *Trade Related Aspects of Intellectual Property Rights*. Selling illegal videos and tapes is still a profitable business in Singapore, despite penalties of five years in jail plus a $50,000 fine for possession of bootleg recordings with intent to sell and a police force that offers rewards up to $150 for fingering violators.[12]

There should be serious concern that the agitation for greater control of intellectual property will endanger the free exchange of ideas. As philosopher and song writer John Perry Barlow warned in *Wired*:

> When the primary articles of commerce in a society look so much like speech as to be indistinguishable from it, and when the traditional methods of protecting their ownership have become ineffectual, attempting to fix the problem with broader and more vigorous enforcement will inevitably threaten freedom of speech.[13]

IT IS UNNECESSARY

Yet we can expect many defenders of the intellectual property paradigm. The idea of business without patents and copyrights turns the faces of publishers, writers and researchers red with anger or pale with terror. They presume that without laws to protect intellectual property there would be little incentive to encourage creative work and that creative people would starve.

Without copyrights, writing a best-seller or having a platinum record might not bring the incredible riches they do now. But that may be a good thing. As Robert H. Frank and Philip J. Cook argue in *The Winner-Take-All Society,* such out-of-proportion awards may be doing serious harm to the general welfare. In any case, I am less interested in protecting billionaires than I am in how ordinary creative people and the business operations that distribute their works will fare in a world without patents or copyrights.

Whether working as an independent contractor or as a partner, the more competent an artist or researcher, the more likely he will be well paid for his services. If an author writes a worthwhile book, a publisher will pay him for it. If the book is very special and the author has an established reputation, several publishers might even bid for it. Of course, without copyright, all the publisher buys is the right to be the first to offer the book to the public. If, after he has published it, other publishers decide to print and sell the same book in a cheaper edition, there is no way to stop them. But by that time, the first publisher should have been able to make a profit.

In other words, people would be paid for their work rather than for their creation's potential. Writers, artists and inventors would be paid for the work they do and for its value to the initial publisher or marketer. But hitting the jackpot would not be as lucrative as it is today. I doubt if that would discourage artists from doing their best. As Barlow argues in the same *Wired* article:

> One existing model for the future conveyance of intellectual property is real-time performance, a medium currently used only in theater, music, lectures, stand-up comedy and pedagogy. I believe the concept of performance will expand to include most of the information economy, from multicasted soap operas to stock analysis. In these instances, commercial exchange will be more like ticket sales to a continuous show than the purchase of discrete bundles of that which is being shown.
>
> The other existing model, of course, is service. The entire professional class—doctors, lawyers, consultants, architects and so on—are already being paid directly for their intellectual property. Who needs copyright when you're on a retainer?[14]

The same process would apply to products now protected by patents. The biologist who discovers a new sulfa drug will be paid for the hours she spent in research and the marketer would make money by selling the drug. If the market for the drug proves profitable, other companies will soon offer a less expensive version. That, too, will not be bad, certainly not for the people who need the medicine.[15]

21. Intellectual Property--Unfair and Unenforceable 377

As to the drug companies' argument that research would be impossible without the handsome returns they get from proprietary prices, I know of no study on the productivity of drug-firm research. I do know that much money is wasted in drug-firm research as happens in any project where funding is generous and productivity difficult to measure. I also know that drug companies frequently kill research projects that lack marketing promise even though they may advance medical science. And I am willing to wager that as many useful drugs have been discovered by independent and academic scientists on small budgets as by big-company employees on high salaries.

In today's marketplace, establishing a beachhead is more important than patents. Since today's technology almost always enables immediate imitators, what counts is winning share of mind by being first. Bayer Aspirin is still sold at a premium price in a market where low-price generic aspirin has been available for years. Clorox still outsells other bleaches.

As marketing evolves more and more from selling products to servicing them, the aftermarket may become the major source of income for creative people. Electronic-information expert Esther Dyson advises Net-users "to distribute intellectual property free in order to sell service and relationships."[16] People will pay for access to authors, to be the first to hear new songs by favorite performers, or to obtain instructions from the expert in using his invention. Consider how little Martha Stewart needs copyright laws.

The elimination of patents and copyright will not allow fraud or false advertising. Names and authorship will be protected. Other companies will not sell *Bayer* aspirin. Martha Stewart will not vanish behind a dozen clones. Nor will publishers be allowed to put a famous byline on somebody else's potboiler.

Though some will miss the big prizes, the majority of creative people will prefer the open-field freedom of skill and reputation to the regulated racetrack of intellectual property. In fact, it is precisely these people who are already facing the problems of surviving in the new economy by arming themselves with the mental and moral tools I describe in the next chapter.

22

PREPARING FOR THE NEW GLOBAL COMMUNITY

"With a breakdown of cultural consensus, an absence of worthy role models, little in the public arena to inspire our allegiance, and disorienting rapid change a permanent feature of our lives, it is a dangerous moment in history not to know who we are or not to trust ourselves."
— *Nathaniel Branden, 1994*[1]

The transformation from a bureaucratic market economy of competing nation-states to a networked gift economy of cooperating partnerships will be slow and painful. The widening gap between rich and poor, increased lawlessness, the population explosion, damage to the environment, information distortion and loss of principles should not distract us from a clear vision of where society is going or our effort to get there. We must be self-reliant: using our strengths, supplementing our weaknesses and achieving both in and through community.

THE AGONY OF ADJUSTMENT

Change is almost always terrifying—partly because it involves facing the unknown, but chiefly because it demands that we forego what we know. The principal trauma of the changes I have described will come from the loss of security systems. In *Beyond Culture,* Edward T. Hall wrote:

> I believe that man in the aggregate resists separations, that he has more things in his life to be separated from than he can ever

achieve, and that one of life's important strategies, albeit an informal, out-of-awareness strategy, has to do with what one is going to give up...[2]

If every separation encounters resistance, we must expect colossal resistance as the changing world asks millions to accept, as their major life strategy, separation from their security systems. Yet that is precisely what the new era demands. Bureaucracies in both business and government have grown and prospered by becoming benevolent parents, binding their children in the silken chains of financial and emotional dependence. The Industrial Revolution gave humanity longer life, wonderful conveniences and many new forms of entertainment, but it also locked the average free citizen in a padded cell of financial dependency.

THE WAGE TRAP

Money has become the central focus of modern life, not as an end, but as the means to everything people want. Without money it is difficult, if not impossible, to attain even rest and recreation. The most pervasive social consequence of the Industrial Revolution was reducing the value of work to what someone will pay for it. It helped to convince most people that money is the only measure of value. Thus money became a dependence-forming drug. Moving to the new era, where money is no longer the sole measure of value, means that almost everyone must go cold turkey.

According to social economist Neva R. Goodwin ...

Much confusion has entered the field of economics through the overloading of one word (*value*) with two theoretical roles and two meanings. The two meanings of value are: (a) the one claimed by economics: "exchange value, or price"; and (b) the one upon which that overt economic value depends: "what people think things are really worth."[3]

The same confusion has invaded our workaday lives in dependence on wage or salary, which shifts the value of work from self-fulfillment to monetary exchange. When you work for another, you let the boss decide the value of your labor. You surrender a large part of your self-esteem: the ability to judge what you are worth and to prove that worth in practical applications of your own choice.

Years ago, when I resigned my job of 15 years to freelance as a management consultant, the question concerned friends asked me most often was not, "How do you know where your next dollar is coming from?" but, "How do you keep working with no one to tell you what to do?" It made me realize how many Americans have lived so long in the padded cell of employment that the idea of leaving it for the world of free enterprise terrifies them. It helped me understand why the pain of being a victim of corporate or government downsizing turns to horror when the unemployed realize that there is no other job to take the place of the one they have lost.

Yet such jobs are disappearing. We are entering an economy in which everyone will be an entrepreneur, in which there will be few, if any, havens where people can depend on someone else to make work decisions for them, as documented by Cliff Hakim's *We Are All Self-Employed* (1994), William Bridges' *Jobshift* (1994) and Jeremy Rifkin's *The End of Work* (1995).

The security blankets extend far beyond wages. Most $250,000-a-year vice presidents are just as dependent as their $25,000-a-year workers. They are lost without the protection of their corporate armor. Thousands of business executives and government officials will do everything they can to retain their current status and incomes. Even professionals, proud of their independence, resist losing their dependence on the corporations and governments that pay their fees, sponsor their projects or support their customers.

In *Creating a New Civilization: The Politics of the Third Wave,* Alvin and Heidi Toffler see a struggle in U.S. politics as Americans determined to preserve the old order battle those who see the future and are anxious to get there. The resistance is not pigheadedness. The current lives and proximate futures of the majority of citizens in the Western world are mortgaged to the status quo. Hence the widespread determination to protect the very entitlements that everyone realizes are sapping the strength of nation-states.

Yet if any people can climb this mountain of resistance, it will be a people who have a long tradition of self-reliance and entrepreneurship. I believe Americans will be the first to break into the new era, but that means Americans will also be the first to suffer the pains of withdrawal.

HOW DANGEROUS IS THE ROAD AHEAD?

In discussing the premise of this book with advisors and friends, the most frequent objection has been: "But we face problems far more critical than the flood of information." When I asked for specifics, these were the six critical problems that were mentioned most often:

(1) The widening gap between rich and poor in our country and throughout the world.

(2) The increase in crime and lawlessness, whether due to ghetto gangs, ethnic strife or the drug trade.

(3) The population explosion with its pressures on financial and material resources.

(4) The growing threat to the natural environment and the difficulty of arriving at a consensus on what to do about it.

(5) The misuse and distortion of information, which is more of a problem than the amount of information.

(6) The loss of guiding principles to help human beings make sense of the world around them.

I agree that all these problems are more critical than the information deluge, if by critical we mean *threatening*. I disagree, if by critical we mean *fundamental*. For example, in AIDS the fundamental problem is the destruction of the immune system. But people seldom die of AIDS, they die of pneumonia or some other disease which easily becomes fatal due to the failure of the immune system. For the AIDS patient, pneumonia is more threatening than the destruction of the immune system, but it is not more fundamental. In Chapter 2, I tried to show how the information flood occasions or intensifies other problems. All six critical problems listed above have been intensified, if not caused, by the information deluge.

Because the transition to the new era is bringing each of these problems to a critical point, there is a danger that one or more of them may seem so critical that it will distract us from the fundamental task of reorganizing society. Only by creating an entirely new system of managing information can we address not just one, but a host of current problems, including the six listed above.

1. THE WIDENING GAP BETWEEN RICH AND POOR

A number of currents in the information deluge are converging to create the turmoil that makes the rich richer and the poor poorer: tricks in manipulating money; technology to make the world a single market; fad merchandising and personality exploitation which milk billions of dollars from millions of people; political and business leverage enabling the privileged to access corporate and even national wealth. Advances in what we know are proceeding at an incredible rate and, as with most new knowledge, destructive use precedes constructive application. Archimedes was famous for his instruments of war before his more constructive inventions were widely applied, and the atom bomb preceded the atomic power plant.

The growing gap between the income of ordinary citizens and that of the very rich has four primary causes related to the changeover period.

First, as is to be expected, increases in information are applied by sophisticates long before ordinary folk catch up with them with a resulting increase in jobs requiring education and a decrease in unskilled jobs.

Second, as large corporations struggle for their lives, rescue operations take the form of downsizing and other economies. This reduces the income of workers and small suppliers while top executives earn higher salaries, bonuses and stock-options for improving the bottom line.

Third, a growing awareness of compensation techniques enables more big-time earners to supplement or replace salaries by bonuses, commissions and percent-of-profits contracts. The most publicized examples are in professional sports and Hollywood, but the really big winners are traders in international currencies, takeover specialists and other money manipulators.

The fourth cause of the income gap is more fundamental than, though related to, the other three. As John Kenneth Galbraith argued at length in *The New Industrial State*,[4] business keeps the marketplace—and the sales of its products and services—healthy by investment. What Galbraith did not consider was that some investments provide more income to the common people than others. When funds are used to make money by constructing factories, building machinery, increasing sales and developing new products, the investment provides employment and fills the pockets of ordinary people. When invested funds are used to make money by securities speculation such as currency trading, takeover wars, corporate spinoffs and new stock-market products, the investment fills only the pockets of the rich. The more the economy tilts toward Wall Street the fewer of its blessings get to Main Street.

Whether the speculative bubble bursts as it did in 1929, or whether it deflates gradually due to investor pressure on pension and mutual-fund managers,[5] I believe it will not last. I am also convinced that the income gap will cease to be a serious problem once appropriate education reaches low-income workers, the new social order is in place, and the disappearance of business and government bureaucracies eliminates the large pools of money which feed speculation and huge discrepancies in income.

2. INCREASING LAWLESSNESS

The problem of crime and violence will plague us as long as there are human beings. But, again as Chapter 2 explained, by undermining authority and feeding alienation, the flood of information makes it harder to control disorder. And the turmoil of social changeover aggravates the situation.

Recent events in former communist lands illustrate how the friction of resistance to change can burst into flames of violence, particularly when bureaucracy becomes too weak to smother it. The confusion, lawlessness and bloodshed we are witnessing in former totalitarian states is likely to be repeated elsewhere as people struggle to find their bearings while the old order is collapsing and the new order is trying to take shape. Consider financier George Soros's plea that Western democracies create a new Marshall Plan for former Soviet lands:

> If there is any lesson to be learned, it is that the collapse of a repressive regime does not automatically lead to the establishment of an open society. An open society is not merely the absence of government intervention and oppression. It is a complicated, sophisticated structure, and deliberate effort is required to bring it into existence. Since it is more sophisticated than the system it replaces, a speedy transition requires outside assistance.[6]

Not only is the society of partnership networks a more complicated and sophisticated structure, but there is no outsider to assist in building it. The leadership, energy and resources to create the new order have to come from within. We alone can quell the insurrections and other outbursts of resistance. We alone can incorporate the alienated into the new society by weaving their concerns, interests and self-esteem into essential social networks.

3. & 4. THE POPULATION EXPLOSION AND THE ENVIRONMENT

No one denies that the surge in the number of people on the earth creates problems. The information deluge is not a direct cause of population growth, yet information—particularly information about hygiene and health care—is a major factor in its recent acceleration.

Worry about the number of people in the world is a prime example of the constant conundrums in the principles by which we live. The supreme value of the human being is a central tenet of our civilization. Murder is considered the most heinous crime. When an aviator goes down at sea or behind enemy lines, we expect our armed forces to do everything possible to rescue him, even if it costs millions of dollars. How can humans so valuable individually be less valuable in the aggregate? They are not, otherwise we would not work so hard to lengthen life and stave off death, nature's tool for population control.

The explanation of the riddle, of course, is that what we fear is not the additional human beings but the consequence of their multiplying. Our fear derives not from the possible number of humans but from a possible shortage of resources. The population problem and the environmental problem are inextricably entwined, for the real question is what can the human race do to keep from exhausting or destroying the natural resources it needs, especially space and food.

The increase of information affects our natural environment in two ways. On one side, it fosters numerous ways to exploit, use up or abuse the environment. On the other, it deepens our knowledge of how nature works, the long-range results of what we are doing to nature and what we can do about it. Business interests argue that we must use the environment to provide jobs and a comfortable living for the population. Environmentalists fight to preserve the population's resources. The solution lies in coordinating the two approaches.

Populations of most developed countries are decreasing or plateauing, because people who are prosperous and unworried about the future tend to have fewer children.[7] Poverty and desperation breed babies. Despite overcrowding, dreadful living conditions and a devastated economy, Rwanda's Tutsis and Hutus are in a competition to procreate.[8] Instead of spending millions to teach birth control to the world's poor, whose only hope is children, maybe we should use the money to give them other objects of hope by helping them to set up partnerships and establish networks.

Unfortunately the turmoil of the changeover period is not conducive to coordination. Among the wildest of the uncoordinated "solutions" is the proposal that we must teach people to feel fulfilled without work because there is not enough work for everyone. Another conundrum? With so many problems, so many people needing help, how can anyone say there is not enough work? The problem is not a lack of things to do. It is a lack of coordination. We must develop networks and partnerships that make it profitable to solve these problems.

5. & 6. ABUSED INFORMATION AND ABSENT PRINCIPLES

Information misuse and the loss of guiding principles is another instance of seeing two faces and forgetting it is one coin. Inability to make sense of the world is a major cause of distorted information, while distorted information makes it difficult to establish principles. The information deluge not only gives us more information to misuse, but the volume and flow of information makes it easier to mangle information even when we do not mean to. And, again as explained in Chapter 2, a major reason for uncertainty about principles is that the flood of information makes more and more people aware of the wide discrepancies in the opinions of people they respect.

But how can we function, if information forces us to be uncertain about the very principles we need in order to make sense of our world? George Soros tries to deal with this problem in his *Atlantic Monthly* article on what he called "the open society":

> The Declaration of Independence may be taken as a pretty good approximation of the principles of an open society, but instead of claiming that those principles are self-evident, we ought to say that they are consistent with our fallibility. Could the recognition of our imperfect understanding serve to establish the open society as a desirable form of social organization? I believe it could, although there are formidable difficulties in the way. We must promote a belief in our own fallibility to the status that we normally confer on a belief in ultimate truth. But if ultimate truth is not attainable, how can we accept our fallibility as ultimate truth?[9]

Soros's answer is that we must make an act of faith in the proposition that our understanding is imperfect, and proceed from there. My answer is a little different. As I explained in Chapter 3, we must recognize our fallibility, but I do not believe we need an act of faith to realize that the human mind is a limited instrument. Experience teaches us that our minds refashion what we perceive, that information, ideas and judgments are mental constructs, useful for dealing with reality but always distortions of reality. When we hear a noise in another room, we do not have to make an act of faith to know that the unknown something that made the noise is real, though unknown. In a sense, our two theories come to the same result. For Soros, too, implies that wisdom comes from testing our judgments by practical use.

A UNIVERSAL PRINCIPLE

If there is a principle that everyone in the world can accept, it is the need for personal integrity, which I define as the unity of the way one lives with the way one thinks: the integration of an honest life with an honest mind. As I see it, ethics is the art and science of using wisdom to maintain one's balance on the tightrope of life. To live with integrity is to follow one's wisdom—what each of us has tested and found effective in fulfilling personal potential.

In communities, integrity tends to be defined as keeping one's balance through the community's wisdom, what the community has tested and found effective. There is so much ethical confusion in today's society because the information deluge has undermined the synchronization of community and personal knowledge. Thus the authors of *The Integrity of Intelligence* warn us that "information technology offers intelligence without integrity."[10]

In fact, much of the confusion in discussing principles (or the lack thereof) comes from identifying principles with dogmas or ideas that became fixed when community wisdom was monumentalized, carved in stone due to fear of change or for political advantage. This happens easily because every community develops its own culture and, as Edward T. Hall pointed out, "one of the functions of culture is to provide a highly selective screen between man and the outside world."[11]

Nothing is more lethal to integrity than the fixed idea. If two people marry and either one of them has a fixed idea of how that marriage should work, the marriage will undoubtedly fail. Because the mind is an imperfect instrument, humans have to be infinitely adaptable. Fixed ideas or doctrines based on absolutes are treacherous because they close the mind against learning, against admitting that there are other possibilities, other circumstances yet unknown.

The honest mind forever admits it can be wrong. That admission is the foundation of integrity. Peter Senge called it "the state of being open," and quoted a student of Zen Buddhism, who said:

> Many people will say that once you recognize that you can never figure life out, you have denied rationality. But that's not true. You have simply recontextualized rationality. To search for understanding, knowing that there is no ultimate answer, becomes a creative process—one which involves rationality but also something more.[12]

PRACTICAL AND PERSONAL

The rest of this chapter describes a *modus operandi* for testing our judgments by practical use to restore that synchronization in the world community and promote progress to the new society. I hope what follows will advance the worldwide evolution I foresee while assisting each reader to find fulfillment on the way.

If our investigation to this point has established anything, it is that human evolution has reached a stage where individuals know too much for blind reliance on bosses and too little for total reliance on themselves. The solution seems to lie in partnering and networking, a system where each individual is free to make decisions while having the advantage of access to and participation in the knowledge of others.

To develop a society that fulfills these insights will take some time, most likely years, considering the many obstacles and probable opposition. For you and me and everyone else, the ultimate question is: "How can I, as an individual, both win the war and survive the battle?"

Since we have no one to rely on but ourselves, we start with Socrates's advice: "Know thyself." No matter what our stage of life, each of us has developed a databank of information, a tool box of abilities and a war chest of wisdom. The more accurately we understand and evaluate all three, the easier it will be to put them to use.

SELF-EVALUATION

Self-esteem begins with positive evaluation: the realization that each of us possesses an incredible number of useful assets. One helpful technique in self-evaluation is to jot down three lists: (1) KNOWLEDGE, or areas of information in which we are reasonably competent (e.g., baseball history; the workings of an automobile, chemistry), (2) ABILITIES, talents or skills in which we are proficient (e.g., tennis, cooking, organizing people), and (3) WISDOM, ideas or judgments that we have put to use and discovered that they worked (e.g., selecting gifts for one's wife, decorating a Christmas tree, applying a computer program).

Inevitably this exercise brings up information, abilities and wisdom we would like to add to our lists but cannot honestly write down. We all have weaknesses in information, ability and wisdom that interfere with our personal potential but would increase that potential if we could turn that weakness into a strength. Here, too, it helps to make a second three-column list for (1) KNOWLEDGE, (2) ABILITIES and (3) WISDOM that can and should be achieved with proper effort and help.

In *Jobshift,* William Bridges makes an important point about noting abilities. He writes that we should avoid thinking in terms of formal skills, like the art of microwave cookery, applying megabank policy, operating spreadsheet programs or speaking French, and concentrate on the underlying aptitudes: ability to grasp and apply instructions, to understand how bureaucrats think, to remember complex steps, to pick up foreign languages.[13]

Imagination is extremely useful in this exercise. Reliving past accomplishments enables us to recognize where our abilities lie. Visualizing future activities enables us to recognize how we can apply them. Unfortunately, imagination can also be the source of three major obstacles to self-realization:

1. Evaluating one's unique personal resources by what we see in others. Comparisons create inferiority complexes. I entered the business world relatively late in life, and the first mistake I made was to contrast my ability with that of my more experienced coworkers. It took me several years to realize that experience is like furniture polish. Its only power is to add luster to the quality of the wood. The path to success lay not in wishing I were like others, but in applying whatever my personal abilities were to the jobs I was assigned.

2. Setting personal goals that do not build on one's personal abilities. Delusions of grandeur are dangerous detours on the road to success. I took writing courses in college and devoted many working hours over several years to writing a novel. I was correct in judging that I had writing potential. But I was dreadfully deluded in believing I could write great fiction. Looking back,

I wish I had taken a more humble, more practical approach. The mistake was not in trying and failing. The mistake lay in refusing to accept failure for such a long time.

3. Riding the fun horse instead of mastering the team. We all have talents that are fun to use and talents that require discipline. If we want to get anyplace, we have to get all our talents to work as a team. I inherited a fast and creative mind and enjoyed using it. But it took me a long time to learn that, unless I exercised this talent with a tight rein, my glib tongue and disregard for people with different thought processes hurt my effectiveness. I had to train this talent to pull in harness with my ability to listen, to use different approaches for different individuals, to retreat in arguments, to realize that cocksureness confronts more often than it convinces.

CAREER CHOICES

When you have listed everything of importance and are satisfied you have eliminated self-delusion, rearrange the items on all your lists according to the working environment in which you think they can be most useful. Is it a PROPRIETORSHIP, a NETWORK, or a PARTNERSHIP? None of these decisions will mean much standing alone. But matching your abilities with different kinds of work and seeing where weaknesses will play a part can generate ideas as to what you can do and what you want to do.

Most people can improve self-analysis by partnering or, at least, networking. Ask someone you trust and who knows you well—a spouse, friend, teacher, or co-worker—to go over your lists and give you their reaction. If you choose the right person, you will find areas that lead to discussion and extremely useful collaboration.

Many older people will find that they have little need to make lists. They have been analyzing their strengths and weaknesses for years. Some will have decided what to do with their strengths and how they will compensate for the weaknesses. The lucky ones will already know how to apply their talents in the knowledge economy. The very blessed will be currently involved in a proprietorship or partnership crafted to prosper in the new era.

DEALING WITH THE INFORMATION DELUGE

Whether young or experienced, everyone faces this major problem: managing the flood of new information. Chapter 3 outlined a life-long learning regimen of (1) controlling attention, (2) evaluating information, (3) storing the useful, (4) interrelating what we learn and (5) applying it. Today this program is more difficult than it has ever been, but we also have a new tool, the computer.

The most disastrous mistake an individual can make in using the computer is to forget that the machine must remain a servant. Because it is a new tool demanding special operating expertise and because it can open up a whole new torrent of information, there is grave danger that the machine will control the user instead of the user controlling the machine.

The computer has enormous potential in dealing with information but, for most of today's users, its most practical application is as a memory extender. It can be an extremely valuable facilitator in steps three and four of our learning regimen: storing information and interrelating what we have learned. When I began the research for this book, I soon learned there were hundreds of books and articles on background subjects. I decided my information area would have to cover close to 300 books and at least as many articles. As my wife commented at the time, I was in danger of drowning in the information deluge before I was equipped to write about it.

The problem was not attention control. I knew how to find all this material and would enjoy reading it. Nor was the problem content evaluation. I had determined what I wanted to find out, and had adequate preliminary theories to focus my search. The real problem was how to remember and interrelate the multitude of facts, ideas and judgments I would gather.

The computer provided the solution. As I read, I entered what I judged important into a database program (in my case Symantec's Q & A), keying each entry both by source and by subject areas to interrelate entries to each other and to the topics on my tentative outline. Entries included ideas, passages, data and examples in the printed material as well as personal ideas and judgments occasioned by what I read. This enabled me to "export" from the database everything I needed before writing each chapter, providing a pool of relevant information much larger and more detailed than I could possibly have stored in my mind or even organized on paper.

I did use the computer for other tasks, such as finding and downloading occasional articles, but for research on what is already in print, technology has not advanced far enough to make the computer an adequate replacement for the assistance one can get from book dealers and librarians, although they used computers to find the books I needed (and the situation may change before this book is printed).

PLANNING, PLANNING, PLANNING

As is evident from this example, effective use of information requires a lot of planning. It is no longer possible to stay in control of one's life and count on someone to tell you what your need to know, if it ever was. Such an attitude is a leftover from bureaucracy.

Not long ago a friend remarked that he admired the self-discipline I showed in reading all those books. What was even more important, and in some ways more difficult, was the self-discipline that kept me from reading an even greater number of other books. Managing the information flow required that I reject some sources of information, and also that I decide which books to skim and which to read closely.

Planning begins with this screening process. Although all of us are already doing it subconsciously, it helps to be consciously deliberate in distinguishing between information that we need for doing what we want to do, information that may possibly be useful in the future and information that we absorb for pleasure. The first tends to be practical information defined by a project one is working on or has in mind. The second tends to be self-improvement information which widens or deepens personal capacity. The last is recreational information, which has the same relationship to the mind that exercise and sleep have to the body. One of these three types of information is not superior to the other two. They all have their place. The goal is to live a fulfilling and successful life by balancing all three.

John Seely Brown, director of Xerox's Palo Alto Research Center, warns that computers encourage us to be satisfied with receiving the information we ask for, while great thinkers depend on serendipity.[14] It is important to browse, to open our minds to the unexpected. The most efficient way to do this is to explore fertile fields, including media we can trust to present the worthwhile and different.

That is only one reason why screening media is indispensable. We have to consider all sources of information, not only books, magazines, newspapers, radio and television, tapes and disks, on-line services and the Internet, theatrical and sports events, but especially people. Subscription periodicals have an advantage in that their subscription departments ask readers to make a decision as to whether the magazine or newspaper should be on their agenda. Scheduling radio and television by time of day works tolerably well for recreational information, while practical and self-improvement information requires selection by program.

But the most important and most difficult source to screen is people. In practice, we screen the information input of friends, business-contacts and consultants less by choosing them than by planning the circumstances of conferring with them. For profitable collaboration or networking, both listener and communicator should be in tune with the conference's purpose.

It is both unnatural for the will and unhealthy for the mind to avoid all information that is not immediately useful for current projects. We need general information that makes us more knowledgeable and we need information that entertains and even has no other function than to feed the mental appetite we call curiosity. Very often a single information package can simultaneously fill several functions. The information in an article or program may be directly useful, self-improving and entertaining. Because so much information can serve multiple purposes, well-disciplined people frequently avoid entertainment unless it is also self-improving and well-focused people get so much pleasure out of their work that the useful information doubles as entertainment.

It is almost as disastrous to avoid certain media categories. For example, broadcasting devotes so much time to news, that there is a strong temptation to eliminate print as a news source. On May 7, 1992, my wife and I watched *Prime Time Live's* report on "Fathers Who Refuse to Pay Child Support." It was a thorough, balanced report, but it left my wife and me with a number of unanswered questions.

The next day I read *Newsweek's* May 4, 1992, cover story on "Deadbeat Dads." It covered the same subject matter and took about the same length of time to read as I had spent watching the television program. But I came away with a much clearer idea of what was happening and why. It is unfair to say that *Newsweek* did a better job than *Prime Time Live.* They were doing different jobs. The human mind needs both the verbal, linear exposition of print and the graphic, non-linear dramatization of broadcasting. Balancing types of media is almost as important as balancing kinds of information.

FINDING ONE'S PLACE IN THE TAPESTRY

If you are unemployed, or on the verge of becoming unemployed, whereas you formerly would have been looking for another job, you now should be planning an individual proprietorship or, better, a partnership. Which? It depends on the type of business and, even more, on your personal knowledge, abilities and wisdom. Partnerships do not need to be two people, although many are born out of two people collaborating on a business idea and then realizing that the project has better prospects for success if there are additional partners to cover the needed knowledge bases.

As I said at the end of Chapter 7, the civilization that is developing is made up of communities of interests that are interwoven like threads in a tapestry. When planning a business, it is important to know where it fits. To succeed it needs networks of customers and suppliers. The future of the undertaking depends on how well you understand how these networks operate, where your points of contact will be and how such relationships will work. It is true that much of the networking will develop as the project progresses, but the more advanced planning you and your partners can do the better the chance of success.

One area of networking that is frequently overlooked in planning a business enterprise is the personal support network of the partners themselves. How will this new community of interests affect all the other communities of concern in which each individual is already engaged? It no longer makes sense to segregate one's personal life from one's business life. The new society will be an organic unit, with each of its organs affecting every other organ. Your goal is to create a successful life, not merely a successful business.

Nor is partnering an exclusively business oriented technique. If you are married, you are already deep in one partnership. Most of us have partnered successfully with friends, teachers and occasionally with doctors, lawyers, realtors and sales people. The secret of raising children is to graduate from instruction to direction to conferring and, if you are a very fortunate parent, to partnering.

23

TOMORROW'S GLOBAL COMMUNITY: A FAMILY OF FAMILIES

"In his ape-like prehistory, man had adopted the habit of forming families: his first helpers were probably the members of his family. ... The love that instituted the family still retains its power; in its original form it does not stop short of direct sexual satisfaction, and in its modified form as aim-inhibited friendliness it influences our civilization."

— *Sigmund Freud, 1930*[1]

Although we cannot predict a precise timetable, we can see how our world is being transformed. Tomorrow's global society will be a network of constantly changing small communities each defined by a single concern. These communities will be independent of geography, allow for degrees of membership, balance responsibilities with benefits, be concerned with members' total welfare and provide for non-contributing members. They will encourage allegiances with other communities, allocate authority naturally, operate as gift economies and connect actually or potentially with every other human community.

CHANGE HAPPENS BY FITS AND STARTS

As examined at length in Chapters 12 and 15, the social structures that were developed to meet the needs of the Industrial Revolution and representative democracy will not disappear overnight. Some old ways may die suddenly, as they did in the Soviet Union. Others will change slowly, as popular attitudes on women's place in society are doing. We can expect relics of bureaucracy, particularly in government, to stay with us well into the next century.

It is impossible to predict when the changes will be complete or precisely how they will take place. What we do know, from everything we have concluded in previous chapters, are the basic outlines of tomorrow's global society. Like the city on the mountain top, the destination is clear, even though the length and difficulties of the road ahead are hidden in the fog of the valley below.

The evidence for the form of the future is all around us. Independent communities organized to manage specific concerns are multiplying. The members of these communities are linked more often by communication than by geography. Most of these communities function independently of traditional corporate or government structures. The great majority of these communities are voluntary and ruled by direct democracy, with every member involved in every community decision.

What sort of world can we expect, if the majority of people invest their energies and talents in such communities? In an *addendum* to this book, I imagine such a community 300 years from now. Although such a story can help us visualize what the future world may be like, it is fiction, owing as much to imagination as to reason. What are the actual probabilities, relying on reason alone? What can we expect, perhaps in our lifetimes, certainly in the lifetimes of our children?

In Chapter 22 we concluded that we all must become entrepreneurs, attaining fulfillment and obtaining income by constructing communities. If we do it right, what will be the nature of these communities?[2]

THE MODEL COMMUNITY

Of all the communities humans have created, fostered and given allegiance to, none is more natural and fundamental than the family. It is the one community that has worldwide recognition, and it is the one established community that fits our concept of the community of the future.

The well-run family:

1. Is created and defined by a common concern. By law and tradition marriage is a mutual agreement to form a life-molding partnership that will fulfill the human potential of the two people involved.

2. Is independent of geography. Not only do families move, but they remain a community even when their members are widely scattered.

3. Allows for different degrees of membership. The daughters and sons who leave to start families of their own remain members of their birth families even though less involved.

4. Balances benefits and responsibilities. The joys of love, companionship, sex and sharing require the obligation of devotion, support, cooperation and sharing.

5. Provides for members unable to contribute and is concerned with the complete welfare of all its members. When this community really works, the original partners realize that their fulfillment and happiness is impossible unless they are concerned with every aspect of the lives of family members, physical, mental, emotional and economic—including the members who do not contribute. Children are a natural consequence, as is mutual care in sickness and in health.

6. Fosters membership in other communities. The healthy family encourages outside involvement, from school to eventual marriage and the formation of new families.

7. Naturally distributes and exercises internal authority. Family government can be called "instinctive democracy," with power shared by mutual consent according to natural ability.

8. Operates as a gift economy. In no community is this more evident.

9. Networks actually or potentially with every other human community. It is a universal conviction in every race and culture that all families are somehow related, descendants of a primordial human couple. Every family with sons or daughters can forge new links with other families through marriage.

1. DEFINED BY A COMMON CONCERN

The spread of information and growth of knowledge has forced society to rely on specialization not only in individual careers but also in the way it makes decisions. In business, in government, even in our personal lives, we rely increasingly on groups of specialists for important decisions. Task forces, committees and support groups are all communities created to enable the collaboration of individual wisdoms in solving specific problems, and the number of these multiplies daily.

All of us have many problems but, considering the complexity of our lives and the current extent of human knowledge, we are more likely to find solutions if we study our problems one by one, and collaborate with others facing the same problem. Human beings have always formed ad hoc communities to solve specific problems. What is changing is that these communities are becoming more necessary, more frequent and, therefore, more formal.

This kind of direct decision making is gradually replacing old systems—feudalism, monarchy, bureaucracy, representative government—in which most people, whether by circumstances or voluntarily, left major decisions to others. One of the effects of the information deluge is a growing demand among individuals to gain personal control of their lives. We already have examined the first signs of atrophy in bureaucracy and representative government. The power and practice of delegating decisions in business and government will continue to decline until society is governed entirely by direct democracy exercised through an uncountable—because ever-changing—number of ad hoc communities.

As in the family, these communities will always be created to attain a single objective. Marriage, whether for love, sex, convenience or financial security, is always ultimately a partnership for the purpose of attaining happiness, fulfillment, and a better life. The partnership communities we are talking about, whether for business, entertainment, philanthropy or education, must be just as focused. A specific purpose, the reason for forming the partnership, creates the community and defines it. Each partner joins to further that purpose.

As in marriage, the members of any community can lose sight of its purpose. When that happens, the community becomes pointless and either falls apart or has to be preserved artificially.

2. INDEPENDENT OF GEOGRAPHY

Early human communities, like early families, were circumscribed by geography, chiefly because travel was difficult and communication predominantly local. Even nomads, who moved with the climate, tended to take their geography with them. Entire families, tribes and villages moved as units. These boundaries were set by the limitations of information. Knowledge itself was circumscribed by geography. But modern technology and the increase of knowledge has scaled the communal walls.

We no longer need constant physical proximity to form a community. On June 4, 1994, in Ojai, California, some 45 members of the Wechsler Family met for a reunion. They traced their origins back to immigrants from the Ukraine who came to the United States around 1900. Surnames at the reunion included Aronson, Glenn, Goldman, Pritzker, Riskind, Scully, Sterling, Vinikour, Wechsler, Wexler, and Zubrinsky. They came from all over the United States: California, Colorado, Georgia, Illinois, New York, and Ohio. But community ties were still strong enough to bring them to Ojai.[3]

There will always be common interests tied to geography: housing, streets, stores, and entertainment facilities. There will always be communities formed to deal with local and regional problems. But as human interests have spread far beyond physical boundaries, so most communities will be dedicated to concerns unrelated to locality.

Hence, as described at the close of Chapter 7,[4] tomorrow's society will be more like a tapestry than a pyramid, a closely woven fabric of intertwined interests. Individuals will belong to many communities, as many as they have serious interests. Since the communities of tomorrow will overlap and interpenetrate, it will be difficult at times to see where one community ends and another begins. In a single partnership, for instance, partners with a unique concern may form their own community within the firm. The possibility for overlapping and interpenetrating is as infinite as the potential of human concerns.

3. DIFFERENT DEGREES OF MEMBERSHIP

Interest and involvement will differ from person to person. Family involvement is different for parents, grown children, grandparents and in-laws. Concerns change according to situation, dependence, and responsibility. There are similar differences among the members of any community. Some are always more involved than others, whether we are talking about an investigative committee, a baseball team, a business partnership or a chess club.

As in voluntary associations today, communities tomorrow will manage degrees of involvement differently. Some will have formal degrees of membership. Others will base dues on involvement. Business communities will determine salaries by the extent as well as the value of participation, and some may distinguish between junior and senior partners. Voting power may be distributed evenly or weighted according to interest and involvement.

We speak of communities of concern being voluntary. Membership in a community can be voluntary even when that membership came about by involuntary circumstances. The great majority of children do not consider membership in their families coercion, even though they are members by the involuntary circumstance of birth or adoption. You may have had no intention of getting involved in specific community decisions when you moved into a neighborhood, but your living there makes you involved. In extreme cases children have sought to divorce themselves from their families. In extreme circumstances you can move out of the neighborhood.

4. BALANCING BENEFITS AND RESPONSIBILITIES

Since each community is voluntary and defined by its purpose, it will be difficult to separate responsibilities from benefits. In marriage mutual love, companionship, sex and sharing are impossible without mutual devotion, support, cooperation and sharing. In business partnerships profit from the joint venture depends on the work of each partner. The effectiveness of administrative communities will be proportionate to the cooperation of their members.

As in families and most voluntary communities today, the communities of the future will be run more by friendly agreement than majority rule,[5] and decisions made by friendly agreement are more frequently reinforced by feelings of obligation and willingness to do one's part.

There will be occasions where members may have to be coerced to cooperate whether by peer pressure or more drastic measures. Preference for friendly agreement tends to avoid such distasteful measures. But coercion no more destroys the voluntary nature of membership than open-heart surgery destroys the average human's desire to stay alive.

5. PROVIDING FOR THE WELFARE OF ALL

The paradox in parenting is that the single purpose of happiness and fulfillment for two individuals becomes the general purpose of welfare for all, children as well as parents. When the community we call the family really works, the original partners realize that fulfillment and happiness are impossible unless they are concerned with every aspect of the lives of family members, physical, mental, emotional and economic.

There is a similar paradox in every partnership community. Although such groups are defined and directed by a single purpose, the members of such groups have to be concerned about other aspects of their partners' lives. The purpose of the partnership is single and limited, but the conditions for achieving that purpose require favorable operating circumstances, i.e., the mental and physical welfare of each partner. Collaboration will succeed in direct proportion to each partner's ability to perform, and each partner's performance depends on physical, mental and emotional health. If my partner is in trouble, so am I.

Consider the contributions of the various partners in a business firm. The partners were chosen precisely because of their different abilities. Hence, in every business decision, some will contribute much and some little, each according to his or her ability. This is the way the partnership was supposed to operate when it was established, and it is the way that every democratic community has to operate. Collaboration is a two-way street. Every partner has to be ready to help the others, and each partner expects to be helped when he or she has need.

In most cases, the need and the help will be directly related to the community's purpose. But there will be many instances when the need and the help will be less direct. A study group waives the dues of a indigent student. A baseball team pays an injured player's medical bills. A quilting club continues to include a woman whose sight has grown too poor to sew. You are right if you see this as compassion, kindness or friendship. You are equally right to see it as a way to retain a helpful mind, a future player, or a morale contributor.

Because each partnership's defining purpose is very specific, and because everything important must be decided by direct democracy, communities will tend to be small and their members very involved. Such an environment demands and encourages personal participation and friendly relationships. This is why tomorrow's society of specialized communities will provide for social problems such as education, insurance, unemployment, health care and crime control.

Tomorrow's communities of concern will create a kinder, more humane world not because humanity has suddenly become more virtuous but because the environment has become more conducive to social virtue.

6. PROMOTING MULTIPLE ALLEGIANCES

A very important consequence of the movement into overlapping and interpenetrating communities, each defined by its own concern, will be the growth of tolerance and the disarming of conflict. In a recent book, *One Nation, After All,* Alan Wolfe reports the results of studies showing that "Americans have revised themselves. However strongly they may judge themselves they are reluctant to pass judgment on others."[6] Even though they have retained moral standards for themselves, the spread of information with its mix of cultural and moral views has taught most people to avoid taking positions that denigrate others. To survive in today's society we have to be tolerant of our neighbor's standards even when they differ radically from our own.

Wolfe's study proves that human beings can be open minded and tolerant without losing their personal values, the moral norms on which they build their lives. Just as the healthy family sees no threat in outside allegiance, and encourages its members to become involved in school, job, social organizations, eventual marriage and forming new families, so the society of multiple single-purpose communities will presume that every citizen has multiple loyalties. The ability to compromise, described in Chapter 5,[7] will become even more important in tomorrow's world.

Since no two individuals have identical interests, everyone will expect his or her neighbor, even his or her spouse, to be involved in many different communities, devoted to many different, and sometimes contradictory, purposes. Such an attitude fosters the virtue of distinguishing individuals from their opinions and even their actions. This growing ability to accept the sinner without accepting the sin, to embrace the prodigal while deploring his profligacy, helps to explain the findings in Alan Wolfe's book. It also explains how a majority of Americans can approve of Bill Clinton's performance as president even while they believe he lies and philanders.

Like Adam Smith's economy, this free market of social interests will be regulated by an invisible hand. The more interrelated individual interests become, the more they will encourage individuals and groups to live in peace, to compromise and reconcile, and to advance the principles of democracy.

7. DISTRIBUTING AND EXERCISING INTERNAL AUTHORITY

In small collaborating teams or partnerships, as in the family, formal designation of authority is the exception. In general, authority spontaneously gravitates to the individual with superior wisdom for the decision at hand. In Jurg Steiner's words, decisions are made by amicable agreement rather than majority rule.[8]

In the Middle Ages and well into the 17th Century, formal authority was rooted in religion. The monarch ruled by divine right and delegated authority to other officers and institutions. The attitude persisted long after 1215, when the English nobles forced King John to sign the Magna Carta limiting his power. Early democracy, including popular rule as seen by America's founding fathers, merely switched the roots of authority from God to the people. They made no essential changes in the way authority was exercised or delegated. In the democratic state, the people were sovereign, but like the divine-right sovereigns they also delegated their authority. Democracy became identified with representative government. Rulers were elected by popular vote and given the authority to make decisions for those who elected them.

Today's social currents move entirely in the direction of enabling people to make decisions for themselves. Hence tomorrow's society will distribute and exercise authority according to the decision to be made. No longer will legislators be given the power to make decisions in many different areas independently of those who elected them. Nor will managers be empowered to make decisions for those who work for them. Instead, each decision will be made by collaboration among the individuals concerned. As sensible parents encourage their children (and each other) to make their own decisions and to cooperate when several individuals are involved, so the community of partnerships will respect and expect independence and collaboration in every decision.

8. OPERATING AS A GIFT ECONOMY

As explained in Chapters 11 and 12,[9] the world cannot move into a knowledge economy without becoming a gift economy. It is precisely because society is reorganizing itself to manage knowledge that partnership will become the dominant form of community and a gift economy the natural way to manage commercial relations.

Since tomorrow's global community will operate as a gift economy, the new society will stress cooperation rather than competition and be characterized by openness and trust rather than secrecy and suspicion.

One result of this is that tomorrow's economy will shrink the gap between rich and poor. It is very difficult, if not impossible, to preserve extreme differences in compensation among people who work closely together and are seriously interested in cooperating with complete honesty.

9. DEVOTED TO GLOBAL NETWORKING

Common lineage and intermarriage unite families. Actual and potential operations networks will unite tomorrow's communities.

Much of the confusion in today's society comes from the impossibility of accommodating the many relationships individuals and groups now have that transcend the boundaries of traditional social structures. Former Secretary of Labor Robert B. Reich put his finger on the problem when he asked: "Who is Us?"[10]—arguing that jobs for our citizens provided by foreign companies are more important than the success of American companies exporting jobs to cheaper labor markets.

The confusion extends to every unit of government. Is the economy of the New York Metropolitan Area distinct from the economies of Connecticut, New Jersey and New York State? Can the North American Free Trade Association become a real economic unit while restricting immigration across Canadian, Mexican and American borders? If a common currency for Europe and the Mercosur countries[11] makes sense, why are our leaders reluctant to adopt a common global currency?

There was a time when "imported" marked a product as very special and usually more expensive. Today supermarkets offer grapes from Chile side by side with grapes from California. Cars sold in one continent are assembled in another with parts from a dozen different nations. Phone calls between continents are almost as common and inexpensive as phone calls between a single country's cities. People see the same movies all over the world. Communities are already networking actually or potentially with communities all over the world.

Tomorrow's global community is not a future dream. In many aspects it is already here.

Addendum

THE WORLD IN 2301 A.D.— A STORY

"Can it be believed that the democracy which has overthrown the feudal system and vanquished kings will retreat before tradesmen and capitalists? ... Whither, then, are we tending? No one can say, for terms of comparison already fail us."
— Alexis de Tocqueville, 1848[1]

According to the evidence presented in this book, several major trends should blossom into new social structures by 2301. Networks of small, transitory partnerships will replace large corporations. Customization and interactive marketing will eliminate the distinction between service and manufacturing. Attitudes on privacy and intellectual property will be transformed. There will be less distinction between rich and poor, and ability to provide higher standards of living will outrace the world's population growth.

IMAGINING SOCIETY IN 2301 A.D.

I wrote the description that follows in 1997, just as reviews were appearing of Arthur C. Clarke's latest book, *3001, The Final Odyssey*. Many scientists love Clarke's science fiction. Some even claim his predictions have influenced their work. NASA's Charles Kohlhase explains, "When you dream what is possible and add a knowledge of physics, you make it happen."[2]

My fantasy, an addendum to this book, could be titled: *2301, The Final Society*. It is my dream of what is possible based on what we have learned in the book.

Imagine:

THE PERSONAL REPORT OF A 24TH-CENTURY RIP VAN WINKLE

"Rip Van Winkle" is what the media have called me since I was resuscitated on April 22, 2301. My real name is Demetrios Sosuonam. I was born in Appleton, Wisconsin, North America, on December 9, 1939. They tell me that my case is one of the few completely successful attempts to revive a human from a state of cryogenic suspension induced before the turn of the 21st Century. I was 60 at the time and in a New York cardiology center.

When they told me that there was no chance of finding a transplantable heart-lung in time to save my life, I asked a doctor friend of mine, who was conducting experiments in cryogenics, if he would freeze me before I died. It was an unusual request. Fulfilling it may even have been illegal. But his freezing me while I was still alive is probably what made my resuscitation possible. There was a complete medical report in my sealed capsule. The 24th Century doctors replaced my heart and both lungs while I was still frozen, and then, as the popular media put it, "defrosted" me.

The psychological shock of "sleeping" for more than 300 years comes not with waking. Time does not exist when you are unconscious. The shock comes when you examine your surroundings and try to relate what is going on around you to what you took for granted before you went to sleep.

Back in New York I had been a writer, consultant and commentator on government, on social problems and on the economy. Hence, once I realized I was not dreaming and that I was actually alive in the year 2301, it was natural for me to ask for information regarding my areas of interest, even before I got used to moving sidewalks, flying taxis, 100-story buildings, elevators that ride on air and television screens that respond to spoken requests and cover entire walls.

I am still a 60-year-old man physically and mentally, and my interests are the same as they were 302 years ago. I was curious as to how people conduct business and govern themselves in this totally new world. I wanted to learn which social problems had been solved and which had grown worse.

The doctor responded to my request by sending me four instructors, not via the digital screen, but in person. The following notes are from the sessions I spent with them. I write them down with the hope they may help other people like myself, for the doctor tells me his colleagues expect to be successful in resuscitating other 20th and 21st Century men and women from cryogenic suspension.

Since the English spoken in my new world has many expressions unfamiliar to people from my century, I've taken the liberty of writing what I was told in the American idiom of the 1990s.

MARIAN TURNER, SOCIAL-STRUCTURE ANALYST

My first instructor turned out to be a very attractive woman in her 40s. She had reddish brown hair under a rose bonnet and was dressed in a mauve, well tailored sort of jump suit. She held out her hand and introduced herself as Ms. Turner, who would answer my questions on business and government. I asked her whether she was on the hospital staff, for her clothing, despite its bright colors, looked somewhat similar to that worn by the doctor who had been attending me.

She smiled. "Oh, this is not a uniform. In fact, Dr. Walder was not wearing a uniform either."

"I guess I was expecting you to wear something quite different, like the women in Buck Rogers and Flash Gordon comic strips."

"I'm acquainted with those cartoons from my course in 20th Century Futurism and Fantasy. Their clothes were colorful but not very practical. Since out-of-home clothes are made from temperature-leveling fabric, designers rely on tailoring rather than on clinging or draping."

"I guess the world is still not ready to dress as daringly as Flash Gordon's ladies."

She laughed. "It has nothing to do with prudishness. We think nothing of being naked at home or in the public athletic centers. But out-of-home clothing is climate controlled. We set it to keep our bodies comfortable by supplying or subtracting heat and moisture in any kind of weather or indoor atmosphere. It would make little sense to leave much skin uncovered."

"Do you buy these wonderful outfits in department stores?"

"Department stores vanished years ago as fewer people were willing to work for wages or salaries and more people began to realize the advantage of dealing with owners. In fact, most clothing today is sold by the tailors who custom design and sew each garment to fit the buyer's needs and taste. We do shop at clothing marts, which somewhat resemble the old department stores but are more like clusters of boutiques, each an independent business."

"Every boutique has a staff of cutters, seamstresses and finishers?"

"After programmable cutting and sewing machines became widespread, designers began doing their own tailoring on the spot in collaboration with the customer. We buy our clothes just as women bought their hairdos 300 years ago. In fact, there is very little you can buy nowadays that is not customized or prepared to order. In retail, hired clerks and salespeople have been replaced by proprietors, who call themselves customer-collaborators."

"Buying made-to-order clothes sounds very expensive. Where do poor people buy their clothes?"

"There are tailoring partners who can charge very high prices due to their reputations for fine work and creative design. But many tailors are less skilled or just beginning and have to compete on price. You shop according to your income and taste. Since both prices and the manner of doing business depend entirely on individual suppliers and customers, there is a very wide variety of arrangements not only in clothing sales but in every type of retail service. There are tailors who come to the customers' homes, others that have traveling showrooms, still others that do all their selling via the digital screen. Some tailors sell footwear as well as clothes. Others make only specialized clothing. Some operate only a few weeks a year."

"Can they make a living working only a few weeks a year?"

"They may be elders who work occasionally for fun or extra cash. Or they may work in a different field the rest of the year. I've friends who keep busy with three or four different occupations, each with different partners."

"What protects me from finding myself with no place to buy a suit or, worse, with no one to go back to when my suit falls apart?"

"There's little danger of that. Cautious customers look for tailors who are approved by one of the established clothesmaker associations. Every business has some sort of association set up by people in that business to protect themselves and provide a guarantee for customers."

"Who keeps these associations from controlling prices, from restricting competition—like the guilds in medieval Europe?"

"Those guilds were chartered by government. They had a monopoly. The business associations today have far less power. If enough tailors don't like the way their association operates, they can either elect new officers or join another association. If the buying public finds that a retail association is not protecting its interests, it looks for firms belonging to competitive associations. I know at least two tailors who are members of more than one clothesmaker association. They find it impresses their customers and makes them less dependent on a single association."

"What's to stop a rogue tailor, who can't meet an association's membership requirements, from setting up his own association?"

"The media would be all over him. Like other businesses, the media are run by small partnerships or sole proprietorships. Today's technology makes it incredibly easy to promote, publish and distribute information. The hard part is making your medium vital enough that people will pay for it. Since there are few things that interest people as much as what they get for their money, consumer-protection stories get extensive coverage."

"What happens when a business cheats the customer? I'm sure that must happen occasionally."

"We've changed a lot of things in the last three centuries, but not human nature. We still have wrongdoers. But the customer who is cheated can sue in the association court. All business associations have guarantees to protect the public. They cover a complainant's loss and punish the wrongdoer either by a fine or expulsion from the association. In 20th Century America the stock exchanges used a similar system as did most state medical societies. Today every association operates that way."

"In the 20th Century many Americans felt that associations were organized to protect their members against the public. State medical groups were very reluctant to censure doctors."

"No one claims we've solved that problem altogether. But it's far less prevalent for four reasons. First, there are no government charters to give professional associations monopoly status. Second, there are client or patient associations, insurance associations, supplier associations, which can put tremendous pressure on a business or professional association. Third, members of medical associations, like everyone else, belong to many other associations. You're less liable to protect a friend in one association if his actions hurt friends in another association. Fourth, there are many associations in every field, and they are all small. In order to preserve democratic control members keep their associations to less than 100 members."

"Do people get that involved? Back in my time half the citizens didn't even vote."

"A number of studies were done in the 2260s on why and how people get involved. The studies found that people got involved in direct proportion to the weight of the individual's vote in organization decisions and the extent that those decisions relate to the individual's primary interests. Associations are kept small enough that each member's vote counts, and people join them only if the association advances some personal interest."

"You say that professional associations have no special authorization from government. Has the government any rules for professional conduct?"

"We have no government in the sense you mean. The associations are the government, the democratically empowered regulators of the group. Each association is something like the nation-state used to be in your day. Each governed its citizens, but not other nations' citizens. When a common concern arose, nations got together and came to an agreement. The same is true of the associations. It's not an accurate comparison because each association is much, much smaller and has authority only over the areas of interest for which it was established. So everybody is a multiple 'citizen,' belonging to and having a say in many of these tiny 'nations'."

"If there's no government outside the associations, who arrests burglars, murderers and other lawbreakers?"

"The security firms. Security and crime control is a business like any other service. Security firms are partnerships that provide policing, some for neighborhoods, others for certain types of businesses, most for one or more multi-residence towers. Everybody pays for policing the same way they pay for waste collection, fire protection, insurance or any other home service. Each tower is divided into commercial and residential areas, each with an association run by the residents to hire firms for maintenance, waste disposal, policing, fire protection and insurance."

"Can the security firm catch a burglar after he leaves the building? And what do they do with him if they catch him?"

"Security firms have their local security association, which belongs to the regional security association, which belongs to the continental security association, which belongs to the Global Security Association. These associations set guidelines for mutual cooperation. It is very difficult for a criminal to hide once a Security Network lists him as wanted. When he's caught, he is turned over to an appropriate justice firm."

"You mean the courts are also run by private companies?"

"Even 300 years ago there were private mental hospitals with the right to judge patients, limit their freedom and prescribe treatment. We consider criminals to be mentally or morally ill. What's changed is that even with mental patients, the three psychologists who decide on the need for treatment never include the professional who will supervise the treatment. They have to be separate to forestall conflict of interest. To open a justice firm, the partners must be qualified in both law and psychology. Usually one or two senior partners belong to a judges' association, while junior partners belong either to an association for prosecutors, for defenders or for investigators. To qualify as a member in any of these associations, you have to pass a very tough exam. People in this field start as investigators and work their way up. Since you cannot take the judge's exam without spending 10 years as an investigator, seven years as a prosecutor and seven as a defender, very few become judges before their mid-40s."

"Who pays for all this?"

"Remuneration for court personnel are set by the associations, and judge, prosecutor and defender are chosen by lot from a calendar of professionals who are free to take a case. Contingent fees are not permitted, nor are complainants or defendants allowed to buy better lawyers or psychologists. To discourage frivolous suits and cover the costs if the defendant proves innocent, complainants must advance a goodwill deposit. Defendants who are found guilty pay all court costs. If they cannot afford the costs or the fine, they must earn the money in jail. If that is not enough, the court garnishees half of whatever they earn after release until the fine is paid."

"I still don't understand how this works without a superior authority to oversee and enforce such arrangements."

"In the 20th Century people tended to make a sharp distinction between private jurisdictions and public jurisdictions. Today every association has both public and private jurisdiction. It has public jurisdiction so far as its authority is recognized by the general public. It has private jurisdiction so far as its rules have to be obeyed by its members. In a democratic society power comes from below, not from above. When there's a conflict between two associations, representatives usually work out a compromise. If they cannot, they ask one of the legal associations to appoint three arbitration specialists. An association that refuses to accept the decision of the arbitration panel is disturber-listed."

"Disturber-listed?"

"Listed as a disturber of the public peace. Such listings are rare. When they happen, they get a lot of publicity. I do not know of a single case where an association remained on the list for more than 60 days. Both suppliers and customers are loathe to do business with firms that belong to a disturber-listed association."

"But what about people who do not belong to any association? Who stands up for their rights? Or forces them to respect other jurisdictions?"

"You would have to be both an oddball and an extremist not to belong to an association. Mothers enroll their children in an association for the benefit of infants before they are born. There are associations for every occupation, for every stage in life, for every special interest. Very few people belong to fewer than 20 associations and many pay dues in as many as 100. The more involved you are in public life, the more associations you join, and the more likely you are to encourage your association to accept compromise when there's conflict."

"Can everyone afford to pay all those dues? Belonging to so many associations must be terribly expensive."

"No more expensive than the taxes people paid in the 20th Century. The difference now is that dues payers know exactly what they are paying for and have direct say in how the money is used. They do not have to join if they do not want to pay for an association's benefits. People can get help when they find it difficult to pay the dues of associations they need. Some associations waive dues under specified circumstances. And almost all associations belong to one of the association-advancement alliances. The AAAs provide insurance to enable member associations to cover dues for individuals or firms in financial hardship. They also provide counseling for association management, arbitrate membership conflicts and conduct publicity campaigns on the benefits of association membership."

"Let me see if I've got this straight. Practically everyone belongs to one or more associations. And the associations are little democracies with jurisdiction only in matters of their concern. And there are associations of associations, and those associations have their own associations. It sounds like the federal system we had in my day: city, county, state, nation."

"It has some resemblances, but power is concentrated at the bottom, not the top. You'll find that the associations of associations have far less influence than the primary associations. They exist largely for coordination and communication. The system is both simpler and more complicated than the federalist system invented in the 18th Century. It's simpler because unlike federalism it does not require citizens to delegate an elected official to make decisions for them. Since each association's power is limited by its specific purpose, membership can be small enough to leave significant decisions to popular vote or conference. It's more complicated because each individual is related to and influenced by associations in many different ways, partly because some associations are for individuals, some are for partnerships or businesses, and some for other associations, but chiefly because every association is constantly networking with other associations to settle disputes and improve matters of common interest.

"What keeps association membership below 100?"

"Since the 2260s it has been customary for associations to split into two when membership rises above 100. There's no law enforcing this, but the public would consider an association undemocratic, even dangerous, if it grew to a size where members did not know each other or group conferences became unwieldy. Many associations have far fewer members. The worldwide Association of Virtuosi on the Virginal has only six members."

"I presume it's easier to run a local association than a worldwide one."

"With meetings conducted by two-way digital screen, distance does not affect operations. Geography is determined by purpose. Associations for real estate, neighborhood services, policing and traffic, roads and parks have to be local or regional. The partnership that takes care of this tower's waste disposal belongs to the Upper Manhattan Waste-Disposal Association, which belongs to the Association of Greater New York Waste-Disposal Associations, which belongs to the North American Alliance of Waste Disposal, Recycling and Public Water Control Associations. Such pyramiding of associations is not uncommon. If there is a global objective, there is probably a global association with 50 or 60 regional association as members. The World Meteorological Alliance, the Global Telecommunications Association and The Global Alliance for Environmental Concerns are examples."

I was so intrigued I did not realize the sun had gone down and the luminous ceiling had come on. Ms. Turner bade me good night and told me that my instructor tomorrow would be an expert on long-term networks.

MAXWELL KERTZ, LONG-TERM NETWORKS COORDINATOR

Dr. Kertz was very different from Ms. Turner. I would have guessed that he was in his 50s, though he told me he was 83. He was a short man with twinkling eyes and a contagious smile. He also wore a temperature-control jumpsuit, but it seemed a little large for him and was threadbare at the elbows. It was evident that appearance was not one of Dr. Kertz's major concerns.

"What," I asked him, "is a long-term network?"

He clapped his hands as he sat down. "Good, let's start there. A long-term network is a network that will last longer than a year. You could say that it is what replaced the large corporations that disappeared in the 2050s and 2060s. I just finished a consulting assignment for one of the three Western Hemisphere networks that manufacture sky taxis. The network is relatively new and manufactures an amphibian model designed by George Calides and Jack Killian. A partnership can build a single taxi, but there has to be a long-term network to build taxis in sufficient numbers to bring prices down to where taxi firms will buy them."

"That means major money to build a factory with an assembly line."

"Exactly. So Calides and Killian set up a new partnership with Mildred Dove and Leopold Wang. Calides and Killian are engineers. Dove is a cost analyst, and Wang specializes in negotiations and contracts. The four partners drew up a business proposal which was presented to a number of investment bankers. Five investment-banking partnerships advanced 20 percent each to guarantee a line of credit. That enabled Calides and partners to engage a construction partnership to build the plant and a plant specialist to supervise the purchase and installation of the machinery. The plant started assembling taxis three years ago."

"Who owns the factory?"

"Calides, Killian, Dove and Wang as managing partners and the five investment partnerships as silent (what used to be called, limited) partners."

"Who hires and pays the employees who work in the factory?"

"There are no employees. Much of Wang's time is spent finding partnerships to take over each manufacturing department and organize a network of partnerships to run it. Contracts usually run from three to five years for the supervisory partnerships and one to three years for the operational partnerships. Each contract specifies production goals with a flat fee for the entire job. The contract is closed with an up-front deposit against the fee, the balance is paid in monthly installments with an incentive bonus upon completion. Bonuses are based on how well the partnership does on the leeway allowed for quantity and schedules. Promotion, sales and delivery teams are engaged in the same way."

"Are there actually unemployed partnerships running around looking for contracts all the time?"

"Not really. A partnership is meaningless without an assignment. Although there are partners who like to work together, most partnerships in manufacturing and construction networks are formed for the specific project. There are firms that help people find partners and assignments. If a factory needs a six-partner team to run the motor-assembly unit, a person interested in that kind of work will look for five qualified partners. The six then draw up a proposal describing how they will do the work and what they will charge for one, two or three years. If the management partnership likes the proposal it leads to a contract."

"There can be several partnerships competing for the same contract?"

"You bet. The team has to match the price of similar teams and the managers have to find a team they can trust and afford. That's what keeps the system efficient."

"You called such networks long-term. Yet some partners sign up for only a year. Doesn't that threaten the life of the network?"

"Good question. A network with a lot of turnover will usually be less efficient than one that keeps turnover at a minimum. Many partnerships ask for a right-of-renewal clause in their contract. You have to remember that each of these partnerships, no matter what it is doing, is an independent business. The partners run their unit as they think best. They agree among themselves how each partner will be paid. And sometimes the partners may not want to continue the partnership beyond a year."

"What happens if one of the partners gets sick or dies?"

"That's the partnership's problem. If the illness is temporary, the other partners usually pitch in. If it is long-term, the partners may want to look for a replacement partner. It's their partnership. They can do as they like, providing, of course, that they meet their contract. If they don't, the managing partners have a right to replace them with another partnership."

"Who takes care of a partner when it's time to retire?"

"We don't talk about retiring anymore. People can work constantly or intermittently, depending on their needs and ability to find partners. Naturally, as people get older or slip into poor health, they work less, or maybe not at all. Most people make sure to invest or save a percentage of their income during their working years. There is a thriving business for personal financial planners and financial-need insurers."

"Unless people have changed considerably, aren't there many individuals who spend more than they save, aren't good at planning or even at making a living?"

"People haven't changed. Society is still burdened with the poor, the incompetent, the profligate and the lazy. There is an entire business sector devoted to caring for the needy and helping the incompetent."

"That's a business? How can charitable work be a business?"

"People who work at helping the poor or caring for the sick have to make a living. In the early 21st Century society began to realize that the distinction between nonprofit organizations and so-called profit organizations had no justification beyond out-of-date tax laws."

"But where does the money come from to pay the partners and cover the costs of helping people in need?"

"Good Samaritan businesses, as we call them, get paid just like any other contracting partnership. They get specific charitable assignments from associations who want to take care of members in difficulty, or from individuals. If you know of a family with a sick child who needs care, you can hire a Good Samaritan partnership that specializes in child care. Private payers are usually helping relatives or friends, but a surprising number of people volunteer to help strangers. In fact, the Good Samaritan firms publish catalogs which describe needy cases for people who want to help. There are Good Samaritan firms that run retirement homes, that provide supplementary retirement-allowances, that provide visiting nurses, that provide food and clothing, that take care of the dying."

"What consulting were you doing for the amphibian taxi network?"

"I was hired to assess their knowledge network. The more relevant information the members of a network have, the more efficient the network will be. This is especially important in long-term networks. The more aware every person working in the network is of what everybody else is doing, the more chance that individuals will foresee problems before they happen and come up with ideas to improve performance. As experienced network initiators, Calides and partners hired a knowledge-network organizer for their amphibian taxi network. That partnership organized the knowledge network, purchased the hardware and designed the software to keep every participant in the operations network informed on everything that was happening or even planned. Several centuries ago knowledge was considered primarily a personal asset. Although each individual learned from others, what he or she knew was of primary importance. Today we realize that the sum of society's knowledge is the mental infrastructure for making human decisions. Just as society creates and maintains a physical infrastructure of buildings, roads, bridges, tunnels and tubes, so society has to create and maintain a mental infrastructure of all kinds of information."

After lunch Dr. Kertz told me to put on my new temperature-leveling suit for a tour of the amphibian taxi assembly plant. We took a sky taxi to the UPTE (Underground Public Transport Express), where we boarded a hover train that traveled underground propelled on a cushion of air by combination jet and magnetic power. I noticed Dr. Kertz paid for our fares by pushing some buttons at the turnstile and inserting a card. He had inserted the same card in the sky-taxi meter.

"Is that a magnetic fare card or a credit card?" I asked.

"It's more like what you used to call a debit card. We call it a money card. These cards are issued by banking firms, which operate something like what you call a mutual fund. As mutual funds provided customers with checks to withdraw money as needed, investment banks provide money cards. A money card can hold up to a million globas, though the routine limit is a thousand. It can make payments as small as a quint, or one twentieth of a globa. When it begins to run low I phone my bank which electronically transfers the globas I request from my account to my card."

"What's a globa?"

"Oh, that's the specie substitute that replaced the old national currencies in the 22nd Century. Non-interest-bearing paper certificates issued by central banks disappeared as people chose to use interest-paying digital money issued by private firms. The globa's value is determined by the Standard of Living Index set by the Alliance of Regional Banking Associations. The SLI changes hourly according to a very complicated formula that involves prices of some 300 basic commodities in 40 different regions modified by a measure of worldwide debt and money-card balances. That's the theory. In practice the globa is a globa and that's that."

Addendum: The World in 2301 A.D.

"Who issues globas?"

"No one. The globa is not really a currency. It's a measurement of economic value, a symbol that says I have credit with a reliable institution."

"But how did you open an account without money? How did you save enough money to open an account?"

"I merely transferred globas electronically from one bank to another. Sooner or later every child has an account opened by parents, who usually arrange to have a limit on the child's card: so many globas and no more each week. As the child grows the limit is increased until he or she is mature enough to take over the account. People so unfortunate as not to have an account opened by parents start with their first salary transfer."

The hover train took us to Fargo in 25 minutes. Dr. Kertz explained that the UPTE runs twice as fast through the tubes to Europe, Africa and Asia, and that jumbo jets and supersonic planes became obsolete in the late 22nd Century. "The lower atmosphere," he grinned, "is left to sky taxis. Above 6,000 thousand feet is for space transport."

The assembly plant was highly automated and the cleanest factory I had ever seen. Most of the taxi parts, from seat cushions and door handles to propulsion packs and plastic bodies were manufactured elsewhere and delivered to the assembly area through something like pneumatic tubes. An operator explained that the attaching of one part automatically triggers delivery of the next. The plant was one big assembling machine with parts going in at the loading dock and finished taxis coming out at ground level.

"It looks like a single operation," Dr. Kertz explained, "but in reality it is a network of cooperating businesses. The secret is teamwork. Once a long-term network is up and running and everybody becomes tuned into the knowledge network, the participants know each other as well or better than players on a champion basketball team know each other. What you see here is just the tip of the iceberg. The network extends to all the suppliers and customers as well as the sales, promotion, and distribution people."

About 3:00 in the afternoon all the machines came to a stop. "Wow," I said, "they have a short workday."

"The machines have a short workday, two hours in the morning and two after lunch. Most of the people work from 9:00 to 5:00 or longer. Time before and after the machine run is for studying, discussing the latest on the knowledge network and inputting new information. One of my principal jobs as an advisor was to show individuals how to improve information input. Note that many of the operators wear earphones with mouthpieces when the machines are in operation. It enables them to tune into the information network, particularly for direct communication with other individuals. When the machines aren't operating, most workers rely on the digital screen."

"What kind of encryption protects all this information?"

"None at all. Encryption is used almost exclusively for signatures to authorize digitalized contracts. Very few people worry about keeping information secret anymore. The only exception is business or engineering plans in their early stages. There is considerable advantage in getting a new idea into the marketplace first. But once you've started selling, it's impossible to keep others from learning about and imitating what you are doing. In fact, the newer and more innovative the product or service, the more advantageous for it to be widely imitated. Imitation increases demand and enlarges the market. Business organizers in one field frequently tune in to knowledge networks in other fields. It stimulates their imaginations and helps them to develop new ideas for their own businesses."

"Aren't there patents, laws to protect intellectual property?"

"There have been no laws to prevent the use of other people's ideas since high tech's revolt against the concept of intellectual property toward the end of the 21st Century."

"High tech revolted?"

"It started with the early pioneers resisting government regulation of the Internet, and spread to digital developers who resented the power of early monopolizers like Microsoft and Intel. Like all revolts, this one wouldn't have succeeded if the time had not been right. Patent and copyright laws became too difficult to enforce just when centralized governments were trying to cut back on legislation and enforcement."

"There must be some way to protect financial information, such as profit margins and how well the network is doing."

"You must realize that the network, as such, has no profit margin. It is made up of hundreds of partnerships, each with its own profit margin. In any case it would be impossible to run a useful knowledge network without including financial data. And it would still be impossible to keep such information secret even if there were no knowledge networks. An individual working on a contract in one operations network today may work in another tomorrow. In fact, it is not uncommon for individuals to be involved in several networks at once. Most supplier firms are."

"You seem very unconcerned about abuse of insider information."

"I've studied enough business history to understand what you are talking about. The benefits of openness, or transparency as business analysts like to call it, began to take hold at the turn of the 21st Century. I have a theory that it grew out of the survival training that business managers took in the late 1980s and 1990s to develop teamwork, which stressed that teamwork requires complete trust and that complete trust requires complete openness. Of course, the difficulty of keeping secrets in an age of advanced copying and transmission technology made it easier to switch from the secrecy paradigm to the transparency paradigm."

We stopped to watch a knowledge network tune-in on a digital screen. Since I didn't know enough about the operation to distinguish the relevant from the irrelevant, I found it hard to follow, especially since I was distracted by frames inserted intermittently in which someone appeared to answer a question that had been asked earlier. At one point the group watching the screen burst into applause. "I knew that would impress the drivers," one of them said, "and I think we could make it even more appealing." This resulted in an immediate conference between five of the viewers and an eventual series of questions being entered into the knowledge network.

"I don't know how that will work out," observed Dr. Kertz, "but I won't be surprised if there is a change in the taxis' acceleration system by the end of the week."

We left the plant shortly after 5:00 for the half-hour trip back to New York.

ELIAS MILLER, FOOD-PRODUCTION SPECIALIST

The next day's instructor was a much younger man. He was all business and seemed very dependent on an electronic pad which simultaneously recorded our conversation, provided data on a small digital screen and had a fluorescent surface on which he wrote notes. He began immediately: "My name is Elias Miller and I'm a food-production specialist. I understand you have some questions about the size of the world's population and whether there are problems of poverty and famine."

"I imagine there must be many more people on earth than there were at the end of the 20th Century."

"On earth and on the moon. The 2300 census put the total human population at 24.6 billion, including the million inhabitants of the moon and the 150,000 colonists on Mars."

"That seems low. In the 20th Century experts predicted 10 billion population by 2050. At that rate it should be over 90 billion now."

"By the end of the 21st Century, history had confirmed the theory that population growth slowed in direct proportion to the decline in poverty. Last year's increase was estimated as 0.6 percent, and that came principally from people living longer."

"You mean society has eliminated poverty?"

"I would not say it's eliminated. We still have pockets of poverty, both in some metro-centers and in a few primitive areas like Chad's Ennedi highlands and western China's Tarim Pendi. But prosperity spread into what were formerly called backward countries as the availability of technology, the spread of education and the collapse of central governments made entrepreneurship a possibility for everybody."

"If governments collapsed, how did education spread?"

"Through the media and technology. Technology not only made access to information easier and less expensive but it eliminated most of the manual labor that deprived so many human beings of the time and energy to educate themselves. The learning factories of the 18th, 19th and 20th centuries were abandoned during the 21st Century. Already in the late 20th Century, young people were dropping out of school, dissatisfied with a regimen of learning they considered archaic and impractical. An increasing number of parents began to teach their children at home or hire private tutors. The effort to introduce more practical courses into elementary, middle and higher education made things worse. To reduce costs and complaints, governments cut school subsidies in favor of school vouchers. This was supposed to make the schools self-supporting and competitive. In practice, it killed the formal school system, because parents campaigned to use the vouchers to pay individual instructors and in some cases themselves. Today private teaching is widespread."

"Who grants degrees? How do you know if a person you hire has the education needed for the job?"

"The degree system died with the formal education system. As partnering increased, people began to realize that the whole accreditation system was a hoax. When you go into partnership with an individual, you soon realize that her contribution to the partnership has very little to do with the time spent studying, whether alone or with an instructor. On the contrary, you usually look for someone who learns fast, not who learns slow."

"I didn't mean to get you off on education. You're a food-production specialist. Even though population growth has slowed, it has grown. There are more than four times as many people as there were in the world I knew. How are they fed and housed?"

"You've seen the housing. We've built higher and deeper. Most of the metro-areas are now contiguous. The entire North American continent, with the exception of the park preserves, a few older sections of Mexico and the Canadian tundra, is covered with residential towers. Most families, even the more wealthy, have to settle for a four-room apartment. Very few have more than two children, which is one reason population growth has slowed."

"Haven't people rebelled against living in such crowded conditions? Doesn't anyone want to flee to the country?"

"You can apply for a permit to spend a week in a park preserve. But there's a waiting list and it's fairly expensive. Most people entertain themselves by using the digital screen to call up scenes from other planets or from earth's wildernesses as they used to be. Virtual travel is always available and enables you to travel not only into space but as easily into the past."

"What about food? The meals I've eaten have been delicious, very like what good restaurants served in the 20th Century."

"Science has perfected nutrition capsules and other forms of condensed nutriment. But they are used only by deep-sea and deep-space explorers plus people on special diets. Most people enjoy eating too much to settle for pills. However, the food you've eaten is far more synthetic than you realized. Even the fresh fruits and vegetables have been genetically enhanced, partly so that they stay fresh longer, but mostly to increase production. The productivity of the average food plant has tripled since 2100."

"But where is all this food grown, if all the farmland and even the great plains are covered with residential towers?"

"Most fresh vegetables are grown on roofs, or underground with artificial sunlight. But the great bulk of food comes from sea farms. Seaculture is a major business and ranges from plankton harvesting and seaweed gardens to fish farms and whale herding. The cream you put in your coffee was processed whale milk."

"And all this is done without a government to designate who farms what part of the ocean and how much can be harvested?"

"The different seaculture associations regulate both how much can be harvested and the technologies used. The big question at the moment is the outcome of the negotiations between the seaculture associations and the seabed mining associations. Today's most productive mines are on the seabed. There's talk of forming a new association to be called the Alliance of Associations for Subsurface Businesses."

"For a society without government there's a lot of regulation."

"You're right. But the regulations are all made by the people being regulated. As one of my instructors used to say, 'Democracy doesn't mean less government; it means self-government.'"

"There's no fear of running out of food, of the growth in food supply falling behind the growth in population?"

"Not yet. At the moment the major food-production problem is guaranteeing a surplus to export to the moon, and to Mars. By 2350, agricultural development on the moon will have been increased enough to feed the lunar population and send fresh produce back to earth. The moon's low gravity makes it much cheaper to export to the earth than to import from the earth. Of course, the lunar population will still depend on earth for seaculture meat and fish. There are no oceans on the moon."

"It's hard for me to imagine that whale herding, sea-bed mines and, for that matter, exports to the moon, can be run without governments or huge corporations. Projects of that size must require huge investment and complex organization."

"They do. Most of those projects are run by long-term networks."

"And the disagreements between networks—or associations—never result in violence?"

For the first time, he smiled. "Not anymore. The last inter-network violence was the Salmon War in 2132. Three Alaskan river-fishing networks hired private coast guard vessels to scare off the North Pacific fishing boats whose fishscoops were intercepting the salmon. Several shots were fired and one fishing vessel was sunk before pressure from a number of associations with interests in the region forced the fresh-water fishing associations, the salt-water fishing associations and the North Pacific Association of offshore security firms to negotiate a permanent compromise."

"Whale herding and overfishing makes me wonder whether the environmental movement that was so strong in the 1980s and 1990s survived.

"There are still a large number of people concerned about how society uses the planet's resources. They break down into three groups. The first and largest group are business people who realize that cooperation is essential to maintain a balanced business environment. The second group, frequently called futurists, argue that it is important to supplement the balanced business environment with long-range planning to guarantee natural resources in greater abundance for our children. The third group wants to preserve as much as possible of what they say is the earth's natural state, that is, environments uncontrolled by humans. They are the main support for the park preserves— and, incidentally, the principal producers of wildlife documentaries and virtual nature adventures for the digital screen."

"Is recycling and keeping your city clean a big thing?"

"I wouldn't call it a big thing. It's more or less automatic. Waste disposal receptacles are built into all the buildings, and the waste is sorted automatically for reuse. As to cleanliness, when you live as closely as we do, peer pressure keeps people from being messy and thoughtless."

"In 1999, I and many other thoughtful people were worried about the growing gap between rich and poor. The wealthy were getting richer and richer while the lower classes became poorer and poorer."

"You lived during one of the economic malfunctions that always accompany severe socioeconomic change. There was a similar expanding gap separating rich and poor in western Europe as it started to shift from an agrarian to an industrial society in the early 19th Century. By 2050 America's transition from the late industrial society to the digital era was just about over and salaries began to even out as large corporations disintegrated and more businesses became partnerships. Salaries of senior partners today may be higher than those of junior partners but nowhere as large as the difference between top executives and wage-earners in the old corporations."

After lunch, Mr. Miller took me upstairs to see the roof farm, nine acres of vegetable gardens divided by walking paths lined with flowers and occasional benches. There were refreshment kiosks at the east and west corners with little tables under plastic roofs. To my surprise the men and women walking and sitting outnumbered those working in the gardens.

"Who brought all the soil up here?" I asked.

"The builders. Soil is basic roofing material. It's about thirty inches deep and is replaced every five years, except on roofs that have orchards where it's six feet deep and replaced only when new trees are planted. Manufacturing prime soil is a full-time business. The basic sand and clay are used over and over, but it is necessary to add chemical fertilizers and purified organic residue from sewerage and garbage treatment plants. The climate determines pretty much what is grown. Here it's largely produce that can mature in the May to September growing season. Because climate is considerably colder at this altitude, most of the new towers and many of the old are installing plexi-firmglass domes, which will turn these roof farms into hothouses and make possible a year-round growing season." He pointed to the north where I could see domes sparkling in the sunlight on some of the towers that stretched to the horizon.

"Where is the produce sold?"

"You can buy it right here, if you wish. The east kiosk sells freshly picked tomatoes, cucumbers, beans and other vegetables in season. But most of what is grown on this farm is packed and delivered to the supermarkets that are usually on 25th and 75th stories in the residential towers. There are farms, of course, that grow grains for flour mills and food processors."

"You mentioned farming on the moon. It's not on rooftops there, is it?"

"There are no 100-story towers on the moon. A few of the domed experimental gardens are on the roofs of three-story residential complexes. But most of the homes and farms are in the moon's volcanic caverns that have been sealed and filled with continually purified air. They are climate controlled and illuminated by artificial sunlight that waxes and wanes to enable plants to grow and inhabitants to have night and day as on earth."

"Was the soil for those gardens transported from earth?"

"That would be far too expensive. The soil is from the moon, but treated with chemicals and organic waste."

I hated to leave the roof, but I promised myself I would visit this place often on my own. Besides the sun was setting.

JANET JUDSON, ANTHROPOLOGIST

The next day's instructor was a tall, gray-haired woman, who told me she had just celebrated her 100th birthday and her 60th anniversary as a member of the North American Anthropological Academy.

I couldn't help but be impressed. "You seem to be in marvelous health. I honestly think you look younger than I, and I'm only 61, if we don't count the 300 years I was frozen."

"Medical science has improved considerably in the last three centuries. The average life span of people who are not killed in accidents is now 114 years, and we have a few individuals who have reached 200."

"You exclude accidental deaths in average lifespan?"

"The medical profession began keeping separate figures just about the time I started working. Although medical science has made tremendous strides in keeping bodies healthy under normal conditions, doctors have not been very successful in accident prevention. So the profession decided excluding accidental injuries and deaths would provide a more accurate measure of progress in health care."

"Do you have more accidents now than we had in the 1990s?"

"Fewer, if you calculate them per person per year. But there are more people and they live longer. So the total number of accidents per person is considerably more. I should add that the percentage of deaths after serious injury has gone way down due to the improvements in trauma treatment and organ replacement."

"Who runs the hospitals and emergency centers?"

"The larger ones are all long-term networks. Many operating rooms and expensive pieces of equipment are owned jointly by several medical partnerships. Others are owned by the technicians who operate them. Like most businesses, caring for the sick and injured is a very cooperative effort."

"Who pays the bills?"

"The patients. Most people have insurance for financial emergencies."

"How do you control costs with a third-payer system? In 1999, everybody worried that skyrocketing medical costs would wreck the system."

"They did wreck the systems of the United States, Canada and most European countries early in the 21st Century. We've learned from the history of health care that insurance payments should never be made to the provider. Healthcare associations blacklist any doctor who asks a patient whether he or she has insurance. In fact, most policies do not specify the nature of the need. They cover inability to pay one's bills rather than specific disasters. The same policy can cover losses from fire, sickness, even unemployment, any unplanned financial bind. But suppliers themselves frequently offer help. When my physician prescribes treatment, she tells me the cost. If I tell her I can't afford it, she can refer my case to her physicians' alliance, which has a fund to recompense members who take on charity cases. Or she may ask me to sign a post-recovery contract. If the operation is a success, I go back to work and she gets paid. If I die, the bill goes unpaid."

"And if you refuse to pay after the successful operation?"

"I'll have a very difficult time finding a doctor when I next need one."

"What about the trauma center? If no one inquires whether the victim has insurance and the victim is not able to sign an agreement, how often do victims pay?"

"The first thing done after taking care of the victim is to try to locate his or her next of kin. Relatives are usually willing to take care of payment arrangements. Health care for all is no longer a major problem in our society. Two factors keep costs under control. Patients have a wide choice of medical partnerships and are involved in treatment decisions. And each link in the medical network has to do cost-benefit analysis when engaging the next link. One result is that in charity cases the network initiator will frequently ask suppliers to absorb part of the cost."

"I can't believe there's such an abundance of charity. Even when Medicare and Medicaid were government-run, there were many people who needed care and didn't get it despite a large number of nonprofit organizations trying to fill the gap."

"There will always be charitable organizations attempting to fill a need when it becomes obvious. The difference today is not in the number of these organizations, but in the fact that people realize there is no overall benefactor who taxes them to take care of this need. In the 20th Century there was much talk about the psychological damage to welfare recipients. The damage to the general populace was far more significant. The more taking care of the needy became government's responsibility, the more it numbed the average citizen's feelings of obligation to and compassion for the unfortunate."

"You mentioned that preventive health care was a major achievement. What has changed there?"

"The biggest overall advance came when doctors began accepting patients on an annual retainer. Doctors who did not want to join a health maintenance organization started the practice, which became widespread after the HMOs ran into financial problems in the 2020s. Today most people pay their physician an annual fee to be their personal health mentor, a sort of combination trainer, dietician, physician as well as consultant and negotiator when a specialist is needed. Although individual physicians have their own patients, they all have partnership arrangements with six to 12 other doctors, each with a different specialty. These partnerships meet at least once a week to discuss patient problems."

"Ms. Turner told me that people go to their tailor as women used to go to their hairdresser. You tell me doctors work on retainers. Are there other services that result in such personal long-term relationships?"

"Many. The one that should interest you most is the psychological savant, who does for your mind what your personal physician does for your body. Psychological savants are something like the psychiatrists or psychologists so popular from 1950 to 2050 but have none of the stigma of being used only when something is wrong. Like psychiatrists the PS can help overcome personality disorders and the strains of life, but most people retain one to help them expand their mental and emotional horizons, to assist them in achieving a full life. They also operate in partnerships to share knowledge and experience. The PS has been called a guide to happiness, but a good PS, like a good personal physician, can demand a lot of hard work."

"Does a PS advise you on recreation?"

"A good PS will recommend mind-expanding recreation just as the physician will prescribe body-building play. My first PS is dead now, but one of her greatest contributions was teaching me how to study history for fun. Since the early 20th Century history became less and less relevant because the world was changing so fast. History used to be studied to help students understand and evaluate what was happenings in their lives. But as change accelerated, the period in which the past seemed relevant to the present became shorter and shorter. Indira told me to look at history as a game for which reality made the rules. The goal of the game is to study all the facts and try to figure out why what took place happened. Why did certain individuals or societies in particular circumstances do what they did? I've been taking trips into history ever since and still find it glorious fun."

"It sounds like a hobby that requires a lot of travel."

"Not really. My digital screen lets me visit locations, view ancient ruins, and interview whoever is willing to talk to me. Many historical events, especially from the last 400 years, have been recorded. If I want to listen to President Kennedy's inauguration address I can see it on the digital screen."

"Kennedy spoke English. Do you also understand de Gaulle's French or Hitler's German or Mao's Chinese?"

"There are times when I have difficulty even with Kennedy's English. I've studied old French and German, but I'm hopeless with Mao's Chinese."

"What do they speak in China now?"

"There are many areas, especially in the Chinese interior, where old Chinese dialects are still used by ordinary people. Today's English has become a world language, but it is still tinted—I like that word better than the pejorative 'tainted'—by local languages in different parts of the world."

"Even the French and Russians have surrendered to English?"

"It was more erosion than surrender. Language was one of the many cultural markers that became less and less significant as communication and travel accelerated the intermingling of peoples. English became the world language just because it happened to be the language of the countries that dominated business and communications when the economy went global. It's a pity in a way, because there were a number of other languages that were more logical in their structure, purer in their origins and easier to learn."

"So today everybody speaks, reads and writes English?"

"Almost everybody speaks and understands it. But there are many people who write it only poorly and relatively few who can read it well enough to enjoy the English classics like Shakespeare's plays or Hemingway's novels. Most of the world has learned English from the digital screen. Signage, that began with traffic signs, figures on washrooms and dashboard symbols on automobiles, has become the global visual language."

"So Le-Mail, developed by Englishmen in 1933, finally succeeded?"

"Le-Mail has about the same relation to Signage that Esperanto has to World English. Signage now has more than a 150 official symbols, and will probably add as many in the next decade. Children learn Signage before they learn to read English. There's even been several rather unsuccessful attempts to translate English literature into Signage."

"At the close of the 20th Century there was a great revival of interest in preserving national cultures and languages. In several parts of the world tribal or ethnic rivalry led to bloodshed."

"I spent a good deal of time studying that period. My conclusion is that the phenomenon was caused by fear in the emotional realm and economics on the rational realm. The changes in society and the growing intermingling of cultural groups put people on the defensive. When you are on the defensive, it is easier to blame strangers than relatives and friends. Economic hardship brings the simmering distrust of strangers to a boil."

"Did that die down while I was in cryogenic suspension?"

"Most, but not all. We've had flareups in Mongolia and central Africa less than 12 years ago. But in most areas, particularly in the metro-regions, people are too interconnected to segregate by groups. There are a large number of heritage associations. Because one of my great grandfathers came from Stockholm and a great, great grandmother was born in Chongqing, I belong to Swedish and Chinese cultural clubs. But they're not political. It's more like belonging to a chess or archeology club."

"I get the impression that people are nicer, that they get along much better than they did in the 20th Century."

"That's because you are looking for the same manifestations of human weaknesses and stupidity that you knew back then. When you've lived in our century for a while, I'm sure you'll find that human beings haven't changed much despite all the changes in the way we live."

"You're an anthropologist. Tell me what you see as the major cultural change since the 20th Century."

"I believe there has been a major shift in value standards. I'm not talking about better or worse values. People can still be selfish, vain, even mean and malevolent. But both their good deeds and their evil deeds are measured on a different value scale. In the 20th Century, possessions, the owning of things, was very important. Social class, living standards, popular esteem revolved around what people owned, the achievement of wealth. Today, the measure of value is experience. People of this age are more interested in experiencing than in owning. Social class and popular esteem are determined by an individual's achievement in mastering experience, in how many areas he or she is expert."

"That's quite a sea change. What occasioned it?"

"My theory is that interest in ownership died as people were forced to live closer and closer together and had less room to store things, conservation became more important than comsumption and economic emphasis shifted from producing material things to providing services, entertainment and information. At the same time money ceased to be a symbol of wealth as it became entirely a means of communication. In olden times money stood for gold or silver or other things you could own. Today money stands for nothing but a promise someone else has made. You can't own promises. You can only take advantage of them. So even when a promise involves the transfer of materials or tools, it is meaningful only because of what you can do with them. I read someplace that 20th Century entrepreneurs used to start companies with the purpose of eventually selling them to large corporations for big piles of money. No one would have such a weird goal today. People organize partnerships to earn a living, but everyone realizes that work has to involve a new challenge. It has to give you new experiences. It has to add to your areas of expertise."

Demetrios Sosuonam's manuscript ends here.

A fable? Yes.

As improbable as Jack's beanstalk?

I do not think so, for the magic beans are sprouting all around us.

BIBLIOGRAPHY

Aaron, Henry J.; Mann, Thomas E.; Taylor, Timothy (editors), *Values and Public Policy*. Brookings Institution, 1994.
Ackoff, Russell L., *The Democratic Corporation: A Radical Prescription For Recreating Corporate America and Rediscovering Success*. Oxford University Press, 1994.
Adams, Dennis. See Hamm, *The Collaborative Dimensions of Learning*.
Adams, Frank T. See Grossman, *Taking Care of Business*.
Adams, Henry.; *The Education of Henry Adams*. edited with an introduction and notes by Ernest Samuels, Houghton Mifflin, 1974. (Originally published in 1918)
Almond, Gabriel A.; Flanagan, Scott C.; Mundt, Robert J. (editors), *Crisis, Choice, and Change: Historical Studies of Political Development*. Little, Brown, 1973.
Appleby, R. Scott. See Marty, *The Glory And The Power*.
Aristotle, *The Basic Works of Aristotle*, edited by Richard McKeon, Random House, 1941.
Armey, Dick, *The Freedom Revolution: The New Republican House Majority Leader Tells Why Big Government Failed, Why Freedom Works, and How We Will Rebuild America*, Regnery Publishing, 1995.
Aronson, Jonathan D. See Cowhey, *Managing the World Economy*.
Arrow, Kenneth, *Social Choice and Individual Values,* Yale University Press, 1963 (second edition; first published in 1951).
Arthur, W. Brian, "Positive Feedbacks in the Economy," *Scientific American,* February 1990, pages 92-99.
Axelrod, Robert, *The Evolution of Cooperation,* Basic Books, 1984.
Bagdikian, Ben H., *The Media Monopoly* (4th Edition), Beacon Press, 1992.
Bahrami, Homa,"The Emerging Flexible Organization: Perspectives from Silicon Valley," *California Management Review,* Summer 1992.
Baldassarri, Mario; McCallum, John; Mundell, Robert, *Global Disequilibrium in the World Economy,* St. Martin's Press in Association with *Revista di Politica Economica,* SIPI, Rome, 1992.
Barnet, Richard J.; Cavanagh, John, *Global Dreams: Imperial Corporations and The New World Order*. Simon & Schuster, 1994.
Barney, Ralph D. See Merrill, *Ethics And The Press*.
Barsamian, David. See Chomsky, *Class Warfare*.
Bateson, Gregory, *Mind and Nature: A Necessary Unity*. E. P. Dutton, 1979.
Bayme, Steven. See Blankenhorn, *Rebuilding the Nest*.
Bell, Daniel, *The Coming of Post-industrial Society: A Venture In Social Forecasting,* Basic Books, 1976 edition (first published 1973).
Bell, Wendell, "World Order, Human Values, and The Future," *Futures Research Quarterly,* XII, 1, Spring 1996, pages 9-24.
Bennett, W. Lance, *The Governing Crisis: Media, Money and Marketing in American Elections*. St. Martin's Press. 1992.
Bennis, Warren, *Beyond Bureaucracy: Essays On The Development and Evolution of Human Organization,* Jossey-Bass Publications, 1993.

Benveniste, Guy, *The Twenty-first Century Organization: Analyzing Current Trends—Imagining the Future,* Jossey-Bass Publishers, 1994.

Bergquist, William, *The Postmodern Organization, Mastering The Art of Irreversible Change,* Jossey-Bass Publishers, 1993.

Berle, Adoph A.; Means, Gardiner C. *The Modern Corporation and Private Property.* Revised Edition. Harcourt, Brace & World, 1968 (First published 1932).

Berry, Adrian; *The Next 500 Years: Life in the Coming Millennium.* W. H. Freeman, 1996.

Bezold, Clement. See Toffler, *Anticipatory Democracy.*

Blankenhorn, David; Bayme, Steven; Elshtain, Jean Bethke (editors), *Rebuilding The Nest: A New Commitment to the American Family.* Family Service America, 1990.

Bliss Jr., Edward, *Now The News,* Columbia University Press, 1991.

Bloom, Allan, *The Closing of the American Mind: How Higher Education Has Failed Democracy and Impoverished the Souls of Today's Students.* Simon & Schuster, 1987.

Blumberg, Paul, *Industrial Democracy: The Sociology of Participation.* Schocken Books, 1973. Originally published in 1968.

Boaz, David; Crane, Edward H., *Market Liberalism: A Paradigm for the 21st Century.* Cato Institute, 1993.

Bogart, Leo, *Commercial Culture: The Media System and the Public Interest.* Oxford University Press, 1995.

Bohn, Thomas W. See Hiebert, *Mass Media II.*

Bok, Derek, *The Cost of Talent: How Executives and Professionals Are Paid and How It Affects America,* Free Press (Macmillan Inc.), 1993.

Bond, Richmond P., *Growth and Change in the Early English Press,* University of Kansas Libraries, 15th Annual Public Lecture on Books and Bibliography presented on 15th November 1968.

Boyd, Harper W., Jr. See Britt, *Marketing Management and Administrative Action.*

Bradley, Stephen P.; Hausman, Jerry A.; Nolan, Richard L. (editors), *Globalization, Technology, and Competition: The Fusion of Computers and Telecommunications in the 1990s,* Harvard Business School Press, 1993.

Branden, Nathaniel, *The Six Pillars of Self-Esteem,* Bantam Books, 1994.

Bridges, William, *Jobshift: How to Prosper in a Workplace Without Jobs.* Addison-Wesley, 1994.

Britt, Steuart Henderson; Boyd, Harper W. Jr., *Marketing Management and Administrative Action,* 3rd Edition. McGraw-Hill, 1973 (originally published 1963).

Brookes, Warren, *The Economy In Mind,* Universe Books, 1982.

Brzezinski, Zbigniew, *Between Two Ages: America's Role in the Technetronic Era.* Viking Press, 1970.

Buhagiar, Marion. See Edelston, *"I" Power.*

Burns, James MacGregor, *The Vineyard of Liberty: The American Experiment,* Knopf, 1982.

Burns, Lee, *Busy Bodies: Why Our Time-obsessed Society Keeps Us Running in Place,* W. W. Norton, 1993.

Carpenter, Edmund, *Oh, What A Blow That Phanton Gave Me!,* Holt, Rinehart & Winston, 1973.
Cavanagh, John. See Barnet, *Global Dreams.*
Cetron, Marvin; Gayle, Margaret *Educational Renaissance: Our Schools At The Turn of The Twenty-first Century,* St. Martin's Press, 1991.
Cherry, Colin, *On Human Communication: A Review, A Survey, and A Criticism,* M.I.T. Press, second edition 1966.
Chomsky, Noam, *World Orders Old And New,* Columbia University Press, 1994.
────── *Secrets, Lies and Democracy,* Odonian Press 1994.
────── (Interviewed by David Barsamian) *Class Warfare,* Common Courage Press, 1996.
Cleveland, Harlan, *The Knowledge Executive: Leadership in an Information Society.* Truman Talley Books, E.P. Dutton. 1985.
────── *Birth of a New World: An Open Moment For International Leadership,* Jossey-Bass Publishers, 1993.
────── "Ten Keys to World Peace," *The Futurist,* July-August 1994, pages 15-21.
────── "The Limits to Cultural Diversity," *The Futurist,* March-April 1995, pages 22-26.
Cogan, John F.; Muris, Timothy J.; Schick, Allen, *The Budget Puzzle: Understanding Federal Spending,* Stanford University Press, 1994.
Cohen, Joel E., *How Many People Can the Earth Support?* W. W. Norton Company, 1995.
Conant, James Bryan, "Education for a Classless Society: The Jeffersonian Tradition," Charter Day Address at the University of California, March 28, 1940.
────── "Education in the Western World," (Copyrighted originally in 1940) Downloaded from AOL on September 2, 1995.
Connelly, Matthew; Kennedy, Paul "Must It Be The Rest Against The West?" *The Atlantic Monthly,* December 1994.
Cook, Philip J. See Frank, *The Winner-Take-All Society.*
Cornish, Edward (editor) *The 1990s & Beyond,* World Future Society.1990.
────── "Is Transcendence Necessary?" *The Futurist,* July-August 1995, pages 49-50
────── (editor) *Exploring Your Future,* World Future Society, 1996.
Cowhey, Peter F.; Aronson, Jonathan D., *Managing The World Economy: The Consequences of Corporate Alliances,* Council on Foreign Relations Press, 1993.
Crane, Edward H. See Boaz, *Market Liberalism.*
Csikszentmihalyi, Mihaly, *The Evolving Self: A Psychology For The Third Millennium,* HarperCollins, 1993.
Czempiel, Ernst-Otto. See Rosenau, *Governance Without Government.*
Dahl, Robert A., *Democracy and Its Critics,* Yale University Press, 1989.
────── & Tufte, Edward R. *Size and Democracy.* Stanford University Press, 1973.
Darwin, Charles, *The Origin of Species, By Means of Natural Selection or the Preservation of Favored Races in the Struggle for Life,* The Modern Library,

1993 (first published in 1859, with the historical note and glossary added after the 1960 second edition).
Davidow, William H.; Malone, Michael S., *The Virtual Corporation: Structuring and Revitalizing the Corporation for the 21st Century,* Harper Business, 1992.
Dawkins, Richard, *The Selfish Gene,* new edition, Oxford University Press, 1989 (first published 1976)
Deal, Carl, *The Greenpeace Guide To Anti-environmental Organizations,* Odonian Press, 1993.
Dennett, Daniel C., *Consciousness Explained,* Little, Brown & Co., 1991.
Denney, Reuel. See Riesman, *The Lonely Crowd.*
Deutsch, Karl W., *The Nerves of Government: Models of Political Communication and Control.* The Free Press, 1966 (first published 1963).
de Tocqueville, Alexis, *Democracy in America,* Henry Reeve text, revised by Francis Bowen, corrected and edited with Introduction, Editorial Notes, and Bibliography by Phillips Bradley. Alfred A. Knopf, 1945. Two volumes.
Didsbury Jr., Howard F. (editor), *The Years Ahead: Perils, Problems, and Promises.* World Future Society, 1993
────── (editor) *Future Vision: Ideas, Insights and Strategies.* World Future Society, 1996.
DiIulio Jr., John J. (editor), *Deregulating the Public Service: Can Government Be Improved?* The Brookings Institution, 1994.
Donnelly, William, *The Confetti Generation: How The New Communications Technology Is Fragmenting America.* Henry Holt & Company, 1986.
Dordick, Herbert S.; Wang, Georgette, *The Information Society: A Retrospective View,* Sage Publications, Sept. 1993.
Downs, Anthony, *An Economic Theory of Democracy,* Harper & Row, 1957.
Doyle, Denis Philip. See Gerstner, *Reinventing Education.*
Drucker, Peter, *The Age of Discontinuity, Guidelines To Our Changing Society.* Harper & Row, 1968.
────── *Concept of The Corporation*: 1972 Edition with a new Preface and Epilogue by the author. The John Day Company. 1972.
────── *The New Realities: In Government and Politics; In Economics and Business; In Society and World View.* Harper & Row, 1989.
────── "The Emerging Theory of Manufacturing," *Harvard Business Review,* May/June 1990.
────── *Managing for the Future: The 1990s and Beyond,* Truman Talley Books/Dutton. 1992.
────── "The New Society of Organizations," *Harvard Business Review,* Sept-Oct. 1992.
────── *Post-capitalist Society,* Harper Business (Harper Collins Publishers). 1993
────── "The Age of Social Transformation," *The Atlantic Monthly,* Nov. 1994, pages 53-80.
────── *Managing In A Time of Great Change,* Truman Talley/Dutton, 1995.
────── *Landmarks of Tomorrow: A Report On The New "Post-Modern" World.* Transaction Publishers, 1996.

Duncan, Joseph W.; Gross, Andrew C., *Statistics for the 21st Century: Proposals for Improving Statistics for Better Decision Making.* Dun & Bradstreet, 1993.
Duncan, William L., *Communication and Social Order,* Bedminster Press, 1962.
Dyson, George B., *Darwin Among The Machines: The Evolution of Global Intelligence.* Helix Books, Addison-Wesley Publishing, 1997.
Easterbrook, Gregg, *A Moment On The Earth: The Coming Age of Environmental Optimism,* Viking, 1995
Edelston, Martin (with Buhagiar, Marion), *"I" Power: The Secrets of Great Business In Bad Times,* Barricade Books, 1992.
Eichengreen, Barry, *International Monetary Arrangements for the 21st Century.* The Brookings Institution, 1994.
Elashmawi, Farid; Harris, Philip R. *Multicultural Management: New Skills For Global Success,* Gulf Publishing, 1993.
Elgin, Duane, *Voluntary Simplicity: Toward a Way of Life That Is Outwardly Simple, Inwardly Rich,* William Morrow, 1981.
Elliott, Osborn, "My Failed Romance With Journalism," Speech given at Harvard Club, New York City, on April 13, 1995.
Elshtain, Jean Bethke. See Blankenhorn, *Rebuilding the Nest.*
Emery, Edwin, *The Press In America, An Enterpretative History of the Mass Media,* Prentice Hall, 1972 edition (also published in 1954 and 1962).
Epstein, Richard A., *Simple Rules For A Complex World,* Harvard University Press, 1995.
Estes, Ralph, *Tyranny of The Bottom Line.* Berrett-Koehler Publishers, 1996.
Etzioni, Amitai (editor) *Readings On Modern Organizations,* Prentice-Hall, 1969.
────── *The Spirit of Community: Rights, Responsibilities, and the Communitarian Agenda,* Crown Publishers, 1993.
Fairtlough, Gerard, *Creative Compartments: A Design For Future Organisation.* Admantine Press (England), Praeger (U.S.), 1994.
Fallows, James, *Looking At The Sun: The Rise of the New East Asian Economic & Political System,* Pantheon Books, 1994.
Flanagan, Scott C. See Almond, *Crisis, Choice and Change.*
Forrester, Jay W., "A New Corporate Design," *Industrial Management Review* (now *Sloan Management Review*), Vol 7, No. 1, Fall 1965. Reprinted as Chapter 6 in *Collected Papers of Jay W. Forrester,* Productivity Press, 1975. Also reprinted in *Internal Markets,* Appendix, pp. 253-275.
Frank, Robert H.; Cook, Philip J., *The Winner-Take-All Society,* Free Press/Martin Kessler Books, 1995.
Franklin, Benjamin, *The Autobiography of Benjamin Franklin, With Sayings of Poor Richard, Hoaxes, Bagatelles, Essays and Letters.* Selected and Arranged by Carl Van Doren. Pocket Books, 10th printing 1948.
Freud, Sigmund, *Civilization and its Discontents* (translated by Joan Riviere), The Hogarth Press, 1949.
Fuller, R. Buckminster, *Education Automation, Freeing The Scholar To Return To His Studies.* Southern Illinois University Press, 1962.
Gaebler, Ted A.; See Osborne, *Reinventing Government.*
Galbraith, John Kenneth, *American Capitalism, The Concept of Countervailing Power,* revised edition (original 1952), Houghton Mifflin, 1956.

───── *Economics and the Public Purpose,* New American Library, 1975. Originally published by Houghton Mifflin, 1973.
───── *The Affluent Society,* Houghton Mifflin, 1976.
───── *The Age of Uncertainty,* Houghton Mifflin, 1977.
Gardner, Howard, *Frames of Mind: The Theory of Multiple Intelligences.* Basic Books, 1983.
───── *Multiple Intelligences: The Theory In Practice,* Basic Books, 1993.
Garfield, Charles, *Second To None: How Our Smartest Companies Put People First.* Business One Irwin, 1992.
Garraty, John A.; Gay, Peter, *The Columbia History of The World,* Harper & Row. Dorset Press edition, 1981.
Gay, Peter. See Garraty, *The Columbia History of The World.*
Gayle, Margaret. See Cetron, *Educational Renaissance.*
George, Henry, *Progress and Poverty,* Everyman's Library/Dutton, 1976 reissue.
Geranmayeh, Ali. See Halal, *Internal Markets.*
Gerstner Jr., Louis V.; Semerad, Roger D.; Doyle, Denis Philip; Johnston, William B., *Reinventing Education: Entrepreneurship In America's Public Schools,* Dutton, 1994.
Gilder, George, *The Spirit of Enterprise,* Simon & Schuster, 1984.
Gilroy, Bernard Michael, *Networking In Multinational Enterprises: The Importance of Strategic Alliances,* University of South Carolina Press, 1993.
Glastonbury, Bryan; LaMendola, Walter *The Integrity of Intelligence: A Bill of Rights For The Information Age,* St. Martin's Press, 1992.
Glazer, Nathan. See Riesman, *The Lonely Crowd.*
Gleick, James, *Chaos: Making a New Science.* Viking, 1987.
Goleman, Daniel, *Emotional Intelligence,* Bantam Books, 1995.
Goodwin, Neva R., *Social Economics: An Alternative Theory,* Volume 1: Building Anew on Marshall's Principles. St. Martin's Press, 1991.
───── "Evolving Values for A Capitalist World," *Human Economy,* Summer/Fall 1996, page 1, 6-10.
Gottlieb, Gidon, "Nations Without States," *Foreign Affairs,* May/June 1994.
Greider, William, *Who Will Tell The People? The betrayal of American Democracy.* Simon & Schuster, 1992.
Gribbin, John, *In Search of Schroedinger's Cat: Quantum Physics and Reality,* Bantam Books, 1984. See page 212!
Gross, Andrew C., *See* Duncan, Joseph W., *Statistics for the 21st Century.*
Grossman, Richard L.; Adams, Frank T., *Taking Care of Business: Citizenship and the Charter of Incorporation.* Charter, Ink, 1993.
Hakim, Cliff, *We Are All Self-employed: The New Social Contract For Working in a Changed World.* Berrett-Koehler, 1994.
Halal, William E.; Geranmayeh, Ali; Pourdehnad, John, *Internal Markets: Bringing the Power of Free Enterprise Inside Your Organization,* Wiley, 1993.
Hale, Sandra J.; Williams, Mary M. (editors), *Managing Change, A Guide To Producing Innovation From Within, Minnesota's Award-winning STEP Approach.* Urban Institute Press, Washington, DC, 1989.
Hall, Edward T.; *Beyond Culture,* Anchor Press/Doubleday, 1976.

Hamm, Mary; Adams, Dennis, *The Collaborative Dimensions of Learning,* Ablex Publishing, 1992.
Hampden-Turner, Charles; Trompenaars, Fons, *The Seven Cultures of Capitalism,* Judy Piatkins, 1994.
Handy, Charles, *The Age of Paradox,* Harvard Business School Press, 1994.
Harrington, Michael, *Socialism,* Bantam Books, 1970.
Harris, Philip R. See Elashmawi, *Multicultural Management.*
Hausman, Jerry A. See Bradley, *Globalization, Technology, and Competition.*
Havel, Vaclav, "The End of the Modern Era," *The New York Times,* Op-Ed, Sunday, March 1, 1992, page E16.
Hawken, Paul, *The Next Economy,* Holt, Rinehart and Winston, 1983.
Heilbroner, Robert, *The Worldly Philosophers: The Lives, Times and Ideas of the Great Economic Thinkers.* [First edition 1953.] Updated Sixth Edition, A Touchstone Book, Simon & Schuster, 1992.
———— *21st Century Capitalism,* W. W. Norton & Company, 1993.
———— & Thurow, Lester. *Economics Explained,* revised and updated, Touchstone/Simon Schuster, 1994 (first published 1982).
Herrnstein, Richard J.; Murray, Charles, *The Bell Curve: Intelligence and Class Structure in American Life.* The Free Press, 1994.
Hiebert, Ray Eldon; Ungurait, Donald F.; Bohn, Thomas W., *Mass Media II, An Introduction To Modern Communication.* Longman, Second Edition, 1979.
Hirsch, E. D.; *Cultural Literacy: What Every American Needs To Know.* Houghton Mifflin, 1987.
Howard, Philip K., *The Death of Common Sense: How Law Is Suffocating America,* Random House, 1994.
Hughes, Robert, *Culture of Complaint: The Fraying of America,* Oxford University Press, New York, 1993.
Huntington, Samuel P., "The Coming Clash of Civilizations: Or, the West Against the Rest," *The New York Times,* Sunday, June 6, 1993, page 19.
Huxley, Aldous, *Brave New World,* Harper's Modern Classics edition. 1950. (Original copyrighted 1932.)
Hyde, Lewis, *The Gift: Imagination And The Erotic Life of Property.* Random House, 1979.
Illich, Ivan, "Why We Must Abolish Schooling," *New York Review of Books:* July 2, 1970, page 6.
———— *Deschooling Society,* Harper & Row, 1971.
———— *Shadow Work.* Marion Boyars, 1981.
Imai, Masaaki, *Kaizen: The Key To Japan's Competitive Success.* McGraw-Hill, 1986.
Innis, Harold Adam, *The Bias of Communications,* University of Toronto Press, 1951.
Itzkoff, Seymour W., *The Decline of Intelligence In America: A Strategy For National Renewal,* Praeger, 1994.
Janis, Irving, *Groupthink, Psychological Studies of Policy Decisions And Fiascoes,* Houghton Mifflin, 1983.
Jaques, Elliott, *Requisite Organization: The CEO's Guide to Creative Structure and Leadership,* Cason Hall and Co., 1989.

Jay, John. See Madison, *The Federalist Papers.*
Jefferson, Thomas, *Thomas Jefferson, Writings.* [edited by Merrill D. Peterson] The Library of America (Literary Classics of the United States Inc.), 1984.
Johansen, Robert; Swigart, Rob, *Upsizing The Individual In The Downsized Organization: Managing In The Wake of Reengineering, Globalization, and Overwhelming Technological Change.* Addison-Wesley, 1994.
Johnson, Wendell, *People In Quandries,* Harper & Row, New York, 1946.
Johnston, William B. See Gerstner, *Reinventing Education.*
Kanter, Rosabeth Moss, *When Giants Learn To Dance: Mastering The Challenge of Strategy, Management and Careers in the 1990s,* Simon & Schuster, 1989.
Kegan. Robert, *In Over Our Heads: The Mental Demands of Modern Life,* Harvard University Press, 1994.
Kennedy, Paul. See Connelly, "Must It Be the Rest Against the West?"
King, Anthony, *Running Scared,* Free Press, 1997.
Korten, David C., *When Corporations Rule The World,* Berrett-Koehler, 1995.
——— "When Corporations Rule the World," *Human Economy,* Winter 1996, pages 1, 4-7.
Kotkin, Joel, *Tribes: How Race, Religion, and Identity Determine Success in the New Global Economy.* Random House 1993.
Kuhn, Thomas, *The Structure of Scientific Revolutions,* 2nd Edition, Enlarged. Foundations of the Unity of Science, 1962.
Kurtzman, Joel, *The Death of Money: How The Electronic Economy Has Destabilized The World's Markets and Created Financial Chaos.* Simon & Shuster. 1993.
LaMendola, Walter. See Glastonbury, *The Integrity of Intelligence.*
Latouche, Serge, *In The Wake of The Affluent Society: An Exploration of Postdevelopment,* Zed Books, 1993.
Lazare, Daniel, *The Frozen Republic: How The Constitution Is Paralyzing Democracy.* Harcourt Brace & Co., 1996.
Lazonick, William, *Business Organization and the Myth of the Market Economy,* Cambridge University Press, 1992.
Lee, Dwight R. See McKenzie, *Quicksilver Capital.*
Lind, Michael, *The Next American Nation: The New Nationalism and the Fourth American Revolution.* The Free Press, 1995
Linstone, Harold A.; Mitroff; Ian I., *The Challenge of The 21st Century: Managing Technology & Ourselves in a Shrinking World,* SUNY Press, 1994.
Lippmann, Walter; *Essays in the Public Philosophy*, New American Library, 1955
Lipnack, Jessica; Stamps, Jeffrey, *The TeamNet Factor: Bringing the Power of Boundary Crossing Into the Heart of Your Business,* Oliver Wight, 1993.
———; *The Age of The Network: Organizing Principles for the 21st Century.* Omneo/Oliver Wight, 1994.
List, Friedrich, *The National System of Political Economy [1885],* Introductory Essay by J. S. Nicholson included as appendix. Augustus M. Kelley, 1966.
Locke, John, *An Essay Concerning Human Understanding.* Abridged and edited by A. S. Pringle-Pattison. Clarendon Press/Oxford University Press, 1924.

Bibliography 443

Lodge, George C., *Perestroika For America: Restructuring U.S. Business-Government Relations For Competitiveness in the World Economy*, Harvard Business School Press, 1990.
Luttwak, Edward N., *The Endangered American Dream:How To Stop The United States From Becoming a Third-World Country and How to Win The Geo-Economic Struggle for Industrial Supremacy*. Simon and Schuster, 1993.
Madison, James; Jay, John, *The Federalist Papers: A Collection of Essays Written in Support of the Constitution of the United States*. Selected and Edited by Roy P. Fairfield. Second Edition. Johns Hopkins University Press, 1981.
Madsen, Richard P., "After Liberalism: What If Confucianism Becomes the Hegemonic Ethic of the 21st-Century World Community?" *Futures Research Quarterly*, XII, 1, Spring 1996.
Malone, Michael S. See Davidow, *The Virtual Corporation*.
Mann, Charles C.; Plummer, Mark L., *Noah's Choice: The Future of Endangered Species*, Knopf, 1995.
Mann, Jim, *Media Management Monographs* 23: "The Care and Feeding of Creative Personnel," July 1980; 47: "The Future of the Magazine Business," July 1982; 70: "Elements of Style in Magazine Publishing," February 1985; 128: "Eleven Laws of Effective Personnel Management," April 1990.
——— *Publishing Trends & Trendsetters*, 151: "Magazines Publishing in the 21st Century," August 1992; 162: "A New Management Technique: Mining the Minds of Your People," September 1993.
Mann, Thomas E. See Aaron, *Values and Public Policy*.
Margulis, Lynn; Sagan, Dorion, *Micro-Cosmos: Four Billion Years of Microbial Evolution*. Summit Books, 1986.
Marty, Martin E.; Appleby, R. Scott, *The Glory And The Power: The Fundamentalist Challenge To The Modern World*, Beacon Press, 1992.
Maslow, Abraham H., *Eupsychian Management: A Journal*. Richard D. Irwin Inc. & The Dorsey Press, 1965.
Mason, Richard O. See Mitroff, *Framebreak*.
McCullum, John. See Baldassarri, *Global Disequilibrium in the World Economy*.
McGregor, Douglas, *The Human Side of Enterprise*, McGraw-Hill Book Company, 1960.
McKenzie, Richard B.; Lee, Dwight R., *Quicksilver Capital, How the Rapid Movement of Wealth Has Changed the World*. The Free Press (Macmillan). 1991.
McLuhan, Herbert Marshall, *Understanding Media: The Extensions of Man*, McGraw-Hill, 1964 (Third Edition).
Means, Gardiner C. See Berle, *The Modern Corporation and Private Property*.
Merrill, John C.; Barney, Ralph D., *Ethics And The Press, Readings In Mass Media Morality*, Hastings House Publishers, 1975.
Meyrowitz, Joshua, *No Sense of Place, The Impact of Electronic Media on Social Behavior*, Oxford University Press, 1985.
Miller, Eric, *The Context of Trends: The Reshaping of America*. EPM Communications Inc. 1994.
Mills, D. Quinn, *Rebirth of The Corporation*, John Wiley & Sons, 1991.
Minsky, Marvin, *The Society of Mind*, Simon & Schuster, 1985.

Mitroff; Ian I. ; Mason, Richard O.; Pearson, Christine M., *Framebreak: The Radical Design of American Business.* Jossey-Bass Publishers, 1994.

───. See Linstone, *The Challenge of The 21st Century.*

Moore-Ede, Martin, *The Twenty-Four-Hour Society: Understanding Human Limits in a World that Never Stops,* Addison-Wesley, 1993.

Mott, Frank Luther, *American Journalism, A History 1690-1960,* Macmillan, 3rd Edition, 1962 (previous editions 1941 and 1950).

Moynihan, Daniel Patrick, *Pandaemonium; Ethnicity In International Politics,* Oxford University Press, 1993.

Mueller, Dennis C., (Editor) *The Political Economy of Growth,* Yale University Press, 1983.

Mueller, Robert Kirk, *Corporate Networking: Building Channels For Information and Influence.* The Free Press, 1986.

Mumford, Lewis, *Technics And Civilization,* Harcourt Brace & World, 1963 reprinted as a Harbinger Book with new introduction. (First edition 1934).

Mundell, Robert. See Baldassarri, *Global Disequilibrium in the World Economy.*

Mundt, Robert J. See Almond, *Crisis, Choice and Change.*

Muris, Timothy J. See Schick, *The Budget Puzzle.*

Murray, Charles, See Herrnstein, *The Bell Curve.*

Naisbitt, John, *Megatrends: Ten New Directions Transforming Our Lives.* Warner Books, 1982.

─── *Global Paradox: The Bigger The World Economy, The More Powerful Its Smallest Players,* William Morrow & Company, 1994.

Nelson, Brent A., *America Balkanized: Immigration's Challenge To Government.* The American Immigration Control Foundation, 1994.

Newman, Joseph (editor), *Wiring The World,* Books by *U.S. News & World Report,* 1971.

Nichols Jr., James H.; Wright, Colin (editors), *From Political Economy To Economics and Back?* (With an epilogue by Allan Bloom), ICS Press (Institute for Contemporary Studies), 1990.

Nirenberg, John, *The Living Organization: Transforming Teams Into Workplace Communities,* Pfeiffer/Business One Irwin, 1993.

Nisbet, Robert, *The History of The Idea of Progress,* Basic Books, 1980.

Nolan, Richard L. See Bradley, *Globalization, Technology, and Competition.*

O'Rourke, P. J., *All The Trouble In The World: The Lighter Side of Overpopulation, Famine, Ecological Disaster, Ethnic Hatred, Plague, And Poverty.* Atlantic Monthly Press, 1994.

Olson, Mancur, *The Logic of Collective Action: Public Goods and the Theory of Groups,* Revised edition. Harvard University Press, 1965.

─── *The Rise And Decline of Nations, Economic Growth, Stagflation, and Social Rigidities,* Yale University Press, 1982.

Ong, Walter J. (S.J.) *The Presence of The Word. Some Prolegomena For Cultural and Religious History.* Yale Univerisity Press, 1967.

─── *Rhetoric, Romance and Technology: Studies in the Interaction of Expression and Culture,* Cornell University Press, 1971.

Osborne, David; Gaebler, Ted A. *Reinventing Government: How The Entrepreneurial Spirit Is Transforming The Public Sector,* Plume, 1992.

Ouchi, William G., *Theory Z,* Addison-Wesley Publishing, 1981.
Paine, Thomas, *The Age of Reason: Being an Investigation of True and Fabulous Theology,* Gramercy Books, 1993. (Originally written 1794-1796.)
Pearson, Christine M. See Mitroff, *Framebreak.*
Peirce, Neal, "Citistates: The True Economic Communities of Our Time," *Points West Review,* October 1993, Center for the New West.
Perelman, Lewis J., *School's Out: Hyperlearning, The New Technology, and The End of Education,* William Morrow, 1992.
Peters, Tom, *Liberation Management: Necessary Disorganization For The Nanosecond Nineties,* Alfred A. Knopf, 1992.
Phillips, Kevin, *Arrogant Capital: Washington, Wall Street, and The Frustration of American Politics.* Little Brown, 1994.
Pinchot III, Gifford, *Intrapreneuring: Why You Don't Have to Leave the Corporation to Become an Entrepreneur.* Harper & Row, 1985.
Pinchot, Gifford; Pinchot, Elizabeth, *The End of Bureaucracy and The Rise of The Intelligent Organization,* Berrett-Koehler, 1993
Pinera, Jose, *Empowering Workers: The Privatization of Social Security in Chile,* Cato Institute, 1996.
Plummer, Mark L. See Mann, *Noah's Choice.*
Postman, Neil, *Amusing Ourselves To Death; Public Discourse in the Age of Show Business.* Elisabeth Sifton Books, Viking, 1985.
Pourdehnad, John. See Halal, *Internal Markets.*
Rauch, Jonathan, *Demosclerosis: the silent killer of American government,* Times Books, Random House, 1994.
Reich, Robert B., *The Work of Nations: Preparing Ourselves for 21st Century Capitalism.* Alfred A. Knopf, 1992.
Renfro, William L., *Issues Management In Strategic Planning,* Quorum Books, 1993.
Riesman, David (with Nathan Glazer and Reuel Denney), *The Lonely Crowd: A Study of the Changing American Character,* (Abridged edition with a new forward; first copyright: 1950) . Yale University Press, 1961.
Rifkin, Jeremy, *The End of Work: The Decline of the Global Labor Force and the Dawn of the Post-Market Era.* G. P. Putnam's Sons, 1995.
Rivers, Caryl, *Slick Spins and Fractured Facts: How Cultural Myths Distort the News.* Columbia University Press, 1996.
Rosell, Steven A., & others, *Governing In An Information Society,* Institute for Research on Public Policy, 1992.
Rosenau, James N.; Czempiel, Ernst-Otto (editors) *Governance Without Government: Order and Change in World Politics,* Cambridge University Press, 1992.
Roszak, Theodore, *The Cult of Information: A Neo-Luddite Treatise on High-Tech, Artificial Intelligence, and the True Art of Thinking.* (Second edition) University of California Press, 1994.
Rothfeder, Jeffrey, *Privacy For Sale: How Computerization Has Made Everyone's Private Life an Open Secret.* Simon & Schuster, 1992.
Sagan, Dorion. See Margulis, *Micro-Cosmos.*
Sahtouris, Elisabeth, *Gaia: The Human Journey from Chaos to Cosmos.* Pocket Books, 1989.

Sakaiya, Taichi, *What Is Japan? Contradictions and Transformations,* Kodansha America, 1993. Published in Japan by Kodansha, 1991. Translated by Steven Karpa.

Salamon, Lester M., "The Rise of the Nonprofit Sector," *Foreign Affairs*, July-Aug. 1994, pages 109-122.

Samuel, Peter, "Highway Aggravation: The Case for Privatizing the Highways," *Cato Institute Policy Analysis*, No. 231, June 27, 1995.

Samuelson, Robert J., *The Good Life And Its Discontents: The American Dream in the Age of Entitlements, 1945-1995,* Times Books, Random House, 1995.

Schick, Allen. See Cogan, *The Budget Puzzle*.

Schrage, Michael, *Shared Minds: The New Technologies of Collaboration,* Random House, 1990.

Schultze, Charles, *The Public Use of Private Interest*, Brookings Institution, 1977.

Schumacher, E. F., *Small Is Beautiful: Economics as if People Mattered*, Harper & Row Perennial Library, 1975, originally published by Blond & Briggs Ltd., 1973.

Schwartau, Winn, *Information Warfare: Chaos on the Electronic Superhighway,* Thunder's Mouth Press, 1994.

Sculley, John, *Odyssey: Pepsi to Apple...A journey of adventure, ideas and the future.* Harper & Row, 1987.

Semerad, Roger D. See Gerstner, *Reinventing Education*.

Senge, Peter M., *The Fifth Discipline: The Art & Practice of The Learning Organization*, Doubleday/Currency, 1990.

Shamos, Morris H., *The Myth of Scientific Literacy*. Rutgers University Press, 1995.

Simon, Julian L., (editor) *The State of Humanity,* Blackwell Publications, 1996.

——— "Why Do We Hear Prophecies of Doom From Every Side?" *The Futurist*, January-February 1995, pages 19-23.

——— "Bet on a Better Future," *The Futurist,* March-April 1997, pages 17-18.

Stamps, Jeffrey. See Lipnack, *The TeamNet Factor & The Age of The Network*.

Smith, Adam, *An Inquiry into the Nature and Causes of the Wealth of Nations.* Edited, with an introduction, notes, marginal summary and an enlarged index, by Edwin Cannan, M.A., LL.D. With an Introduction by Max Lerner. The Modern Library, 1937.

Steele, G. R., *The Economics of Friedrich Hayek.* St. Martin's Press, 1993.

Steiner, Jurg, *Amicable Agreement Versus Majority Rule*, University of North Carolina Press, 1974.

Stoll, Clifford, *Silicon Snake Oil: Second Thoughts on the Information Highway,* Doublday, 1995.

Swigart, Rob. See Johansen, *Upsizing The Individual In The Downsized Organization*.

Tarcher, Martin, *Escape from Avarice*, Chandler & Sharp, 1996.

Taylor, Timothy. See Aaron, *Values and Public Policy*.

Thurer, Shari L., *The Myths of Motherhood: How Culture Reinvents the Good Mother,* Houghton Mifflin, 1994.

Thurow, Lester C., *Head to Head: The Coming Economic Battle Among Japan, Europe, and America.* William Morrow, 1992.
────── See Heilbroner, *Economics Explained.*
────── *The Future of Capitalism: How Today's Economic Forces Shape Tomorrow's World.* William Morrow, 1996.
Toffler, Alvin, *Future Shock*, Bantam Books, 1970. (original with Random House).
────── (with Bezold, Clement) *Anticipatory Democracy, People in the Politics of the Future,* Random House, 1978.
────── *The Third Wave*, William Morrow, 1980.
────── *Previews & Premises: An Interview with the Author of Future Shock and The Third Wave,* William Morrow, 1983.
────── *Powershift, Knowledge, Wealth and Violence at the Edge of the 21st Century,* Bantam Books. 1990.
Toffler, Alvin; Toffler, Heidi, *War and Anti-war: Survival at the Dawn of the 21st Century,* Little, Brown, 1993.
────── *Creating A New Civilization, The Politics of the Third Wave.* Turner Publishing, 1995. Published initially by The Progress & Freedom Foundation in 1994.
────── "Getting Set for the Coming Millennium," *The Futurist,* March-April 1995, pages 10-15.
Trompenaars, Fons. See Hampden-Turner, *The Seven Cultures of Capitalism.*
Tufte, Edward R. See Dahl, *Size and Democracy.*
Ungurait, Donald F. See Hiebert, *Mass Media II.*
United Nations Working Group, *The United Nations In Its Second Half-century: A Report of the Independent Working Group on the Future of the United Nations,* Ford Foundation, 1995.
Veblen, Thorstein, *The Theory of the Leisure Class,* Dover Publications, 1994 (originally published 1899).
Waitley, Denis, *Empires of The Mind,* Excerpt published in *Success,* March 1995.
Waldrop, M. Mitchell, *Complexity: The Emerging Science at the Edge of Order and Chaos,* Simon & Schuster, 1992.
Wang, Georgette. See Dordick, *The Information Society.*
Weber, Max, *The Theory of Social And Economic Organization,* Translated by A. M. Henderson and Talcott Parsons. Edited with an introduction by Talcott Parsons. The Free Press, copyrighted 1947 by Oxford University Press.
Wells, H. G., *The New World Order: Whether it is Attainable, How it can be Attained, and What Sort of World a World at Peace Will Have to Be.* Alfred A. Knopf, 1940.
Wheatley, Margaret J., *Leadership and The New Science: Learning about Organization from an Orderly Universe,* Berrett-Koehler, 1992.
Williams, Mary M. See Hale, *Managing Change.*
Wilson, Edward O., "Back from Chaos," *The Atlantic Monthly,* March 1998, pages 41-62.
Wilson, James Q., *Political Organizations,* Basic Books, 1973.
Wright, Colin. See Nicholas, *From Political Economy To Economics and Back?*
Wurman, Richard Saul, *Information Anxiety.* Doubleday, 1989.

Yankelovich, Daniel, *New Rules: Searching for Self-fulfillment in a World Turned Upside Down.* Random House, 1981.
────── "How Changes in the Economy are Reshaping American Values," *Human Economy,* Spring 1966, pages 1,4-6,13.
Yates, Frances A., *The Art of Memory,* University of Chicago Press, 1966.
Zey, Michael G., *Seizing The Future: How the Coming Revolution in Science, Technology, and Industry Will Expand the Frontiers of Human Potential and Reshape the Planet.* Simon & Schuster, 1994.
──────"The Macroindustrial Era: A New Age of Abundance And Prosperity," *The Futurist,* March-April 1997, pages 9-14.

NOTES

Foreward
1. Wells, *The New World Order,* page 46.
2. Yankelovich, *New Rules.* See introduction, particularly pages 4-6.
3. Havel, "The End of the Modern Era."
4. Naisbitt, *Global Paradox,* pages 273-275.
5. Greider, *Who Will Tell the People?,* pages 406-409.
6. Kanter, *When Giants Learn to Dance,* See chapter on "The New Workforce Meets the Changing Workplace," expecially pages 269-272.
7. Drucker, *Management in a Time of Great Change,* pages 243-250.
8. Peters, *Liberation Management,* particularly chapter 15, pages 226-236.
9. Branden, *The Six Pillars of Self-Esteem.* See pages 232-249.
10. Gardner, *Multiple Intelligences,* especially pages 243-250.
11. Kegan, *In Over Our Heads.* For a better understanding of the relevant ideas read pages 94-97, 102-105 and 314-319.

Chapter 1: We're Drowning in Information
1. T.S. Eliot, "Choruses from 'The Rock', I," *Selected Poems, T.S. Eliot, A Selection by the Author,* The Penguin Poets D4, 1948, page 105. 'The Rock' was a pageant first produced in 1934.
2. Ken Purdy, "The Noise," *The Permanent Playboy,* edited by Ray Russell, Crown Publishers, 1959, pages 469-479.
3. McLuhan, *Understanding Media, page 16.*
4. Perelman, *School's Out, page 59.*
5. Bliss, *Now The News,* page 134.
6. United States General Accounting Office Report to Congressional Requesters, June 1992: *Decennial Census: 1990 Results Show Need for Fudamental Reform,* Executive Summary, page 3.
7. Beth Enslow, "Calling All Reformers," *Forecast,* May-June 1994, page 55. This is a review of *Statistics for the 21st Century,* by Joseph W. Duncan and Andrew C. Gross, worth reading to understand how obsolete government data-gathering systems have become.
8. The Associated Press, May 5, 1994.
9. "How to Get Extra Mileage from Advertising," *Broadcasting,* June 16, 1969, page 18.
10. Nicholas Daniloff "For Political Journalists Only," Project Vote Smart's *Tomorrow's News,* Fall 1993, page 1.
11. Quoted by Daniloff, ibid.
12. John Miglautsch, "There's Such a Thing as Too Much Data," *DM News,* August 15, 1994, page 30.
13. Franklin, "Last Speech in the Constitutional Convention," Franklin, *The Autobiography,* page 378.

Chapter 2: Information Overdose: the Side-Effects

1. Brzezinski, *Between Two Ages,* page xiii.
2. See Bryan Burrough & John Helyar, *Barbarians At The Gate: The Fall of RJR Nabisco.* Harper & Row, 1990, page 510.
3. "Lessons from Louise," *The Economist,* November 15, 1997, page 30.
4. Brzezinski, *Between Two Ages,* page 23.
5. Meyrowitz, *No Sense of Place,* page 141.
6. Berna Miller, "Population Update for April," *American Demographics,* April 1997, page 18.
7. Etzioni, *The Spirit of Community,* pages 34-35.
8. Riesman, *The Lonely Crowd,* pages 49 and 47.
9. Thurer, *The Myths of Motherhood,* pages 262-263.
10. Bill Berkeley, "Sounds of Violence," *The New Republic,* August 22, 1994, page 18.
11. Ibid, page 19.
12. Wurman, *Information Anxiety,* page 226.
13. Cover story, "Kids Growing Up Scared," *Newsweek,* January 10, 1994, pages 42ff.
14. Gary Stix,"Closing the Book," *Scientific American,* March 1998, page 33. The *Science* article appeared in July 1992 issue and was written by H. Keith Florig. See Gary Taubes, "Fields of Fear," *The Atlantic Monthly,* November 1994, page 95.
15. Stix, ibid. See also Sharon Begley, "The Force Is With You," *Newsweek,* November 11, 1996. page 67.
16. Taubes, ibid., page 108.
17. Etzioni, *The Spirit of Community,* page 13.
18. Meyrowitz, *No Sense of Place,* page 141.
19. Lazare, *The Frozen Republic,* pages 266-267.
20. "America, Land of the Shaken," *Business Week,* March 11, 1996, page 64.
21. Meyrowitz, *No Sense of Place,* pages 302-303.
22. Meg Greenfield, "The Cynicism Complaint," *Newsweek,* September 12, 1994, page 72.
23. Quoted by Nisbet, *History of the Idea of Progress,* page 342.
24. John Cunniff, Associated Press wire, Nov. 17, 1994.
25. *Family Concerns,* The Community Action Network, 1995, page 3.
26. Cited by Robert D. Kaplan, "The Coming Anarchy," *Atlantic Monthly,* February 1994, pages 44-45 and 73-74.
27. "Hospital Told to Halt Surgeries," *New York Times,* April 8, 1995, page 7.
28. Raymond Murphy, *Rationality and Nature,* Westview Press, 1994.
29. See Julian L. Simon, "Why Do We Hear Prophecies of Doom From Every Side?" *The Futurist,* January-February 1995, pages 19-23; also "The State of Humanity: Steadily Improving," *Cato Policy Report XVII,* #5, Sept./Oct. 1995. Simon died in 1998. He had a brilliant and amusing mind and will be missed.
30. Gregg Easterbrook, *A Moment on the Earth: The Coming Age of Environmental Optimism,* Viking 1995.
31. From McNamara's *In Retrospect,* excerpt published in *Newsweek,* April 17, 1995, page 46.

Notes: Chapter 2

32. "American Survey: Statistical guessing games," *The Economist,* December 7, 1997, page 25.
33. Quoted by George F. Will, "Inflation Inflated," *Newsweek,* September 30, 1996, page 92.
34. Toffler, *Future Shock,* pages 359-361.
35. Drucker, *The New Realities,* chapter 9, pages 115ff..
36. Toffler, *Future Shock,* page 486.
37. Ibid, pages 343-367, quote page 348.
38. Riesman, *The Lonely Crowd,* pages 168-169.
39. Ted Koppel, commencement address at Duke University's graduation exercises in 1987.
40. Postman, *Amusing Ourselves to Death,* pages 76-77.
41. From Rothfeder, *Privacy For Sale,* pages 161-163.
42. "The Future of Warfare," *The Economist,* March 8, 1997, page 22.
43. For an insightful analysis of how technology can foster physical and mental fatigue, see Moore-Ede, *The Twenty-four-hour Society,* pages 3-5.
44. Cleveland, *The Knowledge Executive,* page 179.
45. Janis, *Groupthink,* pages 31-32.
46. Mark Miller, "Secrets of the Cult," *Newsweek,* April 14, 1997, page 32.
47. Toffler, *Future Shock,* page 314.
48. From Allan Bloom's very perceptive analysis of de Tocqueville's opinion in *The Closing of the American Mind,* pages 246-247.
49. Moynihan, *Pandaemonium.*
50. Joe Klein, "The Threat of Tribalism," *Newsweek,* March 14, 1994, page 28.
51. Myron Magnet, *The Dream and the Nightmare: The Sixties' Legacy to the Underclass,* William Morrow & Co., 1993.
52. Drucker, *Post-Capitalist Society,* pages 152-156.
53. Charles Murray and Richard Herrnstein, *The Bell Curve: Intelligence and Class Structure in American Life.* Free Press, 1994.
54. Ong, *The Presence of the Word,* page 297.
55. Duncan, *Communication and Social Order,* page 76.
56. Meyrowitz, *No Sense of Place,* page 132.
57. Ibid, page 309.
58. Reisman et al., *The Lonely Crowd,* pages 33-34.
59. Charles J. Sykes, *A Nation of Victims: The Decay of the American Character.* St. Martin's Press, 1992.
60. See Marty & Appleby, *The Glory and the Power,* especially page 178.
61. Joe Klein, "The Threat of Tribalism," *Newsweek,* March 14, 1994, page 28.
62. Elijah Anderson, *A Place on the Corner: Identity and Rank Among Black Streetcorner Men,* University of Chicago Press, 1981, and *Streetwise: Race, Class and Change in an Urban Community,* University of Chicago Press, 1990.
63. Elijah Anderson, "Code of the Streets," *Atlantic Monthly,* May 1994, pages 80-94.
64. Ibid., page 94.
65. John Leland, "Gangsta Rap and the Culture of Violence," *Newsweek,* November 29, 1993, page 62.
66. Marty and Appleby, *The Glory and the Power,* page 34.
67. Ibid., page 35.

68. Fallows, *Looking at the Sun*, page 16. The motive behind India's recent atomic-bomb test is an example.
69. Ibid., page 87. Fallows' quote is from *Tokugawa kinreiko*, ed. Shunsuke Kikuchi (Tokyo, Yoshikawakobunkan, 1932), pages 609-610.
70. See Steven Butler,"Japan's Shifting Gears," *U.S. News & World Report*, Nov. 21, 1994, pages 65-66.
71. Transcription #JPRS-JST-91-035-L, Foreign Broadcast Information Service, Washington, D.C., 1991.
72. Barnet & Cavanagh, *Global Dreams*, page 306.
73. Yasuhiro Yoshizaki, "The Value Shift of Japanese Youth," *Comparative Civilizations Review*, Winter 1997. For a preces of the article, see "The New Generation in Japan," *The Futurist*, March 1998, page 17.
74. Tom Abate, "The Midnight Hour," *Scientific American*, January 1996, pages 36-37.
75. Barnet & Cavanagh, *Global Dreams*, pages 306-307.
76. Robert Neff, "Unlocking Japan—At Last," *Business Week*, April 14, 1997, page 56.
77. Brian Bremner, "Toyota's Crusade," *Business Week*, April 7, 1997, pages 104-114.
78. Robert B. Reich, "Who Is Them?" *Harvard Business Review*, March-April 1991, page 81.
79. David Van Biema, "Of Spirit and Blood," *Time*, Oct. 31, 1994, pages 73-74.
80. Hughes, *Culture of Complaint*, page 100.

Chapter 3: Information, Knowledge and Wisdom

1. Minsky, *The Society of Mind*, page 277.
2. See McLuhan, *Understanding Media*.
3. Cleveland, *The Knowledge Executive*, page 22.
4. Idem.
5. Roszak, *The Cult of Information*, page 132.
6. Cleveland, *The Knowledge Executive*, page 22.
7. While Darwinists, like Darwin, believe that species developed without teleology (i.e., conscious planning), they also believe that everything that happens has one or more causes and that natural selection favors species "improvement." Hence they frequently slip into teleological language. In *The Origin of Species*, Darwin (unlike many of his followers) goes out of his way to point this out (e.g., on page 109: "It is difficult to avoid personifying the word Nature; but I mean by Nature, only the aggregate action and product of many natural laws, and by laws the sequence of events as ascertained by us.").
8. "How Many Scientists Does It Take to Screw in a Quark?" *Newsweek*, May 5, 1994, page 54.
9. "For Quark Hunters, a Minute Surprise," *Newsweek*, February 19, 1996, page 64.
10. Csikszentmihalyi, *The Evolving Self*, page 62.
11. See Gribbin, *In Search of Schroedinger's Cat*.
12. See footnote on page 97 of Gregory Bateson's *Mind and Nature*.
13. Gribbin, ibid., page 212.

14. For a good description and history of chaos theory read James Gleick, *Chaos: Making a New Science.* It is my opinion that chaos theory is the study of how linear systems behave when they are affected by externalities whose impact is not fully understood. The theory is frequently (e.g., in the study of fractals) more an explanation of how our minds work than of what reality is.
15. In a leaflet promoting *Butterflies and Hurricanes.*
16. Aristotle, *The Basic Works of Aristotle,* "Rhetoric," page 1337 (text 1359b, 10). I have taken the liberty of retranslating the last sentence.
17. Quoted by Bliss, *Now The News,* pages 106-107.
18. "TV anchorman suspended for Texas rally comments," *Wall Street Journal,* August 31, 1994, page A14.
19. Merrill & Barney, *Ethics and the Press,* Preface, page ix.
20. See Cover Letter by Jim Mann, "Being Human—The Balance Between Bible and Libel," *Media Management Monograph* 59, July 1983.
21. Hall, *Beyond Culture,* page 193. 229. Quoted by Schrage, *Shared Minds,* page 75.
22. Quoted by Hall, ibid., page 12.
23. John Locke, *An Essay Concerning Human Understanding,* Book III, Chapter 9. Readers interested in Locke's analysis of difficulties and errors in the use of language should read the whole of Book III.
24. Colin Cherry, *On Human Communication: A Review, A Survey and A Criticism* (second edition), M.I.T. Press, 1966, page 71.
25. Dawkins, *The Selfish Gene,* Chapter 11: "Memes, the new replicators," pages 189-201. Quotation from page 192.

Chapter 4: Communication Creates Society

1. Thurow, *The Future of Capitalism,* page 3.
2. Quoted by Deutsch, *The Nerves of Government,* page 77.
3. Garraty & Gay, *The Columbia History of the World, page 77.*
4. Michael Rothschild, "Cro-Magnon's Secret Weapon," *Forbes ASAP,* September 13, 1993, pages 19-20.
5. Quoted by Elgin, *Voluntary Simplicity,* page 92, footnote.
6. Webster's *New Universal Unabridged Dictionary,* 1979 edition.
7. Elgin, *Voluntary Simplicity,* pages 92ff.
8. Roszak, *The Cult of Information,* page xx.
9. Yates, *The Art of Memory.* For a helpful summary of the gist of the book, read pages xi-xiii of the preface.
10. Galbraith, *American Capitalism,* page 87.
11. Nicholas Negroponte, "The Next Billion Users," *Wired,* June 1996, page 220.
12. Garraty & Gay, *The Columbia History of the World,* page 122.
13. Harrington, *Socialism,* page 44.
14. Ibid., page 280.
15. Excerpt from Yeltsin's book, *The Struggle for Russia,* published in *Newsweek,* May 2, 1994. page 35.
16. Quoted by Meyrowitz, *No Sense of Place,* page 17.

Chapter 5: Information, Authority and Democracy
1. Madison, *Federalist Paper,* Number 51, page 160.
2. For more on de Beccaria see Garraty & Gay, *The Columbia History of the World,* page 703. Diderot's publication was sold in installments over 22 years, from 1750 to 1772, and had many contributors. It was full of the new thinking about government by reason, about liberty, equality and human rights. It became a best-seller across Europe despite its high subscription price. Idem, pages 698-699.
3. Paine, *The Age of Reason,* "Introduction," page v.
4. Jay, *Federalist Paper* Number 2, page 6. A group of extremists, typified by John Taylor and John Randolph, considered themselves "Pure Republicans" and wanted to keep the federal government as weak as possible. See Burns, *The Vineyard of Liberty,* page 258.
5. Garraty & Gay, *Columbia History of the World,* page 797.
6. Jay, *Federalist Paper* Number 2, page 6.
7. Jefferson, *Writings of Thomas Jefferson,* page 1305. Letter to John Adams, October 28, 1813.
8. Burns, *Vineyard of Liberty,* page 259.
9. Idem, page 511.
10. Peter Drucker, "The Age of Social Transformation."
11. Mott, *American Journalism,* page 180.
12. Burns, *Vineyard of Liberty,* pages 325-326.
13. de Tocqueville, *Democracy In America,* Volume I, page 52.
14. Burns, *Vineyard of Liberty,* page 355.
15. Benjamin Schwarz, "The Diversity Myth: America's Leading Export," *Atlantic Monthly,* May 1995, pages 57-67.
16. Steven Stark, "Too Representative Government," *Atlantic Monthly,* May 1995, pages 57-67.
17. Madison, *Federalist Paper* Number 51, page 160.
18. Rauch, *Demosclerosis,* page 48.
19. Riesman, *The Lonely Crowd,* pp. 213-217.
20. Schultze, *The Public Use of Private Interest,* page 23.
21. Galbraith pointed out this "bureaucratic symbiosis" in 1973. See *Economics and the Public Purpose,* pages 155-158.
22. Toffler, *Previews & Premises,* page 118.
23. Greider, *Who Will Tell the People?,* page 123. See entire chapters 4 and 5.
24. American Values, the parent organization of the Community Action Network, 600 Madison Avenue, New York, NY 10022; and Institute for American Values, 1841 Broadway, Ste. 211, New York, NY 10023.
25. Latouche, *In the Wake of the Affluent Society,* see pages 57-77.
26. Burns, *Vineyard of Liberty,* page 335.
27. Ibid., page 348.
28. Etzioni, *The Spirit of Community,* page 24.

Chapter 6: Adam Smith's Arthritic Invisible Hand
1. Cleveland, *Birth of A New World,* page 137.

2. Adam Smith, *The Wealth of Nations,* page 651.
3. Idem.
4. Ibid., page 423.
5. Neil Postman, *Amusing Ourselves To Death,* page 127.
6. Galbraith, *American Capitalism,* page 17.
7. Idem.
8. Ibid., page 47.
9. Etzioni, *The Spirit of Community,* page 221.
10. Galbraith, *American Capitalism,* pages 32-33.
11. Idem, page 112.
12. Weber, *The Theory of Social and Economic Organization,* page 320.
13. Wilson, *Political Organizations,* page 24.
14. Olson, *The Rise and Decline of Nations,* page 8.
15. The "On Money Illusion" working paper was published in 1994 by Princeton psychologist Eldar Shafir, Stanford psychologist Amos Tversky and MIT economist Peter Diamond. See "Rational Economic Man: The human factor," *The Economist,* December 24, 1994, page 90.
16. Waldrop, *Complexity,* page 44.
17. Ibid., page 47.
18. Parsons' introduction to Weber, *The Theory of Social and Economic Organization,* page 11.
19. Waldrop, *Complexity,* pages 141-142.
20. Marc Levinson, "Dismal Science Grabs a Couch, *Newsweek,* April 10, 1995, pages 41-42.
21. James Mirrlees of Cambridge University in England and William Vickrey of Colombia University in the United States. See "Secrets and the prize," *The Economist,* October 12, 1996, page 86.
22. "Asset-Backed Securities: $30 Billion and Counting," *Business Week,* International Edition, December 16, 1996.
23. Reuter Newsservice, July 11, 1995.
24. For a worthwhile analysis of what happened, see Sandy Tefmen, "Triumph and Tragedy," *Business Marketing,* March 1991, pages 14ff.
25. Toffler, *Future Shock.* Drucker, *The Age of Discontinuity,* page 40: "The new emerging industries, therefore, embody a new economic reality: knowledge has become the central economic resource."
26. Toffler, *Future Shock,* page 486.
27. Mumford, *Technics and Civilization,* pages 218-219.

Chapter 7: The Media: Formed, Fed And Foiled By Information
1. Carpenter, *Oh, What a Blow That Phantom Gave Me!,* page 191.
2. Franklin, *The Autobiography,* page 110.
3. Ibid., page 75.
4. Bliss, *Now The News,* page 11.
5. Page 66.
6. CBS dropped both Brown and Kaltenborn. Bliss, *Now The News,* page 241.
7. Broadcast on CBS but produced by an independent.

8. CBS-TV News Special, February 27, 1968.
9. Bliss, *Now The News,* page 383.
10. John B. Connally, "Advice to the Press,"*New York Times,* May 2, 1977, page 33. (Adapted from an address to the Houston Press Club.)
11. Associated Press, May 2, 1994.
12. "A slow retreat from freedom," *The Economist,* January 4, 1997, page 25.
13. James Boyland, "Punishing the Press," *Columbia Journalism Review,* March/April 1997, page 25.
14. Pages 59-60.
15. Quoted by Mott, *American Journalism,* page 6.
16. John Milton, *English Minor Poems, Paradise Lost, Samson Agonistes, Areopagitica,* Great Books of the Western World, 32, Encyclopaedia Britannica Inc., 1952, page 409.
17. Quoted by Cass R. Sunstein, "Selling Children," *New Republic,* August 21&28, 1995, page 38.
18. Jefferson, Second Inaugural Address, *Thomas Jefferson, Writings,* page 521.
19. "Roger Stone, Republican Public Affairs Consultant," *Newsweek,* May 2, 1994, page 30.
20. Page 64.
21. Quoted by Clive Irving, "All the News That's Fit to Film," *New Statesman,* May 18, 1973, reprinted in Merrill & Barney, *Ethics and The Press,* page 195.
22. Quoted by Amy Bernstein, "The Hush-Rush Law," *U.S. News & World Report,* June 27, 1994, page 12.
23. Tom Rosenstiel, "The Myth of CNN," *The New Republic,* August 22, 1994. pages 27-31.
24. McLuhan, *Understanding Media,* page 309.
25. Meyrowitz, *No Sense of Place,* page 102.
26. Nicholas Negroponte, "Prime Time Is My Time," *Wired,* August 1, 1994, page 134.
27. Merrill & Barney, *Ethics and The Press,* page 109.
28. *Cowles/Simba Media Daily,* America On Line, April 26, 1995.
29. Jonathan Alter, "Growing Up with Nixon," *Newsweek,* May 2, 1994, page 31.
30. Bagdikian, *Media Monopoly,* page 56.
31. Ibid., pages 126-129.
32. 1982 figures from Audit Bureau of Circulations Newspaper FAS-FAX Report for six months prior to March 31, 1982. 1995 figures from *1996 Editor & Publisher International Yearbook.*
33. 1981 figures from Audit Bureau of Circulations Magazine FAS-FAX Report for six months ending December 31, 1981. 1995 figures from Audit Bureau of Circulations for six months ending December 31, 1995.
34. Nielsen average audience estimates for October to December 1981 period vs. September 1995 to May 1996 period.
35. "America's television networks: The dash for the off switch," *The Economist,* June 7, 1997, page 63.
36. Mott, *American Journalism,* page 720.
37. McLuhan, *Understanding Media,* pages 209-210.
38. Debra Goldman, "Mad As Hell," *ADWEEK,* Sept. 6, 1993. page 22.

39. Merrill & Barney, *Ethics and The Press,* page viii.
40. Goldman, "Mad As Hell, op cit., page 22.
41. Quoted in *Capell's Circulation Report,* December 1995, page 4.
42. Toffler & Toffler, *War and Anti-War,* page 169.
43. Referred to by Donald McDonald in his chapter "Is Objectivity Possible?" from Merrill & Barney, *Ethics and The Press,* page 82.
44. Paul H. Weaver, "Crisis Mentality Disturbs the News," *Insight,* March 14, 1994, pages 22-24.
45. Ibid., page 22.
46. Elliott, "My Failed Romance with Journalism."
47. "John Ehrlichman, Nixon Aide," *Newsweek,* January 3, 1994, page 45.
48. See Jim Mann, "What Magazines Can Learn from the Sharon and Westmoreland Suits," Cover Letter, *Media Management Monograph* 77, March 1985.
49. Thurow, *The Future of Capitalism,* page 334.
50. Hughes, *The Culture of Complaint,* page 99.
51. Associated Press, October 21, 1994.
52. *The Reporter's Source Book,* Project Vote Smart, Third Edition, August 1993, page 9.

Chapter 8: Managing Information in the Workplace

1. Cleveland, *The Knowledge Executive,* page 38.
2. Halal et al, *Internal Markets,* page 134.
3. Bennis, *Beyond Bureaucracy,* page 23.
4. John Case, "A Company of Business People," *Inc.* April 1993, page 81.
5. Ibid., page 82.
6. "Labor Unions," *Concise Columbia Electronic Encyclopedia;* also McKenzie & Lee, *Quicksilver Capital,* pages 191-192.
7. Benveniste, *The Twenty-First Century Organization,* page 254.
8. Schrage, *Shared Minds,* page 56.
9. McGregor, *The Human Side of Enterprise.* Chapter 8, "The Scanlon Plan," is particularly perceptive.
10. Drucker was already thinking in terms of management by objectives when he published *The Concept of the Corporation* in 1946.
11. Lipnack & Stamps, *The Teamnet Factor,* page 101.
12. Drucker, *The New Realities,* page 217.
13. Mumford, *Technics and Civilization,* page 416.
14. Toffler, *Previews and Premises,* page 118.
15. Schrage, *Shared Mineds,* pages 83 and 40.
16. "Now you know," *The Economist,* May 27, 1995, page 58.
17. Quoted by Osborne & Gaebler, *Reinventing Government,* page 250.
18. Drucker, "The Age of Social Transformation," pages 71-72.

Chapter 9: Networks of Partnerships

1. Maslow, *Eupsychian Management,* page 66.
2. "CEO Thought Summit," *Sloan Management Review,* Spring 1995, pages 13-21.

3. Idem.
4. Edelston, *"I" Power.* See also *Publishing Trends & Trendsetters,* September 1993.
5. Fallows, *Looking at the Sun,* page 411.
6. Page 52.
7. Hardaker & Ward, "Getting Things Done, How to Make a Team Work," *Harvard Business Review,* November/December 1987, pages 112-120.
8. Harrington, *Socialism,* page 145.
9. "Quality by Choice," *American Demographics Marketing Tools,* June 1993, page 18, excerpted from *The American Forecaster Almanac,* 1993, Business Edition on Disk, c Kin Long.
10. Drucker, *Concept of the Corporation,* pages 190-191.
11. Thurow, *Head To Head,* page 298.
12. Quoted by Peter Senge in Halal et al, *Internal Markets,* page 97, from W. Edwards Deming, *Profound Knowledge,* MIT Center for Advanced Knowledge Study, 1993.
13. Halel et al, *Internal Markets,* page 100.
14. Mann, *Media Management Monograph* 23, page 9.
15. "A New Corporate Design," originally published in *Industrial Management Review* (now *Sloan Management Review*), Vol. 7. No. 1, Fall 1965, pages 5-17; reprinted in Halal et al, *Internal Markets,* pages 253-275.
16. Schrage, *Shared Minds,* page 36.
17. Senge, *The Fifth Discipline,* page 212ff.
18. Olson, *The Logic of Collective Action,* page 54.
19. Tom Peters, "The Magic Number," *Office Systems95,* October 1995, page 39.
20. Peters, *Liberation Management,* pages 260-261.
21. Fairtlough, *Creative Compartments,* pages 52-53.
22. Olson, *The Logic of Collective Action,* page 54, see footnote 4.
23. Ibid., page 54, see footnote 1.
24. Olson, page 54.
25. Schrage, *Shared Minds,* Chapter 11, pages 151-163.
26. Halel et al, "Reconsidering 'A New Corporate Design,'" *Internal Markets,* page 57.
27. What I call decision horizons he calls time spans. See Jaques, *Requisite Organization,* page 20.
28. Pinchot, *Intrapreneuring,* page 309.
29. Ibid., page 310.
30. Quoted by Joel Kotkin, *Tribes,* page 146.
31. Lipnack & Stamps, *The TeamNet Factor,* pages 50-51.
32. Mark Warner, "The Nested Statement," *Executive Excellence,* November 1995, page 8.
33. Osborne & Gaebler, *Reinventing Government,* page 271.
34. Ibid., pages 34ff.
35. Idem.
36. William Taylor, "The Business of Innovation: An Interview with Paul Cook," *Harvard Business Review,* March-April 1990, page 98.
37. Fuller, *Education Automation,* pages 62 & 64.

38. Pinchot, *Intrapreneuring,* page 240.
39. Thurow, *Head to Head,* pages 96-97.
40. Art Kleiner, "The Battle for the Soul of Corporate America," *Wired,* August 1995, page 169.
41. Drucker, *Managing for the Future,* pages 235-236.
42. Idem, page 240.
43. Quoted by Christopher Farrell, "The Boom In IPOs," *Business Week,* Dec. 18, 1995, page 66.

Chapter 10: Organic Networks: Complex Adaptive Systems

1. See Halel et al, *Internal Markets,* page xvi.
2. Ibid., page 164.
3. Ibid., Appendix, page 266.
4. Ibid., pages 6-7.
5. The subject of McGregor, *The Human Side of Enterprise.*
6. As when Ford's chief executive Alex Trotman killed the side-mirror improvement on which his Taurus design team had spent months of effort and test costing $500,000. From Mary Walton, *A Drama of the American Workplace,* W. W. Norton, 1997, as reported by Daniel McGinn, "Lifting Some Hoods," *Business Week,* May 26, 1997, page 56.
7. Pinchot & Pinchot, *The End of Bureaucracy and the Rise of the Intelligent Organization,* page 134.
8. Halal et al, *Internal Markets,* page 57.
9. See Ouchi, *Theory Z,* page 63.
10. Halal et al, *Internal Markets,* page 34.
11. Ibid., page 31.
12. Ouchi, *Theory Z,* page 211.
13. Idem.
14. Mitroff et al, *The Radical Redesign of American Business,* page 47.
15. Halal et al, *Internal Markets,* page 161.
16. Gary Hamel, Yves Doz & C. K. Prahalad, "Collaborate With Your Competitors and Win," *Harvard Business Review,* January-February 1989, page 139.
17. Halal et al, *Internal Markets,* page 254.
18. Thomas Stewart, "The Search for the Organization of Tomorrow," *Fortune,* May 18, 1992, page 97.
19. Schumacher, *Small Is Beautiful,* page 64.
20. Bergquist, *The Postmodern Organization,* page 181.
21. Senge, *The Fifth Discipline,* page 296.
22. Pinchot, *Intrapreneuring,* page 88.
23. Galbraith, *American Capitalism,* page 87. See my earlier reference in Chapter 4, page 52.
24. Pinchot, *Intrapreneuring,* page 89.
25. Ouchi, *Theory Z,* page 196.
26. Page 62.
27. Bell, *The Coming of Post-Industrial Society,* page 276.
28. Wheatley, *Leadership and the New Science,* page 13.

29. See Waldrop, *Complexity,* pages 146-147.

Chapter 11: Superpartnering
1. Hyde, *The Gift,* page 39.
2. Perelman, *School's Out,* page 59.
3. Mueller, *Corporate Networking,* page 137.
4. Sculley, *Odyssey,* page 92.
5. Intel Corp. CEO Andrew S. Grove described it as "The Rich Ecosystem of Silicon Valley," *Business Week,* August 25, 1997, page 202.
6. Sculley, *Odyssey,* page 234.
7. Ibid., page 260.
8. Ibid., page 391.
9. Kanter, *When Giants Learn to Dance,* page 50.
10. Sculley, *Odyssey,* pages 392-393.
11. Bart Ziegler, "How Do Joint Venutres Go Wrong? Ask Kaleida," *Wall Street Journal,* Nov. 22, 1995, pages B1 & B8.
12. Peter Burrows, "Will Gray Hair be an Asset to Apple?" *Business Week,* July 22, 1996, pages 38-39.
13. On *Business Week's* latest annual list of the S&P 500 according to performance, Apple Computer ranks 147th, among the bottom 10 in sales, earnings , margin and return on investment. "The Best Performers," *Business Week,* March 30, 1998, pages 76-158.
14. Stanley Reed, "Percy Barnevik Passes the Baton," *Business Week,* October 28, 1996, page 66.
15. Peters, *Liberation Management,* page 47.
16. Although still on the board of ABB, Barnevik has turned its management over to others. In April, 1997, he accepted the chairmanship of Investor, a Swedish company with major stakes in companies worth close to $100 billion.
17. Hyde, *The Gift,* page 80.
18. John A. Byrne, "Management Meccas," *Business Week,* September 18, 1995, pages 122-132.
19. Hyde, *The Gift,* page 273.
20. See Yankelovich, , "How Changes in the Economy are Reshaping American Values," page 5; also *New Rules,* page 7.

Chapter 12: Three Economies
1. Wheatley, *Leadership and the New Science,* page 86.
2. Editorial, "Europe Must Nourish Its Startups," *Business Week,* International Edition, May 6, 1996.
3. Julia Flynn, "Startups to the Rescue," *Business Week,* March 23, 1998, pages 50-51.
4. Bill Vlasic, "Can the UAW Put a Brake on Outsourcing?" *Business Week,* June 17, 1996, pages 66-70.
5. Mueller, *Corporate Networking,* page 38.
6. Donnelly, *The Confett Generation,* page 188.
7. Franklin, *The Autobiography,* page 111.

Notes: Chapter 12

8. Bagdikian, *The Media Monopoly*, page 23.
9. Aronson & Cowhey, *Managing the World Economy*, page 97.
10. Ibid., page 62.
11. Idem.
12. Brian Brenmer, "Cozying Up to Keiretsu," *Business Week* International Edition, July 22, 1996.
13. Part of the problems Japan and Korea are now facing arise out of their efforts to wed their traditional "family" economies with the bureaucratic systems of the West. As events prove, the mix has the vices of both systems.
14. Toffler, *Power Shift*, pages 226-227.
15. Brenmer, op. cit.
16. Lipnack & Stamps, *The TeamNet Factor*, page 22,
17. *Nikkei Weekly*, October 26, 1991, as quoted by Peters, *Liberation Management*, page 115.
18. Brenmer, op. cit.
19. Lipnack & Stamps, *The TeamNet Factor*, page 22.
20. Drucker, *Managing For The Future*, page 32.
21. Aronson & Cowhey, *Managing the World Economy*, pages 105-107.
22. Toffler, *Power Shift*. page 226-227.
23. Lipnack & Stamps, *The TeamNet Factor*, page 18.
24. Ibid., page 22.
25. Aronson & Cowhey, *Managing The World Economy*, page 175.
26. Imai, *Kaizen*, page 100.
27. Stewart Toy, "Chargeurs: The Spin-Off Heard 'Round the Continent," *Business Week* International Edition, July 8, 1996.
28. "Pepsi Challenge," *The Economist*, June 14, 1997, page 5.
29. Toy, idem.
30. Quoted in Reuter News Release, September 21, 1995.
31. Latouche, *In The Wake of the Affluent Society*, pages 127-148.
32. Ibid., page 138.
33. Hyde, *The Gift*, page 75.
34. The ideas from Lerner's *Passing of Traditional Society* are taken from Chapter I in Almond, *Crisis, Choice and Change*, page 9.
35. Latouche, *In The Wake of the Affluent Society*, page 130.
36. Ibid., page 154.
37. Wheatley, *Leadership and the New Science*, page 22.
38. "Employee Self-Management Without Formally Designated Teams," *Organizational Dynamics*, Winter 1992, pp. 48-61
39. Lipnack & Stamps, *The TeamNet Factor*, page 82.
40. Pinchot, *Intrapreneuring*, page 186.
41. Joel Kotkin, "Urban Renewers," *Inc.*, March 1996, page 23.
42. Idem.
43. For a detailed history and analysis of the Grameen Bank see Susan Higinbotham Holcombe's *Managing To Empower: The Grameen Bank's Experience of Poverty Alleviation*, Zed Books, 1995.
44. See Chapter 19, "The New Superpower: The Overseas Chinese," in Drucker, *Managing in a Time of Great Change*.

45. Richard Madsen, "After Liberalism: What If Confucianism Becomes the Hegemonic Ethic of the 21st Century World Community?" *Futures Research Quarterly*, Spring 1996, pages 25-39.
46. Ibid., page 27.
47. Ibid., page 33.
48. "Crony Capitalism Takes Its Toll," *Business Week*, July 22, 1996, page 106.
49. Rosell et al., *Governing in an Information Society,* page 98.
50. "The U.S. Sets IBM Free," *Business Week* International Edition, July 15, 1996. The Justice Department's moves against Microsoft do not counter this trend. Rather it is a parallel trend to revise the application of antitrust laws to fit the new knowledge economy.
51. Gilroy, *Networking in Multinational Enterprises,* page 124.
52. Ibid., pages 124-125.
53. Peters, *Liberation Management,* page 121.
54. Robert J. Samuelson, "Beyond the Budget Fuss," *Newsweeek*, November 28, 1988, page 33.
55. Amy Cortese, "Here Comes the Intranet," *Business Week,* February 26, 1996, pages 76-84.
56. The author has read descriptions of the McGraw-Hill intranet in company publications.
57. James Brian Quinn, Thomas L. Doorley & Kenny C. Paquette, "Technology and Services: Rethinking Strategic Focus," *Sloan Management Review,* Winter 1990, pages 79-87.
58. Peters, *Liberation Management,* page 152.

Chapter 13: Rediscovering Government

1. Jefferson, Letter to Samuel Kercheval, July 12, 1816, *Thomas Jefferson, Writings,* page 1401.
2. John Herbers, "Throwing Out a Million Babies With the Bathwater of 'Big Government,'" *The Washington Spectator,* September 1, 1996, page 2.
3. William Ophuls, "Requiem for Representative Democracy," *The Good Society,* Winter 1997, page 1. The article is adapted from the author's book, *Requiem for Modern Politics,* Westview, 1997.
4. Bogart, *Commercial Culture,* pages 175-176.
5. Tarcher, *Escape From Avarice,* page 7.
6. See especially Chomsky's "Democracy's Slow Death" in *In These Times,* November 28, 1994, pages 25-28.
7. King, *Running Scared.* See Lippmann's *The Public Philosphy*, Chapters 1 & 2
8. "Survey of Democracy: Happy 21st Century, Voters," 14-page insert in *The Economist,* December 21, 1996.
9. Fallows, *Looking At The Sun,* page 214.
10. Toffler & Toffler, *Creating a New Civilization,* page 91.
11. Chomsky, *Secrets, Lies and Democracy.*
12. Greider, *Who Will Tell The People,* page 11.
13. "Consensus Democracy," page 2, leaflet issued by the Center for Communities of the Future, 1319 Heatherloch Drive, Gastonia, NC 28054.
14. Associated Press newsrelease, Nov. 7, 1994.

15. "Citizen Consensus Conferences Point to Better Political Decisions," *On The Horizon,* February/March 1995, page 10.
16. Toffler & Toffler, *Creating a New Civilization,* pages 96-99.
17. Associated Press release, November 15, 1994.
18. Associated Press release, October 29, 1994.
19. William F. Weld, "Release Us From Federal Nonsense," *Wall Street Journal,* December 11, 1995, page A12.
20. Rosell, *Governing in an Information Society,* page 91.
21. Howard, *The Death of Common Sense,* page 7.
22. "Oink Inc.," *The Economist,* March 11, 1995, page 28.
23. Mann & Plummer, *Noah's Choice,* pages 22-23.
24. Epstein, *Simple Rules For A Complex World,* page 297. To understand how this happens, read Greider's *Who Will Tell The People,* page 334.
25. Howard, *The Death of Common Sense,* page 19.
26. Ross Sandler & Sheila P. Murphy, "Are You a Lobbyist?" *City Law,* February 1995, page 1. Published by the Center for New York City Law at New York Law School.
27. "Overregulating America," *The Economist,* July 27, 1996, page 20.
28. Wilson, *Deregulating The Public Service,* page 43.
29. Idem.
30. Toffler, *Future Shock,* pages 472-473.
31. Idem.
32. Idem.
33. *The World Almanac and Book of Facts 1983,* Newspaper Enterprise Association, page 924.
34. "Gurus in the government," *The Economist,* May 20, 1995, page 21.
35. Thomas A. Bass, "The Future of Money," *Wired,* page 202.
36. McKenzie & Lee, *Quicksilver Capital,* page 10.
37. Cleveland, *Birth of a New World,* page 33.
38. Toffler & Toffler, *Creating a New Civilization,* page 100.
39. Bell, *The Coming of Post-industrial Society,* page xxiii.
40. Drucker, *Managing in a Time of Great Change,* page 244.
41. Drucker, *The Age of Discontinuity,* page 176.
42. Drucker, *Managing in a Time of Great Change,* page 245.
43. See editorial, "Abolish D.C.," *The New Republic,* December 5, 1994, page 7.
44. Phillips, *Arrogant Capital,* page 113.
45. DiIulio Jr., *Deregulating The Public Service,* page 187.
46. *A Region At Risk: An Executive Summary of the Third Regional Plan for the New York-New Jersey-Connecticut Metropolitan Area,* published by the Regional Plan Association, 1996.
47. *The Calumet Crescent Corridor of Southeast Chicago and Northwest Indiana: A Brief Look at What's In the Corridor,* published by City Innovation, 1994.
48. "Who is a German?" *The Economist,* April 5, 1997, page 45.
49. "The New Trade in Humans," *The Economist,* August 5, 1995, page 45.
50. Idem.
51. "Kicking (out) the habit," *The Economist,* August 5, 1995, page 46.

52. Ben A. Franklin, "The Melting Pot Escapes Total Meltdown," *The Washington Spectator,* June 1, 1996, page 2.
53. McKenzie & Lee, *Quicksilver Capital,* page 232.
54. "Global Gangsters," *U.S. News & World Report,* November 28, 1994, page 33. A more complete account of the First World Ministerial Conference on Organized Transnational Crime appeared in the *U.N. Chronicle,* March 1995, page 89.
55. "Getting Together," *The Economist,* June 29, 1996, pages 42-43.
56. Thurow, *The Future of Capitalism,* page 127.
57. Peirce, "Citistates," page 3.
58. Ibid., page 11.
59. Quoted by Etzioni, *The Spirit of Community,* page 122.
60. Garrett Hardin, "The Tragedy of the Commons," *Science,* December 13, 1968, pages 1243-1248.
61. Pages 99-101.
62. Osborne & Gaebler, *Reinventing Government,* pages 285-289.
63. "Oink Inc." *The Economist,* March 11, 1995, page 28.
64. Cogan et al., *The Budget Puzzle,* pages 24-25.
65. Bergquist, *The Postmodern Organization,* page 54.
66. Naisbitt, *Global Paradox,* page 273.
67. See Paul A. Samuelson, "The Pure Theory of Public Expenditures," *Review of Economics and Statistics,* November 1954, pages 387-389.
68. See Julius Margolis, "A Comment on the Pure Theory of Public Expenditures," *Review of Economics and Statistics,* November 1955, pages 347-349.
69. Pages 67-68.
70. Herbers, "Throwing Out a Million Babies With the Bathwater of 'Big Government,'" op. cit., page 2.
71. Drucker, *Managing in a Time of Great Change,* pages 255-257.
72. Benveniste, *The Twenty-First Century Organization,* pages 252-253.

Chapter 14: Restoring the Supremacy of the Individual

1. de Tocqueville, *Democracy In America,* Volume 1, page 70.
2. Steiner,*Amicable Agreement versus Majority Rule,* page 4.
3. Ibid., page 5.
4. Garfield, *Second To None,* page 174.
5. Steiner, *Amicable Agreement versus Majority Rule,* page 6.
6. Ibid., page 66.
7. Pages 97-98.
8. Lehner, *The Political Economics of Growth,* page 206.
9. Steiner, *Amicable Agreement versus Majority Rule,* page 67.
10. Cleveland, "Ten Keys to World Peace," pages 15-16.
11. Toffler & Toffler, *Creating a New Civilization,* page 92.
12. Pages 109-110.
13. Drucker, *Post-capitalist Society,* page 49.
14. Pages 170-179.
15. "NYPD, Inc," *The Economist,* July 29, 1995, page 50.
16. McKenzie & Lee, *Quicksilver Capital,* page 99.

17. Rachel Dickinson, "The Rush to Sell Off Government," *American Demographics*, February 1996, page 41.
18. Drucker, *The Age of Discontinuity*, page 180.
19. Randy Gragg, "High-Security, Low Risk Investment, *Harper's Magazine*, August 1996. page 50.
20. Rachel Dickinson, op. cit., page 81.
21. Tom Herman, "U.S. May Explore Private Tax Collection," *The Wall Street Journal*, November 22, 1995, pages A2, A12. More examples can be supplied by Americans For Responsible Privatization, 1401 I Street, N.W., suite 925, Washington, DC 20005.
22. "From highway to my way," *The Economist*, Nov. 18, 1995, page 29. See also "Living with the car: No room, no room," *The Economist*, December 6, 1997, pages 21-22, where the editors conclude that "governments all around the world, faced by worsening traffic congestion and pollution, are steeling their nerves and forcing motorists to pay for road space."
23. Peter Samuel, "Highway Aggravation: The Case for Privatizing the Highways," *Cato Policy Analysis* No. 231, June 27, 1995, page 12.
24. Bell, *The Coming of Post-Industrial Society*, pages 322-323.
25. Idem.
26. Osborne & Gaebler, *Reinventing Government*, page 260.
27. Pages 120-121.
28. Patricia Vowinkel, "Catastrophic Risk Exchange Planned," Reuter News Service, July 26, 1995.
29. Pages 181-182.
30. Drucker, *The Age of Discontinuity*, pages 234-235.
31. Kevin Kelly, "Anticipatory Democracy," *Wired*, July 1996, page 187.
32. Toffler & Toffler, *Creating a New Civilization*, page 92.
33. Thomas A. Bass, "The Future of Money," *Wired*, October 1996, page 202.
34. Bennett, *The Governing Crisis*, page 18.

Chapter 15: The Death Struggle of Government

1. Lodge, *Perestroika For America*, page 211.
2. Ibid., page 212.
3. David Mercer, "Global Forces That Will Shape Our Economic and Political Lives," *Futures Research Quarterly*, Winter 1997, page 85.
4. Lodge, op.cit., page 67.
5. Ibid., page 15.
6. Ibid., page16.
7. "More neighbourly government," *The Economist*, January 3, 1998, page 25.
8. "One Europe, up to a point," *The Economist*, September 14, 1996, page 48.
9. "Blair on the Constitution: Democracy's second age," *The Economist*, September 14, 1996, pages 55-58.
10. "Polls to nowhere," *The Economist*, November 23, 1996, page 20.
11. Cowhey & Aronson, *Managing The World Economy*, page 217.

12. *The United Nations In Its Second Half-Century: A Report of the Independent Working Group on the Future of the United Nations,* Ford Foundation, 1995, page 51.
13. Ibid., page 10.
14. Michael Lind, "The Twilight of the U.N.," *The New Republic,* October 30, 1995, pages 25-30.
15. W. Bell, "World Order, Human Values and the Future," page 16.
16. Charles S. Maier, "Democracy and Its Discontents," *Foreign Affairs,* July-August 1994, page 64.
17. "One Europe, up to a point," *The Economist,* September 14, 1996, page 48.
18. "Policing for Profit," *The Economist,* April 19, 1997, page 21.
19. *The United Nations In Its Second Half Century,* pages 46-47.
20. Speech at the conference of the World Future Society held in Atlanta in 1995.
21. Chomsky, *World Order Old and New,* page 159.
22. Richard N. Cooper, "What Future for the International Monetary System?" in Baldassarri et al., *Global Disequilibrium in the World Economy,* page 344.
23. See William Davidow, "Does Money Exist," *Forbes ASAP,* June 3, 1996, page 26. The local script exchanged in Ithaca, New York, was called Ithaca Hours because it originally represented hours of labor pledged as payment. Its primary purpose was to encourage economic activity locally. For a complete explanation see, Paul Glover, "Ithaca Hours: Creating Community Economics with Local Currency," *The Good Society,* Winter 1997, page 56. A similar experiment has been tried in Montpelier, Vermont. See "What's an hour worth?" *The Economist,* June 28, 1997, page 29.
24. Introduction by James A. Dorn, editor of *The Future of Money In The Information Age,* Cato Institute, 1997.
25. Cato Institute's Fourteenth Annual Monetary Conference on "The Future of Money in the Information Age." downloaded from the Cato Institute's Internet Page, September 24, 1996.
26. Dennis Logue, "When Theory Fails: Globalization as a Response to the (Hostile) Market for Foreign Exchange," *Journal of Applied Corporate Finance,* Fall 1995, pages 39-48.
27. Quoted by Theodore J. Forstmann, "The Paradox of the Statist Businessman," *Cato Policy Report,* March/April 1995, page 1.
28. Steele, *The Economics of Friederich Hayek,* pages 22-23.
29. Kurtzman, *The Death of Money,* page 18,
30. Davidow, "Does Money Exist," op. cit., page 26.
31. Thomas A. Bass, "The Future of Money," *Wired,* October 1996, pages 201-202.
32. Walter B.. Wriston, "Incredible Future," *Executive Excellence,* November 1995, pages 6-7.
33. Aldous Huxley, *Brave New World,* Harper's Modern Classics edition. 1950. (Original copyrighted 1932.) Introduction, page (11).
34. Naisbitt, *Global Paradox,* pages 22-23.
35. Kellas, *The Politics of Nationalism and Ethnicity,* page 114.
36. Quoted by Robert D. Kaplan, "History Moving North," *The Atlantic Monthly,* February 1997. page 22.

37. J. Orstrom Moller, "The Future of Europe: Economic Internationalization, Cultureal Decentralization, Soft Security Policy," *Futures Research Quarterly,* Winter 1995, pages 83-92.
38. Epstein, *Simple Rules For A Complex World,* page 3.
39. Davidow & Malone,*The Virtual Corporation,* pages 261-262.
40. Epstein, *Simple Rules For A Complex World,* page 46.
41. PR Newswire, "Schering-Plough in Settlement Agreement in Retail Pharmacy Class Action Suit," February 9, 1996.

Chapter 16: Solving the Problem of Social Insurance

1. Drucker, *Managing In A Time of Great Change,* page 255.
2. Page 271.
3. Pages 263-264.
4. Olson, *The Logic of Collective Action,* page 94.
5. Ibid. page 94, footnote 81.
6. D. Bell, *The Coming of Post-Industrial Society,* page 283.
7. Pages 266-268.
8. Russell Hardin, "Special Status for Groups," *The Good Society,* Spring 1996, page 15.
9. See Garraty & Gay, *The Columbia History of the World,* page 609.
10. "Hunger—A National Shame in the World's Richest Country," *Hunger,* Community Action Network, 1995, page 4.
11. Drucker, *Managing For The Future,* page 204.
12. "Outreach Worker," *Health Care,* Community Action Network, 1995, page 11.
13. "Citywide Drug Program Enlists Five Local Agencies," *Street Crime,* Community Action Network, 1995, page 14.
14. "Prudential Bestows Grants Sponsored by Individual Agents," *Disadvantaged,* Community Action Network, 1995, page 30.
15. Drucker, *Managing In A Time of Great Change,* pages 255-256.
16. Yankelovich, "How Changes in the Economy are Reshaping American Values," page 6.
17. Gene Koretz, "Fewer at the Charity Ball," *Business Week,* October 28, 1996, page 36.
18. "The People Behind the Money," sidebar to Jerry Adler, "He Gave at the Office," *Newsweek,* February 3, 1997. pages 34-35.
19. "Guilt Affects Giving," *Target Marketing,* April 1988, page 61.
20. Dr. Demo, "Why Donors Give," *American Demographics,* June 1996. page 4.
21. Drucker, *Managing For The Future,* page 211.
22. "Families are taking care of each other," *AARP Bulletin,* May 1997, page 4.
23. Jonathan Alter, "Think Before You Give," *Newsweek,* September 29, 1997, page 38.
24. Pages 120-121.
25. Gary S. Becker, "A Social Security Lesson from Argentina," *Business Week,* October 21, 1996, page 25. This should not be considered an unconditional recommendation for Chile's system. For its negatives see Stephen J. Kay, "The Chile Con," *The American Prospect,* July-August 1997, pages 48-51.

26. Elisabeth Malkin, "Private Pensions Worked in Chile, But in Mexico . . . ," *Business Week,* International Edition, November 25, 1996.
27. "Retirement Revolution," *The Economist,* November 23, 1996, page 95.
28. Pages 289-291.
29. See Peter Coy, "The Closest Thing to a Crystal Ball," a review of Peter L. Bernstein's *Against The Gods, Business Week,* October 21, 1996, page 20.
30. See "Dunning by the Numbers," *Newsweek,* October 28, 1996. page 86.
31. Michael J. Mandel, "Gurus for the Information Age," *Business Week,* October 21, 1996, page 60.
32. Delegates from 100 countries met in December 1977 to discuss establishment of a permanent International Court. "A criminal court for the world," The Economist, December 6, 1997, page 18.
33. Christian Parenti, "Pay Now, Pay Later," *The Progressive,* July 1996, page 26.
34. "Dan Coates, senator for charity," *The Economist,* February 15, 1997, page 32.
35. Paul Magnusson, "Commentary: Why Privatizing Welfare Could Actually Work," *Business Week,* October 21, 1996, page 94.

Chapter 17: Transforming Education

1. D. Bell, *The Coming of Post-Industrial Society,* page 171.
2. Cited by Armey, *The Freedom Revolution,* pages 197-198.
3. Cetron & Gayle, *Educational Renaissance,* page 5.
4. Idem., pages 6-7.
5. "World Education League: Who's top?" *The Economist,* March 29, 1997, page 21.
6. Boaz & Crane, *Market Liberalism,* page 197.
7. Armey, *The Freedom Revolution,* page 199.
8. Hughes, *Culture of Complaint,* pages 61-62.
9. Cetron & Gayle, *Educational Renaissance,* page 83.
10. Ibid., page 82.
11. "The Endangered Summer Vacation," *U.S. News & World Report,* May 16, 1994, page 12.
12. Jonathan Alter, "Busting the Big Blob," *Newsweek,* April 8, 1996, page 40.
13. Hall, *Beyond Culture,* page 166.
14. Perelman, *School's Out,* pages 126-127.
15. Associated Press release, September 21, 1994.
16. Hirsch, *Cultural Literacy,* page 134-135.
17. Ibid., page xv.
18. LynNell Hancock, & Pat Wingert, "A Mixed Report Card," *Newsweek,* November 13, 1995, page 69.
19. Drucker, "The Age of Social Transformation," pages 68-69.
20. Bill Gates, Excerpt from *The Road Ahead,* published in *Newsweek,* November 27, 1995, page 66.
21. Drucker, "The Age of Social Transformation," page 68.
22. Gardener & Blythe, *Multiple Intelligences,* pages 71-72.
23. Quoted by Reich, *The Work of Nations,* page 60.
24. Ong, *Rhetoric, Romance, And Technology,* page 118.
25. Branden, *The Six Pillars of Self-esteem,* pages 206-207.

26. James Bryant Conant, Charter Day Address at the University of California on March 28, 1940.
27. Gardner & Blythe, *Multiple Intelligences,* page 8-9.
28. E.g., Charles Handy lists nine, in *The Age of Paradox,* pages 204-205.
29. See Karen Pennar, "How Many Smarts Do You Have?" *Business Week,* September 16, 1996, pages 104-108.
30. Gardner & Blythe, *Multiple Intelligences,* page 71.
31. Ibid., page 72.
32. Ibid., page 74.
33. Marc Levinson, "Hire Education," *Newsweek,* September 30, 1996, page 52.
34. Drucker, *Managing For The Future,* page 5.
35. Hamm & Adams, *The Collaborative Dimensions of Learning,* page 2.
36. William E. Halal & Jay Liebowitz, "Telelearning: The Multimedia Revolution in Education," *The Futurist,* November-December 1994, page 23.
37. Shamos, *The Myth of Scientific Literacy,* page 14.
38. Bogart, *Commercial Culture,* pages 150-151.
39. Hughes, *The Culture of Complaint,* page 108.
40. Quoted by Riesman, *The Lonely Crowd,* page 5.
41. Maslow, *Eupsychian Management,* page 65.
42. Jerry Adler, "The Tutor Age," *Newsweek,* March 3, 1998, page 47.
43. Ackoff, *The Democratic Corporation,* page 214.
44. Tibbett L. Speer, "A Nation of Students," *American Demographics,* August 1996. pages 32-38, 45.
45. Illich's ideas are well summarized by Guy Benveniste, *The Twenty-First Century Organization,* pages 419-420.

Chapter 18: The Need for Paradigm Change

1. Veblen, *The Theory of the Leisure Class,* page 119.
2. Ibid., pages 117-118.
3. Kuhn, *The Structure of Scientific Revolutions,* page 77.
4. Ibid., page 208.
5. Garfield, *Second to None,* page 9.
6. For a good definition of the differences see *Business Incorporating Guide* published by Corporate Agents, Inc., 1996, 1013 Centre Road, Wilmington, DE 19899.
7. For a useful discussion of this see Marc F. Plattner's "Natural Rights and the Moral Presuppositions of Political Economy," in Nicholas & Wright, *From Political Economy to Economics and Back?,* pages 35-56.

Chapter 19: The Bottom Line—A Deception

1. Adams, *The Education Of Henry Adams*, page 4
2. Bridges, *Jobshift,* page 33.
3. Halal et al., *Internal Markets,* page 202-203.
4. Galbraith, *The New Industrial State.* See especially Chapters III and IV.
5. Daniel McGinn, "Deadbeat Nation," *Newsweek,* April 14, 1997, page 50.

6. From Keynes' *General Theory*, as quoted by Heilbroner, *21st Century Capitalism*, page 126.
7. Quoted by Heilbroner, ibid., page 127.
8. "Panel Discussion: The Role of the Corporation," *Journal of Business Strategy*, July/August 1996, page 54.
9. Drucker, *Managing In A Time of Great Change*, page 84.
10. Korten, "When Corporations Rule the World," page 1.
11. Goodwin, "Evolving Values for A Capitalist World," page 8.
12. See Betty Jane Dunn, "The Scott Paper Saga," *Directorship*, June 1995, page 4.
13. See "Panel Discussion: The Role of the Corporation," op. cit., page 54.143.
14. See Drucker, *Managing In A Time of Great Change*, page 84.
15. See Kurtzman, *The Death of Money*, page 164.
16. Chomsky, *Class Warfare*, page 125.

Chapter 20: The Corporation—Legalized Irresponsibility

1. Acceptance speech, Democratic National Convention, June 27, 1936.
2. Bell, *The Coming of Post-Industrial Society*, page 362.
3. Berle & Means, *The Modern Corporation and Private Property*, page 3.
4. Ibid, page 64.
5. The authors spell out these seven points at greater length, ibid, pages 64-65.
6. Ibid, page viii.
7. Ibid, page xxvi.
8. Ibid., page 309.
9. Galbraith, *The New Industrial State*, See especially pages 258-259.
10. Ibid., pages 126-127, footnote 14.
11. Berle & Means, *The Modern Corporation and Private Property*, page 313.
12. Korten, *When Corporations Rule The World*, page 54.
13. To say that businesses should be run *by* their stakeholders is far different than saying they should be run *for* their stakeholders. See John Plander's *A Stake In The Future; The Stakeholder Society*, Nicholas Brealy, 1997.
14. Drucker, *Managing The Future*, page 4.
15. Quoted by Richard L. Grossman & Frank T. Adams, *Taking Care of Business: Citizenship and the Charter of Incorporation*, Charter, Ink (P.O. Box 806, Cambridge, MA 02140), 1993, page 10.
16. Op. cit.
17. Barnet & Cavanaugh, *Global Dreams*.
18. Idem.
19. Chomsky, *Class Warfare*.
20. See Lance E. Davis and Robert A. Huttenback, *Mammon and the Pursuit of Empire: The Political Economy of British Imperialism*, Cambridge University Press, 1987.
21. Grossman, *Taking Care of Business*.
22. Lance E. Davis and Robert A. Huttenback, op. cit.
23. Korten, *When Corporations Rule The World*.

Chapter 21: Intellectual Property—Unfair and Unenforceable
1. John Perry Barlow,"The Economy of Ideas," *Wired,* February 3, 1994, page 86.
2. Cleveland, *The Knowledge Executive,* page 78.
3. Jim Mann, "Managing Magazine Research & Development," *Media Management Monograph* Number 61, September 1983, page 4.
4. Letter to Isaac McPherson, August 13, 1813, *Thomas Jefferson, Writings,* pages 1291-1292.
5. Mumford, *Technics and Civilization,* page 108.
6. Otis Port, "Headliner: Douglas Engelbart, The Man Behind the Mouse," *Business Week,* April 21, 1997. page 48.
7. Peter Coy, "India Calls It Patent Absurdity," *Business Week,* August 12, 1996, page 83.
8. "The Trustbusters Get One Right," editorial, *Business Week,* January 20, 1997, page 104.
9. Barnet & Cavanaugh, *Global Dreams,* page 145.
10. Don Steinberg, "Digital Underground," *Wired,* January 1997, page 107.
11. "Intellectual Property," a special supplement to *The Colby Report,* July 1994.
12. Barnet & Cavanaugh, *Global Dreams,* page 142.
13. John Perry Barlow, op.cit., page 86.
14. Ibid., page 128.
15. For an example of a life-or-death drug that could be kept from patients while two companies fight over the patent see Michael Myers & Tara Weingarten, "A Deadly Serious Fight," *Newsweek,* May 19, 1997, page 60.
16. Esther Dyson, "Intellectual Value, *Wired,* July 1995, page 136.

Chapter 22: Preparing for the New Global Community
1. Branden, *The Six Pillars of Self-Esteem,* page xi.
2. Hall, *Beyond Culture,* page 199.
3. Goodwin, *Social Economics,* page 33.
4. Galbraith, *New Industrial State,* see especially chapter XX, "The Regulation of Aggregate Demand," pages 230-242.
5. Fund managers are already feeling such pressure according to "Just what the patient ordered," *The Economist,* January 18, 1997, pages 69-70.
6. George Soros, "The Capitalist Threat," *The Atlantic Monthly,* February 1997, page 53.
7. For a lengthy discussion of this pehnomenon see "Why there is a perplexing shortage of rich kids," *The Economist,* February 22, 1997, pages 89-90.
8. "Rwanda: Be fruitful," *The Economist,* Feb. 1, 1997, page 43.
9. Soros, op. cit., page 55.
10. Glastonbury & LaMendola, *The Integrity of Intelligence,* page 3.
11. Hall, *Beyond Culture,* page 74.
12. Senge, *The Fifth Discipline,* page 282.
13. Bridges, *Jobshift,* pages 86-87.
14. "John Seely Brown," interview by Eric Nee, *Upside,* December 1993, page 28.
15. Galbraith, *The New Industrial State,* page 332, footnote 2.

Chapter 23: Tomorrow's Global Community: A Family of Families

1. Freud, *Civilization and Its Discontents,* pages 65 and 71.
2. Beginning on page 387.
3. The facts on the Wechsler reunion were provided by family member Norman R. Glenn, founder chairman of The Community Action Network.
4. Page 149.
5. See Chapter 14, pages 270-273.
6. Quoted by Ben A. Franklin, "Public Opinion As the Fourth Branch of Government," *The Washington Spectator,* April 15, 1998, page 1.
7. Pages 87-89.
8. Page 271.
9. See pages 223-225 and 233-238.
10. Robert B. Reich, "Who Is Us?" *Harvard Business Review*, January-February 1990, pages 53-64.
11. Kerry Capell, "What a 'Euro' Could Do For the Latins," *Business Week,* April 13, 1998, page 100.

Addendum

1. de Toqueville, *Democracy In American*, Volume I, page 6.
2. Quoted by Steven V. Brull and Neil Gross, "The Next World Accordingly To Clarke," *Business Week*, Feb. 24, 1997, page 123.

Index

A
ABB Asea Brown Boveri, 212, 218-21, 223, 243
ABC, 147, 188
Abilities, in self-evaluation, 388
Ackoff, Russell L., 192, 337
Acquired immunodeficiency syndrome (AIDS), 381
Adams, Henry, 347
Ad hoc administration, 290
Ad hoc communities, 278
Administration, 200-201, 290
  welfare, 314-15, 400-401
Adolescent society, 153-54
Advertising, 23, 113-14
Adweek, 140
African Americans, 47, 69, 104-5, 237-38
"After Liberalism," 238
The Age of Discontinuity, 284
Agreement, amicable, majority rule vs., 270-72
Agriculture, 357
AIDS, 381
Alexander, Herbert E., 99
Alger, Horatio, 94
Alienation, 46-56, 147
Allen, Robert, 233
Alliances, corporate, 230-32
Alter, Jonathan, 320
Amelio, Gilbert F., 217
American Capitalism, 78, 111, 115
American democracy, 84-107
American Indians, 55, 104, 112
American Journalism, 139
American Values, 102
Amicable agreement, majority rule vs., 270-72
Amoco Oil, 254
Amusing Ourselves to Death, 41-42, 92
Anarchy, 81
Anderson, Bob, 204
Anderson, Elijah, 50-51
Animistic fallacy, 62
Anxiety, 30
Apathy, 40-41, 146-47, 251-53
Appleby, R. Scott, 51
Apple Computer, 212, 214-18
Archer Daniels Midland, 255
Archimedes, 382
Areopagitica, 134
Argosy, 141
Argument, definition of, 61
Aristotle, 64, 65, 344
Arthur, Brian, 118, 373
The Art of Memory, 78
Asian economy, 238-39
Asians in America, 238
Asian view of power, 252
Associated Press, 253
AT&T, 107, 233, 242
Atlanta, 261
The Atlantic Monthly, 50, 385
Attention, control of, 70, 390
Attitude, 67, 196-98

Attucks, Crispus, 85
Authority
  communication and, 79-81
  decline of, 34-36
  distributing and exercising, 402
  division of, 267-68
  information and democracy and, 84-107
  knowledge and, 268-69
  in partnership networks, 276
  public vs. private, 179
Automobile industry, 21, 230-31
B
Bagdikian, Ben H., 138
Ballestrini, Bill, 212-14
B&O, 212-14, 228
Bangladesh, 238
Bankruptcy, 351
Banks, 183
Barlow, John Perry, 368, 375, 376
Barnevik, Percy, 218, 219, 220, 241
Barney, Ralph D., 66
Barter, 347-48
Bartol, Julio R., 193
Bayer Aspirin, 377
Bay of Pigs, 44
Beccaria, Cesare Bonesma de, 85
Beedham, Brian, 252, 253
Behavioral economics, 119
Bell, Daniel, 207, 258, 281, 305, 316, 355
Bell, Wendell, 293
The Bell Curve, 47
Benefits
  business, profits vs., 352-53
  loss of, 277
  responsibilities balanced with, 399
  social vs. individual, 305-6
Benetton, 232
Bennett, Bill, 316
Bennett, James Gordon, 93
Bennis, Warren, 156
Bentham, Jeremy, 78
Benveniste, Guy, 159, 269
Bergquist, William, 203, 264-65
Berkeley, George, 64
Berkeley, William, 133-34
Berle, Adolf A., 355-60, 363
Beyond Culture, 67, 321, 378
The Bias of Communication, 82
Birth of a New World, 257
Blacks, 47, 69, 104-5, 237-38
Blair, Francis Preston, 93
Blair, Tony, 289
Blanqui, Auguste, 79-80
Bloom, Allan, 45, 334
Blythe, Tina, 327-28
Bobbit, Lorena, 28
Bogart, Leo, 333-34
Bosnia, 300
Bosses, 174, 175
Bottom-line paradigm, 343, 347-54
Bourne, Randolph, 95
Boycott, 277
Branden, Nathaniel, 326-27, 378

Bratton, William, 280
Brave New World, 299
Bridges, William, 380, 388
Broadcast journalism, 130-31, 392-93
Brodeur, Paul, 32
Brown, Cecil, 131
Brown, John Seely, 391
Brzezinski, Zbigniew, 26, 29
Buhagiar, Marion, 170
Bureaucracy
  attitude in, 196-98
  competition and, 198-99
  of corporations, 361
  dealing with complexity in, 161-63
  disillusion with, 253-54
  flexibility and, 188-89
  human needs and, 158-60
  law and, 255, 301
  professionals in, 160-61
  rise of, 156-57
  secrecy and, 222
Burke, Edmund, 132
Business
  balance, 354
  benefits, profits vs., 352-53
  media and social structure and, 75-76
  media criticism of, 138
Business Organization and the Myth of the Market Economy, 111
Business Week, 222, 227, 239, 373
Byrne, Robert F., 214
C
Campbell, Bill, 217
Canada, 254
Cancer, 32-33
Capitalism, 109-11, 352
Career choices, 389
Career exploration in schools, 332-33
Carpenter, Edmund, 128
Cato Institute, 124, 295-96, 309
Cavallo, Domingo, 297
CBS, 66, 131, 142
Cetron, Marvin, 317
Change, fear of, 125, 226-27
Character, building, 334-35
Chargeurs, 233
Charitable donations, 310-11
Charitable groups, 308-10
Cherry, Colin, 68
China, 238, 257, 374-75
Chomsky, Noam, 251, 252, 354
Christ, Jesus, 309
Chrysler, 227
Citistates, 261-62
Civil Disobedience, 335
Civilizations, societies and cultures and, 76-77
Claris, 217
Clarke, Arthur C., 405
Clay, Henry, 110
Cleveland, Harlan, 43, 60, 61, 108, 257, 268, 274, 368-69
Clients, 182-83
Clinton, Bill, 23, 101, 135, 256, 281, 401

Clorox, 377
The Closing of the American Mind, 45, 334
CNN, 135, 148
Coaches, development, 330-32
Coca-Cola, 205
Cocheiro, Antonio Alonso, 300
"Collaborate With Your Competitors and Win," 198
Collaboration, 178-80, 400
The Collaborative Dimensions of Learning, 328-29
Columbia Broadcasting System, 66, 131
The Coming of Post-Industrial Society, 207, 258, 281, 305, 355
Commercial Culture, 333
Common Sense, 86-87
Communication. See also Media
  acceleration of, 22
  authority and, 79-81
  culture corrupting, 67-69
  defensive, 97-99
  distortions in, 65-67
  forms of, 210-11
  loss of control by media, 143-44
  manipulation in, 59-60, 65, 68
  methods, 64-65
  power in, 133-34
  revolutions, 73-75
  skills, 136
  society created by, 72-83
Communication and Social Order, 47
Communism, 159, 383
Community
  communication creating, 72-73
  compassion and, 308-11
  cooperation and, 304-5
  culture and, 306-7
  definition of, 62, 148-49, 262
  enforcement of power in, 276-77
  global, 378-404
  of interests, 148-49
  knowledge and, 82
  networks as, 273-74
  new kind of, 148-49, 262
  society vs., 259
  types of, 278
Compassion, community and, 308-11
Competition
  business, 115, 116, 189, 199-200
  cooperation and, 239-40
  employee, 198-99
  knowledge vs., 240-41
Complex adaptive systems, 208-9
Complexity, 118
Compromise, in government, 87-89, 270-73
CompuScore System, 42
Computers, 241, 390-91, 392
Conant, James Bryant, 327
Conference, 154, 155
Congress, 21-22, 28
Connally, John, 132
Consultants, 28

Consumer Price Index, 38-39
Contino, Ronald, 168
Continuing education, 337
Control Data Corp., 198
Cook, Paul, 188
Cook, Phillip J., 375
Cooper, Richard N., 295
Cooperation
  community and, 304-5
  competition and, 239-40
  global, 289
  in government, 87-89
  independence and, 172-73
  in industry, 199-200, 222-23
Copyright, 374-77. See also Intellectual property
Corporate alliances, 230-32
"Corporate Integrity and Internal Market Economies," 193
Corporate Networking, 211
Corporate structure
  arguments for, 203-5
  attitude and, 196-98
  lack of, 244
  transition and, 232-33
Corporation paradigm, 343-44, 355-67
Counselors, guidance, 330, 331
Crawford, Richard, 244
Creating a New Civilization, 257, 380
Credit, 121-23, 226-27, 350-51
  actuarial vs. guaranteed, 296-97
Crime, 313-14
Crockett, Jim, 204
Cro-Magnons, 73-74, 75
Cronkite, Walter, 132
Crowds, following (groupthink), 43-46
Csikszentmihalyi, Mihaly, 63
Cuberly, Elwood P., 326
The Cult of Information, 77
Cults, 44
Cultural Literacy, 322, 324
Cultural literacy, 322-24
Culture(s)
  alienated, 47-56
  American, 95-96
  as communication corrupter, 67-69
  community and, 306-7
  economics and, 299-300
  popular vs. elite, 333-34
  preservation, 307-8
  value change and, 103-7
Culture of Complaint, 55, 334
Cunniff, John, 35
Currency, 295-99
Currents of Death, 32
Customers, 182-83
D
Daedalus, 35
Darwin, Charles, 62, 119
Davidow, William, 298
Dawkins, Richard, 62, 68-69
Day, Benjamin H., 93
Deacon, Robert, 280
The Death of Money, 297

Debt, 121-23. See also Credit
Decision division, 257-58
Decision horizons, 182
Decisions
  authority and, 402
  social nature of, 305-6
Declaration of Independence, 86, 285
Delegation, 162
Deming, W. Edwards, 174
Democracy
  American, 251-53
  business organizations and, 363-64
  information and authority and, 84-107
  in network vs. representative government, 273-74
  transforming, 285
Democracy in America, 45
The Democratic Corporation, 337
Democratic insurance, 312-13
Democratic justice, 313-14
Demosclerosis, 98, 263
Deregulating the Public Service, 256
Design, definition of, 61
Despair, 49
De Tocqueville, Alexis, 45, 95, 270, 405
Development coaches, 330-32
Devolution, government, 289-90
Dewey, John, 323
Dichter, Ernest, 113
Diderot, Denis, 85
Direction, 154, 155
Distrust, 33-36, 140-41, 146
Dividends, 349
Doe, Samuel, 36
Dole, Bob, 148
Domain, concept of, 358-59
Dominion, public vs. private, 279-80
Dorn, James A., 295
Douglas, Stephen Arnold, 92
Downs, Anthony, 304
Doz, Yves, 198
Drucker, Peter, 39, 46, 93, 125, 159, 161, 168, 190, 194, 220, 238, 244, 259, 268, 278, 284, 289, 303, 308-9, 311, 324, 328, 353, 364
Drugs, proprietary, 372, 377
Duncan, Hugh G., 47
Durkheim, Emile, 29, 155, 206
Dyson, Esther, 377
E
Easterbrook, Gregg, 37
Economics, 108-27. See also Money; Taxation
  bottom-line paradigm, 343, 347-54
  Consumer Price Index, 38-39
  culture and, 299-300
  currency, 295-99
  financial controls, 186-87
  financial markets, 190
  gap between rich and poor, 382-83
  ownership and, 356-60
  three economies, 226-45
Economic Theory of Democracy, 304

Index

The Economist, 28, 38, 42, 108, 133, 289, 293
Edelston, Marty, 170-71, 172
Edgell, Bob, 123
Education, 316-37
Educational Renaissance, 317, 320
Ehrlichman, John, 145
Elecrical power lines, cancer and, 32-33
Electronic Data Systems, 314
Elgin, Duane, 76, 77
Eliot, T. S., 19
Elite culture, 334
Elliott, Osborn, 145, 146, 147
Emerson, Ralph Waldo, 92
Emotional withdrawal, 40-41
Employee ideas, 171-72
Encyclopedie, ou Dictionnaire raisonné des arts, des sciences et des méltiers, 85
The End of Bureaucracy and the Rise of the Intelligent Organization, 195
The End of Work, 380
Engelbart, Douglas, 372
Engels, Friedrich, 288
  England, 89-90, 95, 110, 130, 233.
  See also Great Britain
English bias in American culture, 95
Entertainment, literacy and learning and, 91-92
Entitlement programs, 264
Entrepreneuring in money system, 295-96
Environment, 384-85
Environmentalists, 37
Envy, 46
Epstein, Richard A., 302
Equality, 86-87
Escape from Avarice, 251
Ethics and the Press, 140
Ethnicity. *See also* Culture; Minorities
  economic cohesion and, 299-300
Etzioni, Amitai, 29, 34, 107, 115, 148
Eupsychian Management, 335
Euro, 295-96
Europe, immigration to, 260
European Union currency, 295-96
Evaluation, self-, 387-89
Exclusion, 277
Experimentalistic fallacy, 63
Extranets, 242
Exxon, 229

F
Faitlough, Gerard, 178
Fallows, James, 52, 53, 252
Family, 105-6, 155-56, 395-96
Family Media, 122
Fear, 30-33
  of change, 226-27
  of fragmentation, 282-83
  in media, 146
Federal government, 250, 263-64. *See also* Government
Federal Register, 100, 301

Federal Reserve, 35-36
  Federalist Papers, 89, 97
Federalist Party, 90-91
Feudalism, 357-58, 360
The Fifth Discipline, 171, 176
Financial commons, 263-65
Financial controls, 186-87
Financial markets, 190
Financing partnerships, 183-84
Firms, teams vs., 181-82
Fisher, Rosalind, 296
Fitch, John, 371
Foerster, David W., 42
Food packaging, 21
Force, 275-76, 277
Ford, Henry, 112, 157, 351
Ford Motor Co., 158-59, 227
Foreign policy, 292-93
Forrester, Jay W., 175, 181, 194, 195, 200
Fragmentation, fear of, 282-83
Framebreak, 197
France, 89, 289, 345
Frank, Reuven, 135
Frank, Robert H., 375
Franklin, Benjamin, 24, 88, 92, 129, 130, 229
Freedom
  to listen, 369-70
  moral, 304
  for print journalism, 129-30
Free-market theory of Adam Smith, 109-11, 112, 116, 124
French Revolution, 89
Freud, Sigmund, 113, 394
Fromm, Erich, 334
Fuller, Buckminster, 188
Fulton, Robert, 371
Fundamentalism, religious, 51-52
Future Shock, 13, 39, 40, 125

G
Gaebler, Ted, 186, 188, 263-64, 282
Galbraith, John Kenneth, 78, 96, 111, 113, 115-16, 205, 350, 362, 363, 382
Gallatin, Albert, 90
Galloway, Carl A., 66-67
Gallup, George, 113
Gangs, ghetto, 50-51
Gardner, Howard, 325, 327-28
Garfield, Charles, 271-72, 343
Gates, Bill, 324
Gayle, Margaret, 317
General Electric, 161
Generalists, 324
General Motors, 171, 174, 184, 227, 231
Genetic materials, patenting of, 372
Geographic communities, 278
Geography education, 322
Geranmayeh, Ali, 193
Germany, 98, 115, 260, 287, 289
Ghetto gangs, 50-51
The Gift, 221, 223
Gift economy, 239, 403
Gifts, 223-24

Gingrich, Newt, 137, 148
Globa, 286
Global community, 378-404
Global cooperation, 289
Globalist foreign policy, 292, 293
Global Paradox, 299
The Glory and the Power, 51
Goldhirsh, Bernie, 204
Goldwater, Barry, 87-88
The Good Society, 307
Goodwin, Neva R., 353-54, 379
Gore, Bill, 236-37
Governing in an Information Society, 240, 254
Government
  activist central, 90-91
  Adam Smith's view of, 109
  controls on corporations, 362-63
  by cooperation through compromise, 87-89
  death struggle of, 286-302
  distrust of, 34
  economics and, 124-25
  free market and, 283-84
  growing complexity of, 100-101
  information overload in, 21-22
  media criticism of, 138
  organic, 273-75
  outsourcing of functions, 280-82, 289
  paralysis in, 33
  rediscovering, 249-69
  representative, 250-51, 273-74
  societal needs and, 311-12
  supporting industry, 226-27
  territorial, 258-62
  world, 290-92
Grameen Bank, 238
Great Britain, 85, 132-33, 228, 287, 289. *See also* England.
The Great Good Place, 262
Greenfield, Meg, 35
Greider, William, 13, 101-2, 252-53
Groupthink, 43
Groupthink, 43-46, 147
Grove, Andrew S., 22
Guidance counselors, 330, 331
Guilt, 30
Gutenberg, Johann, 74, 75, 371

H
Hakim, Cliff, 380
Halal, William E., 330
Hall, Edward T., 67, 321, 378-79, 386
Hamel, Gary, 198
Hamilton, Alexander, 90, 91, 106, 110
Hanoukai, Moose, 28
Hardaker, Maurice, 171
Hardin, Garrett, 263
Hardin, Russell, 307
Harding, Warren G., 111
Hare, A. Paul, 178
Harrington, Michael, 171
Harris, Mike, 170
Harrison, Michael, 135
Havel, Vaclev, 13-14

Hayek, Friedrich, 297
Head to Head, 189
Heaven's gate cult, 44
Henderson, Hazel, 290, 294
Henry, Patrick, 87
Herbers, John, 266
Hillers, Isaac, 93
Hirsch, E. D., 322-23
Historical knowledge, growth of, 20
History, American, 84-107
Hobbes, Thomas, 113, 344, 345
Holland, John H., 208
Holmes, Oliver Wendell, Jr., 134
Hoover, Herbert, 139
Hughes, Robert, 55, 96, 334
The Human Side of Enterprise, 159
Huxley, Aldous, 299
Hyde, Lewis, 210, 221, 223-24, 234
I
"I" Power, 170, 172
Iacocca, Lee, 289
IBM, 165, 184, 240, 314
Ideas
 definition of, 60-61
 from employees, 171-72
 ownership and, 344-45, 368-77
Illich, Ivan, 234, 337
Immigrants, 260
Income gap, 382-83
Incorporation, 361
Independence, 83, 172-73
Independent Working Group on the Future of the United Nations, 291, 294
Index of Leading Cultural Indicators, 316
Indians, American, 55, 104, 112
Indifference, 40-41, 146-47, 251-53
Individuals, supremacy of, 270-85
Industrial Revolution, 379
Inertia, 226-27
Informal economy, 233-38
Information
 abused, 385-86
 application, 70
 authority and democracy and, 84-107
 definition of, 60
 evaluation, 70
 force-feeding of, 22-23
 knowledge and wisdom and, 57-71, 166-68
 management in workplace, 153-68
 relations, 70
 revolutions, 73-75
 storage, 70
 technology, 241-42
 tools and, 77-79
 understanding vs., 23-24
Information Anxiety, 31
Information overload, 17, 19-25
 dealing with, 389-91
 side effects, 26-56, 146-47
 threatening problems and, 381-86
Innis, Harold Adam, 82, 135
In Over Our Heads, 14
Instruction, 154, 155

Insurance
 democratic, 312-13
 networks, 283
 social, 303-15
Insurance industry, 21, 120-21
Integrity, personal, 386-87
The Integrity of Intelligence, 386
Intellectual property paradigm, 344, 368-77
Intelligence Quotient testing, 47
Interest
 definition of, 61-62
 shared, 148-49
Interest groups, 98-100, 268
Interest rates, 35-36
Intermodal Surface Transportation Efficiency Act, 255-56
Internal Markets, 193, 195, 196, 348
Internal markets, 193-95
International authorities, 267-68
Internet, 54, 242, 374
In the Wake of the Affluent Society, 103, 233
Intranets, 242
Intrapreneuring, 183, 204
Intuition, 329
Invisible hand, 109-10, 112, 116
IQ testing, 47
Ishihara, Shintaro, 171
Isolationism, 48
J
Jackson, Andrew, 91, 93, 104, 144
Jackson, Jesse, 47
Jacques, Elliott, 181-82
James, John, 178
Janis, Irving, 43-44
Japan, 52-54, 98, 171, 184, 196, 205-6, 230-31, 240
Jay, John, 90
Jefferson, Thomas, 90, 91, 134, 249, 370
Jesus Christ, 309
Jobs, positions vs., 186
Jobs, Steve, 214, 215, 216, 218
Jobshift, 380, 388
Johnson, Prince, 36
Joint ownership, 365
Journalism. *See also* Media
Journalists, 131-32, 146
Judgment, 61, 173
Jury system, 28-29, 37-38
Justice, democratic, 313-14
K
Kaizen, the Key to Japan's Competitive Success, 196
Kalb, Marvin, 149
Kaleida Labs, 217
Kaltenborn, H. V., 131
Kamuhanda, Emmanuel, 31
Kant, Immanuel, 63
Kegan, Robert, 14
Keiretsus, 230
Kellas, James G., 300
Kelly Services, 314-15
Kendall, Amos, 93, 106

Kennedy, John F., 34, 44
Keynes, John Maynard, 117, 119, 297, 352
King, Anthony, 252
Kirchner, Bruce, 55
Klein, Joe, 46, 49
Knowledge
 authority and, 268-69
 community and, 82
 competition vs., 240-41
 definition of, 61
 independence and, 83
 information and wisdom and, 57-71, 166-68
 in self-evaluation, 387-88
 thirst for, 24-25
The Knowledge-Creating Company, 166
Knowledge economy, 125-26
The Knowledge Executive, 43, 60, 368
Knowledge networks, 210-25, 243-45
Knowledge warp, 36-40, 146
Kohl, Helmut, 293
Kohlhase, Charles, 405
Koppel, Ted, 23, 41
Korten, David C., 353, 363
Kuhn, Thomas, 342, 343
Kurtzman, Joel, 297-98
L
Labor, ownership and, 344
Labor unions, 106, 159, 227
Labor-vs.-management problems, 187
Ladies' Home Journal, 141
Language, 68, 74
Latin-American culture, 55
Latinos in America, 238
Latouche, Serge, 103, 233-36
Law and order, organic, 300-301
Law enforcement, 35
Lawlessness, 383
Laws, 101-2, 106, 130, 255-56, 266, 301-2
Lazonick, William, 111
Leadership, 33-34, 174-78, 244
Leadership and the New Science, 236
Learning, 70, 91-92. *See also* Education
Lee, Dwight R., 257, 260
Legislation, 101-2, 106, 130, 255-56, 266, 301-2
Legislators, 38
Lehmbruch, Gerhard, 271
Lehner, Franz, 272-73
Lerner, Daniel, 235
Levy, Frank, 328
Lewin, Kurt, 159
Liberalism, in media, 137-38
Liberation Management, 24, 218
Liberty, 86
Liebowitz, Jay, 330
Life style, 44-45
Lincoln, Abraham, 92, 105
Lind, Michael, 292
Lindahl, Goran, 218
Lindsey, Lawrence, 254

Index

Lipnack, Jessica, 185
Lippmann, Walter, 252
List, Friedrich, 110
Literacy, learning and entertainment and, 91-92
Lobbying, 98-100
Local government, 264-65
Locke, John, 68, 85, 344, 345
Lockheed Information Services, 314
Lodge, George C., 286, 287, 288
The Logic of Collective Action, 118, 304
The Lonely Crowd, 30, 41, 48, 98
Looking at the Sun, 52, 252
Louisiana Purchase, 94, 345

M

Macias, Aurelia, 28
MacLeish, Archibald, 21
Madison, James, 84, 97, 253-54
Madsen, Richard, 238
Magazines, 138, 139, 141, 148, 204
Magnet, Myron, 46
Maier, Charles S., 293
Majority rule, amicable agreement vs., 270-72
Malone, Thomas, 169-70
Management. *See also* Bureaucracy
 corporate, function of, 194-95
 total quality, 171
Management by objectives, 159, 194
Management-vs.-labor problems, 187
Manipulation
 in communication, 59-60, 65, 68
 economic, 123
Mao Tse-tung, 80
Marketing, rise of, 112-14
Markets
 financial, 190
 internal, 193-95
Marriage, 274, 397
Marshack, Alexander, 73
Marshall, Alfred, 113
Marshall, John, 91
Marty, Martin E., 51
Marx, Karl, 78, 344
Masaaki, Imai, 196
Maslow, Abraham H., 169, 335
Mason, Richard O., 197
Massachusetts Institute of Technology, 169-70, 184, 281
Matrix structure, 218
Maurer, Gilbert, 369
Mauss, Marcel, 223
McCarthy, Joseph, 131
McClure's Magazine, 141
McDonald's, 205
McGregor, Douglas, 159, 194
McKenzie, Richard B., 257, 260
McKinsey & Co., 201
McLuhan, Marshall, 19-20, 59, 135, 140
McNamara, Robert S., 38
Mead, George Herbert, 47
Means, Gardiner C., 355-56, 359-60, 363
Mechanical models, organic models vs., 207-9

Media, 128-49
 broadcast vs. print, 392-93
 business and social structure and, 75-76
 complaints about, 58-60
 education influenced by, 321
 information overload and, 23
 objectivity in, 66-67
 screening, 391-92
 tuneout and, 41-42
The Media Monopoly, 138
Medieval Europe, 357-58, 360, 402
"Meet the Mayors," 371
Megatrends, 265
Melton, William, 296
Membership communities, 278
Memes, 69
Mergers, 170
Merrill, John C., 66
Meyerowitz, Joshua, 34, 47-48, 136
Microsoft Windows, 374
Middle Ages, 357-58, 360, 402
Miglautsch, John, 24
Milton, John, 134
Mind, 62-64
Minorities, 47, 48, 69, 104-5, 237-38
Minsky, Marvin, 57
Mirriees, James A., 313
Mission statements, 185
Mitroff, Ian I., 197
The Modern Corporation and Private Property, 355-56, 359
Moller, J. Orstrom, 300
Money. *See also* Economics
 global, 296-99
 management, 116-17
 manipulation of, 123
 as misused tool, 120-21
 in modern life, 379
 mystery of, 117-18
 privately issued, 295-96
 profit and, 347-46
Money system, entrepreneuring in, 295-96
Monopoly, 189
Morison, Robert, 35
Morse, Samuel, 94
Motivation, 186
Mott, Frank Luther, 139
Moynihan, Daniel Patrick, 13, 38, 46, 299
Mueller, Robert K., 211
Multiple Intelligences, 327
Mumford, Lewis, 78, 126, 157, 163, 371
Murder, 30-31
Murdoch, Rupert, 148
Murnane, Richard, 328
Murphy, Raymond, 37
Murray, Charles, 47
Murrow, Edward R., 20-21, 131
Musa, Solomon Anthony Joseph, 36

N

Naisbitt, John, 265, 299-300
Names, ownership of, 372

National Assessment of Educational Progress, 318
National Basketball Association, 374
National CompuScreen, 42
National Rifle Association, 269
The National System of Political Economy, 110
A Nation at Risk, 317
A Nation of Victims, 49
The Nature and Necessity of a Paper Currency, 130
Negotiation, force vs., 275-76
Negroponte, Nicholas, 78, 136
Nelson, Kent, 353
Networking
 partnering vs., 164-66
 purpose and, 202-3
Networks
 as communities, 273-74
 history and development, 228-30
 knowledge, 210-25
 organic, 192-209
 of partnerships, 169-91, 279
 types of, 210-12
The New Industrial State, 350, 362, 382
The New Realities, 39, 161
News and the Culture of Lying, 144
Newspapers, 129-30, 138, 139, 141
Newsweek, 31, 51, 63, 119, 336, 392
Newton, Isaac, 207
New York City, 91, 167, 259, 280, 318
New York Herald, 93
New York Sun, 93
The New York Times, 147
Nirenberg, John, 148
Nissan, 230, 231
Nixon, Richard M., 134, 138, 145, 256, 295
Noer, David M., 198
"The Noise," 19
Nonaka, Ikujiro, 166
Normlessness, 29-30
No Sense of Place, 34, 47, 136
Novak, Michael, 137

O

Objective of partnership, 176-77
Odyssey, 214
Ohmae, Kenichi, 231, 240-41
Oldenburg, Ray, 262
Oligopoly, 189
Olson, Mancur, 98, 117, 118, 177, 178, 272, 304
One Nation, After All, 401
Ong, Walter J., 47, 326
On Human Communication, 68
Onorato, Jim, 212-14
Openness, in industry, 222-23
Operations network, 211
Ophuls, William, 250-51
Organic governance, 273-75
Organic models, mechanical models vs., 207-9
Organic networks, 192-209
Organization, post-hierarchical, 201

Osborne, David, 186, 188, 263-64, 282
Ostroff, Frank, 201
Ouchi, William, 194, 196, 197, 206
Outsourcing, 227, 280-82, 289
Overhead departments, 187-88
Overstimulation, 40
Ownership, 344-46, 356-57, 364-66
P
Paine, Thomas, 87
Pandaemonium, 13, 299
Paradigms
  bottom-line, 343, 347-54
  corporation, 343-44, 355-67
  intellectual property, 344, 368-77
  need for change in, 341-46
Parents, education influenced by, 320
Parsons, Talcott, 118
Partnering
  educational, 336
  networking vs., 164-66
  power of, 200-201
Partnerships, 274-76, 393-404
  networks of, 169-91, 279
  property and, 364-66
Passing of Traditional Society, 235
Patents, 371-72, 375-77. *See also*
  Intellectual property
Pavlov, Ivan, 113
Paye, Jean-Claude, 290
Pearson, Christine M., 197
Peer pressure, 277
Peirce, Neal, 261
PepsiCo, 214, 233
Perelman, Lewis J., 20, 211, 321
Perestroika for America, 286
Perry, Matthew C., 52
Personnel motivation, 186
Persuasion, 200
Pessimism, 96-97
Peters, Tom, 177, 218, 241, 244
Philanthropy, 310-11
Piaget, Jean, 326
Pinchot, Elizabeth, 195
Pinchot, Gifford, 183-84, 188, 195, 204, 205, 237
Planning, 200, 391-92
Plato, 60
Police, 35, 293-94
Political Organizations, 116
The Politics of Nationalism and Ethnicity, 300
Poole, Charles, 33
Poor, gap between rich and, 382-83
Population explosion, 384-85
Population shifts, 46
Positions, jobs vs., 186
Postman, Neil, 41-42, 92, 111
The Postmodern Organization, 264
Prahalad, C. K., 198
The Presence of the Word, 47
Presidential Campaign Hotline, 143
Pressure groups, 114-16
Prime Time Live, 392
Principles, 385-87

Printing history, 74
Print journalism, 129-30, 392-93
Prisons, 281
Private sector, growth of, 289
Privatization, 280-82, 289, 312-13, 314-15, 336
Problems, threatening, 381-86
Professors, careers and, 332-33
Profit(s), 187
  bottom-line, 347-54
  from fear, 32-33
Profit motive, 351-54
Programs, government, 266-67
Property, 344-46, 364-66, 368-77
  Prudential Insurance Co., 281, 308
Psychonomics, 119
Publicity, 144
The Public Use of Private Interests, 124
Purdy, Ken, 19
Purpose
  of networks, 278-79
  of partnership, 176-77, 185-86
  as ultimate power, 202-3
Q
Quality control, 186
Quicksilver Capital, 257, 260
R
Radio Act, 130
Railroads, 94
Randolph, John, 89
Rapid Reaction Force, 291, 293
Rathenau, Walther, 360
Rationality and Nature, 37
Rauch, Jonathan, 98, 263
Realist foreign policy, 292, 293
Reconstruction Finance Corp., 264
Reich, Robert B., 54, 403
Reinventing Government, 186, 188, 263, 282
Religion, 86, 87, 402
Religious fundamentalists, 51-52
Remuneration in partnerships, 180-81
Representative government, 250-51, 273-74
Reprivatization, 284
Resentment, 49
Responsibility
  avoiding, 43
  benefits balanced with, 399
  corporations and, 355-67
  personal vs. corporate, 366-67
  social, 303-5
  splintering of, 282-83
Rewards, 181
Rhetoric, 65, 67
Rich, gap between poor and, 382-83
Riesman, David, 30, 41, 48, 98
Rifkin, Jeremy, 380
Rights, 49, 86-87
Riordan, Bob, 122
The Rise and Decline of Nations, 98
Risk of splintering responsibility, 283
Risk taking, 175-76
RJR Nabisco, 28

Rogers, Carl, 159
Roosevelt, Franklin D., 139, 146, 355
Rosenstiel, Tom, 135
Roszak, Theodore, 61, 77, 78
Rothschild, Michael, 73-75
Rousseau, Jean Jacques, 85, 323
Rules and regulations, 276
Rwanda, 30-31, 384
S
Sahlins, Marshall, 223
Sakai, Kuniyasu, 184
Salaries, 379-80
Samuelson, Paul, 265
Samuelson, Robert J., 241
Sanders, Irene, 64
San Diego, 261
Sapir, Edward, 68
Savage, Charles, 244
Savings, 350
Schering-Plough, 302
Schlesinger, Arthur, 44
Schools, 316-37
School's Out, 321
Schrage, Michael, 164-65, 176, 178-80
Schroedinger's cat, 64
Schultze, Charles, 98, 124, 126
Schumacher, E. F., 203
Schumpeter, Joseph Alios, 352
Schwarz, Benjamin, 95
Science, 32
Scientific knowledge, growth of, 20
Scientific paradigms, 342-43
Screening, 391-92
Sculley, John, 214-17
Second to None, 343
Secrecy, 222
Self-evaluation, 387-89
Self-image, 47-48
Self-interest, 303-5
The Selfish Gene, 62, 68
Self-regulation, 268-69
Senge, Peter, 171, 176, 204, 387
Shapiro, Robert, 264
Shared Minds, 165, 178
Sharon, Ariel, 147
Shuttleworth, John, 174
Sias, John, 188
Simon, Julian L., 37
Simple Rules for a Complex World, 302
Singapore, 375
Sioux, 48-49
Six Pillars of Self-Esteem, 326
"60 Minutes," 66-67
Slavery, 86, 104-5
Sloan Management Review, 244
Smith, Adam, 109-10, 112, 116, 124, 275, 344
Smith, Clifford, 190
Snoop Doggy Dogg, 49, 51
Snyder, Mike, 66
Social adolescence, 153-54
Social change, 394-95
Social insurance, 303-15
Society

Index

communication creating, 72-83
community vs., 259
de-schooling, 337
heterogeneous vs. homogeneous, 205-7
Socioeconomic paradigms. *See also* Paradigms
Socrates, 387
Soros, George, 383, 385, 386
South Africa, 47
Sovereignty, central, 256-58
Special interest groups, 98-100, 268
Specialists, 39, 324-25
Speculation, economic, 122
Spencer, Herbert, 103
Spinoffs, 233
Spirit of Community, 29, 115
Stamps, Jeffrey, 185
Standard Oil, 106, 229
Star, John, 154
Stark, Steven, 96
State government, 250
State sovereignty, 89-90
Steiner, Jurg, 270-73, 275, 402
Stewart, Thomas A., 201
Stockholders, 362, 363
Stone Age Economics, 223
Stowe, Harriet Beecher, 92
Stress, 30
Structure. *See also* Corporate structure
The Structure of Scientific Revolutions, 342
Study of History, 76
Subordination, government, 290
Sumerians, 74, 75
Superfund, 255
Super-simplifiers, 39, 40
Supreme Court, 91, 104, 106, 361
Switzerland, 270-71, 272-73
Sykes, Charles J., 49

T
Takeuchi, Hirotaka, 166
Tarcher, Martin, 251
Tariffs, 106, 110-11, 124, 139, 240
Taxation, 99, 263-65, 294, 310
Taylor, Frederick Winslow, 157, 194
Taylor, John, 89
Teaching the New Basic Skills, 328
The Team/Net Factor, 185
Teams, firms vs., 181-82
Technics and Civilization, 78, 157, 371
Technology
  advantages and disadvantages of, 241-42
  intellectual property and, 374-75
  phases in use of, 157-58
Telecommunications, 22
"Telelearning," 330
Teleological fallacy, 62
Television
  impact of, 134, 135
  tuneout and, 41-42
  viewer dropout, 138-39
Territorial government, 258-62
Theory of Moral Sentiments, 110
The Theory of Social and Economic Organization, 118
The Theory of the Leisure Class, 341
Theory Z, 194, 196, 206
Thoreau, Henry David, 335
Thurer, Shari L., 30
Thurow, Lester C., 72, 172, 189
Time, 146-47
Tocqueville, Alexis de, 45, 95, 270, 405
Toennies, Ferdinand, 259
Toffler, Alvin, 13, 39, 40, 44, 101, 125, 143, 163, 244, 252, 253, 257-58, 274-75, 284, 285, 380
Toffler, Heidi, 252, 253, 257-58, 274-75, 380
Tools, 77-79
Total quality management, 171
Toynbee, Arnold, 76, 77
Toyota, 54, 230, 231
Trademarks, 372. *See also* Intellectual property
"The Tragedy of the Commons," 263
Tribalism, 46-47
Triviality, 41
Trust
  actuarial, 297
  lack of, 33-36, 140-41, 146
Tuneout, 40-43, 146-46
The Twenty-First Century Organization, 159, 269

U
Uncertainty, 27-30, 146
Uncle Tom's Cabin, 92
Understanding
  information vs., 23-24
  mind and, 62-63
Understanding Media, 19-20, 140
Undeveloped countries, 234-36
UNESCO, 132
Unions, 106, 159, 227
United Auto Workers, 227
United Nations, 249, 267, 290-94
United Parcel Service, 184, 353
U. S. Congress, 21-22, 28
U. S. Constitution, 86-87, 89, 97, 104, 250, 262, 361, 369
United Steel Workers, 159
UPS, 184, 353

V
Value systems, 102-7
Veblen, Thorstein, 113, 341-42, 343
Venture capital partnerships, 183
Vickrey, William, 313
Vietnam War, 38
Villanueva, Danny, 238
Violence, in ghetto gangs, 50
Vision, shared, 176
Voluntary Simplicity, 76
Volunteers, 308-10

W
W. L. Gore & Associates, 236-37
Wages, 379-80
Walden, 335
Waldrop, M. Mitchell, 118-19
Wall Street Journal, 254
WalMart, 232
Ward, Bryan, 171
Warner, Mark, 185
War of 1812, 90
Washington, D.C., 33, 98-100, 259, 261
The Wealth of Nations, 109, 110
We Are All Self-Employed, 380
Weaver, Paul, 144
Weber, Max, 116, 118, 196
Wechsler Family, 398
Weick, Karl, 244
Weld, William, 254
Welfare administration, 314-15, 400-401
Wells, H. G., 13
Wertheimer, Nancy, 32
West, Frederick, Jr., 138
Wheatley, Margaret J., 207-8, 226, 236
Wheeler, John, 64
When Corporations Rule the World, 353, 363
Who Will Tell the People?, 13, 101
Widgren, Jonas, 260
Wiener, Norbert, 73
Wigner, Eugene, 64
Wilkie, Wendell, 139
Williams, Roger, 85
Williamson, Gilbert, 287
Wilson, James Q., 96, 116, 256
Windows (Microsoft), 374
The Winner-Take-All Society, 375
Wired, 374
Wisdom, 172-74
  definition of, 61
  information and knowledge and, 57-71, 166-68
  in self-evaluation, 388
Wolfe, Alan, 401
Workplace, information management in, 153-68
World Future Society, 290
World Court, 267, 314
Wriston, Walter, 256, 285, 298-99
Writing history, 74
Wurman, Richard Saul, 31

Y
Yankelovich, Daniel, 224, 310
Yates, Frances A., 78
Yeltsin, Boris, 80

Z
Ziff, Bill, 142-43

About the author

Jim Mann is president of Jim Mann & Associates, a consulting firm specializing in the marketing problems of communications media, which he founded in 1974. From 1978 to 1996, he was founding editor of *Publishing Trends & Trendsetters*, an advisory service for periodical publishing executives, which he sold to Oxbridge Communications in 1991. He began his career in this field in 1959 working for *The Gallagher Report*, a journal addressed exclusively to magazine publishing executives. As a consultant, he has advised media CEOs of many companies, including ITT, Matsushita Electric (Panasonic), *The Reader's Digest*, ABC's Fairchild Publications, *The Ladies' Home Journal*, Cablevision Inc., and Harcourt Brace Jovanovich. Mr Mann has also been adjunct professor of marketing and advertising at the University of New Haven and director of its business school's New Products & Concepts Laboratory. He holds a Master of Fine Arts in creative writing from Fordham University and has also studied writing at Columbia University. He has written three books on magazine management: *Solving Publishing's Toughest Problems* (1982), *Magazine Editing: Its Art and Practice* (1985), and *Ad Sales: Interviews with 23 Top Magazine Editors* (1987). He and his wife live in Connecticut.

About Harlan Cleveland

Mr Cleveland, political scientist and public executive, is president of the World Academy of Arts and Science. After graduating from Princeton University in 1938, he was a Rhodes Scholar at Oxford University. In 1952, he was the Washington-based supervisor of the last stages of the Marshall Plan for European recovery. Under President Robert F. Kennedy, he served as Assistant Secretary of State for International Organization Affairs, and was later appointed by President Lyndon B. Johnson as US Ambassador to NATO. He also served as President of the University of Hawaii, founder of the Program in International Affairs of the Aspen Institute, and dean of the University of Minnesota's Hubert H. Humphrey Institute of Public Affairs. He is the author of hundreds of magazine and journal articles, as well as eleven books, mostly on executive leadership and world affairs.